WE DO NOT WANT THE GATES CLOSED BETWEEN US

NATIVE NETWORKS AND THE SPREAD OF THE GHOST DANCE

Justin Gage

UNIVERSITY OF OKLAHOMA PRESS : NORMAN

Publication of this book is made possible through the generosity
of Edith Kinney Gaylord.

Library of Congress Cataloging-in-Publication Data

Names: Gage, Justin R., 1981– author.
Title: We do not want the gates closed between us : Native networks
and the spread of the Ghost Dance / Justin Gage.
Description: First. | Norman : University of Oklahoma Press, [2020] | Includes
bibliographical references and index. | Summary: "Examines how Native
Americans created vast intertribal networks of communication to control
their own sources of information, spread and reinforce ideas, and collectively
discuss and mobilize resistance against government policies during the late nineteenth
century"—Provided by publisher.
Identifiers: LCCN 2020019283 | ISBN 978-0-8061-6725-1 (hardcover) ISBN
978-0-8061-8636-8 (paperback)
Subjects: LCSH: Indians of North America—Communication—History—19th century. |
Indians of North America—Social networks—History—19th century. | Ghost dance.
Classification: LCC E98.C73 G34 2020 | DDC 970.004/97—dc23
LC record available at https://lccn.loc.gov/2020019283

The paper in this book meets the guidelines for permanence and durability
of the Committee on Production Guidelines for Book Longevity
of the Council on Library Resources, Inc. ∞

Copyright © 2020 by the University of Oklahoma Press, Norman, Publishing Division
of the University. Paperback published 2022. Manufactured in the U.S.A.

All rights reserved. No part of this publication may be reproduced, stored in a retrieval
system, or transmitted, in any form or by any means, electronic, mechanical,
photocopying, recording, or otherwise—except as permitted under Section 107 or 108 of
the United States Copyright Act—without the prior written permission of the University
of Oklahoma Press. To request permission to reproduce selections from this book, write
to Permissions, University of Oklahoma Press, 2800 Venture Drive, Norman OK 73069,
or email rights.oupress@ou.edu.

In memory of my loving mom and dad, Gail and Steven Gage

Contents

List of Illustrations   vii
Acknowledgments   ix

Introduction   1

Part I. Networks of Correspondence
Chapter 1. Acquiring and Using Literacy   17
Chapter 2. Connecting Reservations   50

Part II. Networks of Visitation
Chapter 3. Remaining Mobile   79
Chapter 4. Dangerous Influences   113

Part III. Communicating the Ghost Dance
Chapter 5. "Go and Tell All the Tribes"   141
Chapter 6. Suppressing the Spread   169
Chapter 7. The Ghost Dance in a Continental Network   192
Chapter 8. Continuing the Movement   213

Conclusion   239

Abbreviations   247
Notes   249
Bibliography   325
Index   347

Illustrations

Figures

Turtle Following His Wife's letter to his son Little Man, early 1880s   21

Drawing accompanying James Bear's Heart's letter to his former teacher   40

Uncompahgre Ute chiefs at Los Piños Agency Post Office with Agent J. B. Thompson and interpreter, c. 1878   43

Take Way From Crow's letter written in Dakota to his sister-in-law, March 1, 1890   59

Pretty Owl, Red Cloud's wife, with their books, paper, and ink   72

Native American men on horseback in front of Taos Post Office   74

Three Native men on railroad tracks in the Southwest   95

Kicking Bear and Young Man Afraid of His Horses, 1891   182

Casper Edson and Apiatan and his wife   232

Jack Wilson (Wovoka) and Northern Arapaho men on the set of the film *The Thundering Herd*, 1924   240

Maps

1. Selected reservations and western rail lines, 1890   12
2. Known trips made with and without permission, 1880–1890   80
3. Known trips concerning the Ghost Dance, 1888–1891   151
4. Known links of correspondence concerning the Ghost Dance, 1889–1894   167

Tables

1. Reservations Most Frequently Referenced in This Book   10
2. Number of Indians Who Could Read at Selected Reservations in 1880 and 1889, along with Literacy Rates   32
3. Native Americans Reading in English and a Native Language at Selected Reservations, 1886   33
4. Origin and Number of Known Surviving Native American Letters Sent to the Commissioner of Indian Affairs, 1890   47
5. Number of Known Trips to and from Lakota Reservations, 1880–1890   84

Acknowledgments

No one wants to read the history of a history book, so I will be brief. The seeds of this book were planted twelve years ago, unwittingly, and I would like to thank those who have contributed along the way. In 2007, I began thinking about Native American communication while enrolled in a research seminar at the University of Arkansas led by Elliott West. After reading about the rapid and extensive spread of the 1890 Ghost Dance, I wondered how the ideas of a religious movement that originated in Nevada spread so quickly across the entire West. If Native Americans were confined on reservations, how did the news and information about the Ghost Dance move from reservation to reservation? I could not find a satisfactory answer in existing literature, so I decided, with the cautious encouragement of Dr. West, to provide an answer in my short seminar paper. Several years later, with the guidance of my professors Beth Schweiger, Patrick Williams, and Elliott West, my research morphed into a dissertation about something much larger. I want to thank those three special teachers.

After graduation, I continued teaching at the University of Arkansas as an adjunct instructor while working on this book. As my professors became my colleagues (and I struggled to call them by their first names), they still offered advice and support. Elliott West, in particular, has tolerated unannounced visits in which I try to siphon as much wisdom from the man as I can. I also want to thank Patrick Williams, Michael Pierce, and my fellow instructors Benjamin Purvis, David Schieffler, Robert Brubaker, Ronald Gordon, Louise Hancox, and Aaron Moulton for our conversations and their interest in my work. I cannot say enough about other folks at the University of Arkansas, including Calvin White, Brenda Foster, Melinda Adams, and Jeanne Short. The chair of the History Department, Jim Gigantino, has done everything he can to support my work (from digging up some funding for research trips to offering me an office of my own), which is not typical for other contingent faculty members across the country. This book was also supported by a University of Arkansas Fulbright College Humanities Summer Research Stipend in 2017, which was, through the efforts of Kathy Sloan, also made available to contingent faculty members.

I owe many thanks to the folks at the University of Oklahoma Press, and I am honored to be included in their prestigious catalog. The talented Alessandra Jacobi Tamulevich, especially, has been incredibly supportive (and patient). Thanks to copyeditor Abby Graves and indexer Chris Dodge for their thoughtful work. I also appreciate the fine work of cartographer Erin Greb, who produced some challenging maps in a short amount of time.

I have also been helped by a number of people who kindly offered their expertise, criticism, and encouragement. Rani-Henrik Andersson deserves special thanks. Rani was kind enough to quickly answer an email from a foreign graduate student in 2015 who asked him if he could, in his spare time, translate a letter written in the Dakota language before a dissertation deadline. Since, Rani has been generous with his time, and his support has been invaluable to this project. In fact, the final weeks of my revisions were completed while I was a part of Rani's Humana Project out of the University of Helsinki, funded by a Kone Foundation Grant. Another terrific historian, Jeffrey Ostler, went above and beyond what I expected from a reader. His thorough assessment and wise advice are much appreciated. Both Jeffrey and Rani have books of their own that have greatly influenced my work. Speaking of influential historians, I also want to thank Alejandra Dubcovsky and Brian DeLay. Their encouragement and advice were a boost during the long slog. Robert Brave Heart also delivered a boost during the homestretch; thank you, Bob. Alessandra Link and Cameron Blevins, whose dissertations I relied on, have graciously passed along beneficial sources over the years. I should also thank Thomas Connors for making me aware of the drawing by James Bear's Heart featured in this book.

Most of the work here comes from the archives, and I was lucky to visit many great institutions across the country, often thanks to their financial support. This project was a recipient of the American Philosophical Society's Phillips Fund for Native American Research, which is one of the rare sources of funding dedicated to research on Native American history. I am incredibly grateful for that support. I also benefited from a month at the Beinecke Rare Book & Manuscript Library at Yale University, funded by the Beinecke's Archibald Hanna Jr. Fellowship. My thanks to the outstanding staff there, including Anne Marie Menta and George Miles. Not only was George, the curator of their Western Americana Collection, a great supporter of my project, but his essay "To Hear an Old Voice: Rediscovering Native Americans in American History," in *Under an Open Sky*, was a revelation to me as a grad student. I also spent a wonderful month at the Huntington Library in San Marino because of the Huntington Library/Western History Association Martin Ridge Residential Fellowship. I appreciate the help of Peter Blodgett there. Much appreciation also to the staffs at the National Archives in Kansas City, Denver, Riverside, San Bruno, and Washington, DC, and to the staffs at the Oklahoma Historical Society, History Colorado, and the Bancroft Library. The excellent staff at my home library, Mullins Library at the University of Arkansas, have processed hundreds of my requests, especially the folks in the Interlibrary Loan Department.

My deepest thanks goes to my family. My father, Steven, passed away a year before this book was finished, but it would not have been possible without his support over the years. Kristen, my wife, has lived a life with me and this project for nearly ten years now. Her encouragement has never wavered, and I am forever grateful. By the time this book hits the shelves, our daughter, Cora, will be six months old. I am told that a six-month-old still can't read, even my six-month-old, but I hope one day she will read this and know that she was a part of this book as well.

Fayetteville, Arkansas
October 2019

Introduction

In the 1860s and 1870s, after years of resistance, most western Native Americans were forced to settle onto ever-shrinking pieces of land created by the United States government to relocate, contain, and separate them. Native Americans were colonized peoples living on reservations, which, the US government hoped, would keep them away from each other and from the white populations coursing through the plains. Despite this colonial control and confinement, Native Americans were able to remain mobile in the late nineteenth century. This tenacious mobility, defined not only as the freedom of geographic movement but also the ability to share ideas and information widely, allowed western Native Americans to create vast networks of communication that traversed the boundaries of the US government's reservations. These intertribal networks, threaded together in the 1870s and 1880s by intertribal visiting and letter writing, facilitated the dissemination of important information and ideas to Natives on a continental scale, often in opposition to US colonialism, including religious knowledge and practices like the Ghost Dance.

US officials were afraid of ideas that might diminish the government's power over tribal nations, and they often tried to suppress communication among the diverse tribes of the West. For the US government, the solution to the so-called Indian Problem depended on geographic isolation—keeping Native Americans in a space where they could be controlled and set distant. As the secretary of the interior put it in 1865, Indians had to give up their "wandering life" and remain within their imposed borders. As part of the effort to suppress Native identities and engender Americanized assimilation, the US government hoped to end the intertribal interaction that had always been an important part of Native life. In 1874, Francis Walker, by then a former commissioner of Indian affairs in the Grant administration, stated his hope that Indians "be resolved into the body of our citizenship."

After a few generations, if all went according to Walker's plan, "Indians, as a pure race or a distinct people, shall have disappeared from the continent."[1] This could only be accomplished if Indian agents kept the people "upon the reservation," segregated from white communities, and did not allow them to stray off "for the occasional debauch" at white settlements.[2] Without colonial confinement and authority, what he defined as an "adequate system of moral and industrial correction and education," the Indians would "break away in their old roving spirit" and form "gypsy-camps all over the frontier States and Territories, to be sores upon the public body."[3] The US government had to keep Indians in a controlled setting where they and their children could be changed.

The US government created more than one hundred isolated reservations designed to confine Native Americans. The Pine Ridge Reservation was described by a white educator as a "forlorn, straggling concentration camp in the middle of the vast empty spaces of Dakota Territory," but the reservations of the West were not static points on the map encircled by the dynamism of white society.[4] Native Americans did not allow themselves to be kept prisoners on reservations. They thought that they would have the freedom of movement, and they expected reservation agents to give it to them. When that freedom was threatened, Natives fought to keep it. In 1888, Oglala Lakota leaders Little Wound, Young Man Afraid of His Horses, and Red Cloud sent a letter to President Grover Cleveland that complained about geographic restrictions. "We should be permitted to make friendly visits among each other as the white people do," they argued; after all, the president "said he wanted us to be at peace with each other and to be friendly."[5] They insisted, "We do not want the gates closed between us."

Even though reservations were constructed by the federal government, they were ultimately altered by the people living within them. Despite the intentions and racist strategies of policy makers at the Office of Indian Affairs, government employees could never wholly control the populations on reservations. The Office of Indian Affairs was an expansive, radically bureaucratized Reconstruction-era reform program, but it did not have the administrative capacity (initiative, funding, manpower, or otherwise) to accomplish its goals.[6] While Native peoples undoubtedly faced limitations on their movement and communication in the last quarter of the nineteenth century (they were not allowed to pass through the reserve borders at their will), they found ways to interact with those outside. Native Americans on reservations constantly submitted requests to visit foreign tribal nations on other western reservations. Native Americans made at least twelve hundred trips between western reservations, and probably many more, from 1880 to 1890. At least one-third of those trips, made by parties ranging in size from one to hundreds, were made without the permission of Indian agents and outside US government authority.[7] Historians and anthropologists have painted a picture of an animated world west of the Mississippi before and after the arrival of Europeans, documenting the trade networks, kinship ties, and political alliances that united Indian peoples across the West.[8] Those face-to-face relationships did not cease after tribes were forced onto the reservations.

The written language, passed along in letters through the US Postal Service, also bridged the gaps among reservations, allowing men and women to communicate efficiently across the vast distances that separated them. With their own words, distant contacts could share news and express their thoughts and beliefs outside of colonial control, accelerating the development of larger intertribal communities. Natives used the US government's suppressive education to communicate for their own purposes, to limit colonial control, direct their own lives, and expand their cultures. By 1889, nearly 12,000 Lakotas, Santees, Yanktons, Yanktonais, Mandans, Assiniboines, Gros Ventres, Utes, Paiutes, Shoshones, Bannocks, Arapahos, Cheyennes, Kiowas, Comanches, Apaches, Wichitas, Poncas, Pawnees, Otoes, Sac and Foxes, Nez Perces, Blackfeet, Crows, Omahas, Ho-Chunks, and others could read in English or their Native language.[9] Only nine years earlier, fewer than 3,500 had been able to read.[10] Four percent of the individuals from those tribes could read in 1880, but by 1889, the number reached 18 percent.

As far as many Native Americans were concerned, acquiring literacy could be a means of preserving culture, not losing it. Men, women, and children used new sources of knowledge that were now open to them in the ways that they chose, accessing and distributing information independent of the US government. Natives saw that the mail offered practical benefits, and as more and more Natives learned to read and write, the usefulness of literacy became more apparent. Intertribal (and intercultural) communication was no easy matter in the nineteenth century. Many miles separated reservations, and even related tribes and bands faced separation. Cheyennes and Arapahos were both divided between northern and southern nations, with their northern nations occupying reserves in Wyoming and the Dakotas and their southern nation living hundreds of miles south in Indian Territory. The diverse Shoshones were dispersed on various reservations in parts of Wyoming, Idaho, and Nevada, and dozens of other tribes were spread throughout the West. The seven major bands of Lakotas, who shared parts of what is now South Dakota, were separated by reservation boundaries and multiple days' travel over rough terrain. Even among tribes living on the same reservation, communication could be difficult because of the number of languages in the West. For instance, on the two reservations in western Indian Territory, the Cheyenne-Arapaho and the Kiowa, Comanche, and Wichita Agencies, there were at least eight languages being spoken from five distinct linguistic families.[11] But, as a lingua franca, English could ease intertribal communication among the hundreds of exceptionally diverse Indigenous groups of the West.

Part 1 of this study begins with a survey of education and the early usage of literacy by western Native Americans. They acquired literacy in a variety of ways during the 1870s and 1880s: from early missionaries, in day schools on the reserves, at eastern boarding schools, and on their own initiative without white involvement. Chapter 1 also describes how Indians understood the written language within the framework of colonization, using it to maintain some sense of sovereignty. Letter writing and the postal system were wielded as anticolonial weapons to question the power of the US government, to demand change, and to remind officials about the government's obligations. Like eastern Native Americans before the mid-nineteenth century, western tribes used literacy to acquire information independent of the US government. Newspapers created for Native audiences, by whites and by Natives, became vital resources. Natives also consumed white newspapers and magazines, connecting themselves to white sources and the national web of communication.

Chapter 2 explores how Native Americans used literacy and letter writing as important tools for communication while living through the unforeseeable consequences of colonialism. Because of the forced separation of peoples and the inevitabilities that carried individuals away from their people, long-distance communication was increasingly valuable to Natives. Networks of correspondence formed, linking individuals to their families, families to their tribes, and tribes to other tribes throughout the West. Kinship was critical in Native communities, intertribal marriage was common, and those ties needed to be sustained. Divided tribal nations could stay informed of others' affairs. They exchanged advice and strategies for managing their changing worlds, often in defiance of the US government. Nations without a previous relationship could forge new bonds, and those with a history of conflict could make peace. Leaders used correspondence to spread influence, sway minds, and hash out disagreements. Men and women exchanged cultural ideas that were under attack by the US government, especially religious ones; they planned visits and dances, which further developed extratribal life. All of this written-down information—the good and bad news, the mundane reports about the weather, or the serious appeals for support—could be created and relayed outside the control of whites. Although literacy was meant to be a tool of American colonization, the writing that was produced by Native Americans, conveying their thoughts and expression, could not be colonized.

Native Americans also remained geographically mobile even though they were forced onto reservations, challenging the government's efforts to isolate tribes from one another. Part 2 of the book, chapters 3 and 4, demonstrates the prominence of another means of forging bonds: the intertribal visiting among many different nations during the last quarter of the nineteenth century.[12] Natives throughout the West, particularly those living great distances apart, visited continuously, some more than ever before, in part because of the growing networks of intertribal correspondence and the transportation provided by new western railroads. Intertribal visits were made for social, economic, political, and religious reasons. Men and women from different backgrounds shared knowledge (often anticolonial in nature), related experiences, and exchanged aspects of their cultures. But intertribal visiting persisted only because Natives demanded it. Office of Indian Affairs agents tried to limit the movement of men and women across agency boundaries, but visiting was never outright banned. Those who could not or did not care to obtain permission to visit other reservations often traveled anyway, despite the threats of punishment that might result.

Native Americans had common concerns, and they shrewdly used the US government's repressive education system and the mechanisms of American settler-colonialism, notably the railroads and the US Postal Service, to protect and expand elements of their ways of life. Unfortunately, US government officials believed that some of the ideas that spread through these intertribal networks might undo their efforts to control and assimilate Indians. Agents knew that tribes shared their experiences dealing with the federal government and the strategies they used to resist government control. Intertribal interaction often gave Natives advantageous knowledge as they negotiated government demands. Intertribal letters and visits were also used to collectively discuss and mobilize resistance against government policies, such as the Dawes General Allotment Act of 1887, and to combat land cession. Moreover, intertribal communication spread and reinforced Indigenous concepts that were seen to be uncivilized by the US government, especially religious concepts. New religious knowledge and practices were continually acquired and adapted by tribes and individuals during the reservation years. Indian agents tried to put up roadblocks to prevent their dissemination, but they could not suppress Native culture. Intertribal dancing was the most common purpose for intertribal visits involving large groups in the late nineteenth century, and it persisted into the twentieth century. Religious ideas and practices like the Sun Dance, the Omaha Dance, or the Ghost Dance were carried to new places.

Thus, communication was often an effort toward decolonization. Native Americans spread information that might limit colonial control. The US government thought such knowledge could be dangerous and thus limited intertribal contact to prevent its spread. Besides restricting visiting, there are instances where agents surveilled and censored the mail coming into their reservations, which forced at least one group of Lakotas at Standing Rock to leave the reservation, cross the Missouri River in the dead of night, and mail letters at the nearest white settlement.[13]

Part 3 takes a look at the intertribal networks of communication in action on a continental scale. By tracing the rapid spread of a particular set of ideas that informed a religious movement, eventually known as the Ghost Dance, we can see the extent and effectiveness of the networks that were operating despite the limitations of the reservation system. This is a project of Indigenous intellectual history, but ideas are difficult things to trace. Historians who hope to trace the path of an idea might encounter a complex web of connections, something resembling the tangled mess of wires behind a television, where sorting out the knots informs the path of transmission. But for those who study the intellectual history of the colonized, the wires are not always apparent. The process of colonization can erode the histories of the peoples who faced its impact. It can be difficult to understand the past experiences of the colonized because their stories were most often described, recorded, and then collected by the dominant white society, which has led to inaccurate assumptions about how humans responded to oppressive power structures. Historians know, for instance, that the Ghost Dance made its way into the minds of tens of thousands of Native Americans between 1888 and 1891 and beyond. But it has been difficult for historians to explain the spread of the Ghost Dance because we did not understand how Native Americans created connections that could carry ideas across reservation boundaries. The network remained hidden. Many have imagined that reservations left Natives cut off from the world and thus cut off from other tribes, but new sources, many written by Natives themselves, reveal the connections and prove that this is not the case.

In November 1890, anthropologist and conservationist George Bird Grinnell reported that tribes living in Indian Territory "frequently" received letters from "Northern Indians . . . touching on religious topics."[14] He noted that Northern and Southern Cheyennes, separated by a thousand miles, regularly visited "back and forth" and kept "a constant correspondence by letter" with each other.[15] Shoshones and Northern Arapahos at the Wind River Reservation in Wyoming were sending "reports and letters . . . relative to the second coming" of Christ, which created interest among Southern Cheyennes and Arapahos. "The new Messiah excitement had taken possession" of the Cheyennes, Arapahos, and Pawnees he visited, "and fills their minds to the exclusion of everything else."[16] Some of the letters, Grinnell said, contained "most extravagant statements, which, however, are received by the Indians with implicit faith."[17] Grinnell also noticed that "a lot of letters" were being received by Pawnees from the "Sioux," who were "trying to get the Pawnees to unite with them." Grinnell thought the intertribal correspondence regarding this new Ghost Dance religious movement was "one of the disadvantages, perhaps, of the Indian education."[18] Using skills learned in government schools, Indians were spreading information that seemed to conflict with the goals of Americanization and was outside the control of the US government.

The intertribal networks of correspondence and off-reserve visitation that formed in the 1870s and 1880s facilitated the rapid dissemination of the Ghost Dance in 1889 and 1890. By the time Grinnell noticed what was going on at the Cheyenne-Arapaho Reservation, most Native Americans in the country had already heard about the Ghost Dance, and thousands believed in its decolonizing promises to make their world better. No other religious movement reached so many Native Americans in such a short amount of time. Information was sought, gathered, and relayed across a network that spanned the continent. Some Natives defended the movement, and others criticized it, but because of the well-established networks among tribes, a set of ideas originating in the mind of a Paiute in western Nevada named Wovoka (or Jack Wilson) became part of a continental, Native-controlled conversation (with believers from southern Arizona to Saskatchewan).

Part 3 begins by taking a detailed look at how the Ghost Dance spread.[19] Intertribal visitation and correspondence brought the news from the Nevada agencies, out of the Great Basin to the Fort Hall Reservation of Idaho, and through the Rockies to the Wind River Reservation in Wyoming. From those locales, Wovoka's message was sent via letters down to the Southern Plains reservations in Indian Territory and to the Northern Plains reservations of Montana and the Dakotas. Correspondents who for years had used letters to share news with friends and family on other reserves exchanged ideas about the new Messiah. By tracing the information about the movement that was gathered and relayed, we can see the intertribal networks that were in place, revealing the links among Paiutes, Utes, Shoshones, Northern Arapahos, Southern Cheyennes, and many other groups. Chapter 5 details the intricate and deliberate spread of the movement and how it crossed reservation boundaries via numerous sources in 1889 and 1890. Letters about the new religion interested tribal leaders, and investigators were sent west, often on railroads, to find Wovoka and discover the truth of his words. Some proponents of the movement wrote letters or traveled to spread the news. Others simply informed their friends or relatives of what they knew about it all.

As chapter 6 illustrates, things began to change once federal authorities found out about the movement. Agents, who were already tasked to limit the perpetuation of so-called savage ways, feared that the Ghost Dance movement would lead to dissent or outright rebellion. Agents tried to limit communication between reservations by tightening visitation, arresting those traveling without permission, and, eventually, censoring the mail. They knew that they were losing control of geography and the flow of information.

Chapter 7 explores how Natives, both believers and skeptics, broadcast their ideas regarding the Ghost Dance, attempting to convince or dissuade others and control the flow of information. Natives throughout the American West were brought closer together with the shared purpose of communicating what the Ghost Dance was to others within their developing intertribal community. Some Natives wrote to Indian Affairs and to the press to declare their right to practice their religion. Many stayed informed of the dance through newspapers, and some challenged the inaccurate reports that the dance was leading to violent outbreaks.

Chapter 8 reveals how the Ghost Dance's spread persisted after the infamous massacre at Wounded Knee Creek in late 1890.[20] The early 1890s were years of dynamic communication among Native men and women despite the US government's efforts to curb intertribal relations by severing connections. Reservation agents went to great lengths to suppress the Ghost Dance, seeing its persistence and the intertribal connections that sustained its ideas as an affront to US government control, but the Ghost Dance survived the nineteenth century, and Natives continued to exchange anticolonial notions.

Together, these chapters reveal that Native Americans' ability and desire to communicate with people outside their own tribes or language groups created intertribal networks—a web of interconnectedness—during the early reservation years. These networks fostered a growing sense of community among tribal nations and made the rapid spread of the Ghost Dance possible. A closer look at western Indian agency records and Native American letters reveals a dynamic world in motion, where long-distance intercultural communication among Native Americans was ongoing and where Native Americans challenged colonialism by controlling their own sources of news and information. Through these networks, Native Americans were trying to decolonize their lives—meaning they hoped to reduce US government power and restore their sovereignty—in ways large and small.

This study of communication in the early reservation period relies on a vast and largely untapped archive.[21] By utilizing more than one hundred nineteenth-century letters written by or for Natives, it brings to the fore a great record of Native life, much of which has never been seen by scholars. It reveals the activism prevalent among western Natives before the twentieth century that has largely been unexplored. Unfortunately, it is not easy finding Native voices in our archives, a point that scholars of Native American history have persistently complained about. In his study on Indian education, David Wallace Adams found the challenge of representing Indian children's voices "almost unsurmountable." The documentary record of the Native voice is "both sparse and unreliable," he wrote.

Texts written by Native Americans in English during the late nineteenth century are more commonly found in library archives and governmental records than those written in a Native language. Many Native groups did not have a written form of their language until the twentieth century. Several Siouan-language nations did (Dakotas and Lakotas, Omahas), but Cheyennes, Arapahos, Kiowas, and others did not. They wrote their letters in English.[22] Most Native-language texts from the nineteenth century were letters that were written by Natives to other Natives, but personal correspondence between Native peoples was kept private and was seldom preserved in archives. Only sometimes would government officials, anthropologists, or other interested whites, like James Owen Dorsey, somehow acquire and preserve a letter written by a Native individual intended for another Native individual.[23]

Many Native-produced letters used in this study are written artifacts of people learning on the go—some were expressing ideas on paper for the first time. Letters written by Natives in English are rarely incoherent, and most Natives were quite adept at writing in their second language, but some of the meaning that writers tried to convey in their second language could be lost.[24] Word usage and sentence structure in many letters can seem unusual to English speakers; the writings reflect Native speech patterns and figures of speech. Letters written by Native people in any language offer a rare peek into their personal histories, but anyone hoping to find the

Table 1
Reservations Most Frequently Referenced in This Book

Reservation (agency)	Location	Tribes or bands	Population, 1889
Blackfeet	Montana Territory	Blackfeet Nation (Southern Piikani)	2,293
Cheyenne-Arapaho	Indian Territory	Southern Cheyenne, Southern Arapaho	3,598
Cheyenne River	Dakota Territory	Miniconjou (Lakota), Two Kettles (Lakota), Sans Arc (Lakota), Sihásapa (Lakota)	2,846
Crow	Montana Territory	Crow	2,456
Crow Creek and Lower Brule	Dakota Territory	Mdewakanton (Eastern Dakota), Lower Brulé (Lakota), Lower Yanktonai	2,171
Devil's Lake (Spirit Lake)	Dakota Territory	Sisseton, Wahpeton (Eastern Dakota)	2,947
Flathead	Montana Territory	Pend d'Oreille, Kootenai, Flathead, Lower Kalispel	1,914
Fort Belknap	Montana Territory	Assiniboine, Gros Ventre	1,793
Fort Berthold	Dakota Territory	Mandan, Hidatsa, Arikara	1,195
Fort Hall	Idaho Territory	Shoshone, Bannock	1,600
Fort Peck	Montana Territory	Assiniboine, Upper Yanktonai, Sisseton, Wahpeton, Hunkpapa (Lakota)	1,891
Kiowa, Comanche, and Wichita (or Kiowa, Comanche, and Apache)	Indian Territory	Kiowa, Comanche, Apache and Wichita, Caddo, Delaware (after 1879)	4,088
Mescalero	New Mexico Territory	Mescalero Apache	474
Navajo	New Mexico Territory	Navajo, Hopi	20,200
Nevada (Pyramid Lake and Walker River)	Nevada	Paiute	959

Nez Perce	Idaho Territory	Nez Perce	1,450
Omaha and Winnebago	Nebraska	Omaha, Ho-Chunk	2,347
Pine Ridge	Dakota Territory	Oglala (Lakota), Northern Cheyenne	5,611
Ponca, Pawnee, and Otoe	Indian Territory	Ponca, Pawnee, Otoe	1,780
Rosebud	Dakota Territory	Upper Brulé (Lakota)	7,586
Sac and Fox	Indian Territory	Sac and Fox	2,180
Sac and Fox	Iowa	Sac and Fox	393
San Carlos	Arizona Territory	San Carlos Apache, Pinal Coyotero Apache, White Mountain Apache, Tonto Apache, Yavapai	3,940
Santee and Flandreau	Nebraska	Mdewakanton (Eastern Dakota), Wahpeton (Eastern Dakota), Ponca	1,354
Sisseton (Lake Traverse)	Dakota Territory	Sisseton and Wahpeton (Eastern Dakota)	1,487
Southern Ute	Colorado	Southern Ute	1,814
Standing Rock	Dakota Territory	Hunkpapa (Lakota), Sihásapa (Lakota), Upper and Lower Yanktonai (Western Dakota)	4,610
Tongue River (Northern Cheyenne)	Montana Territory	Northern Cheyenne	867
Uintah and Ouray	Utah	Uintah (Northern Ute), Uncompahgre (Northern Ute), Whiteriver (Northern Ute)	1,904
Western Shoshone	Nevada	Western Shoshone, Paiute	477
Wind River	Wyoming Territory	Shoshone, Northern Arapaho	1,945
Yankton	Dakota Territory	Yankton (Western Dakota)	1,760

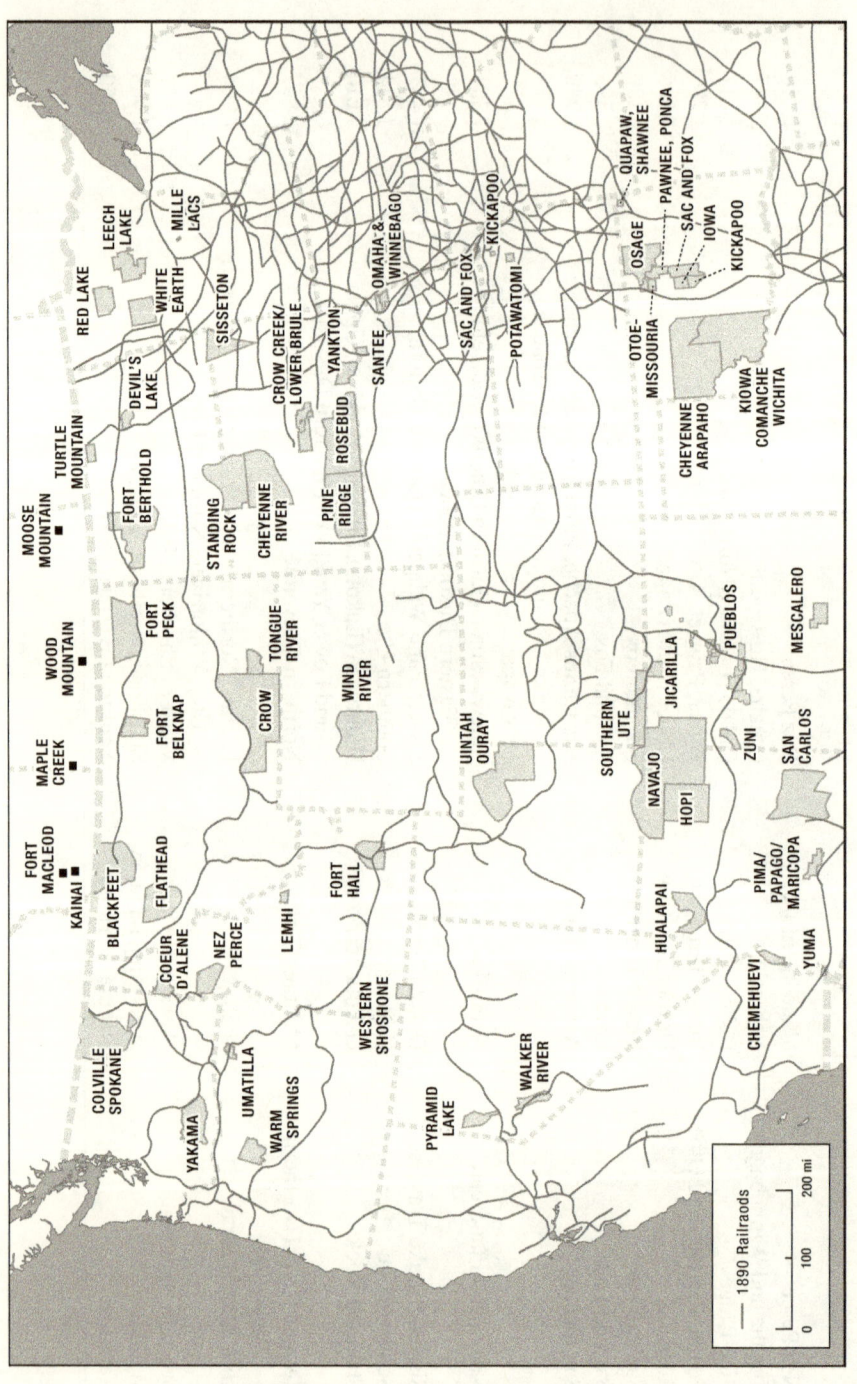

Map 1. Selected reservations and western rail lines, 1890

"authentic voice" in a Native text will be disappointed.[25] There are a number of different types of Native texts, and interpreting the meaning in each can be problematic. There are texts composed entirely by Native people, written either in a Native language or in English; some use both a Native language and English. There are also texts that were dictated by Natives and transcribed (and sometimes translated) by a literate individual, either white or Native. The transcription of a Native language into the written form of that language might alter the original language. And a translation into English always disrupted the original language.[26] Nevertheless, this study recognizes the usefulness of letters that were written for the illiterate or for those not proficient in written English. The "authenticity" of those letters should not be denied because the ideas of a Native were to put to paper by a non-Native.

Another problem this study faces is the large variety of cultures it describes. This book makes use of sources and letters from individuals representing dozens of tribal nations, each considerably different from the others. Each author came from a background unique to his or her nation. It is also difficult to provide adequate context for the intricate histories of the Kiowas, Northern Arapahos, Oglala Lakotas, Southern Utes, and the many other nations this study covers. It may be easy to see these groups as one people, but it is not my intention to present them in that way.

Nevertheless, it is clear that Native Americans were beginning to see themselves as similar people in the late nineteenth century. In 1888, Young Man Afraid of His Horses demanded that "the gates" should not be "closed between" the tribal nations of the West.[27] Three years later, he told a council between his people and government officials, "We want to live up to the Great Father's words. There are fifty-nine agencies altogether, and the Great Father has asked us all to be one.... Indians are all one.... These people who came here from the other agencies are of the same blood that we are and want to be one.... We want the doors left open so that we may have permission to visit these different agencies if we want to.[28] Young Man Afraid of His Horses ended his appeal by saying, "Now, we consider ourselves as one," indicating the growing connections among tribes during his lifetime.

PART I

Networks of Correspondence

CHAPTER 1

Acquiring and Using Literacy

In an 1895 council with the commissioner of Indian affairs, Southern Arapaho leader Little Chief expressed that he was not entirely in line with white men's ways. He acknowledged that the white man's suit he was wearing that day did not "feel natural"; it made him "seem to be tied up all the way through." Little Chief also spoke of the "two roads" that his people were facing.[1] He saw that the "educated boys follow this road and the ignorant boys that road" and said he had made up his mind to "follow the educated boys and not to grope like a blind man." For Little Chief and other Native leaders, managing their changing world was complicated. While some whites might label him a "traditionalist" because of his preference for comfortable traditional clothing, Little Chief's choice to follow the road of education would have been considered a "progressive" one by the commissioner of Indian affairs. But Little Chief fell under neither of these labels. The injustice of colonization required Native Americans to live complicated lives and make difficult decisions, but for most Natives, acquiring literacy did not mean leaving their cultures behind. Unfortunately, the road to English-language literacy for many was through government-controlled Indian schools, where erasing Native cultures was the priority. But during the last quarter of the nineteenth century, thousands of western Natives used literacy to communicate for their own purposes, often to strengthen their ways of life.

Before the 1870s, the large majority of western Native Americans (excluding some eastern tribes that had been removed to the West, like the so-called Five Civilized Tribes: the Cherokees, Choctaws, Seminoles, Creeks, and Chickasaws) had little opportunity to become familiar with reading or writing in any language. As the US government became more committed to Indian assimilation during the late 1870s, however, the Office of Indian Affairs' commitment to Indian education deepened. Indian adoption of the English language, which was understood to be the key to assimilation, became the primary goal of government schools. Although Native men and women resisted many aspects of Americanized assimilation, written language was an exception. During a period of intense colonial pressures, Pawnees, Lakotas, Arapahos, Paiutes, Kiowas and dozens of other groups living west of the Mississippi found they had a practical use for written language. Literacy rates increased quickly, and tribal nations began to rely on new sources of information in their fight against the repression of reservation life. Natives knew that English was the only language that white America understood. The written word gave them another way to condemn governmental structures and push for self-determination. Native Americans used literacy pragmatically to communicate extratribally and within their own smaller communities.

Innovations in Communication

Before the reservation years, Indigenous peoples confronted their dynamic and diverse trans-Mississippi world with continuous adaptations and innovations in communication. Many western Native Americans were multilingual before and after European contact. Native groups were exposed to multiple languages during their intertribal interactions, especially with tribes in close association. Among tribes with mutually unintelligible languages, communication required that some individual or individuals learn the language of the foreign group, which allowed them to maintain the social, political, and economic relationships required in their diverse regions. Sometimes the communication gap could be bridged through a third language, one that both parties understood, called a lingua franca. In fact, regional lingua francas developed throughout the West. For instance, Santee bands became familiar with the Ojibwe (Chippewa) dialect (which became a lingua franca because of its use by fur traders) in Minnesota. During the nineteenth century, the Lakota language was commonly used among members of Northern Plains tribes and Comanches in the southern plains. Also, Great Plains Sign Language had become a sophisticated lingua franca for Natives west of the Mississippi at least two centuries before that. With the arrival of Europeans, Spanish, French, and English would be also used as lingua francas. A French-Lakota pidgin language was in use for a period of time, and during the early years of American westward expansion, Natives encountered English and various forms of pidgin English (Indian-modified and even "Black English" from Buffalo Soldiers).[2]

Most reservations were culturally and linguistically diverse places, which required communication in a common tongue. On two neighboring reservations (the Cheyenne-Arapaho and the Kiowa, Comanche, and Wichita Reservations) in western Indian Territory, for instance, Natives spoke the Caddo and Wichita languages (Caddoan family); the Comanche language (Uto-Aztecan); the Delaware, Cheyenne, and Arapaho languages (Algonquian); the Kiowa-Apace language (Athapascan); and the Kiowa language (Kiowa-Tanoan family). Multilingualism took on a new importance as different tribes lived in close proximity on the same reservations or within the same communities. Intertribal visiting also remained critical in Native life. Spoken and written English provided Natives an opportunity to communicate across tribal boundaries more effectively, which created stronger connections, but Native languages in the West did not die out in the process (though many grew endangered during the twentieth century). In the last thirty years of the nineteenth century, American English was an addition, not a substitution for existing languages.

Long before the US government began its assimilation program west of the Mississippi, Natives were adapting to new forms of communication, including written forms. Early missionaries found that Dakotas had some experience with the concept of scripted communication. In 1834, a missionary reported Indians using *wowape*, which "consisted of rude paintings and hieroglyphs. . . . Figures of men and horses, of battle-axes and scalps, drawn with coal or cut in bark, told the story of a war-party . . . told a man's history."[3] Native Americans used pictographs for centuries to express themselves and explain their world. Lakota winter count pictography, *waniyetu wówapi*, one of many forms of Native pictography, has received attention from scholars and museums. Winter counts are pictographic calendars that served as records of tribal or family history. Important events from each year are represented by sequentially arranged images that hold a complex meaning. The origins of the winter count are unknown, but at some point, probably around the turn of the nineteenth century, Lakotas decided to rely on a written record rather than just on oral tradition alone when maintaining their history. The count was used periodically to retell past events and mark the passage of time.[4] Blackfeet, Mandans, and Kiowas also used these pictorial calendars.

Pictographs that served as a writing system were also commonly used by Natives to communicate ideas to those outside a linguistic family. Before and after European presence, North Americans used pictographic messages to communicate a wide variety of ideas to foreign groups, including complex messages of war, peace, trade, and religion.[5] Early on, Europeans described the exchange of letters with picture writing. In the 1840s, for instance, Mandans wrote letters to European fur traders, using symbols that represented "I will barter" and the particular animal they could provide or what they desired. One letter pictured a gun next to thirty strokes, which meant the man would barter thirty beaver skins and a gun for the skins of a buffalo, weasel, and otter, which were also pictured.[6]

Western Native men and women recognized the practical benefit of written communication before becoming literate in phonologic (alphabetic or syllabic) writing systems, and some began to use dispatched correspondence containing pictographs as early as the 1870s to communicate with members of their own tribes when they could not have face-to-face interaction. In 1877, Crow hunting parties sent pictograph letters to their people back home to describe hunting routes and areas that might offer the best hunting conditions (as well as areas where there might be lodges of Lakotas and Arapahos, who were Crow rivals).[7] Others used pictographic letters to overcome the separation caused by colonialism. From 1875 to 1878, seventy-two Southern Plains Indians were held as prisoners of war at Fort Marion, Florida, hundreds of miles away from their Kiowa, Comanche, Southern Cheyenne, and Southern Arapaho families and friends.[8] Many of those men became literate in English while imprisoned, but some also communicated with home through pictographic letters. Minimic, a Southern Cheyenne prisoner, received from his family a letter with detailed pictographs that passed along an incredible variety of news.[9] Likewise, an Arapaho sent a letter to a Cheyenne prisoner that told of his involvement in the Great Sioux War. A map with pictorial descriptions communicated his movement through Wyoming, Montana, and Canada.[10]

Post offices were established at every Indian reservation in the West, and pictographic correspondence continued well into the reservation period. A Southern Cheyenne named Turtle Following His Wife living in Indian Territory at the Cheyenne-Arapaho Reservation used a pictograph to communicate to his son Little Man living seven hundred miles away at the Pine Ridge Reservation.[11] Little Man easily understood the meaning of the picture upon receiving it. Turtle Following His Wife was telling Little Man that he had sent fifty-three dollars (represented by the drawing of fifty-three silver dollars) to the agent at Pine Ridge to pay for his journey to his father's home in Indian Territory.

Kiowas were particularly adept at pictographic correspondence. Below (or Belo) Cozad's wife wrote to him in pictographs while he was at an off-reservation boarding school, and he claimed that "a good many" Kiowas knew "how to write in this way."[12] Cozad's letters imitated Plains Indian Sign Language, and some were "very long." One of Cozad's surviving letters from home detailed good news (such as a relative getting a freighting

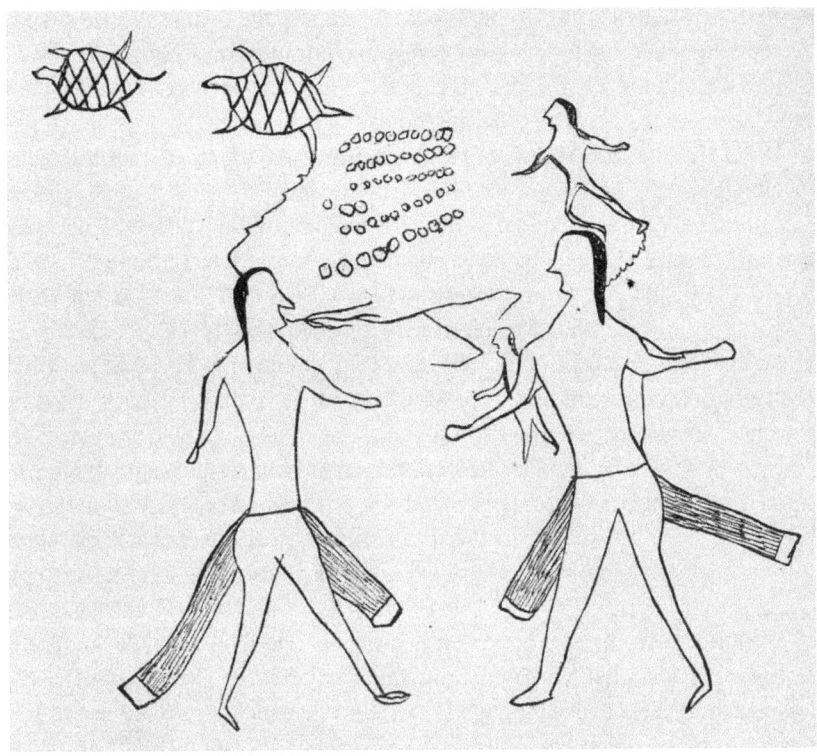

Turtle Following His Wife's letter to his son Little Man, sent from the Cheyenne-Arapaho Reservation in Indian Territory to the Pine Ridge Agency sometime in the early 1880s.

First published in Garrick Mallery, "Picture Writing of the American Indians," *Tenth Annual Report of the Bureau of Ethnology to the Secretary of the Smithsonian Institution, 1888–'89* (Washington, DC: Government Printing Office, 1893).

job) and the bad news that his brother had died. The letter also imparted complex religious ideas: that Jesus was watching out for them, that Cozad should pray to Him, and that one relative had been singing peyote songs.[13]

A few western groups created their own phonologic written language outside of white involvement. Plains Cree oral history recounts how they created their own Cree syllabary; it was not the sole invention of missionary Rev. James Evans in 1840 (as historians have repeated).[14] Raining Bird, a Plains Cree man living at the Rocky Boy Reservation in 1959, told an anthropologist that well before 1840, Crees "were very pleased with their new accomplishment," developing their own symbols on white birch bark.[15]

They "knew that the white traders could read and write," Raining Bird stated, "so now they felt that they too were able to communicate among themselves just as well as did their white neighbors." Historian Winona Wheeler (née Stevenson) reasons that by the time James Evans translated hymns into Cree in 1840, Crees had been in contact with Europeans for two centuries and "were well aware of the power of the written word."[16]

Intertribal contact resulted in at least two other nations developing their own syllabaries without white participation. In the winter of 1883–84, a group of Sac and Fox from Iowa visited Ho-Chunks (Winnebagos) on their reservation in Nebraska. The pioneering ethnologist Alice C. Fletcher was at the reservation at the time. She was told by Sac and Fox that some of their people could read and write in their Native language. This surprised Fletcher because no white person had developed an alphabet for them. She learned that the Sac and Fox had created their own written alphabet (now known as Western Great Lakes Syllabary or Great Lakes Algonquian Syllabics) decades before, but to the disappointment of Fletcher, the Sac and Fox on that particular visit to the Ho-Chunks were not among those who could use it.[17]

Within the next year, however, a group of Ho-Chunks independently learned the alphabet while visiting the Sac and Fox Reservation, then adapted it to their own language (Ho-Chunk or Hoocąk). In August 1885, the agent in charge at the Winnebago Reservation wrote to Fletcher: "The tribe have suddenly taken to writing their own language.... Most of them can read and write it. People who have never learned English have acquired this. The people claim they took the basis of it from the Sacs and elaborated it themselves ... illustrating the surprising facility with which they acquire what they want to learn. The acquisition is very recent and sudden."[18] A single Ho-Chunk man had "discovered" the Sac and Fox alphabet's "adaptability," put it to use, and taught other Ho-Chunks how to use it. The "knowledge spread rapidly" among Ho-Chunks in Nebraska and Wisconsin. "At the present time the principal correspondence of the tribe takes place by means of these characters," Fletcher observed in 1890.[19] She concluded that Ho-Chunks were inspired to "preserve their own language" in writing because of the education of the younger generation in English.

Indian Education

Ho-Chunks continued to develop their written language—today there is a smartphone app that teaches Hoocąk—but before the 1870s, the large majority of Native Americans living west of the Mississippi (outside the so-called Five Civilized Tribes) and east of the Pacific coastal region had little opportunity to learn to read and write, despite many decades of contact with Europeans and Americans. Although French Jesuits had contact with the eastern Plains people since the late 1600s, the first significant effort to evangelize to them came during the 1830s. Missionaries developed systems of writing as a way to get Indians to read the Bible, a normal route toward Indian conversion east of the Mississippi for two centuries. Protestant missionaries produced Indian-language primers that presented an Indian-language writing system along with translations of English words and stories from the Bible. Rev. Asa Smith, working among the early missionaries to Oregon Country, put together a Nez Perce dictionary in the late 1830s with the invaluable help of a Nez Perce man named Lawyer.[20] Primers were also printed for Siouan-language tribes living in the eastern plains: the Osages in 1834, the Santees and Sissetons (Dakotas) in 1836, the Otoes in 1837, the Iowas in 1843, and the Omahas in 1850.[21] Catholic missionaries began educating Santees of the eastern plains in the 1840s with Dakota-language prints of catechism, prayers, songs, and biblical messages.[22]

In the 1830s and 1840s, a trader of French and Dakota descent named Joseph Renville created multiple translations of biblical material for the Protestant-led Dakota Mission, which spurred efforts to educate Santees. The first Dakota school, built by Renville for use as a mess house for his traders, began at Lac qui Parle (in present-day Minnesota) in December 1835. Missionary Thomas Wilkerson asked Renville to help create a written Dakota language. Within three months, Wilkerson and Renville had their students writing to each other "on scraps of paper and birch bark. These epistles were brief, and not elegant, but intelligible."[23] In 1851, the Lac qui Parle school reported that "the greater part" of their sixty students were learning to read their own language while only six were learning English. Also in 1851, the mission school at Kaposia, a Dakota seasonal village in present-day Minnesota, reported that their thirty-seven students of Dakota descent were making good progress in learning to read and write.[24]

Under the tutelage of missionaries, around two hundred Santees confined in a government prison learned to read and write during the winter of 1862–63.[25] The prisoners wrote one hundred to two hundred letters per week to their families, who were camped nearby. The families likewise received instruction from missionaries living with them in order to read the letters.[26] In one early Dakota-language letter in January 1869, a young Santee named John Wapaha told his former pastor, Episcopal missionary Rev. S. D. Hinman, that he would never throw away the words of God: "If I can only make them mine I will be happy." Wapaha, one of the missionary's first converts, had not seen Rev. Hinman in two years. Delighted with the letter, Rev. Hinman translated it into his journal in order "to show that Indians" could "be steadfast."[27]

For many Natives living farther west, the possibilities of literacy were apparent before the arrival of missionaries. Missionary work did not begin in earnest in the western plains until the reservation years of the 1870s, but Lakotas had begun using written text to their political advantage as early as 1846.[28] In the 1840s, white Americans began migrating through Lakota lands on their way to Oregon Territory and later California. The streams of white travelers put strain on the ecology of the plains, and Lakotas found it more difficult to find game, especially bison, near the traffic. In January 1846, sixteen Brulé and Oglala Lakota headmen made their marks on a petition to the president that asked for compensation for their loss of subsistence and for Lakotas "getting killed on several occasions."[29] The headmen's letter proved to be sophisticated statesmanship. It initiated diplomatic relations with the United States and, according to historian Kingsley Bray, directly resulted in the First Fort Laramie Treaty in 1851 (the Horse Creek Treaty).

In the 1850s, the federal government began negotiating treaties with western Plains tribes that were standing in the way of western migration. Tribes were forced to surrender territories for much smaller reservation lands with the goal of keeping Natives on their lands within Indian Territory and out of the way of white settlement. In the Medicine Lodge Treaty of 1867, for instance, Kiowas, Comanches, Apaches, Southern Cheyennes, and Southern Arapahos agreed not to harm whites and consented to railroad construction (although only a minority of the members of those tribes actually consented to the treaty).[30] In return, the US government agreed to provide food and clothing and to fund the employment of agency workers like carpenters, farmers, and most important, teachers. Medicine Lodge provided for the construction of schools, with teachers "competent to teach the elementary branches of an English education." Educators' progress was slow during the 1870s, however. Many Native groups were reluctant to settle near the agencies, making it difficult to attract children to the schools. But by the late 1870s, after a series of Indian wars, most groups were living on reservations. Congress, however, did not always provide the appropriations to build and support schools despite the treaty obligations (church missions often fit the bill instead). For instance, the Yanktons were promised a school in an 1858 treaty (at their request), but it was not established until 1870 despite their chiefs' repeated requests to have their children educated.

By the mid-1870s, Native-language literacy "began to flourish" at the Yankton Reservation.[31]

The Yanktonais at the Crow Creek Agency (the Upper Missouri Agency until 1874) got their first school in 1872 after an Episcopal mission was established.[32] The Sissetons and Wahpeton Sioux at Devil's Lake Agency began attending a Catholic school in 1874.[33] Most of the children of the Lakota bands, the Northern Arapahos, and the Northern Cheyennes did not begin attending school until after 1875, once they were forced onto reservations. Farther west, the Shoshones at the Wind River Reservation had contact with traveling teachers for years before a permanent day school opened for thirty-two students in 1878. Government agents in the Southwest reported in 1880 that education among Apaches, Mojaves, Chemehuevis, Navajos, Hopis, and Pimas was making good progress.[34] Those at the Colorado River Reservation got a boarding school, and the San Carlos Apaches got a new schoolhouse.

In the southern plains, formal education began among the Southern Cheyennes and Arapahos in 1871 at a day school, although instruction began through sign language because the Quaker teachers did not speak the students' language. At least one Arapaho chief, Little Raven, encouraged his band's children to learn to read and write in these early years.[35] A visitor to the new school at the Wichita Agency in 1873 wrote that the nearly seventy children were "learning English very fast."[36] A school started at the Kiowa Agency in 1871, but its students did not yet include Kiowas (sixteen were Caddos, seven were Comanches, and one was a Delaware).[37] The Kiowa chief Kicking Bird would eventually welcome a Quaker missionary into his camp in 1873 to start a school. Kicking Bird believed Kiowa children needed to confront the "new road" that was being forced upon his people by the federal government by learning "white skills."[38] In 1875, there were only forty Kiowa and Comanche children enrolled at the single school, but fifty-seven Kiowas and Comanches learned to read that year (out of a population of 3,180).[39] At the nearby Cheyenne-Arapaho Reservation, only twenty-one could read in 1875, but thirteen had learned in the previous year.[40] Most Southern Cheyennes remained unenthusiastic about sending their children to school until the late 1870s, after the Red River War.[41] Twenty years later, however, Arapaho headman Left Hand (the younger) said that the schools were "doing good" for the Arapahos and Cheyennes and that it was "the school boys that lead me around . . . and tell me what is going on and what will take place hereafter. . . . We can see the good of schooling."[42]

The English Language

Bringing the English language to the Native populations of the West became a governmental concern in 1869 as part of President Grant's "peace policy." As white American settlers took stretches of the West in the 1860s, conflicts between Native groups and the US military became all too common. Grant's policy intended to remedy the violence while protecting the whites migrating westward.[43] The Peace Commission, which determined that it "costs less to civilize than to kill," saw education as a humane way to solve white America's so-called Indian question, to help the Indians understand the supposed superiority of white civilization, and to bring the Natives into American life.[44] According to one member of the Peace Commission, government schools needed to introduce the English language because the "sameness of language" would produce the "sameness of sentiment and thought."[45] If Indians spoke English, then Indians would think like whites, and future war could be avoided. "In the difference of language to-day lies two-thirds of our trouble," he believed. The Office of Indian Affairs agreed, and most policy makers argued that assimilation was impossible for an Indian who could not read, write, and speak English. They thought learning English would benefit Natives economically, socially, and politically, giving them the ability to participate in the white world.

During much of 1870s, however, the mission schools that drew support from federal funds instructed their Native students in their own Native languages and often taught Siouan speakers how to read and write in their own Siouan languages. Because the missionaries' primary goal was to convert, they needed Indians to read the Bible, and that could be accomplished more quickly if the Bible was written in their vernacular. This technique was nothing new, but Indian Afairs officials hoped that mission schools would produce English-speaking Indians. In 1878, the agent at the Yankton Reservation lamented that "the study of English is too much neglected, and it is rarely spoken by the children," which was "a serious evil."[46] But the missionary at the Yankton Reservation insisted that instructing in the Native tongue was more practical. It would take "three or four years in a boarding school, and twice as many in a day-school, for them to learn enough English to make it a fit medium for the conveyance of ideas to their minds."[47]

The federal government began to invest more in Indian assimilation and Indian education in the 1880s. In 1876, for instance, Congress appropriated only $20,000 for education, but by 1885 it appropriated $75,000, and nearly $1 million more came from the general fund. By 1890, Congress's commitment to education skyrocketed to close to $1.4 million per year, nearly half of Indian Affairs' total budget.[48] In 1881, President Grant's policy of giving single denominations monopoly rights at each agency ended, giving any church the ability to build mission schools at any agency they wished. Government-run schools were also built with increased frequency during the 1880s. Unlike the mission schools, however, the government schools made Indian adoption of the English language the primary goal. Indian pupils were prohibited from using their own languages in the classroom. Their teachers could only speak in English, leaving the students to figure out how to read, write, and speak the new language with a blank slate.

The US government's fervent English-only policy can also be seen as a part of the Americanization movement that intensified during the wave of European immigration during the 1880s.[49] Policy makers believed that the Indian populations should adopt English as readily as the immigrants arriving at US shores. Unlike immigrants, however, Native Americans often saw the English language as an imposition from a colonizer. But Commissioner of Indian Affairs J. D. Atkins believed that because the "superior ... laws and institutions of the United States" operated in English, Indians had to learn English in order to become Americans.[50] English-only became a point of national pride, as Commissioner Atkins wrote in 1886, "the English language as taught in America ... the language of the greatest, most powerful, and enterprising nationalities beneath the sun ... is good enough for all her people of all races."[51] The English language was the foundation of assimilation, and its introduction to every tribe was seen as the key to erasing the differences between Natives and whites.[52]

Educators with religious backgrounds tended to favor Native-language instruction, while government educators nearly all argued for English-only instruction. This debate lasted throughout the 1880s, even after Indian Affairs mandated English-only, but because of years of Native-language instruction, many of those who had a written language, like Siouan-speakers Dakotas, Lakotas, and Omahas, read and wrote in their own languages.[53] In February 1887, Commissioner Atkins ordered every school on an Indian reservation to commit fully to the English-only approach. Some missionaries, like Alfred Riggs, refused to stop using Native-language instruction because of its effectiveness. His school stopped receiving federal funding in 1893 as a result.[54] Despite opposition, English literacy became the groundwork of the US government's classroom instruction. The superintendent of Indian schools believed that the most "prominent features of the school room drill" should be "English conversation and intelligent English reading, ... first, last and always."[55]

Taking Advantage of Literacy

But government officials' efforts to entirely acculturate Native Americans into some general notion of American culture did not succeed. Native languages, in this case, continued to be spoken and written. In fact, Native Americans used the Americanized education instilled at Indian schools as an anticolonial tool. Many western Natives sent their children to schools throughout the 1870s and 1880s to acquire the skills of reading and writing and did so for a variety of reasons, many willingly and hopefully.[56] They did not believe, as white educators did, that US government schools could eradicate their Indigenous identities. Some wrote to officials to ask for more schools and teachers. General petitions from tribes usually contained requests for more schools, and some sent personal letters asking for the same.[57]

But government agents also manipulated or coerced parents who were hesitant to send their children to schools, even though influential Native leaders, including Red Cloud, argued that such actions were unjust.[58] Agents were on the reservations to unravel the knotty bonds of Native culture. Their job was to convince the Indians, through bribery or punishment or shaming, that assimilation was the only way forward for their people. Since the government was responsible for much of the Indians' material well-being, agents could convince parents to send their children to school (and keep them there) by providing extra benefits and rations, or they could threaten to take rations away. In 1882, the commissioner of Indian affairs told the agent at Standing Rock that he could withhold rations from the families of children who did not attend school, because it was permitted by the government's 1876 agreement with the Lakotas.[59] He repeated that assertion the following year.[60] In 1884, the teacher at the Porcupine Creek School at Pine Ridge asked the agent to "punish" the families of eight students who did not send their children to his school.[61] Besides direct pressure from the US government, some parents enrolled their children for political reasons, such as gaining or maintaining favor with their agents. Historian Jeffrey Ostler points to an instance in 1882 when many Brulé Lakotas "concluded that it would be best to gain (or avoid losing) political capital" by sending their children to an off-reservation boarding school.[62]

It is also important to understand that from the very beginning, many educators relied on physical and mental abuse to try to eradicate Native ways of life from their students (government policies were dedicated to that end). Parents condemned the mistreatment of their children, and they expressed their concerns in letters regarding whom the US government hired to teach their children. They wanted some control over the hires.[63] While fewer parents were opposed to sending their children to on-reservation day or boarding schools, where they could better protect their children, many were often understandably unwilling to send their children to off-reservation boarding schools. The traumatic cultural change, the great distance from home, and real threats of sickness and death were a few of the most common reasons parents refused.[64]

Separating themselves from their children was an impossible choice for some, especially when on-reservation schools could provide education. In 1884, for instance, the agent at Rosebud reported that he was having a difficult time inducing parents to send their children away to school because they wanted to have a boarding school at the agency. Parents wrote their agent: "We have been promised for a long time by the Great Father that we should have a boarding school at this agency. Why do we not have it? Have one built here as on other agencies and we will send our children. We do not want to send our children from home. . . . Why has not the oft-repeated promise been fulfilled?"[65] Some at Pine Ridge and Cheyenne River made similar requests in 1890.[66] A number of Western Shoshone parents were worried about their children heading off to a school in Carson City, Nevada, because they would be living among whites in a large, corrupting town. According to their agent, the Shoshones were "afraid of the contaminating influence of a town" where other Shoshones had "acquired most of the white man's vices and none of his virtues."[67] The agent tried to convince the parents that their children would be "surrounded" with "the best of people," but they thought it best that a new boarding school be built on their reservation instead.

Army officer Richard Henry Pratt was among the first to convince the US government to invest in off-reservation boarding schools for Indian students. Pratt's view of white society was much different from that of the Western Shoshone parents. He reasoned that the surest way to rid Indian children of their "savage" ways was to immerse them in a "civilized" environment, in a white town, separate from their past. Pratt had his first experiences with Indian education while stationed at Fort Marion from 1875 to 1878, where he interacted with the Southern Plains prisoners of war.[68] He experimented with different methods to teach the male Kiowa, Cheyenne, Arapaho, and Comanche prisoners, some well into their forties and fifties, and to assimilate them to white ways. Manual labor and English classes (both important in Pratt's mind) took the bulk of the prisoners' time. For many of them, this instruction was their first experience with the written word. They were taught how to read and write, and some corresponded with their families back in Indian Territory. Some of the men used their newfound skill to write to Washington to ask for their release.⁶⁹ Pratt believed that education had reformed the Southern Plains prisoners. Satisfied with the prisoners' progress and convinced that holding the men in a controlled, civilized environment aided assimilation, Pratt continued his methods with Native students at the Hampton Institute in Virginia (established by the American Missionary Association for African Americans in 1868) and then at his own Carlisle Indian Industrial School in Pennsylvania.⁷⁰

For nearly four decades, Carlisle was the home to thousands of Native children from nearly every Indian agency in the West.⁷¹ In 1879, Pratt was able to convince chiefs at Rosebud and Pine Ridge to send eighty-four children to Carlisle for the school's first class. Eighteen Southern Cheyenne and ten Southern Arapaho boys and girls were also immersed in Pratt's program in 1879. During its first year, 147 students were at Carlisle, and the total reached 239 by 1880. Demand for a spot at Carlisle was so great at the Cheyenne-Arapaho Reservation that one boy was smuggled onto the train to Pennsylvania by his father, Antelope, a returned Fort Marion prisoner.⁷² In 1880, the Cheyenne-Arapaho agent reported that "not a day passes, hardly, but some one asks that his child may be included in the next lot called for, for Carlisle."⁷³ Forty-two Southern Cheyennes and twenty-one Southern Arapahos attended off-reservation schools in 1880. In 1881, there were sixty-eight Cheyenne and Arapaho students at Carlisle alone, and ninety-one attended in 1882.⁷⁴ In 1887, several Crow boys wrote to Pratt themselves, asking that they might be allowed to attend Carlisle.⁷⁵ For the students who had the choice to attend a boarding school or not, many saw it as an opportunity to help their people. Benjamin Stago, a San Carlos Apache student at Hampton, explained in a letter he wrote home that he and three other Apaches "study very hard" because they wanted to "learn good so when they go back to Arizona they teach other people."⁷⁶

But Native children experienced the greatest threat of assimilation at off-reservation boarding schools, and there was not universal enthusiasm for Carlisle and the like.⁷⁷ Native parents understood the often devastating aspects of schools because of what their sons and daughters told them about their experiences. Scholars of Indian education have correctly labeled boarding schools as sites of "cultural genocide."⁷⁸ Many have examined Native students' negative experiences at boarding schools and their resistance to assimilation.⁷⁹ Some scholars, such as Ruth Spack, have argued that Indians used education, and literacy in particular, as a tool to control their own fates and foster their own culture.⁸⁰

Despite the undeniably detrimental aspects of Indian education, the number of Indians who attended boarding and on-reservation day schools rose steadily throughout the 1880s. By 1892, 15.56 percent of Indians living on agencies in North and South Dakota were enrolled in a day or boarding school (this statistic includes all ages, not just children; the percentage of children would have been much higher), up from just 0.56 percent in 1873 and 3.95 percent in 1882. The percentage of students who attended those schools increased sharply from 1887 to 1892. In 1892, 8 percent of all Indians in the United States were enrolled in a school (excluding the Five Tribes).[81] Government officials were becoming more successful at persuading and coercing parents to send their children to school, and more parents were willing to face white education. In 1880, the agent at Devil's Lake reported that "a change, however is gradually taking place, as is shown from the fact that in the past they strongly opposed schools and religious teachings, but now they are either reconciled or indifferent, and allow their children to attend school."[82] During the same year at the Lower Brule Reservation, the agent reported a disappearance of opposition to education. At Pine Ridge, Agent McGillycuddy reported "a strong desire" for education of their children, but he believed that "the nature and habits of these Indians . . . do not justify the belief that they will make very rapid progress in the way of education."[83]

Although progress was gradual, hundreds of Native Americans were learning to read every year, and government officials seemed more positive by the mid-1880s. In 1885, Southern Cheyenne headman Whirlwind wrote to Richard H. Pratt with news that his people had decided in council to send more children to schools.[84] In 1887, the Cheyenne River agent noted that attendance and desire for instruction were larger than ever. Likewise, the progress at Lower Brule was "all that could be asked."[84] The Blackfeet agent was astonished how quickly the children at his agency picked up English and how fast some learned.[86] In the Great Basin at the Western Shoshone Agency (Duck Valley), the teacher at the day school reported that half of his Shoshone students could read and write and the chiefs were "very anxious that the school should be a success that the children may be able to speak English."[87]

Thousands of Indians living on reservations in the Dakotas, Wyoming, Montana, Idaho, Nevada, Nebraska, Iowa, and Indian Territory (excluding the Five Civilized Tribes) learned how to read in the 1880s, according to Indian Affairs estimates. By 1889, nearly 12,000 Lakotas, Santees, Yanktons, Yanktonais, Mandans, Assiniboines, Gros Ventres, Utes, Paiutes, Shoshones, Bannocks, Arapahos, Cheyennes, Kiowas, Comanches, Apaches, Wichitas, Poncas, Pawnees, Otoes, Sac and Fox, Nez Perce, Blackfeet, Crows, Omahas, Winnebagos, and others could read in English or their Native

Table 2
Number of Indians Who Could Read at Selected Reservations in 1880 and 1889, along with Literacy Rates

Reservation	Number of residents who could read in 1880	Percentage of residents who could read in 1880	Number of residents who could read in 1889	Percentage of residents who could read in 1889
Blackfeet	24	0.3	90	3.9
Cheyenne-Arapaho	249	4.2	500	13.9
Cheyenne River	320	18.1	1,175	41.3
Crow	9	0.3	120	4.9
Crow Creek and Lower Brulé	155	6.83	740	34.1
Devil's Lake	109	10.0	812	27.6
Fort Belknap	18	0.9	144	8.0
Fort Berthold	26	1.9	225	18.8
Fort Hall	10	0.7	150	9.4
Fort Peck	7	0.1	200	10.6
Kiowa, Comanche, and Wichita	143	3.5	450	11.0
Nevada	8	0.3	295	30.8
Nez Perce	110	9.1	400	27.6
Omaha and Winnebago	376	14.8	250*	NO DATA
Pine Ridge	50	0.7	1,580	28.2
Ponca, Pawnee, and Otoe	111	6.0	427	24.0
Rosebud	NO DATA	NO DATA	330	4.35
Sac and Fox (in Iowa and Indian Territory)	480	27.6	910	35.3
Santee and Flandreau	407	34.8	862	63.7
Sisseton	258	17.2	700	47.1
Southern Ute	10	0.4	40	2.2
Standing Rock	70	2.7	700	15.2
Tongue River	NO DATA	NO DATA	47	5.42
Uintah and Ouray	23	5.1	16*	NO DATA
Western Shoshone	NO DATA	NO DATA	45	9.4
Wind River	61	3.0	170	8.7
Yankton	350	17.3	410	23.3
TOTAL	**3,384**	**4.2**	**11,788**	**18.0**

*Not every resident was counted.
Source: Office of Indian Affairs data from *ARCIA*, 1880 and 1889.

Table 3
Native Americans Reading in English and a Native Language at Selected Reservations, 1886

Reservation	Can read English only	Can read Native language only	Can read both
Cheyenne River	260	380	160
Crow Creek and Lower Brule	10	150	190
Devil's Lake	5	85	150
Pine Ridge	634	361	405
Rosebud	350	150	100
Sisseton	NO DATA	250	450
Standing Rock	200	50	170
Yankton	NO DATA	120	180
Nez Perce	90	45	85
Fort Peck	19	NO DATA	115
Santee and Flandreau	133	150	361
Omaha and Winnebago	350	100	50

Source: Office of Indian Affairs data from *ARCIA*, 1886.

language.[88] Only nine years earlier, fewer than 3,500 could read.[89] Only 4 percent of the individuals from those groups could read in 1880, but by 1889, the number reached 18 percent. In the Dakotas alone, nearly a quarter of Native Americans could read English or the Dakota language in 1890, compared to only 5 percent ten years earlier.[90]

Despite the emphasis on English education, a significant percentage of those Plains Natives who could read did so only in their Native language. Many Siouan-speaking people (Dakotas, Omahas, Poncas) took advantage of their early contact with missionaries. Eastern Dakotas (Santees and Sissetons), Western Dakotas (Yanktons and Yanktonais), and Lakotas were all taught to write Dakota.[91] Many communicated with one another using both written Dakota and English. However, several languages, including Kiowa, Cheyenne, Arapaho, and Shoshoni, did not have a written form until the twentieth century.[92] These groups relied on English. In their annual reports to the commissioner of Indian affairs, agents typically counted the number of Indians who could read on their reservations, lumping together those reading in English and Native languages. But in 1885 and 1886, some agents distinguished between the two and included numbers of each in their reports. In 1886, the agent at Pine Ridge tallied 634 who could read only

English, 361 who could read only Dakota, and 405 could read both English and Dakota.[93]

Statistics do show that Native youths were much more likely to learn to read, but a surprising number over the age of twenty-one learned to read in 1886. Many of the children attending schools had known life only on the reservations. Although their parents and older siblings experienced long-established ways of life, hundreds of Native youths were born into a world influenced by US colonialism. By 1892, there were 5,217 dwelling houses on reservations in the Dakotas; 64.5 percent of Indians were "wholly" wearing "civilized dress" (14 percent in part), and 21 percent could "use English enough for ordinary intercourse."[94] In 1882, by comparison, 20 percent of Indians on Dakota reserves had worn civilized dress, and only 1.47 percent could use English. Farm life, new modes of dress, or newspapers might have been oddities to the older generations, but those things had become a part of life to many Native youths. This generational shift was never out of the minds of policy makers. The strategies on which the reservation system was founded depended on this trend.[95]

Using Literacy

Though aware of the damaging effects that Americanized education could have on their children, many Native Americans still expressed a desire to have them educated so that they could use literacy to their advantage. In 1877, Red Cloud personally told President Rutherford B. Hayes, "I also wants schools to enable my children to read and write, so they will be as wise as the white man's children. . . . We would like to have Catholic priests and nuns, so that they could teach our people how to read and write."[96] The famous chief, along with other Lakota leaders, repeated this demand to their agent in 1879.[97] In 1884, Lakota headman Standing Elk (Hehaka Najin) sent six of his children to school because he thought "that is best way," and he wanted other Lakotas to do the same. He wrote to the Standing Rock agent, "If we don't send our children to school how can they get education and how can be they like white children when they are grown enough they won't try the white mens way so I think we better send our children to school now so they can learn some thing good before they grown up."[98] The following month, an Episcopal missionary reported to the agent at Standing Rock that he had been receiving messages from Standing Rock Lakotas for two years asking for a mission house and school there.[99]

While visiting the Hampton Institute, Red Cloud told students that they should listen to the superintendent: "He has brains, he has eyes, he will take good care of you. I like all his work, and I am very glad to see it."[100] When asked what the parents back home thought about Hampton, Red Cloud, who believed that the US government should not forcibly educate children, responded, "The Indians love their children but they sent them here, a great ways off, to learn the white man's ways. This shows what we think of it." The Hampton Institute was always sure to publish the good words of visiting chiefs. In August 1880, the *Southern Workman*, a Hampton publication, reported that visiting Lakota Like-the-Bear told the Hampton superintendent in a speech, "I see you are making brains for my children; you are making eyes for them so they see well. That is what I reach out to the Great Spirit for."[101] Likewise, Chief Wizi hoped that education would benefit Lakotas: "Looking at our children here, I think how sometimes I put seeds into the ground. If I don't see them growing after a time I feel uneasy. Then I look again, and if I see them sprouting, I feel glad, so I feel about our children. I see the seed is growing here now, and by and by it will do good among my own people."[102] Percy Zadoka, a twenty-year-old Kichai (Keechi or K'itaish) Carlisle student, wrote to his people's agent that he would "make use of my education" and "come home and help the good work that is going on . . . and will speak for them as long my tongue is in good order."[103]

Of course, no Native leader argued in favor of English-education because they wanted to see their cultures destroyed. They viewed it practically. Reading, writing, and speaking English would allow their nations to protect their interests. White Swan at Cheyenne River, for example, wrote Sen. Henry Dawes to ask for a copy of the past treaties between his people and the US government and a copy of the Dawes Act. "We don't know what is coming to us," White Swan wrote, "but there is some Educated Indians we can keep the paper of promises and if any of them come untrue we can see to it ourself."[104] Likewise, Oglala chief American Horse told a crowd of whites and Indian children that education was useful as a means of detecting the fraudulent activities of settlers and the US government.[105] Southern Arapaho headman Left Hand (the younger) believed that learning English would give his people power in the court of law against the US government and the flood of white settlers in Oklahoma. "The white man speaks his own language and understand the ways of giving testimony in the case," Left Hand reasoned, "and the Indian has not got much intelligence to tell his own case and so he gets beaten."[106] Indians had "been beaten in every case that has been up in the courts," but if there were more literate English speakers, "the Indian would have a better show in the courts, and if the Indians' evidence was good . . . it would go all right."

Natives knew that the written words of whites were critical within the framework of colonization, so they acquired literacy to challenge reservation life.[107] They were faced with situations that demanded some knowledge of the language of their adversary. The broken treaties, the stacks of congressional legislation and reservation regulations, and all the day-to-day bureaucratic paperwork that controlled their lives were only accessible to those who were literate in English. Presidents and commissioners of Indian affairs wrote to tribes and responded to their letters. Indian agents often informed, assured, and instructed their Indian populations with notes and letters, especially when those dispatches proved most efficient because of the size of reservations.[108] Letters were written by agents to gather opinions, gauge the Indians' attitudes, or admonish certain actions, but they typically served as official commands or requests.[109]

If a tribe did not have a man or woman who could translate a letter from an official, then it would only be done by their agent or a government-paid translator. Some Natives relied on trustworthy whites to write letters for them. The Yanktons told the commissioner of Indian affairs that they got a man to write a letter for them "who will tell what we want to say and not what he thinks."[110] But these translators were not always trustworthy. American Horse and others insisted that educated Natives should replace white employees, particularly the translators, on the reservations.[111] For extremely urgent matters, relying on white men to relay concerns seemed risky. Southern Cheyennes Whirlwind, Cloud Chief, Wolf Face, and Red Wolf wrote a dire letter to Richard Pratt at Carlisle, asking that he would send home their kin, Calvin Red Wolf and Charley White Shield, so that those literate, English-speaking young men could help them interpret, as they were considering important questions that might decide their future welfare, "even the existence of" their people.[112] Nearly a decade later, Cloud Chief, after repeating his people's demand for another day school, told the commissioner of Indian affairs that "the good results of education" were "their only salvation now."[113] By the end of the 1880s, Native leaders came to rely on the educated to confront governmental structures, and most letters received by government officials were written by literate Indigenous men and women.

Native leaders also knew that US government officials had the ability to record the words said (and the obligations set) during their councils with generals and agents. It became common for leaders to request that a written record be made of discussions with the US government and that the record be sent to the president and/or a copy kept for the tribe themselves. Little Wound, the Lakota chief, asked for a copy (to be kept by No Flesh) of the council proceedings with officials during a gathering of the Sun Dance in 1879.[114] The previous year, printed copies of the proceedings in Washington between Lakota leaders and officials circulated in Red Cloud's camp. That printed record of the president's promises was so important to the Lakotas that they were sure to put the document directly in the faces of the government officials who came to their camp as a flagrant reminder. As Jeffrey Ostler put it, Lakotas "turned the written text, so often an enemy, to their advantage."[115]

With the possible benefits of literacy, Native leaders were forced to make difficult and complicated decisions regarding assimilationist education. Red Cloud for a time refused to send children to school because it was compulsory, but he also thought that literacy was necessary. Similarly, Sitting Bull, who regularly resisted US government attacks on his culture, did not equate literacy with conceding to colonization. He wanted his people to learn to read and write. Mary Collins, a missionary to Sitting Bull's camp at the Standing Rock Agency, wrote that Sitting Bull was "very much opposed to the Indians becoming civilized" and he did not want Collins to try to persuade his people to "leave their old ways of living" or to "abandon their dances," but he still wanted her to teach them how to read.[116] Stanley Vestal (aka Walter Campbell) attributed this statement to Sitting Bull: "If you see anything good in the white man's road, pick it up and keep it. But if you find something that is not good, or that turns out bad, leave it alone."[117] There was plenty that Sitting Bull did not want to pick up, but he believed that his people "must teach the children to read and write, so that the white men cannot cheat us, and we must hang on to our land until the young folks can speak English and look out for our own interests."[118]

Sitting Bull did not become a fluent English speaker, and he could only write his name, but he found the written word useful. He received and replied to letters from as far away as France and Germany in 1882. Maj. George Ahern, who was among those (both white and Native) who translated his correspondence, recalled that letters "included requests for his autograph, his tomahawk, pipe, etc."[119] Sitting Bull "only occasionally [deemed] a reply necessary." It seems Sitting Bull was charging two dollars per mailed autograph in 1887; one particularly persistent Baltimore resident sent three letters to Standing Rock in six weeks, trying to obtain the Hunkpapa headman's signature.[120]

Other Lakotas adopted correspondence with enthusiasm early on. In 1879, the agent on the Cheyenne River Reservation reported that he "occasionally" saw "writing material" in the cabins of Lakotas.[121] In that year at the Pine Ridge Agency, Oglala Lakota chief Little Wound sent a letter to his agent, asking that something be done about whites stealing their horses.[122] In 1880, American Horse at Pine Ridge began a long correspondence with a twelve-year-old white boy named Edwin Landy, the son of Cincinnati photographer James Landy. In an April 1880 letter to Edwin, American Horse wrote, "Although I have received a great many letters from other little boys in the East, yet I consider you my first."[123] American Horse later met Edwin and James Landy in Chicago, and a friendship developed. In December 1880, American Horse's wife was sick; he wrote that she was "not likely to live."[124] He confessed, "I am afraid I shall be sad hearted." The two also exchanged gifts through the mail. Edwin sent American Horse rings and a watch, and Edwin was given moccasins and beaded Indian work. American Horse's relationship with the Landys was not exclusive; he regularly used the mail, corresponding with several whites during his lifetime.

New Sources of Information

Gaining new sources of information was another advantage of literacy. Like eastern Native Americans before the mid-eighteenth century, western tribes used literacy to acquire more information independent of the US government. Plains Indians had newspapers printed in their own language as early as 1871. From 1871 to 1939, a Dakota-language newspaper run by the Dakota Mission called *Iapi Oaye* operated at the Santee Reservation (alongside the English-language version called the *Word Carrier* from 1884 to 1939).[125] Although not produced by Sioux, it claimed eight hundred Sioux readers in 1877 and became the longest-running Native-language paper. The paper began to print the same material in both English and Dakota as a way to encourage Sioux readers to learn English. Because the paper was run by Christian missionaries, its contents did not always represent the viewpoint of Dakotas or Lakotas. Nonetheless, *Iapi Oaye* still provided Sioux readers with news, education, and entertainment. Raymond J. DeMallie claims *Iapi Oaye* was "circulated widely and served as an important means of communication among the various Sioux agencies."[126]

Episcopalians began printing the Dakota-language *Anpao* in 1878, and the Catholic Church established *Sina Sapa Wocekiye Taeyanpaha* in 1892, both aimed at Christian Sioux.[127] Newspapers and periodicals printed at Carlisle, Hampton, the Genoa Indian Industrial School in Nebraska, and other boarding schools made their way onto the reservations as well, allowing parents and former students to be informed of the happenings at the schools.[128] They were English-only publications intended for both white and Native audiences, but they offered Natives from all parts of the country news that was relevant to them. Michael Burns, an Apache, said he valued Carlisle's the *Indian Helper* because he "learned much interesting news... about Indians throughout the United States."[129] Ten thousand copies of the *Indian Helper* were being printed weekly by 1890.[130] Also, Indians in western Indian Territory undoubtedly read the *Cheyenne Transporter* out of Darlington, near Fort Reno and the Cheyenne-Arapaho Reservation. It was issued at the agency during its run from 1879 to 1886.[131] Other nineteenth-century Indian Territory papers were published by missionaries (the *Indian Advocate, Indian Methodist, Our Brother in Red*) and printed by or for citizens of the Five Tribes (*Cherokee Advocate, Indian Chieftain, Indian Journal*), which were available to all Indians in the Territory.

The first newspaper created by Natives on a western reservation (outside of the Five Tribes) was called the *White Earth Progress*, launching in 1886. The editor of the paper, Theodore Hudon Beaulieu, an Ojibwe (Chippewa) on the White Earth Reservation in Minnesota, wanted to "advocate constantly and without reserve ... for the interests" of White Earth residents and all tribes "wherever they now are residing."[132] But Beaulieu accurately predicted that the US government would "fear" that their printed information might "be revolutionary in character." The White Earth agent did in fact accuse the *Progress*, which was critical of the Dawes Act, of "the voicing of incendiary and revolutionary sentiments." The agent prevented the publication of the next issue of the paper for a year and a half by raiding the press office and kicking Theodore and Augustus Beaulieu off the reservation. But, after a district court ruling and a hearing by the subcommittee of the Senate Committee on Indian Affairs, the paper ran again weekly, changing its name to *The Tomahawk* in the twentieth century.

Natives were also devoted readers of white newspapers and magazines and used them to inform themselves about American culture, politics, and concerns more immediate to them.[133] Connecting themselves to white sources, Natives snagged beneficial knowledge out of the national web of communication. Some, for example, became aware of US troop movements because of media reports.[134] Lakotas were aware of and troubled about the false newspaper reports about them as early as 1881. After an inaccurate report in the *Bismarck Tribune* that Indians were going off the reservation and causing trouble, the agent at Standing Rock telegraphed the editor that the Indians were instead "very indignant and mad" about his "groundless article."[135] Several years later, Sitting Bull was amused by a false report that claimed that he and his followers threatened to kill an educated Indian who was arguing for the acceptance of civilized ways during a council. Sitting Bull was visiting the Lower Brule Agency at the time of the council, four hundred miles away, which led him, after hearing that news, to quip, "Bull great man; Bull everywhere."[136]

Native Americans also used white newspapers to spread their own information and appeals for justice. They understood that English was the only

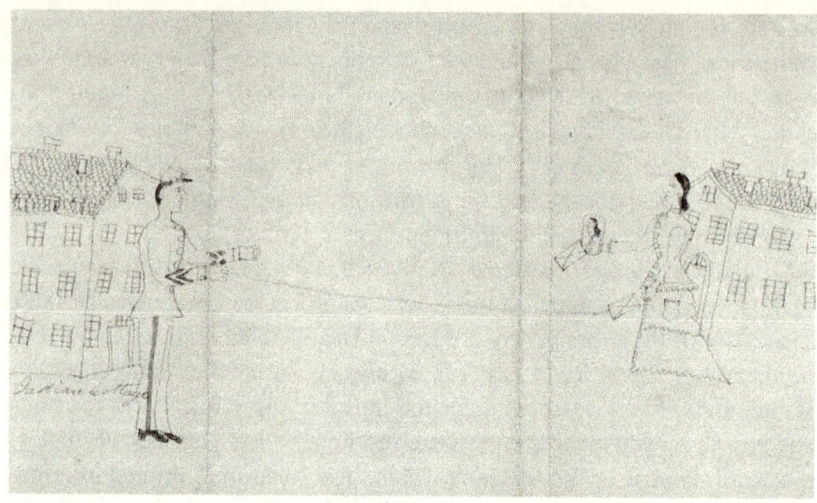

James Bear's Heart (Nacoista), a Cheyenne and former Fort Marion prisoner at the Hampton Institute, wrote a letter in English to his former teacher Helen Ludlow along with this drawing, asking for a return letter and a picture of Ludlow. For more on Bear's Heart, see Lookingbill, *War Dance at Fort Marion*, 169, 181. Courtesy of Thomas G. Connors.

language that white Americans paid any attention to. In December 1889, Sam White Bird, Iron Nation, Killing White Buffalo, and nine other Lakotas from Lower Brule wrote to the office of W. H. Wills & Co., pension, patent, and claim attorneys in Washington, DC, to seek assistance in their fight with the US government. Their people were poor, but they did not want to sell their land. They hoped that a lawyer could make public the injustices done to them. They wanted the press to get involved. "We give you this letter and you going to send it some newspapers in every cities," they directed.[137] "That is the reason we give you this letter," White Bird wrote, closing the letter with a pledge: the men were "going to get the mail to it."

Frustrated with government injustice and finding nowhere else to turn for help, others appealed to the American public through newspapers. In August 1879, a group of Omaha men wrote to the journalist Thomas Tibbles of the *Omaha Daily Herald* in order to convey their criticisms of President Rutherford B. Hayes to the white public. In a letter written in the Omaha language, the men stated, "We used to think that the oversight which the President exercised over us Indians was a good thing, but now it is not apt to be so."[138] The Indians "ought to be human beings," they wrote, "we desire you to make us human beings!" "Though I have a different skin, I hope that I may live in the land as do the people with white skins," the men pleaded. They told Tibbles that the letter was written so that whites could understand their condition. Other Omahas also tried to publicize in newspapers that same year. Hupeȼa, a thirty-two-year-old Omaha man, dictated a letter to William M'Kim Heath, who hoped to have it printed in the *Cincinnati Commercial Tribune*.[139] Hupeȼa described the crops he grew and the animals he raised and the house he had built but said he still saw his people dying in poverty. "Help us," he pleaded. "If you aid us, we ought to live." He accused the whites of craving Indian lands, wishing them dead, and killing the deer, buffalo, antelope, and elk, "which abounded for our good." Hupeȼa hoped that "the people in the whole world hear of" his letter, "and by the time that the people have heard about me, give me a letter and send it." The letter was not a petition to the US government; it was a direct plea to the people of the United States.

Indians and the Mail

During the early reservation years, Natives saw that the mail offered practical benefits, and as more and more Natives learned to read and write, the usefulness of literacy became more apparent. It is important to recognize that the growth of Native literacy coincided with the westward expansion of the US Postal Service. Spurred by population booms and the efficient reach of the railroads, post offices tied the trans-Mississippi into the national network, making daily communication among Indian reservations possible. The federal government quickly expanded the postal network in the 1870s and 1880s by employing private agents, often merchants, to manage the post in thousands of communities.[140] In 1877, the postal service used most of its new appropriations to deliver mail to the Black Hills of South Dakota, and more and more small towns in the West received mail during the 1880s.[141] In 1888, 1,068 post offices were operating in Dakota Territory, nearly doubling in six years. That same year, 219 post offices operated in Indian Territory, 173 in Wyoming Territory, 296 in Montana Territory, and 136 in Nevada.[142] In 1890 alone, 667 new post offices opened in Indian Territory, Nebraska, Colorado, North and South Dakota, Montana, Wyoming, Idaho, and Utah.[143]

Even before western Natives were living on reservations, the mail stations of the West saw frequent visits from Natives and often served as a meeting ground between whites and tribes. Beginning in 1860, Southern Plains Indians, including Kiowa chief Santana, Cheyenne chief Black

Kettle, and Arapaho chief Little Wolf, were regulars at the mail station at Pawnee Fork (Fort Larned) along the Santa Fe Trail in Kansas, even after Kiowas and Comanches threatened the presence of the post the previous year. James Brice, who worked as an overland mail contractor in those years, remembered Cheyennes, Arapahos, and Kiowas coming to the mail station "at all hours," not yet there to send and receive correspondence, but to interact with the men there (often telling Brice how badly the white people were treating them, killing their bison and spoiling hunting), rest their ponies, or even to sleep ("expecting the same courtesy as a guest at a hotel").[144]

Western Natives soon began to use the post for correspondence in the early reservation years. Each Indian agency had at least one post office, some established within the agency offices. Some reservations had multiple in service, and they became the focus of tribal communication.[145] In 1876, the doctor at the Santee Agency in Nebraska reported that half of the Santees (Eastern Dakotas) there could read and write and that more than half of the mail received at the agency post was for Santees.[146] Most of that mail was written in the Dakota language. The doctor noted that the Santees were prompt in their correspondence and they took pleasure in writing. That same year but farther south in Indian Territory, the clerk at the Pawnee Agency commented on the rush that accompanied mail day at the agency. Pawnees aiming to send and receive correspondence swamped his office. "The people are anxious to get their letters," the clerk wrote, "and when they do get them [they] often sit down and read them or the papers."[147] Because of the volume of mail, servicing the postal demands of Natives became a responsibility of reservation employees early on. In 1890, the agent at the Western Shoshone Agency in Nevada told the commissioner of Indian affairs that one of the jobs of his agency clerk was to write and read letters, to carry on "an extensive correspondence," for illiterate Shoshones.[148]

Natives also used the mail to ship gifts to friends at distant agencies.[149] Young Man Afraid of His Horses at Pine Ridge (more properly translated as Young Man Whose Enemies Are Afraid of His Horses or They Even Fear His Horses) sent a box express with two pipes to High Chief at the Cheyenne-Arapaho Reservation in Oklahoma.[150] Red pipestone pipes also seemed to be an important item among Omaha and Ponca letter writers. Several letters specifically asked for them to be sent by mail. In 1879, the Omaha chief Mantcu-nanba wrote to his Yankton friend Feather-in-the-Ear (Wi Ya Ko Mi) to "beg" for "some claws of grizzly bears, send them to me in the mail-bag from your post-office."[151] Pawnees in Indian Territory had sent Mantcu-nanba a letter wanting a necklace of bear claws, and he wanted

Uncompahgre Ute chiefs (including Captain Billy, second from left) at the Los Piños Agency Post Office with Agent J. B. Thompson and an unnamed interpreter, c. 1878. Denver Public Library, Western History Collection, Z-1543.

to oblige them. Mantcu-nanba promised Feather-in-the-Ear that he would "do my best and get something in return from them." Many packages were exchanged with white acquaintances. Keeps the Battle, a Lakota man at Pine Ridge, wrote to a white settler at Fort Keogh, Montana, saying that he never received the bison robe he had been promised in exchanged for a war club (nor had Young Man Afraid of His Horses received his field glasses).[152] It seems that Keeps the Battle's robe was not the postal service's only failed delivery to a reservation. In 1890, the postmaster general reported that "Indian pipes and tomahawks" occupied the service's Dead Letter Office.[153]

Even though reservations had post offices, many Natives still had to travel a good distance to reach the nearest one, and demand for better access to the post grew.[154] In 1888, an agent asked for the establishment of a post office at the Lower Brule Agency, which shared a post office with the Crow Creek Agency across the Missouri River. "The employees and Indians are very anxious for its establishment," he wrote to the commissioner of Indian affairs, "which will give them the security of a regular mail pouch."[155] The agent claimed that the Lakotas received more mail than any white town within a fifteen-mile radius of Chamberlain, Dakota Territory (present-day South Dakota), which had a distributing office.

Similarly, in 1891, Luther Standing Bear, while visiting relatives at Pine Ridge, got into a discussion with other Lakotas about the inadequate mail service in a section of the reservation along Medicine Root Creek, where letters were frequently delayed. Standing Bear decided to write to John Wanamaker, a man he had worked for in Philadelphia while a student at Carlisle, who happened to be the US postmaster general in 1891. Standing Bear asked if they could establish a new post office at the Medicine Root Creek; he proposed calling the place Kyle because it was short and "easy to spell."[156] Wanamaker was "pleased" with the idea, but he would not allow Standing Bear to be the postmaster at Kyle because he was not white.[157] Instead, a local missionary was appointed, but Standing Bear did all of the work at the office, which began in the corner of his uncle's store. Standing Bear remembered that they were glad they "were at least on the map." Kyle, South Dakota, still has a post office, zip code 57752.

An Anticolonial Weapon

Native Americans did not always utilize literacy and the US Postal Service in the ways whites expected. Natives questioned the power of the federal government and made their thoughts known to white America. They knew that English literacy was meant to be a tool that would contribute to the destruction of their culture, yet many came to use it as a tool of self-determination instead. The Office of Indian Affairs was created by the US government to control the Native populations of the west. Agents, special agents, subagents, assistant farmers, clerks, superintendents, teachers, and other government employees were hired to manage the thousands of Indians living on reservations in the West. Hundreds of employees and millions of federal and private dollars supported a system of education, food rations, and other forms of assistance, but Indians still had a difficult time getting what they required. The US government built a system that required rules and regulations, documents, receipts, and record keeping. Permissions had to be obtained, letters had to be sent, communication between the West and Washington, DC, had to transpire. All of this was done to limit Native American independence, to keep them away from the white world while the younger generation could be assimilated through education and agriculture. But letters gave Indians another path to Washington. Even if agents wrote letters on their behalf, they could not always be trusted to write what Indians asked them to write. An Omaha man named Two Crows complained to another Indian that agents did not write to the president when Omahas asked them. "They say that they have written for us," Two Crows wrote, but "the agents do not speak the truth."[158] Two Crows and other Omahas needed to be heard by the president, so they sent their own letters. Native Americans could write to the commissioner of Indian affairs, the president, congressmen, or white allies directly, no matter their standing with their people.

Letter writing gave Natives additional weight in the balance of power on reservations. In letters to white officials or allies, Natives criticized government policies and employees, demanded assistance, and offered their opinions on agency decisions, like the hiring and firing of agents, farmers, and teachers.[159] Because agents were the most significant government force in their lives, Natives tried to influence who would be hired to direct their reservations, and letters became an easy tool with which to do that. Complaints against agents filled the commissioner's desk as Native writers hoped to undermine the power of their agents and expose corruption. There are hundreds of examples of these particular late-nineteenth-century letters. Just one example of the everyday corruption exposed because of literacy comes from the summer 1890. In a letter to the secretary of the interior, a group of Western Shoshones accused their agent of selling them grass seed that belonged to the government. The agent's wife, according to the men, was using government rations to supply her restaurant on the reservation.[160] Letters also make clear that Natives had many types of criticism against agents under many different circumstances, from specific complaints about not providing government jobs for their people, especially those recently returned from boarding schools, to general complaints about unfairness or malice on the part of the agent.[161]

Moreover, the conduct and performance of all agency employees, from whites to the Indian police, were frequently criticized via letter.[162] Natives took to the mail to attack or recommend government interpreters (who had to be trusted to relay communication accurately and honestly). There were also written protests against licensed Indian traders. The morality of agency employees was also regularly questioned. For instance, in one particularly biting letter, Fast Horse at Pine Ridge reported that "nearly all the agency employees were drunk, intoxicating around the agency" on Christmas.[163] Letter writing also allowed Indians to report horrible crimes, like sexual abuse, that otherwise may have been concealed by white authorities.[164] In early 1891, William Selwyn (Wicahaokdeum), a Yankton at the Yankton Reservation, accused a missionary of sexually abusing a boy.[165] Similarly, Running Bull and a group of Yankton headmen asked the commissioner to discharge Henry E. Dawes, the superintendent of the Yankton Boarding School, because he "had taken improper liberties with six of the girls."[166]

Of course, land rights were a common topic in Indian letters to government officials. Tribes wanted to be sovereign bodies that controlled their own lands, but they usually had little say over agency operations on their lands, such as the location of the agency headquarters, the creation and location of subagencies, or boundary lines between agencies.[167] Some, especially Northern Cheyennes in the 1880s, wrote to demand to be moved to new reservations. Many individuals, especially Lakotas, wrote to officials in order to be transferred to other agencies, particularly to be closer to family and friends.[168] Natives used the mail to gather information about the US government's strategies to obtain Indian lands and to protest the ever-changing shape of reservations.[169] Letters were also sent to government officials to report land violators like white trespassers, whites illegally using Indian land to graze cattle, and agents or headmen using grazing land to line their own pockets.[170]

Letter writers also contested legislation. Between January 1889 and March 1890, more than one hundred letters regarding allotment and the Dawes Severalty Act were sent to the commissioner of Indians affairs by Native Americans (or those claiming to be of Native American descent), at least twenty-four came from Native American women.[171] Many also used the mail to fight the endless battle against hunger on the reservations.[172] The US government intentionally created a reservation system that left Indians dependent on the federal government for basic necessities. Not only did the US government dictate what foods Indians received, it also controlled the flow of manufactured goods, livestock, farming implements, and medicines entering the reservations. Letter writers tried to convince the federal government that their people deserved more rations, especially after Congress reduced the appropriations for rations in 1889 and ignored recommendations from Indian Affairs to increase appropriations in spring 1890. Besides

Table 4

Origin and Number of Known Surviving Native American Letters Sent to the Commissioner of Indian Affairs, 1890

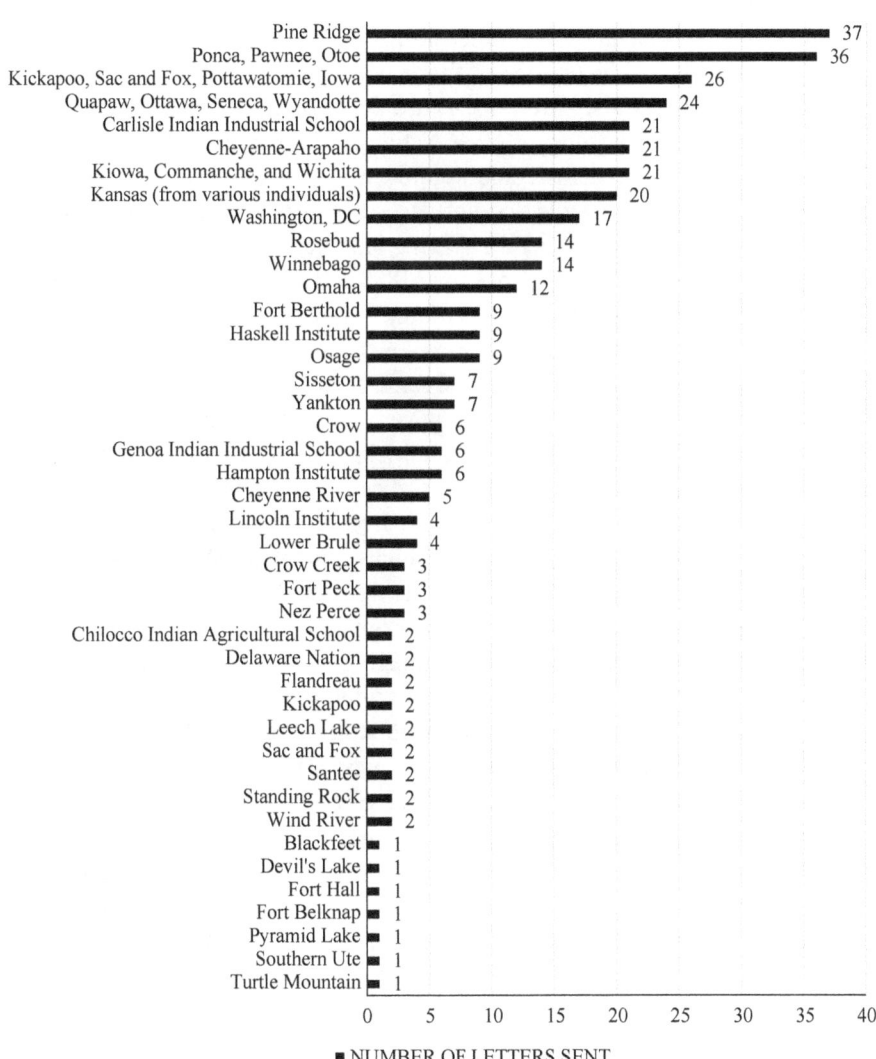

■ NUMBER OF LETTERS SENT

food, writers also asked for items they could not acquire on the reserves or reported shortages of necessities, including medicine.[173] Wagons were a hot commodity for many.[174] Horses were also needed. Newton Big Road, a thirty-two-year-old Oglala at Pine Ridge, needed reapers, wire fences, plows, mowing machines, and other farm tools to earn any money on his farm. "And besides," he reasoned, "this is not a good farming country."[175]

Western Natives also wrote to secure debts owed to them by the US government, white citizens, or other Natives.[176] Letters and petitions were often the only way Indians could secure owed funds. Kiowas, Yanktons, and men from Fort Berthold and Fort Belknap all demanded money owed to them for things like leasing for grazing land, railroad rights-of-way, and promised annuities. Between November 1888 and February 1891, more than one hundred letters regarding annuity money were sent to the commissioner of Indian affairs by Native Americans (or those claiming to be of Native American descent). At least thirty-one came from Native American women. But getting money owed by the US government was rarely an easy task. Wolf Chief at Fort Berthold, for example, had to write multiple letters to government officials to convince the Office of Indian Affairs to pay the $80,000 owed to his people.[177] John Half Iron, a Santee, believed the government owed his people thousands of dollars of interest ($15,000 a year for more than two decades). "We think we are men, not beast," he implored.[178]

Letters allowed Natives to express their opinions on government policies, but if those opinions were seen to be damaging to the US government's civilizing efforts, an agent could use those written records of opinion against letter writers.[179] Some letter writers were worried about retribution from their agents.[180] Ponca chief White Eagle, worried that his letter of complaint to Washington, DC, might eventually be read by his agent, told the commissioner, "The agent now here as he does not like me and would seek to injure me if he knew this letter was written."[181] Others wanted to keep their agents out of the loop. Cloud Chief, Starving Elk, and White Antelope, three Southern Cheyennes at the Cheyenne-Arapaho Reservation, had written to the commissioner before, but their agent never let them know if the commissioner replied. In December 1890, they asked the commissioner to reply to them, his "Indian friends," instead of forwarding it to the agent.[182] Additionally, surveillance and censorship of the mail seem to be common tactics used by some agents to control the Indians they managed (Gahige, an Omaha man, wrote to a Ponca friend that his agent would "usually conceal from the Ponkas the letters that we sent them.... They do not give them the letters"), but letter writing still became a tool used by Natives to improve their situation and to give them a sense of control over the governmental decisions made on their behalf.[183]

In July 1890, Feather-in-the-Ear, a Yankton, wrote to the secretary of the interior and the commissioner of Indian affairs to ask if he could get a horse and a wagon that were not being used at the Yankton Reservation. "My grandchildren have all died this summer and I am a poor old man," he wrote, "but I want to go and see some of my friends at other Agencies, but I have no good horse."[184] Feather-in-the-Ear usually asked his agent for such things, but the agent "always says he will write to Washington about it and it is so long before we hear so I thought I would get a man to write a letter straight to you." He added, "When you answer me I want you to send the letter to me because we wrote a letter to Washington once and the answer came back to the Agent and he never showed us the letter but told us about it and we did not like that way of doing business."[185] Why rely on an untrustworthy agent of the US government when you can make the communication yourself? he asked. By writing a letter directly to Washington, Feather-in-the-Ear, like many Natives in the late nineteenth century, found a way to carry his voice through the maze of bureaucracy that had been built around his people.[186]

This chapter has demonstrated that western Native Americans turned the educational goals of the US government on its head, and used literacy to reestablish a sense of sovereignty, decolonize some aspects of their lives, and protect their tribes and families from colonial abuses. The next chapter will show how Natives also corresponded with other Natives who were facing common concerns, which allowed them to actively manage and contest colonialism collectively. Groups outside of a common language family communicated via English-language letters. Kiowas could read letters from Cheyennes, Arapahos could send letters to Shoshones, and so on. English literacy allowed for the creation of an open inter-Indian media community where all Native peoples could congregate.

CHAPTER 2

Connecting Reservations

The US government created artificial boundaries to limit tribal lands and to separate tribal nations, which would supposedly ease the US government's effort to Americanize the Indians by keeping intertribal peace and eliminating distractions. But Native Americans used the tools acquired at Americanized Indian schools to express themselves beyond reservation boundaries, overcoming the segregation that the reservations of the West were designed to create. Native Americans employed education, namely literacy, as an anticolonial tool. Letters written by Native men, women, and children passed over reservation borders (courtesy of the US Postal Service) to other Natives, bridging the distance between reservations, largely outside the control of colonialism.

During the 1870s and 1880s, a series of local communities networked into larger, growing intertribal communities. Native networks of correspondence tied individuals to their families, families to their tribes, and tribes to other tribes. Nations divided by language used written English as an effective common language. Related peoples separated by geography and by the consequences of colonialism, like the Northern and Southern Cheyennes, Northern and Southern Arapahos, Southern and Northern Utes, or divisions of Lakotas living at different agencies, could stay in constant communication and be informed about the affairs of other groups. Nations without a previous relationship could forge new bonds, and those with a history of conflict could make peace. Correspondence was used by leaders to spread influence, sway minds, hash out disagreements, and inform others about the dirty dealings of the US government. Letters spread warnings of disease, plans for improvement, and ideas of change. Cultures were exchanged, especially religious concepts; visitations and dances were planned; and extratribal life developed.

Boarding School Networks

Many western Native Americans began to correspond for the first time out of necessity. With hundreds of boys and girls sent off to live at boarding schools, often hundreds of miles from the reservation, concerned parents wrote to communicate with their children. Parents exchanged letters with their children living in dormitories at off-reservation boarding schools across the country, providing children at least one tether to their accustomed life back home. Students regularly sent letters home at the request of their parents, as an exercise in English class, or of their own free will.[1] Parents also corresponded with school administrators and government officials concerning their children. Beginning in the 1870s, a great chain of correspondence was created throughout the country among superintendents and parents, parents and students, and students and superintendents and agency officials.

Letter writing was a specific skill taught alongside general literacy at most Indian schools. The practical benefits of writing a good letter were obvious to educators in the late nineteenth century. In 1883, Laura Tileston, a fifth division English teacher at the Hampton Institute in Virginia, reported, "These are exceedingly bright boys.... They are giving more particular attention to letter-writing, as that will be of the greatest service to them when they go home."[2] In his report of the Ponca School to the commissioner of Indian affairs, the agent at the Ponca, Pawnee, and Otoe Reservation in Indian Territory boasted, "The system of pupils writing business and social letters is, in my mind, very advantageous as it gives them an insight to business that older men and women would be glad to possess, many of these letters are simply grand both in composition and penmanship. Such proficiency is rarely observed in the states among white children."[3] The Hampton Institute claimed that in a few months, its average student was able "to form short sentences, either in conversation or in little letters to his teachers or the friends at home."[4]

From the earliest years of the western Indian schools, students used that letter-writing skill to communicate with their parents. In 1875, the teacher at the Crow Creek Mission School wrote that her five English-speaking Yanktonai boarding school students had "learned to write and now write to their parents very often."[5] Students at Carlisle Industrial School in Pennsylvania began writing home in English (on the backs of monthly reports) in the first months of that school's existence in 1879.[6] By the 1880s, most boarding school students were required to write letters home.[7] Children at White's Institute in Wabash, Indiana, sent monthly letters to their parents along with their report cards.[8] Roscoe Conkling, a Kiowa, sent his father his report card that showed "Very good" in the areas of work, neatness, conduct, recreation, and health. "I send my to love to my mother and sister," Conkling wrote. "I want you to wide a letter to me."[9] Topics varied, but students tried to keep their parents informed.[10] According to the agent at Pine Ridge, parents took "great interest" in the letters from Carlisle students, a "custom" that "accomplished" "much good."[11]

Parents missed their children, and letters allowed them to connect. Some parents desperately asked for letters from their children. This distress can be seen in the report of the agent in charge of the Nevada Agency (the Pyramid Lake and Walker River Reservations in Nevada) who had to comfort the parents of a group of Paiute boys at the Grand Junction boarding school:

> Judging from letters received of recent date by relatives and friends from these boys, they are apparently better contented with their new home than was anticipated.... The parents of those who are in Colorado mourn them as lost, or as they would the dead, and are frequently at the office at daylight making inquiries as to their (the children's) welfare and asking for letters. It is really a pitiful sight to witness their distress and sorrow at times when they come to talk about the children and ask how many "moons" before they come home, while their appearance indicates that they had passed a restless night, or perhaps not slept any. At times I really feel sorry, and console them in every possible manner, by pointing out the advantages their children will derive by the change, and refer them to the letters of encouragement they receive.[12]

Despite efforts to reassure parents, plenty of them asked their children to come home. Felix Iron Eagle told his father to "keep quiet" in reply to a request to come home: "I have a good chance to learn the English language, when I learn it better, then I can go home and help him all I can."[13]

Students received important news from home, learning of illnesses or deaths of loved ones.[14] Students also wrote to friends in order to hear news from the reservation.[15] Sometimes the distance between friends was unbearable. A boy at the Kiowa Agency wrote to his friend Orry Giving at the Haskell Institute in Lawrence, Kansas, "I will let you know that my mother is dead, today is the third day since she die. I thought that I would like to see you little while and then you will return to school again because I do not feel well, may be when I meet you I will feel better, this is all I have to say."[16] One Carlisle student complained in a letter back home that she was tired of writing letters each month without getting any replies. "If you should ask me a question when I get home and I will not answer your question would you think that I was very polite or impolite?" she asked.[17] Another student understood that those back home could not "write letter as well as we can because you never went to school like we. But you could get somebody to write for you and you can do the talking for yourself."[18]

Parents did write back, and many familiarized themselves with the written word for the first time during their exchanges.[19] Parents often encouraged their children to succeed at boarding schools and do their work, even though many were hesitant to trust white educators. Brave Bull, a Lakota, wrote his daughter (using the hand of his friend Big Star), "If you could read and write, I should be very happy."[20] Another wrote to his daughters, "I told you both before you went away how much I wanted you to learn English to read and write like white people."[21] One Ponca man wrote to his son at Carlisle in their Native language: "I say what I think in order to urge you to persevere. If you do well one of the good things which the white people teach you, you may become rich. Though it generally gives me much trouble not to see you for a single day, yet when they cause you to do one good thing, one thing which you can find, for the sake of your improvement, attend to it! I think that alone is good."[22] Besides the prospect of personal improvement, letters also reflected the practical benefits parents hoped education would bring to their nations. Torlino, a Navajo man, wrote (with the help of the Navajo agent) to his son Tom that the Navajos wanted him to learn all he could, "for they will need you when you come back so you can do our business for us."[23] Likewise, a Cheyenne named Bobtail wrote his son, "Those who went to Carlisle are on a good road. I think they will learn English fast and understand the white man's road quickly. So they can bring it back to their people."[24]

In 1880, Hampton superintendent Samuel C. Armstrong provided the commissioner of Indian affairs several letters from parents to their children that illustrated the "Indian interest in the improvement of the children."[25] No doubt, the most favorable letters were selected, as Armstrong was quite the fund-raiser, but all seem to be authentic. A father from Crow Creek wrote, "My Son: I am going to write you a letter again. I want you to write letters to me often. I am glad that you are trying to learn. . . . The boys down there, their fathers would like to go down and see them. . . . Then they would like to send all their children. Learn to talk English; don't be ashamed to talk it."[26] Another father wrote, "I want you to learn how to be a printer. I want you to learn to talk English. . . . I hope some of the boys will learn to be a teacher, when they come back that they can teach the boys and girls." A brother told his sister, "I want you to learn all you can and learn something good, and God watch you all the time. . . . That's the reason I let you go to

Hampton."[27] Yanktonai chief Wizi told his half brother that he wished he were young again so he "could go down and learn too. I want you to learn all you can and come back and teach your brothers. Try to learn and talk English, too."[28]

White educators were not pleased with all the letters from home, especially those that asked students to do things forbidden by schools.[29] Also, some parents wrote to their children in their Native language, and those letters could be left unread. In 1887, for instance, two Carlisle girls received letters from their mothers that were written in Dakota. According to the Carlisle newspaper, the *Indian Helper*, nobody at Carlisle could translate for the girls, but the paper was not telling the truth.[30] Carlisle simply wanted to discourage the use of the Sioux "vernacular." The previous year, Slow Bull's letter to Carlisle superintendent Richard H. Pratt that was written in Dakota was translated at Carlisle by Slow Bull's grandson, Frank Locke.[31] Furthermore, in 1888, an editorial in a weekly Congregationalist magazine called *The Independent* stated that the writer had heard "that boys at Carlisle are interfered with as their liberty of receiving letters in the vernacular from their parents."[32] Superintendent Pratt replied to the editor of *The Independent*, saying that any letter sent to a Sioux student that he "apprehend[ed might] be written in their vernacular [would] be opened." If the letter was written in English, it would be delivered "without further espionage." If it was written in the Dakota language, Pratt would have the letter interpreted "to gain some general idea of the character of the correspondence" because, as he reasoned, "about nine out of ten" of the letters sent to his students in "vernacular" were "the twaddle and scurrility of boys and girls to each other under the cloak of darkness, and not best as a school influence." Those who wrote to the students in Dakota were asked to thereafter write in English. Pratt assured the editor that this practice only related to the 92 Sioux (Dakota and Lakota) pupils, because the other 481 were not members of tribes with a written language.

It is clear that Pratt interfered with his students' correspondence when he thought it necessary. In at least one instance, he even encouraged the censorship of his students' letters to their parents.[33] Conversely, in another instance, Pratt worried that letters sent by students were being interfered with by reservation employees. After Pratt learned that Fannie Charging Shield's letters were not getting into the hands of her family at Pine Ridge, he assured the Pine Ridge agent that all letters were stamped and addressed directly to the parents. Pratt, having similar "complaints at other agencies," wondered if there was "something more than carelessness" at hand.[34] White officials did have the opportunity and incentive to peruse the Indian mail.

Nevertheless, because letters that might damage the reputations of schools made it into the hands of parents, it seems that most boarding school students could write home without someone scrutinizing their words. Many students wrote home to the parents to report their bad health, for instance, often asking to be sent back to the reservation.[35] A group of pupils at the Haskell Institute was able to inform the parents of Hugh Antelope, a Southern Cheyenne, that he was seriously ill via letter.[36] Apparently the school had failed to do so.

Also, parents regularly wrote directly to school superintendents to inquire about the health of their children.[37] Superintendent Pratt's most frequent correspondents were concerned parents. Blue Tomahawk wanted his son Dennis, who was ill at Carlisle, to come home to Rosebud. He had recently lost two daughters to the same illness on the reserve. However, Pratt did not think that Dennis would survive the journey home, particularly in the cold winter weather (though Pratt typically wanted gravely ill students to return home). "I will write to you every day and tell you about your son," Pratt promised Blue Tomahawk, but Dennis would not return home.[38] Dennis Blue Tomahawk, who had come to Carlisle with the first group of students from Rosebud and Pine Ridge in 1879, died on January 19, 1881, eleven days after Pratt's letter to Blue Tomahawk.[39] There are dozens of such surviving letters to and from the parents of sick children at Carlisle from the early 1880s alone. At least one Oglala Lakota parent sent medicine to her son Herman Arrow Maker.[40] Some parents also wrote to ask for the bodies of their recently deceased children.[41] Most students who died at Carlisle were buried at the school because of the high cost of transporting the body back west. Some students chose or were asked to write letters to the parents of their deceased classmates to let them know the particulars of the death or more about the life of the child while at school.[42]

Students informed their parents via mail when they were ready to leave school and return home permanently.[43] Some students wrote to their agents, asking to be released from school, sometimes only for a short spell.[44] If requests to visit home were denied, some students used the mail to supersede the authority of their school superintendents by asking their agents or the commissioner of Indian affairs for the privilege.[45] Parents also took to the mail to have their children returned to them.[46] Long Pumpkin, a Rosebud Brulé, wrote to the commissioner in October 1890 to ask that his son be returned from the Genoa Indian Industrial School in Nebraska.[47] He claimed the superintendent had promised him that if he sent one of his daughters to the school, the son could go home. Long Pumpkin said he was "lame and not able to work" (he had been shot in the leg during the aftermath of Spotted Tail's murder by Crow Dog in 1881), his "old lady" was "not able to work" either, and all five of his children were in school.[48] "Please ask the superintendent to allow my boy to come," he wrote. "I will help you all I can and am a friend to you all."

Students also wrote to their agents back home, asking for information or assistance.[49] Others wrote home to their agents just to let them know how things were going.[50] Students who had already returned home kept in touch with friends and teachers back east, reporting news of employment, illness, or important life events like marriage.[51] The mail also allowed the eastern boarding school students who were married to keep their families together. John Running With at Hampton received a letter from home that his wife and son were having a hard time and were sick with no one to take care of them, which made him "feel very sorry."[52] Running With told the superintendent that he wanted to finish school, "but such a news from home made me think of going home."

Intratribal Correspondence

Even with their compulsory confinement on reservations, western Natives traveled across their boundaries, a topic discussed in the next chapter. Those traveling on their own accord used the postal service to keep in touch with their families back at the reservation. Men and women on visits to other reservations commonly let their people know how their travels were going. For instance, Hairy Chin, a Hunkpapa from Standing Rock, made sure to write home on his arrival to the Rosebud Agency for a visit in 1889 (he was being "[treated] like a king," he wrote).[53] In 1874, three Prairie Band Potawatomis traveled from Kansas to Indian Territory and Texas to visit Potawatomis and Southern Kickapoos. While at a stopover at the Wichita Agency, they wrote a letter home to provide an update of their travels. But, weeks later, Pee Shee Dwin, a Potawatomi headman back in Kansas, after not hearing from his traveling friends in a while, wrote a letter to the Wichita agent, asking if he knew their whereabouts. He asked the agent to give the traveling Potawatomis a message, a few lines written in their Potawatomi language, if he ever saw them. "Please do not fail to give us some information whether they are there or not by the first mail," he added.[54]

Many western Natives participated in the market economy before the twentieth century, working off-reservation, traveling with Wild West shows, freighting government supplies, or laboring on white farms. Some corresponded to stay connected to their homes. George Miller, an Omaha man who was off the reservation trying to earn money, instructed his wife (in letters written in the Omaha language) to attend to their children, take care of their corn, and "do whatever you think is right."[55] He was upset that his wife did not write more letters to him. "Day after day I am constantly thinking about my children, and I wish to hear how they are," he wrote.[56] A month later, in reply to a letter from his wife, Miller wrote that his efforts to make money were a "total failure," but he still was able to stuff ten dollars in the envelope.[57] He told his wife that he thought of her every day and that he was sad, but he would return home.

Others used the mail to communicate their emotions to absent loved ones. Kaxé-¢ᴺba, a Ponca, wrote to his child who had left the reservation: "My child, before you went, I was not poor at all. When you departed, I was very poor. I always remember you, and I greatly desire to see you. It is not probable that there will be any way for me to get to see you. I am sad because you went so far away. I hope to hear good words from you. I send you this when there is no moonlight."[58] Letters were also written to convey romantic love. David Pendleton Oakerhater (Making Medicine), a Southern Cheyenne who had been away from his people for years, wrote his wife, Nomee (Thunder Woman), "O my dear wife I not forget—I love you."[59] One boy wrote to a prospective sweetheart, "I have thought in writing to you and request whether we can agree and constant of friendship or not. Please see about the matter and give the information with cause."[60] Letters also carried heartbreak. A non-Native man in 1888 was worried that news of his infidelity would reach his Lakota wife at Standing Rock, "told her by Indians about me."[61] He asked the Standing Rock agent to tell his wife that those "letters written to her by outside parties will be nothing but what is not so." Letter writing was a regular practice for Lakotas by 1888, and according to this man, there was a chance that his wife would be informed about his actions via an already established network of correspondence.

Other Lakotas corresponded to apologize for their actions. In 1890, Take Way From Crow, who was in Stacyville, Iowa, working with an Indian medicine company, wrote a number of letters to his sister-in-law at Pine Ridge, "Miss Pte Sa," or the wife of Red Cow, in order to resolve a family schism (Red Cow, an Oglala, was also known as Charles Picket Pin and also Spotted Horse).[62] Take Way From Crow seems to have done something to hurt his sister-in-law, and his letter (written in Dakota) was a way to make amends. It begins, "Eya ha ka wowapi (in modern Lakota syllabary: eyá haŋká wówapi)," or "My sister-in-law, I write to you." It continues in Dakota, but here is a portion of the letter in an English translation:

I have written to you a number of times but some reason I have received no word from you in reply. Still I am writing to you. I received a letter from my brother, Spotted Horse, in which he says: "My brother, I do not want you to write any more because they do not like you and that makes me feel bad. I have been feeling very badly about it. I said that I was ashamed, but really I am not, and I am all right." My sister-in-law, in thinking of myself I feel that I am not good and that you had the right to say what you did about me. . . . You will not see me again for a long time. I guess your heart will be good. . . . You make me feel ashamed of myself but it is nothing. . . . Do not think any more of this affair but keep quiet about it. . . . I shake hands with you with a good heart. Write me at this address.[63]

The written Dakota language was the medium in which Take Way From Crow chose to express his remorse. Perhaps it was the only way he could communicate with his family, but the letter demonstrates how Lakotas readily adapted literacy to their own, often personal, purposes.

Native men and women journeyed to distant places on their own accord, but in many instances, tribes were separated for reasons outside their control. Letter writing kept tribes in contact despite the consequences of settler colonialism. The Pawnees, for instance, were forced to leave their territory in Nebraska in 1873–74 and relocate with the Wichitas in Kansas because, as Sun Chief told a council, "the white men were getting too thick up there, and were taking our wood and other things," and the "northern tribes would steal our horses and sometimes kill our men."[64] Some Pawnees decided to head south to Kansas, while others remained in Nebraska, which separated the tribes for months. By 1873, the Pawnee population had already dwindled to less than three thousand, and the continued raiding by the Lakotas, along with competition with white settlers, pressed the remaining Nebraska Pawnees to reluctantly head to the Wichita Agency in Indian Territory. Pawnee chiefs' letters to the Wichita Agency allowed the Pawnees to coordinate this transition while the tribe was geographically divided. In 1874, Pawnee headmen Sun Chief, Captain Chief, Good Chief, and Turse-le-con-wa-ho sent a letter to the Pawnees at the Wichita Agency to inform them that forty lodges of Pawnees were on their way to settle there.[65]

In 1876 and 1877, Pawnees were again caught in circumstances that kept around seventy men away from their people. These men volunteered to serve as scouts in the US Army's attempt to take the Black Hills from the Lakotas and Northern Cheyennes (which had led to the Great Sioux War in 1876).[66] In January 1877, several Pawnee scouts who were chasing "hostile"

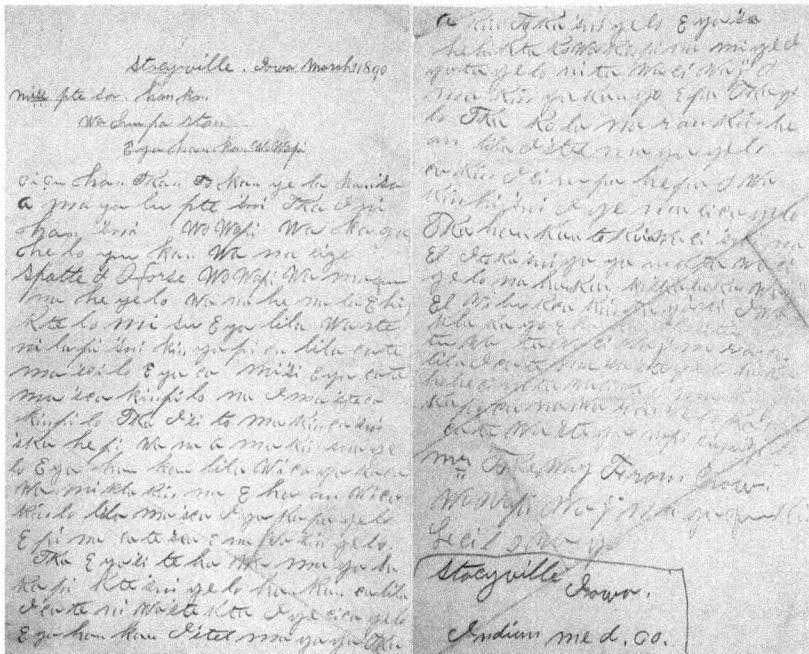

Take Way From Crow's letter written in Dakota to his sister-in-law, the wife of Red Cow, March 1, 1890. Smithsonian Institution, National Anthropological Archives, MS 1748.

Lakotas in Powder River country sent letters written in English (there was not yet a form of written Pawnee) home to the Pawnee Agency in Indian Territory. The non-Native clerk at the agency read the letters for Pawnees (his English was, in turn, interpreted by the agency interpreter). One scout wrote home, "God looks down on us, we have had revenge for some things that the Sioux have done to us."[67] A few weeks later, Pawnees received a twenty-eight-page letter from the scouts about their exploits (written by Maj. Frank North and dictated by several of the scouts). After the reading of the letter, Pawnees "commenced and made big enough noise to be heard a long distance," and "some old men commenced singing and started off in different directions singing about the exploits as they went."[68]

Others who were forced to be away from their people corresponded home. After two Sans Arc Lakota men fled their Cheyenne River Reservation in 1880, they used the mail to let others know the reasons for their decision. Crow Feather and Whip wrote to a Santee woman named Mary Trimmer, who lived in Hill City, Dakota Territory, in the Black Hills. Trimmer had corresponded with the men before (the previous letter she received had already been opened by an unknown reader), but now the men were living at a new agency, Rosebud. Crow Feather and Whip explained that they had been denied rations at Cheyenne River, and their agent and interpreter were mistreating their people. They reported that Agent Theodore Schwan and the interpreter "pretended to be priests" and forced "all the young unmarried women" onto "the wagons and carried them off."[69] The letter continued, "They cry and don't want to go, but they take them any way, and the agent told us if we would not let them go he would not give us any rations. The whole tribe did not like this and left the agency. We left without doing any trouble. Don't keep this to yourself. Tell the lawyers if they have not shut the court up yet."[70]

It is not entirely clear what Agent Schwan had done, but it is likely that he forced the girls to live at a boarding school. Months before Crow Feather and Whip's letter, Schwan had told the commissioner of Indian affairs that he believed that "children must be separated from the own people" in order to learn English; "the greater the separation the better. The scheme recently adopted of placing Indian children at school in the East is a most excellent one."[71] A boarding school for girls was in operation at the Cheyenne River Agency, and the agent believed that attendance at schools "should be compulsory, and no parent or relative should be permitted to take a child home, even for one night." But because of mailed correspondence, Crow Feather and Whip could, from more than one hundred miles away, try to prevent Lakota children from being forcibly sent to boarding schools.

Other families were separated by misfortunes caused by colonialism, but letters brought hope of reconnection. In 1881, Pawnee Woman, a Northern Cheyenne at Pine Ridge, wrote to the agent at the Cheyenne-Arapaho Reservation in Indian Territory, looking for her son High Back Wolf, who was with the Dull Knife party of Northern Cheyennes who were forced by the US government to settle south of their homelands in Indian Territory.[72] Similarly, Mazantanka (John Lynde), who used the then common term "halfbreed" to describe himself, wrote to the agent at Fort Totten in search of his mother. In 1868, as a boy, he had been taken by soldiers from Fort Totten (Devil's Lake Reservation) to Fort Bennett (Cheyenne River Reservation). Separated by more 350 miles, he had not seen his mother since the day he was kidnapped. "I also wish that you would find out whether my mother is still living or not," he requested. "I forgot my mother's name I was very small when I left Fort Totten *with the Soldiers*."[73] Frank Black Hawk also used letter writing as a means to find lost loved ones. Black Hawk worked off the reservation for two months in a coal mine and then as a farmer for one dollar a day, but he could not get his brothers at Standing Rock to reply to his letters. He had to write to the agent there to find out where they were.[74]

The dislocation caused by US colonialism separated entire tribes, but letters could keep them in touch. More than five hundred Northern Paiutes were forced to live apart from their people in a concentration camp for several years at Fort Simcoe on the Yakima Agency in Washington Territory, hundreds of miles from their homelands in Nevada and southeast Oregon. The US Army marched them there as prisoners of war in 1878 following the Bannock War, in which these Paiutes seem to have been only marginally involved. In the years that followed, the Paiutes constantly faced starvation, and dozens died from disease. Lee Winnemucca, the son of Chief Winnemucca (Old Winnemucca) and half brother of Sarah Winnemucca, was among those held at the Yakima Agency, and he used the post to communicate with his people down south.[75] In 1881, Lee wrote to his half brother Natchez to update him on the awful conditions at Yakima and ask what was being done to get them out of there. The Paiutes believed that a government inspector might help, but Lee also expected his brother to keep pressing for their return. "We want to get back to our home, as our people are dying off rapidly," Winnemucca wrote. "Do what you can for us. Our hearts are heavy and I think if you work hard for us we can get there."[76] The Winnemuccas corresponded frequently as a family and with newspapers about problems concerning Paiutes.[77] Unfortunately, the Northern Paiutes at Yakima were not allowed to reunite with their people until 1886, but their dilemma received public attention because of Sarah Winnemucca's popular 1883 book, *Life among the Piutes: Their Wrongs and Claims*, the first autobiography written by a Native American woman.

With all the movement, forced relocation, and imprisonment of "hostile" Indians, the whereabouts of fellow tribesmen could be lost, but letters could facilitate the search for them. The Nez Perces in Indian Territory, because of their confinement there, did not know the fate of all of their tribesmen who had fled into Canada because of the threat of confinement to a reservation, but letters offered a means to investigate. In 1877, several bands of Nez Perces resisted settlement in a new Idaho reserve, leading to what is known as the Nez Perce War. The Nez Perces headed north to avoid the US Army and fought in a long series of engagements until most of the resisters, including Chief Joseph, surrendered at Bear's Paw in Montana. Those who surrendered were kept in exile down in Indian Territory on the Ponca reserve, 1,500 miles from their Columbia River Plateau homelands, while around 100 Nez Perces avoided capture and made it to Canada, where they camped with Lakota refugees under Sitting Bull.[78] While many of those Nez Perces remained in Canada, an unknown number might have joined Sitting Bull on his return to the United States in 1881 and his eventual settlement at the Standing Rock Agency. In 1883, Archie Lawyer, a Presbyterian Nez Perce from the reservation in Idaho who was ministering among the Nez Perces exiled to Indian Territory, wrote to the agent at Standing Rock to learn how many Nez Perces were there with Sitting Bull. "We like to hear from them," Lawyer wrote, "who is chiefs there. . . . We like to know of them."[79] Lawyer continued, "Here in Ind. Terr. they are not very good health here. They are sick all the time and die."

Like Lawyer's, letters were frequently used to convey bad news. Some expressed their writers' last thoughts or wishes before death.[80] In 1879, an Omaha man on his deathbed and surrounded by his loved ones dictated a letter (written in the Omaha language) to a Yankton man named Tuqmaxa-witcayutapi (Honey Eater). "Though I am very ill I send you a letter by some one," he wrote. "Often in the past, when I returned home after visiting you, a letter would come from you, just like a person (to ask for presents for the Yanktons). . . . I am ill, but I do not know at all whether I shall live or die."[81] Young Spotted Tail (or Spotted Tail Jr., the son of Spotted Tail) had his last will and testament put to paper before he was to "travel the 'starry trail' in route to the happy hunting grounds" in 1888.[82] He promised dozens of his possessions to friends and family. Luke Shield (Hunkpapa Lakota) left a suicide letter before he took his life in May 1890. According to an agent, Shield, who had been struggling to find his place at Standing Rock after his return from an eastern boarding school, wrote that he "knew he had done a great wrong and was now going to punish himself for his weakness."[83] Shield reportedly felt immense shame for abandoning his first wife at Standing Rock (whom his agent compelled him to marry because of one night of romance) and marrying another woman at Pine Ridge who did not know about his first marriage.[84]

Intertribal Correspondence

Corresponding became a normal part of life for many Indigenous peoples of the West during the 1870s and 1880s. This practice, which was once a specialized skill, developed into a collective routine. As a result, correspondence began to connect those who lived on different reservations, those who were members of different tribes, and those outside of kinship networks. Between 1881 and 1893, for example, at least sixty letters were received by the Southern Utes in southwest Colorado from the Northern Utes at the Uintah and Ouray Agency in Utah (distinct groups of people who shared relatives and friendships).⁸⁵ The letters carried news, information, and well-wishes. At least two dozen letters from the Northern Utes to the Southern Utes relayed bad news.⁸⁶ Sapporrano and Red Moon wrote to Buckskin Charley and Ignacio that one of their headmen, Touasanca, had drowned in the Green River ("he was a very good old man and everybody here regrets his death"), two others had died, and two girls were sick, but "everything is all right here and the Utes are fat, happy, and contented and would like you to write them a letter."⁸⁷ In November 1890, the Northern Utes reported two deaths. "We will inform you of all deaths that may happen here at anytime in the future," they promised. "All my brothers and sisters have died and left me all alone and I will have to die sometime can't help all from dying sometimes, the Dr can't help people from dying sometime. . . . All die sometime large and small, old and young."⁸⁸ A Northern Ute man wrote that his brother had drowned in the Grand River on their way to visit the Southern Utes in Colorado (he had found the body and buried it). The man asked his friends at the Southern Ute Agency "to write me a letter as I am all alone and want something to comfort me."⁸⁹ His wife and son, his last, had died earlier in the year. "I think it is to God that I should loose so many of my children," he grieved.⁹⁰

Utes were not the only people who built long-distance networks of correspondence. Other tribes were in communication with one another during the 1870s and 1880s, keeping relationships linked despite government efforts to disconnect them. The seven bands of Lakotas were separated by distance and agency boundaries. In the 1870s the US government organized agencies on the Sioux reservation to establish a presence near the seven bands of Lakotas (and hundreds of Yanktonai Sioux) where treaty annuities could be distributed.⁹¹ After the Great Sioux War the government, having dispossessed more of their land, became more dedicated to assimilating Lakotas. To more efficiently facilitate that process, the five Lakota agencies began to function independently of one another. Lakota bands were assigned, or "enrolled," at respective agencies within the larger Great Sioux Reservation (those five agencies officially became separate reservations in 1889 within the boundaries of the new state of South Dakota). Pine Ridge Agency (formerly Red Cloud Agency) became the home of most Oglalas; Rosebud Agency (Spotted Tail Agency) was for the Upper Brulés (Sicangu); Cheyenne River Agency was for the Miniconjous, Sans Arcs, and Two Kettles; Standing Rock Agency was for the Hunkpapas and Sihásapas (along with some Yanktonais); and the Lower Brule Agency (which was across the Missouri River from the older Crow Creek Reservation home of Santee Sioux) was for the Lower Brulés. There were also Lakotas living at Fort Berthold in what became northwestern North Dakota and at Fort Peck in northeastern Montana.[92] Also, many Lakotas lived at reservations where the majority of their band did not live (they were separated because of marriage, a decision by the US government, or personal choice).

Travel between agencies in Dakota Territory was restricted (see the next chapter) and difficult. Many, like Charging Eagle at Rosebud, chose to use letters to communicate with those at other agencies, often for very practical purposes. Matters of money and horses, for instance, were common topics in Lakota correspondence.[93] Crazy Elk at Rosebud wrote to Pine Ridge in 1880 to ask if Iron Tomahawk would send the eight dollars that he was gifted at a dance.[94] That same year, Charging Eagle sent a letter to Three Bear at Pine Ridge, asking if he would bring his horses at Pine Ridge over to Rosebud.[95] In 1885, the sister of Yellow Horse at the Cheyenne River Agency wrote a letter to Takes the Bear at Standing Rock to inform him that his horse was actually Yellow Horse's horse.[96] The following year, Good Woman at Cheyenne River wrote (through her agent) to Eagle That Was Scared Away at Standing Rock to retrieve her pony. Even though the sister of Yellow Horse was literate and Good Woman was not, both Cheyenne River women used the mail to see their property returned.

The policy of enrollment at Sioux agencies, that is, belonging to and being confined to a single agency, also divided many families because intertribal and interband marriage was common. A Lower Yanktonai man might marry a Hunkpapa woman, for instance, which might require the Lower Yanktonai man and his immediate family to live at Standing Rock rather than Crow Creek. But familial situations changed, and there was a continuous demand for transfers between agencies. Some Natives were able to initiate that process through a persuasive letter to their agent or the agent in charge at their anticipated destination. If that did not work, some asked influential friends for their help. In 1880, White Ghost at Crow Creek wrote Yankton chief Strikes the Ree for help on behalf of his Yankton friends who wished to transfer to Standing Rock (he also wrote unsuccessfully to President Rutherford B. Hayes).[97] Strikes the Ree, writing from the Yankton Reservation, was able to convince the Standing Rock agent to approve the transfer. Letter writing gave Native leaders like Strikes the Ree another outlet to wield their influence.

Native Americans also used letters to stay informed of the political affairs of tribal nations hundreds of miles away. In 1879, Cañge-skă, an Omaha man, wrote in his language to his Yankton friend Feather-in-the-Ear, hoping to hear "a correct account of the various affairs of the Dakota tribes up the Missouri River" and "of the various affairs of you own nation, and what they are doing."⁹⁸ Another Omaha man wrote to a Yankton friend, "I hope that you will send and tell me exactly how you are, and what you are doing. I wish to see those young Dakotas whom I made my children (in the pipe-dance)."⁹⁹ The Omaha man asked to acquire a calumet, "such as they use in the pipe-dance," from another Yankton family "and dance the calumet dance for his children."¹⁰⁰ The Omaha man also addressed the Oglala chief Red Cloud in the letter. He asked Red Cloud to "ask that my petition be granted as a personal favor to you" when he went to Washington. The Omaha man wanted to talk to the president "about several matters," he explained. "When the Omahas reach the Yankton village, tell them what you will give me. When you come to the Yankton lodges, send me a letter quickly. I wish to hear from you."¹⁰¹ Indians also discussed intertribal relations in letters to members of their own tribes. In 1878, an Omaha wrote to his grandson that he had shaken hands with the Brulé Lakota Spotted Tail. "It was for no special reason that I shook hands," he said, "yet it was good. It was very good for me to shake hands with him."¹⁰² The man also wanted to hear "which of the nations" his grandson was "on good terms" with.

Written correspondence was also used to express disagreements between western nations and perhaps hash out those conflicts. Intertribal relations in the West were complicated by long histories of competition for resources, raiding, violence, and alliance making.¹⁰³ One early surviving exchange of letters between two western groups in conflict came in 1844. In a letter that crossed international boundaries, a number of Sisseton Sioux leaders, whose territory included what is now northern North Dakota and southern Manitoba, wrote to Red River Métis in Manitoba to finally settle a long-simmering feud that had recently resulted in the deaths of several Métis and Sioux. Some Sioux had killed a number of Métis during unsuccessful peace negotiations, and the Métis responded by killing four Sissetons and four Yanktonais.¹⁰⁴ The Sissetons described their mourning in the letter (in English), "We hang down our heads; our wives mourn, and our children cry," and they asked the Métis to offer four carts of supplies as recompense for their dead "relations."¹⁰⁵ They asked, "Tell us if we are to be friends or enemies, is it to be peace or war?" The Sissetons continued, "Let your answer make our wives happy and our children smile," but they also emphasized that they were "not frightened. We are yet many and strong. Our bows are good."

The Métis responded three weeks later with their own poignant letter that placed much of the blame on the Sioux. "Your young men have killed, and, what we regard worse than death, scalped many belonging to us," they wrote, "not that we were afraid to retaliate, but because we are Christians, and never indulge in revenge."[1106] The Métis pointed out that the Sisseton did not "express . . . regret" in their letter for their treacherous actions. They would not compensate the Sioux with the four carts of supplies because it would be unjust, for the Métis had "violated no faith" and did not break the peace. The Métis wanted peace and would "always respect the laws of humanity," but they wrote that they would "never forget the first law of nature: we will defend ourselves, should you be numerous as the stars, and powerful as the sun. You say you are not frightened: we know you are a brave a generous people, but there are bad people among you."

After holding a council, the Sioux responded two months later. The Sissetons and Yanktonais who had lost relatives in the conflict provided their own statements in a reconciliatory letter. Each wanted to adopt the Métis who had killed their kin. "You killed my son, he was brave," Netai Ope wrote. "He who pointed the gun at him, I wish to be my son."[107] Haitokeyan wrote, "You killed my brother-in-law. He was braver than the bear. . . . Whoever killed him, I wish him to be my brother-in-law for ever." Bonds of kinship were initiated through the written word, and the Sioux and the Métis found peace for at least another year. They hunted together and visited each other in 1845, but according to historian David McCrady, periods of peace and conflict came and went until the Dakota War in 1862.[108]

Letters became a diplomatic tool for western tribes before the American Civil War, although there is more evidence of intertribal correspondence after the war. Relations were further complicated in the 1860s and 1870s with the increased presence of white Americans in the West, the settlement of reservations, and the constant pressures of colonialism. Tribes were forced onto reserves, and some found themselves with new neighbors, tribes that might have been longtime enemies or distant strangers. Osages, for instance, were forced to relocate onto a reserve in Indian Territory in 1870, a territory with eventually more than two dozen other tribal nations, several of which were rivals. Like other nations in the territory, Osages had to consider other groups diplomatically and figure out the best path toward harmony. An early reservation-era letter, sent in 1873 from Osages to Wichitas, was an attempt to solve a dispute stemming from the murder of Wichita chief Isadawah by a couple of Osages.[109] Wichitas wanted the Osages to hand over the men responsible, and according to the white press, war was "imminent" between the two tribes in May 1873.[110] The murder of the Wichita chief became an intertribal incident that could have brought violence into the Indian Territory, affecting all the tribes there. Shawnees who lived Indian Territory, having gotten a copy of the Osage letter, sent their own letter to the Osages in June that demanded the men be handed over.

The Sac and Foxes did the same. Eventually a council was held, and the Osages begrudgingly agreed to pay for Isadawah's life with ponies. "There have been many words," an annoyed Osage headman said at the council. "Wichitas have sent many words from their tongues; they have said little," which perhaps referred to an exchange of letters that resulted in an unfavorable council for the Osages.[111]

Tribes understood that letters could carry diplomatic messages that might ease tensions with old rivals. Several Northern Plains groups with long histories of violent conflicts exchanged such peacekeeping letters. In 1884, Indians at the Fort Berthold Reservation, where Arikaras, Hidatsas, and Mandans lived, wrote several letters to the Hunkpapa and Sihásapa Lakotas at the Standing Rock Agency to invite them to visit Fort Berthold.[112] Arikaras, Hidatsas, and Mandans were old enemies of the Lakotas in the 1800s, but increased communication between the tribes during the early reservation years cooled tensions.[113] In 1883, a party of more than one hundred Standing Rock Lakotas and Yanktonais made a "friendly visit" to Fort Berthold. Their interactions with the Arikaras, Hidatsas, and Mandans were described as "mutually agreeable" by an agent who hoped that the "relations of friendship" would continue.[114] It was no easy matter following generations of conflict, but the letters sent by Fort Berthold Indians in 1884 and the visit that came out of that invitation strengthened the peaceful relationship between the Lakotas and their former enemies.

Some tribes attempted a firmer diplomatic strategy. In 1879, two Northern Cheyenne leaders, Tall Bull (the younger) and Spotted Wolf, and two men of both Miniconjou Lakota and Cheyenne descent, Hump and Horse Roads, who lived around Fort Keogh (present day Miles City, Montana), wrote in English to Young Man Afraid of His Horses and Little Big Man, both Oglala Lakota leaders at the Pine Ridge Agency. In a remarkable example of intertribal communication in the early reservation years, the men wrote with concern for their Northern Cheyenne friends and relatives who had been living at Pine Ridge for a year. Northern Cheyennes had been separated since 1878, when they fled Indian Territory—some were arrested at Fort Robinson and sent to Pine Ridge while the others made it farther northwest, closer to their homelands, but were confined at Fort Keogh. The Fort Keogh Cheyennes had "heard" that some of their relatives at Pine Ridge were being mistreated by Lakotas, even being kept "prisoners" by Young Man Afraid and others. When the Cheyennes were hungry, they claimed, "There is no one to give them food."[115] The authors of the letter used intimidating language to convince the Lakotas to treat the Cheyennes better. "You think you are soldiers but you are not, We are soldiers here and treat everybody right," they wrote.

Hump demanded that his Lakota relatives leave his Cheyenne friends at Pine Ridge alone, writing that "in the old times" he was "a soldier and is a soldier now and we do not want any Indians to interfere with our friends" at Pine Ridge. They asked the Lakotas to influence the Pine Ridge agent and the Indian police to allow eighteen Cheyennes to join their relatives at Fort Keogh. After all, the Northern Cheyennes argued, they were living a promising life: "We earn our living here and would like to have some of our relatives with us—no rations or annuities are given to us but we raise our food and we have our cattle, there is Buffalo plenty yet, and we expect someday to raise an abundance of food and have many cattle and we want you to do the same as we have done." Although more than one hundred Northern Cheyennes were allowed to transfer to Fort Keogh in 1879, perhaps because of this letter, more than five hundred Northern Cheyennes still resided at Pine Ridge a decade later, even after the Fort Keogh Northern Cheyennes received their own Tongue River Reservation in 1884.[116] Correspondence and visiting kept them connected until the Pine Ridge Cheyennes were allowed to join their people at Tongue River in 1891.[117]

Tribes also wrote to exchange advice and strategies in managing their changing worlds. Some letters urged recipients to pursue traditional ways of life while others recommended so-called progressive paths. In 1871, Bradford Porter, a Ho-Chunk (Winnebago) who opened the first school for his people in 1866, wrote from the Winnebago Reservation in Nebraska to his uncle Par-Thee (Elk Chief), a Kickapoo living in Kansas. Porter told his uncle to "ask your Agent make him get up big school for you like we do here. . . . Get all your childrend education and go in to work farming."[118] Some exchanged news about farming techniques and their results, which could serve as valuable economic advice. Taokahah, an Omaha man, told White Eagle, a Ponca friend, that he had "broke 7 acres of prairie" that year and raised "237 bushels of wheat, 21 loads of corn, 7½ loads of potatoes, 1 load of turnips, 7 bushels of beans," and "sold $17 worth of melons."[119] He expected "to raise more next year" on twenty-five acres. Taokahah wanted the Poncas to "work and do as we are doing; try to improve and make a good living."[120] Tribes also passed along information about surviving diseases, including warnings of outbreaks and recommendations for vaccines. Mantcu-nanba, wrote to Feather-in-the-Ear to warn the Yanktons of an outbreak of smallpox that was spreading in the south among the Omahas. Mantcu-nanba instructed the Yanktons to ask "for medicine among the white people. . . . If you are vaccinated you will not have the small-pox."[121] Smallpox devastated Omahas and Poncas in 1878, and the letters exchanged reflected the loss and allowed the nations to grieve collectively. "Your elder brother is dead. . . . Your daughter had twins. Both died. . . . Scabby Horn, your father, is almost dead. He will die before you see him," one wrote.[122] Another letter, from October 1878, was sent to "tell you that the people have died."[123] Four were dead, including the recipient's father. "Our people are very sick, so my heart is not very good. . . . The people usually die in five days. The sickness is bad," an Omaha told a Ponca. "My heart is far more sad than tongue can tell," another wrote.[124] Letters in return allowed friends to offer condolences, but the Omahas and Poncas also exchanged good news in 1878.[125]

Some used the mail to ask other tribes for assistance, even across international borders. In 1885, Sitting Bull received a letter from Gabriel Dumont, one of the Métis leaders of the North-West Rebellion in Saskatchewan. Dumont hoped that Sitting Bull could help the Arikaras and Gros Ventres (living in at the Fort Berthold and Fort Belknap Agencies, respectively) to secure a pass to Canada to help the Métis, Crees, and Assiniboines in their revolt against the Canadian government. The letter was written in a combination of French, English, and Native language, and Sitting Bull asked Aaron Wells, an assistant farmer at Standing Rock of Native and European descent, to read it to him. "They must think I am a fool," Sitting Bull reportedly said after hearing Dumont's wishes.[126] He knew that the US government would never allow Arikaras and Gros Ventres to enter a rebellion against the Canadian government.

Letters sent by Sitting Bull still survive, even those from his prereservation life. During 1876's Great Sioux War and less than three months after the Battle at Little Bighorn, Sitting Bull, camped along the Yellowstone River, delivered a letter to a US Army battalion escorting a supply train to a cantonment on Tongue River. Passed along by an old woman on a hilltop, the letter read:

> I want to know what you are doing traveling on this road. You scare all the buffalo away. I want to hunt in this place. I want you to turn back from here. If you don't I will fight you again. I want you to leave what you have got here and turn back from here.
> I am your friend, Sitting Bull. . . . Wish you would write as some as you can.[127]

Col. Elwell Otis directed a scout to reply that his men would keep heading toward Tongue River and that they would be "pleased to accommodate them at any time with a fight."[128] Sitting Bull, Gall, and other Lakotas met with Gen. Nelson Miles soon after under a flag of truce, but Miles would not grant the wintertime truce that the headmen asked for.[129]

Sitting Bull continued to correspond in the years that followed the conflict, even as his people fled into Canada, where they lived for four years.

In 1882, while detained at Fort Yates after his return to the United States (and before he lived at the Standing Rock Agency), Sitting Bull wrote to the agent at Rosebud to ask permission for his relative there to visit him.[130] The following year, Sitting Bull had to petition in writing to live with his Hunkpapa relatives at Standing Rock.[131] Another Lakota leader, the Brulé chief Spotted Tail, used letters to communicate with other Indian groups like the Omahas as early as 1879.[132] He was using interpreters to send letters as early as 1877.[133]

By the mid-1880s, intertribal letter writing was regularly used by Lakotas as a political tool and an anticolonial weapon. In 1886, as Lakotas were debating the merits of the Dawes Severalty Act (a disastrous plan of individual allotment of lands passed by Congress in late 1887 that dramatically hastened land loss for most tribes in the West), a letter was reportedly circulating "among the Sioux for the purpose of preventing their acceptance of the Dawes' Bill."[134] Just after the Dawes Act was passed and as a Dawes Sioux Bill was under consideration (which would bring allotment to the Lakota agencies and open nearly ten million acres for white settlement in the Dakotas), there was a movement among Lakotas, as the Standing Rock agent described it, to collect money to pay for a delegation of headmen from several agencies to visit and influence politicians in Washington, DC. "Many letters from Indians of the other Sioux Agencies" were received at Standing Rock in the weeks after the Dawes Severalty Act was passed, "imparting" the Standing Rock Lakotas "to join in the movement."[135] And in May 1889, as the Lakotas were confronted with the reality of the revised Dawes Sioux Bill, a white trader at Pine Ridge reported to the commissioner that an "anonymous letter originally sent to Red Cloud" was being circulated among the Pine Ridge Indians.[136] The letter suggested that the Sioux should "get together" to organize a united front against the bill before the commissioner visited the Sioux agencies.

In the decades before the twentieth century, western Native Americans living many miles apart were already using letters to discuss and organize protests against government policies like the Dawes bills. But many Natives did not want the US government to read their private letters, especially letters that could be used against them by agents. Their letters were kept private and, consequently, are rarely found in government archives today. But Indian Affairs records reveal that Natives throughout the West communicated with one another in order to combat colonial injustices like land cession. In September 1889, a special agent told the commissioner of Indian affairs that Red Cloud, because of his "strong influence," received a lot of letters "from those of influence scattered over the Indian nation asking his advice not only in relation to this Bill but on many of the topics that pertain to the Government and the Indians."[137] Natives who could not travel the distance to Pine Ridge could council with Red Cloud via letter.[138]

In 1881, the agent at Standing Rock complained to the commissioner of Indian affairs that his Hunkpapas received two troublesome letters from Red Cloud and No Water, respectively. Brought by couriers from Pine Ridge, both letters were written on official Pine Ridge Agency stationery and enclosed in Pine Ridge Agency envelopes. Because of the official stationery, the agent supposed that the letters were written by "some one closely connected with the agency office" even though they were signed "Red Cloud" and "No Water."[139] But the agent could not understand why a government official would compose letters that were "flagrant acts" fostering a "spirit of discontent." It can be assumed that Red Cloud and No Water borrowed stationery for their own purposes and had a literate Native or sympathetic white man or woman write the letters to Hunkpapas at Standing Rock.

It seems that the written language became a part of Red Cloud's daily life. A photograph of Red Cloud's home, taken in 1890 or 1891, shows a small shelf above a cast iron stove next to the chief's quilt-covered bed. On the shelf sit books, stacks of paper, and two bottles of ink.[140] Although thought to be illiterate, Red Cloud made good use of the pen and paper with the help of literate Lakotas and white friends. As early as 1877, he regularly corresponded with Lakotas, distant tribes, and whites and government officials.[141] In 1878, Red Cloud and fifteen other Lakotas sent a letter to Dakotas at the Crow Creek Reservation that reportedly appealed "to them to remember that they must act as one people when they get into trouble with the whites."[142] Red Cloud's reputation and influence gave weight to his many letters that criticized government policies and the whites that implemented them. He regularly wrote to presidents and cabinet members.[143] He wrote to newspapers to publicize the problems his people were facing.[144] Because of the many letters of complaint from Red Cloud and a petition he circulated among Pine Ridge Oglalas, Red Cloud forced the Pine Ridge agent to concede to the inspection of his agency in the summer of 1882.[145]

For agents, letters arriving at their reservations from outside tribes could be a nuisance. Sometimes the simple act of sending or receiving a letter was complicated by the colonial reach of the US government. Agents often used their authority to contest communication. In 1879, the Ponca agent asked the Omaha agent to prevent Omahas from sending letters to Poncas because they "create much uneasiness and dissatisfaction among the Indians and a desire to return to Dakota," as the Poncas were unhappy on their reservation in Indian Territory.[146] The Ponca agent knew that the letters were

Red Cloud's wife, Pretty Owl, sits on their bed. Along with books, paper, and ink on the shelf, the couple's wall was decorated with Catholic imagery, American flags, and even a Japanese samurai sword. Denver Public Library, Western History Collection, X-31434.

largely written through dictation by the missionary and ethnologist James Owen Dorsey, and he hoped that Dorsey could be informed "of the evil effects of such letters" and that he should not "be used by the Indians for such a purpose." The concern of the agent surprised Dorsey, who claimed to his boss at the new Bureau of Ethnology, John Wesley Powell, that the letters were harmless (some would, in fact, be published in Dorsey's *The Ȼegiha Language* in 1890). Dorsey knew that the Poncas were dissatisfied with their reserve regardless of the letters from Omahas, but he also denied ever transcribing letters about such matters. Nevertheless, Dorsey told Powell that he would stop writing the letters to the Poncas for Omahas, but correspondence between members of the tribes continued.

Agents also had to put limits on newer modes of communication. As telegraph lines reached their reservations, Natives did not hesitate to communicate close to the speed of light. A primary function of western telegraph lines was to more effectively coordinate the subjugation of Indians in times of war and peace.[147] The Office of Indian Affairs relied on telegraphs to better surveil Indian movements and send updates from the reservations to eastern officials, but as with other emblems of white modernity, Natives readily used the telegraph for their own purposes. When the telegraph line opened between the Pine Ridge Agency and the Rosebud Agency in 1881, for instance, the Rosebud agent complained that it was "overrun with requests from Indians to forward messages upon the most trivial subjects," which created "a serious annoyance" for the agent and "a hinderance to legitimate business."[148] Rosebud began charging one cent per message for the transmission of private messages "to prevent such general use of the wires." Of course, Lakotas kept using the wire between the agencies, sometimes for more "legitimate" reasons like to ask for fresh horses or an interpreter.[149] Other telegrams relayed more urgent matters. Two Strike at Rosebud sent word to White Blanket, who was off at Deadwood, that his son was very sick.[150] Yellow Breast at Rosebud sought information about his son's health from Lighting Bear, who was off-reservation.[151] Thunder Hawk at Rosebud asked No Flesh at Pine Ridge, "Is my father going to die? I heard he sent for me, answer."[152] Days later, Thunder Hawk, for unknown reasons, telegraphed Annie Edwards in Deadwood (the deputy superintendent of Deadwood schools and the wife of Deadwood's first school superintendent, newspaper owner, and city leader) to let her know that ten dollars had been sent to her by registered mail. Perhaps the money was meant for a doctor.[153] In that same month, May 1882, Brave Bull at Rosebud telegraphed Pine Ridge that he had eighty-six dollars and four horses (worth forty dollars each) to pay Crow Dog's lawyer (Crow Dog had famously murdered Brulé chief Spotted Tail and was convicted in a territorial court that May but was later released after the Supreme Court's *Ex parte Crow Dog* decision).[154]

The telegraph also played an important role in Lakota politics. Young Spotted Tail (the son of Spotted Tail) became the head chief of the Brulés after his father's death. During the Crow Dog trial, Young Spotted Tail was asked to testify in Deadwood. In those same weeks, Lakotas were debating an agreement that would allow Poncas to settle on a portion of the Great Sioux Reservation. The Rosebud Brulés would lose half their lands. With Young Spotted Tail off the reservation up in Deadwood, the debate between Rosebud headmen was carried by Morse code. Crazy in the Lodge and Good Eagle telegraphed Young Spotted Tail, "You told us if any new business came up to wait till you come back. Four days after you left authority came to change the Ponca agreement to suit the demand of our people. . . . What should we do you are the chief of this people?"[155] Spotted Tail replied that same day to Crazy in the Lodge as well as Swift Bear and Two Strike: "I want my people to sign the agreement but will write in full what I want them to do by this days mail."[156] These urgent instructions were sent in an

Native American men pose on horseback in front of the Taos Post Office, date unknown. McCracken Research Library, Buffalo Bill Center of the West, P.438.0434.

instant, whereas the letter from Deadwood to Pine Ridge would have taken two days or more.

Whatever the medium of transmission, written correspondence became an important component in the communications of nineteenth-century western Native Americans. Although literacy was meant to be a tool of American colonization, the writing that was produced by Native Americans conveying their thoughts and expressions could not be colonized. Natives corresponded to make connections while segregated on reservations. They wrote to keep in touch with loved ones separated because of the circumstances of their changing world. They wrote intertribally to spread information, to make new alliances with former rivals, to solve problems, and to organize opposition to government policies. Even those considered to be nonprogressive used the skill in ways that they determined. Maqpiya-qaga, an Omaha man who apparently considered himself a traditionalist, wrote the Ponca chief Standing Grizzly Bear that he was "disgusted" with the progressive group of his people "because they do not wish to be Indians."[157] He was upset that progressive Omahas wanted to diminish the influence of chiefs, "to live as white men and to throw away the Indian life." But Maqpiya-qaga used literacy, a crucial component of white education, to tell a member of a foreign tribe about the political divisions within his own tribe. Even though he was a traditionalist, Maqpiya-qaga considered the written word a useful feature of Indian life.

PART II

Networks of Visitation

CHAPTER 3

Remaining Mobile

In 1882, Captain Jim, a Paiute leader at the Pyramid Lake Reservation in Nevada, sent a message to the *Reno Evening Gazette* to have his thoughts broadcast to both Natives and whites. Jim expressed a pan-Indian notion of brotherhood among Indians "from the Rocky Mountains to the Pacific, from British Columbia to Mexico."¹ He thought that North America's Indigenous people, all of whom had common concerns, should "visit each other" in order to "consult together for our mutual benefit." His notion, that diverse nations that were facing common concerns could improve their lives through an exchange of ideas, was not an unusual one during the early reservation years. Another Paiute named Johnson Sides told the *Reno Evening Gazette* and the *News Reporter* in Dayton, Nevada, that Bannocks, Shoshones, Arapahos, and Paiutes throughout the Intermountain West (including Wyoming Territory) wanted to "visit each other more often and keep up the good understanding now existing."² This face-to-face communication strengthened intertribal relationships.

Native Americans remained mobile even though they were forced onto reservations, challenging the US government's efforts to isolate tribes from one another. During the last quarter of the nineteenth century, many Natives throughout the West, particularly those living great distances apart, visited each other more than ever before. Long-distance visiting increased, in part because of the growing networks of intertribal correspondence and the transportation provided by new western railroads. Native Americans made at least twelve hundred trips between western reservations from 1880 through 1890, trips that varied from parties of one to parties of hundreds. Many of the parties in those years, at least one-third, traveled off-reservation without permission. Map 2 visualizes each one of these trips and the intricate networks of mobility that connected reservations across the West.³

Native American men and women traveled off-reservation to feel independence, to experience life outside their reservations, to find economic

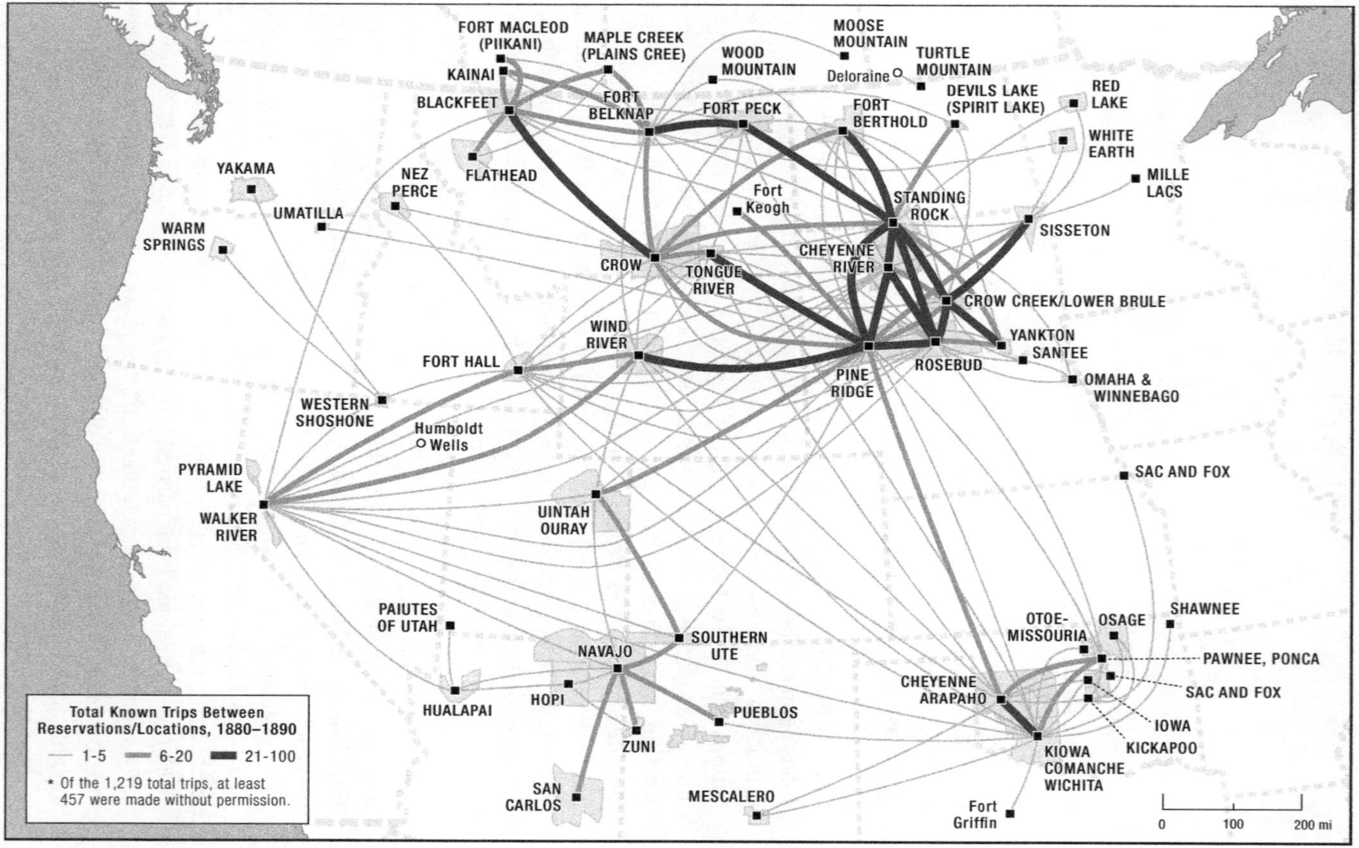

Map 2. Known trips made with and without permission, 1880–1890

opportunities, to create and support bonds of kinship, and to expand their connections with other tribal nations. Intertribal visits were made for social pleasure, business, politics, and especially religion (more often than not, if a large party was making a visit to another reserve, a dance would be held). Interaction among tribes was a vital part of prereservation life. Now on reservations, Native Americans demanded the freedom to leave those reservations in order to visit other Natives and secure the benefits that came with it.

Captain Jim believed that creating connections among foreign tribes could improve life for all Indians. He also thought that his people's habit of leaving the reservation to network with distant nations was entirely within their rights. In fact, he told the *Reno Evening Gazette* that Indians should "above all things, obey the laws of the United States." Unfortunately, during the last quarter of the nineteenth century, the United States government used its power to discourage Native Americans from visiting one another (and often tried to forbid it). When visiting was curbed by the Office of Indian Affairs, some took to the mail to express their displeasure. "We are here on this land like prisoners that's what I don't like now," John Half Iron wrote to the Indian Rights Association from the Santee Reservation in 1889.[4] In December 1888, Oglala Lakota leaders Little Wound, Young Man Afraid of His Horses, and Red Cloud sent a letter of complaint to President Grover Cleveland. "We should be permitted to make friendly visits among each other as the white people do," they argued.[5] After all, the president "said he wanted us to be at peace with each other and to be friendly." They insisted, "We do not want the gates closed between us." Reservation life presented plenty of challenges for Native peoples, but they did what was needed to maintain intertribal relationships. Only Native activism kept the gates open.

Interregional Connections

Johnson Sides described greater connections among tribes living on the west side of the Rockies, but those Intermountain Indians also developed contacts with the east-siders on the Great Plains. Those eastward, the Lakotas, Crows, Northern and Southern Cheyennes, Northern and Southern Arapahos, Kiowas, Pawnees, and many other nations, were already mingling peacefully in the late 1870s, but their presence west of the Rockies increased during the 1880s. They made connections with foreign nations that had been loose or nonexistent before. For example, Oglala Lakotas at the Pine Ridge Reservation in Dakota Territory and Northern Utes at the Uintah and Ouray Reservation in Utah, once longtime adversaries, were among those who exchanged letters and annual visits in the 1880s. Their new relationship might have been established in September 1886, when more than four hundred Oglala Lakotas arrived unannounced at the recently consolidated Uintah and Ouray Agency some six hundred miles from their home. Led by the son of Red Cloud, Jack, the Oglala travelers went directly to the agency office upon arrival, presented their papers to Agent Eugene White, and asked for some rations. The group had "a great many papers of the nature of testimonial, or certificates of good character," White wrote several years later, but the only travel pass they held was issued by Capt. James Bell, an army officer who was acting as a temporary agent at Pine Ridge.[6]

The pass, which was required by Indian Affairs regulations, only gave the party permission to visit the Shoshones at the Wind River Reservation in Wyoming (where they also met up with some Southern Utes), but the Oglalas had decided to travel a great deal farther without authorization.[7] The Pine Ridge agent had no idea about their extended travel plans when he issued the pass to Wind River.[8] However, once the Lakotas made it to Wind River, Chief Red Cloud, who led the first leg of the trip, informed the Pine Ridge agent that he wanted his son Jack to continue westward to see the Uintah and Ouray Utes. Jack and only a few other Oglalas would go "to send the Utes some messages," but the Pine Ridge agent denied the request.[9] Nevertheless, not only did Jack Red Cloud ignore his agent's instructions, most of the Oglala party traveled more than three hundred miles south to see the Utes.

Agent White at the Uintah and Ouray Reservation knew that the Oglalas came in peace, and he was hospitable to the men (although he would not give them government rations) and allowed them to stay a week to allow their horses to rest. The Oglalas told Agent White that they came to "swap" with the Utes. They wanted to exchange red pipestone long-stem pipes, moccasins, tobacco pouches, and "other trinkets made of buckskin and ornamented with beads and porcupine quills" for ponies and buckskin.[10] Three or four days after their arrival, the Utes held a feast at Chief Sowawick's camp that was attended by two thousand persons in all. Sowawick addressed the Oglalas using sign language, the only way many of them could communicate (Agent White could not understand any of it). Three hundred men participated in a dance—one hundred Oglalas and two hundred Utes—that lasted several hours. At midnight, a medicine man named Wash brought the Utes and Oglalas closer into the ring. The dancers remained at the edge of the ring, and meat was served with certain ceremony. During their weeklong visit, the Oglalas and Utes must have shared customs, told stories (perhaps stories relating to their long history of hostility), and related experiences, creating a lasting relationship between the groups.

Oglalas and Utes kept in touch through the US Postal Service, and they met at least nine more times by 1891, often without permission from their agents. In 1887, Sowawick received a letter in English from Red Cloud. "He writes his people are making good progress," Sowawick told the Southern Ute chief Ignacio in his own letter. "He also wrote me they would come down part way from his land and wanted me to meet him half way and have a visit. I should like very much to know you come up here and we will go up together and meet him and his friends that may accompany him and have a good visit."[11] Red Cloud most likely wanted to meet Sowawick at the Fort Hall Reservation in Idaho, a halfway point between their reserves with various railroad connections. Several visits were exchanged in 1888, 1889, and 1890 (with and without permission, some involving more than one hundred travelers), journeys that would have been much more difficult without rail travel.[12] Because of the connection built by the two tribes, some Utes were able to share their knowledge of a new set of religious ideas (eventually called the Ghost Dance) with Oglalas during a visit to Pine Ridge in the late fall of 1888.[13]

The interaction among Utes and Lakotas also drew in other tribes. In March 1890, for instance, Red Cloud wrote a letter to Marcisco, inviting the Utes to meet him at the Wind River Reservation in Wyoming. Ute chief Marcisco asked Buckskin Charley in a letter to "tell this to all of the Utes, so that they will all know."[14] Northern Utes received other visitors from the plains as well. In August 1889, a large party from Wind River visited them in Utah (Northern Utes had visited Wind River in the years prior).[15] Close to 100 Northern Arapahos (including Black Coal and Sharp Nose), 7 Shoshones, and 11 Lakotas (perhaps led by Little Wound) returned to Wind River with 235 horses they received from the Utes.[16]

Diplomatic Visiting

It is no small thing that Lakotas and others were interacting peacefully with former enemies. Diplomacy in the West had always been complex; tribes held evolving alliances with outside groups while they wrestled with longstanding rivalries. Intertribal warfare, mainly limited to horse raiding and retaliatory assaults, accelerated in the nineteenth century as tribes competed for diminishing resources in the West.[17] As the nineteenth century progressed and bison became a limited resource because of white presence, Lakotas in particular menaced bands of Crows, Mandans, Hidatsas, Arikaras, Poncas, Pawnees, Wind River Shoshones, and Utes. But most Plains

Table 5
Number of Known Trips to and from Lakota Reservations, 1880–1890

	Cheyenne River	Crow Creek and Lower Brule	Pine Ridge	Rosebud	Standing Rock
Cheyenne River	—	17	22	51	69
Crow Creek and Lower Brule	17	—	51	46	59
Pine Ridge	22	51	—	97	25
Rosebud	51	46	97	—	31
Standing Rock	69	59	25	31	—
Blackfeet	2	—	—	—	—
Cheyenne-Arapaho	—	—	6	—	—
Crow	—	2	18	3	8
Devil's Lake (Spirit Lake)	—	3	—	—	8
Fort Belknap	—	—	—	—	1
Fort Berthold	1	2	1	1	33
Fort Hall	1	—	2	1	—
Fort Keogh	—	—	6	—	—
Fort Peck	—	—	—	1	49
Kiowa, Comanche, and Wichita	—	—	3	—	—

Nevada	1	—	1	1	—
Omaha and Winnebago	—	—	—	2	1
Ponca, Pawnee, and Otoe	—	—	2	—	—
Ponca (Nebraska)	—	—	—	3	—
Red Lake	—	1	—	—	1
Santee	1	—	—	4	—
Sisseton	30	—	2	—	4
Southern Ute	—	—	1	—	—
Tongue River	3	—	20	2	2
Uintah and Ouray	1	—	8	—	—
Umatilla	—	—	1	—	—
Wind River	4	—	22	3	—
Yankton	—	45	2	19	6

TOTAL TRIPS TAKEN: 768
TOTAL TRIPS TAKEN WITHOUT PERMISSION: 257 (33%)

Sources: These data come from a variety of sources, mostly agency documents such as letters between two agents. Agency records were not always reliably kept or preserved in the 1880s. Generally, the records at Lakota agencies were better kept and preserved than similar records at other agencies in the northern plains and intermountain regions.

leaders decided, with the urging of Indian Affairs and the military, to sort out new intertribal dynamics in the 1870s and early 1880s.

In the reservation era, visits continued to be opportunities for tribes with a history of conflict to make peace. Although these interactions required skilled diplomacy, by the end of the 1880s, almost all western tribes were on agreeable terms, individual grudges notwithstanding. Several tribes made peacemaking a priority early on. In 1871, for instance, Pawnees set up a series of visits on the same journey meant to cultivate friendly relations with the Kiowas, Comanches, Southern Cheyennes, and Southern Arapahos.[18] According to James Mooney, the visit between the Pawnees and Kiowas was their first friendly meeting within the memory of those living in the mid-1890s. A Kiowa calendar (by Sett'an or Little Bear) that recognizes important events in their history recorded the 1871 Pawnee visit.[19] Two years later, Kiowas and Comanches proposed a visit to make permanent peace with Utes, and they invited Southern Cheyennes and Southern Arapahos to join.[20] West of the Rockies, a Paiute headman named Bargotzin set up a visit with the Navajos in 1882 "to establish friendly and peaceable relations," promising to give up his "former marauding practices."[21]

Up in the northern plains, relations between the alliance of Mandans, Hidatsas, and Arikaras and their traditional Sioux enemies, Yanktons, Yanktonais, Santees, and Lakotas, had softened by the end of the 1870s. In 1874, four hundred Cheyenne River Sioux raided an Arikara village, killing eight and losing one man, but by 1875, the Cheyenne River agent reported that the Sioux were losing interest in such raids.[22] In 1870, White Shield, an Arikara chief who was angry with Sioux raiding, told the agent at Fort Berthold that "the Sioux will never listen to the 'Great Father' until the soldiers stick their bayonets in their ears and make them," but by 1879, a new agent at Fort Berthold reported that "his" Mandans, Hidatsas, and Arikaras loved to visit other tribes, "especially their old enemies the Sioux."[23] As mentioned in the previous chapter, the Mandans, Hidatsas, and Arikaras and the Hunkpapa Lakotas were on good diplomatic terms by the mid-1880s because of the diplomatic one-two punch of letter writing and visiting.

Farther west, tension still existed in the 1880s among the various tribal nations in Montana Territory and into the Northwest Territories of Canada.[24] Agents had a difficult time controlling the great mobility of Natives in that transnational region, which mostly consisted of hunting and friendly visits between foreign groups. But horse raiding was still common, which helped keep antagonism aflame among some Crows, Northern Cheyennes, Assiniboines, Gros Ventres, Plains Crees (living on both sides of the international line), and people of the Blackfoot Confederacy: Blackfeet Nation

Piegans at the Blackfeet Reservation in Montana (Southern Piikanis, referred to in this study as the Blackfeet), Northern Piikanis around Fort Macleod in southern Alberta, Kainais (Bloods) at and around the Blood 148 Reserve in southern Alberta, and Siksikas in southern Alberta. In 1885, efforts were made, as a government agent described it, to negotiate through visiting runners more peaceful relations among the groups, eventually leading to a council.[25] In 1886 and 1887, Kainais in Canada and Gros Ventres and Assiniboines from the Fort Belknap Reservation exchanged visits to make peace.[26]

Crows and their eastern neighbors, the Lakotas from Pine Ridge and Standing Rock, also exchanged visits in the 1880s, calming relations that had been rocky for generations.[27] In June 1883, a party of Crows visited Standing Rock, and Standing Rock Lakotas visited the Crow Reservation the following summer.[28] Among the Lakotas, these peacemaking visits were initiated with the delivery of tobacco as a gesture of goodwill.[29]

Among Lakotas and Pawnees, who shared generations of hostility, relations were much improved by the end of the 1880s. Harry Kuhns (Pawnee) was with the Pawnees who visited Pine Ridge in 1889. George Bird Grinnell, an anthropologist who corresponded with Kuhns and other Pawnees, asked Kuhns how strange it must be visiting the Oglala Lakotas, "talking over the old times when you were the bitterest of enemies and were always fighting with the other."[30] The entirety of Kuhns's return letter (which he wrote from Pine Ridge) does not survive, unfortunately, but he undoubtedly discussed with the Oglalas the "old wars of the Pawnees and Sioux" and the "last massacre down on the Republican [River] in 1873" (the Battle at Massacre Canyon in Nebraska where more than one thousand Lakotas killed more than seventy Pawnees), which was the result of increasing competition on the plains because of the collapsing bison population.[31] There are not many details about Kuhns's experiences at Pine Ridge, but discussing such tragedies from the recent past with Lakotas must have been difficult. He did return to Pine Ridge the following year, so things probably went well.[32]

The interactions between visitors and hosts could also complicate intertribal relations. In 1888, a visit between some Paiutes and Shoshones reportedly became tense. According to the *Silver State*, Johnson Sides and another Paiute were asked to leave a Shoshone council because they expressed their opinions despite not having been asked to attend. The Shoshones reportedly "resented" Sides's "interference." Another Paiute headman (and son of Winnemucca) who was also at the Shoshone gathering, said that Sides "had no business to assume the direction of Shoshone affairs."[33] But Johnson Sides claimed in the *Reno Evening Gazette* (the

Silver State's competition) that the Shoshones had, in fact, invited the Paiute leaders to council in eastern Nevada, as is evident by a letter Sides showed the newspaper. According to Sides, the friction during the visit actually came from a single Shoshone who objected to the presence of the Paiutes at the council, which led Sides to leave despite other Shoshones asking him to stay.[34]

As Johnson Sides's letter also demonstrates, Natives sent invitations to distant tribes via the mail, a practical way to propose a visit to a group living many miles away. They could be written by an agent, but invitations and plans were commonly made outside the US government's auspices. In 1882, for instance, Buena Vista John, a Paiute, received a letter from Captain Sam, a Shoshone from the Duck Valley Reservation, asking if John and his people would like to visit.[35] Farther east, in 1879, an Omaha man wrote to a Ponca friend, directing him to get ready for a visit from his people (and he asked the Yanktons already visiting the Poncas if they would also "entertain" his Omahas).[36] He also wanted to know about the Poncas' visit with Red Cloud and the Oglalas. Letters sent by the Omahas or Poncas to friends or relatives in other tribes usually spoke of future visits or offered apologies for not making past visits.[37] On a single day, August 22, 1878, nine letters were written by Omahas in their Native language, and several of them referred to an anticipated visit from Poncas.[38] "When we Indians meet, we ought to do something for one another," an Omaha wrote to a Ponca friend.[39] People also kept in touch with their guests via letter after they traveled back home, which allowed them to continue communication, cultivate relationships, and resolve any unfinished business from the visit. In one instance, Omahas wrote letters to quell tensions with another tribe after a disastrous visit.[40]

Communicating across Cultures

Tribes visited other tribes to communicate a wide variety of things, but how did tribes communicate face-to-face, considering that there were dozens of languages spoken on the dozens of western reservations? English eventually became a common language used by tribes on their visits, but before the wider use of English in the 1880s, Plains Indian Sign Language allowed tribes to communicate effectively. In 1876, for instance, a group of Kiowas (who speak a Tanoan-family language) visited the Pawnees (who speak a Caddoan-family language), and they conversed "entirely by signs," according the agency clerk.[41] "They have no difficulty in readily and rapidly understanding each other," the clerk wrote to his wife. "The motions are not extravagant but often very slight and with one hand more than with both." The Pawnees had also conversed through signs with some visiting Southern Cheyennes several weeks earlier. Although several Pawnees signed, one Pawnee who understood the language well did most of the interpreting. He was "far ahead of the others in ease and rapidity," the clerk wrote, motioning "very fast and gracefully."[42] The following year, the agency clerk described how Pawnees would often travel up from Indian Territory to Arkansas City, Kansas, to trade with whites and to visit Poncas. There were two Poncas who could speak Pawnee, which, along with the aid of sign language, "made it easy for the two tribes to communicate."[43]

Regardless of the language spoken, tribes also faced a cultural barrier. Although centuries of interaction among neighboring tribes created cultural commonalities, tribes were nevertheless very different, especially region to region. Perhaps during that 1876 Pawnee-Kiowa visit, two young Pawnees, Mark Evarts (who would go to Carlisle in 1883) and David Gillingham (Gray Eagle), spent time in a Kiowa tepee and communicated with their hosts as best as they could despite their clear cultural divide.[44] As Mark described to anthropologist Alexander Lesser decades later, he and David could not speak Kiowa but were welcomed into the tepee by a Kiowa man. Upon entering, the man's wife put down a blanket and two pillows for the boys. A black pipe was lit and passed to David.

> Mark nudged David and whispered to him that he should not make any gestures with the pipe. Both knew that the Kiowa had special ways and motions in using their pipes; Mark was afraid David would try them and make a mistake. He knew David was a great show-off. The Kiowa pipe-smoking was very complicated. David nudged Mark back and told him to keep quiet. David wanted to show off, so he made some motions with the pipe, imitating Kiowa motions he had seen somewhere. The Kiowa watched him with astonishment. Then David handed the pipe to Mark, who took it and smoked it quietly and without ceremony.

As Mark and David discovered in their first encounter with Kiowas, visiting tribes that spoke different languages also communicated through custom and ceremony, but cultures varied. Having experienced their first interaction with the Kiowas, Mark and David could better understand the foreigners.

The ability among foreign tribes to exchange meaning without words was also evident to Quaker missionary and teacher Thomas Battey, whose published journal offers a rare description of a visit between two Plains tribes. In 1873, Pawnees visited Kiowas in Indian Territory, continuing the friendly relations established during their 1871 visit. Battey, who was asked by Kiowa headman Kicking Bird to start a school near Fort Sill, witnessed the arrival of the Pawnees on the evening of March 2, 1873. The main party remained two or three miles behind while a headman and a few others approached the Kiowa village with a white flag that had the letter *P* painted on it. Presumably, the *P* stood for "peace," but Battey did not provide any additional information.

Next, the Pawnees planted their flag into the ground and "sat down in a line on each side of it, facing the village."[45] A half hour later, after the Kiowa headmen made their arrangements, a group of Kiowas, including women and children, greeted the Pawnees next to the flag. "Upon drawing near to them," Battey recorded in his journal, "the Kiowa chiefs walking with a slow step and dignified mien, some of the old women set up a chant in a shrill voice, whereupon the head chief of the Pawnees, and two or three others perhaps the nearest in rank, arose, and with a quick firm step approached the Kiowa chiefs, and after embracing them, retire to their former position." Other Pawnees arrived and were "embraced" by the Kiowa headmen. Some Pawnees "occasionally placed a shawl or embroidered blanket upon the shoulders of a Kiowa, while several of the old men passed along in front of the whole line of the visitors, shaking hands with them."

Next came a demonstration of the hosts' generosity, which was typical of intertribal visits on the Great Plains. The Pawnees sang while small Kiowa children (carried by men), young girls, and "occasionally a woman" presented Pawnees with a stick.[46] To receive the stick, a Pawnee would "place his hands upon the donor's head in a solemn, reverential manner, as if blessing, pass them down the sides, following the arms, take the stick, and sit down." The sticks represented "a pledge from the giver to the receiver for a pony" before the visit's end. Old Kiowas urged their people "to show the largeness of their hearts, the warmth of their friendship" by giving ponies as gifts to the "poor" Pawnees (who had arrived on foot). According to the account of a Pawnee Agency clerk in 1876, whenever Pawnees hosted guests, they used a different ceremony to initiate the gifting of a horse. After a mock war demonstration for their Southern Cheyenne guests, Pawnee men rode up to individual Cheyennes, handed them the reigns, then struck the horses with a whip, signifying that the guests would be given a horse before they left.[47]

At the end of the gift-giving ceremony during the 1873 visit, the Pawnees arose and took the white flag out of the ground and followed the Kiowas to their lodges, where they would intermingle. The Pawnee headman became the guest of Kicking Bird. Also typical of intertribal visits, the Pawnees and Kiowas danced. Among the dancing that Battey witnessed was a Pawnee "war dance." The ceremony was interpreted by the outsider Battey as an emblematic sign of peace, the burial of the hatchet.[48]

Rail Networks

It is not clear whether the Pawnees traveled from their Nebraska reservation to the Kiowas in Indian Territory via the railroads in 1873. There was not a direct route down to the Kiowas yet, but Pawnees were taking advantage of the efficiency of rail travel very early on. In 1872, the Pawnee agent reported that the Union Pacific, running close to the Pawnee Reservation, allowed Pawnees to ride their freight cars for free, which brought "idle and vagrant members of the tribe to visit the towns and hang around the depots along said road."[49] For western tribes, the railroads made the trips from the Dakotas to Idaho, Utah, and Nevada, across the Rockies and into the Great Basin practical. Many used this modern means of transportation to move around a continent increasingly bound together by rail lines. Between 1870 and 1890, railroad mileage west of the Mississippi increased six times over, from 12,000 to 72,000 miles. Improved transportation brought more settlers, farming, and industry into the West, which were all detrimental to Native life. The white population of Nebraska increased nearly nine times, and the Dakotas nearly thirty-six times during that twenty-year span, but Natives also used the rail to their advantage.[50] Besides benefiting Native communication through more efficient mail service, railroads also constantly moved Native travelers.[51]

Of course, the railroad was the primary tool of American expansion into Indian territories, and some tribes attempted to confound its early construction.[52] Lakotas, Cheyennes, and Arapahos attacked the construction of the Kansas Pacific and Union Pacific lines during the late 1860s, leading to military intervention. Gen. William Tecumseh Sherman once told President Ulysses S. Grant that his army was not going to let a "few thieving, ragged Indians stop and check the progress of the railroad."[53] Most Plains Indians, however, kept their distance from the tracks as they were laid. Soon the bison disappeared, in large part due to the railroads, and tribes were often forced away from the land that railroads required. The Office of Indian Affairs was supposed to deal with railroad companies in the interests of Indians first, but granting rights-of-way through reservations became the priority. In 1872, Indian Affairs recognized that transcontinental railroads were "of the first importance in the solution of the Indian problem."[54]

Native Americans, however, did not run away from the iron horse once it was in place. Most, in fact, used the technology in opposition to whatever solution to the so-called Indian problem government policy makers came up with. By the end of the 1870s, railroads were familiar to most Native Americans in the West. Even Sitting Bull, who had harassed Northern Pacific Railroad surveyors in the Yellowstone Valley as early as 1871, attended the completion ceremony of the Northern Pacific in 1883.[55] In the same year, Red Cloud made the train ride to Virginia to visit the Hampton Institute. Similar to their introduction to literacy, many Plains Indians experienced long-haul railroad travel for the first time because of the Indian boarding school system. By the early 1880s, delegations from the Crows, Shoshones, Bannocks, Cheyennes, Arapahos, Lakotas, Ojibwes, Pueblos, and others had all visited Carlisle or Hampton. The schools paid for the eastern excursions to promote their institutions among the tribal leaders and the white public.[56] Indian delegations to Washington, DC, also traveled over rail.[57]

When possible, Natives chose the most practical mode of transportation on their visits to foreign tribes. Of course, trains were faster than horses, which meant that travelers could spend more time at their destinations than on the trail or that travelers could stop at more destinations in the same time frame. As soon as the rails were laid near reservations, visiting became easier and perhaps more frequent. Tribes living in the Intermountain West were especially connected by rail. Shoshones, Bannocks, and Paiutes regularly used the railroad to visit each other beginning in the late 1870s.[58] The Central Pacific snaked through the Great Basin, meeting the Union Pacific in northern Utah in 1869. Branches off those lines were constructed in the decades after, giving the residents of several reservations a quick path to the West's main artery. The Utah & Northern Railway, built to connect the Union Pacific line from Utah to the Northern Pacific in Montana (and the mined products therein), ignored requirements of treaties with Shoshones and Bannocks at the Fort Hall Reservation and built through their lands in 1878. A Union Pacific branch line heading toward Portland also passed through Fort Hall in 1882, making that reservation one of the most easily accessible in the West. Also accessible were the Paiute reservations at Pyramid Lake, near the Central Pacific, and Walker River, right on the Carson & Colorado line beginning in 1883.

These western lines carried Native men, women, and children to visits and dances. In 1883, the first year of the C&C, six hundred Natives met in Winnemucca, Nevada.[59] In September 1887, Shoshones living in east Nevada and Bannocks from Idaho headed west to visit Paiutes during the pine nut harvest. According to Nevada newspapers, the westbound train platforms were crowded for several days with Natives on their way to the Paiutes' dance.[60] Men wore hats "adorned with gaudy ribbons and feathers," and the women wore "white calicoes, and have their raven-hued tresses adorned with red, blue, green or yellow handkerchiefs." Another "big dance" at Pyramid Lake in May 1888 also carried crowds on the Nevada railroads.[61] Nevada Paiutes were at Fort Hall later that year, where Bannocks, Shoshones, and visiting Nez Perces and Lemhis held a large dance.[62] The Paiutes from Pyramid Lake and Walker River, the Shoshones from the Western Shoshone Reservation in Nevada, the Uintah and Ouray Reservation Utes in Utah, the Flatheads and Lemhis in the Northern Rockies, the Nez Perces and Umatillas in the Columbia Plateau, the Bannocks and Shoshones from Fort Hall, and others were all connected via rail networks.

Because of the railroads, Fort Hall became a bridge connecting Intermountain and Plains tribes. During the 1880s, there was "constant visiting back and forth between" the Natives coming from Fort Hall, over the Continental Divide, to the Wind River Reservation in Wyoming Territory.[63] Four rail lines eventually merged at Fort Hall (and it was only a short distance from the main Union Pacific line), making it a routine stop for Indians traveling by rail from all directions.[64] Fort Hall, after all, was the halfway point where Red Cloud chose to meet Sowawick in 1887. Before the reservation years, the camas prairies around Fort Hall in the Snake River Plain were an annual intertribal meeting place for bands of Bannocks, Shoshones, Paiutes, Nez Perces, and Umatillas, where they would trade and dance while women gathered camas and yampa roots.[65] That tradition continued in the 1870s and perhaps became even more important for a time because of the diminished game and fish caused by white encroachment. In 1872, around 2,500 Nez Perces, Umatillas, Shoshones, and Bannocks left their reservations and met in the camas prairie, which made whites in the region apprehensive.[66] The importance of camas eventually lost ground during the reservation years, but the area remained a hub of intertribal connection.

Railroad companies often needed to lay their rails through Indian lands. Facing tough negotiations with tribes, some companies began to accept their demands for free service.[67] In order to convince the Bannocks and Shoshones at the Fort Hall Reservation to allow a right-of-way on their reservation, the Utah & Northern Railway Company offered them free rides from 1878 to 1908.[68] The Southern Utes on the Denver and Rio Grande railroad, the Crows on the Northern Pacific, and several tribes on the Southern Pacific and Santa Fe Railroads were among those riding for free, for a time, on western railroads.[69] In Nevada, Paiutes and Shoshones made an agreement with the Central Pacific Railroad that offered employment and allowed them to ride freight cars anytime free of charge (chiefs got to ride in coach). For the privilege of crossing the Walker River Reservation, the Carson & Colorado Railroad agreed to carry all its residents and any goods they wanted to ship for free.[70] Indians rode the line "almost incessantly," often on the top of the boxcars.[71]

The agent in charge at Pyramid Lake and Walker River complained to the secretary of the interior about the mobility of Paiutes, or their "Gypsy life" as the *Reno Evening Gazette* labeled it.[72] According to the agent, Paiutes' ability to ride the rails for free might have been to their "detriment." They were riding to Reno and Wadsworth, where they fell in "with bad classes" of whites, but the agent also recognized that many were heading to these towns to find work, making those individuals "self-supporting" rather than dependent on the limited resources of the reservation. Paiutes found economic benefits from the rails as many became wage laborers on white land operations, some regularly traveling west across the Sierra Nevada on the Central Pacific to the Sacramento Valley.[73] Hops growers in Sacramento recruited Paiutes and other Indians, at least one thousand on one occasion in 1887, to pick for one cent per pound.[74] Around two hundred Paiutes were riding the Colorado & Carson line south to mine borax and salt at the Rhodes Salt Marsh in 1890.[75] Paiutes also worked at rail stations, loading and unloading freight. In Winnemucca, Nevada, they were paid one dollar a day in 1877 according to *Leslie's Magazine* (the same rate as Chinese laborers).[76] Paiutes also transported the products of their own labor: in November 1887 alone, several Paiutes carried two tons of pine nuts onto the Virginia and Truckee Railroad through Reno.[77] The amount of tonnage brought aboard by Paiutes over the years annoyed the railroad company, which argued that the Paiutes' freight was not included in their ride-for-free agreement.[78]

Paiutes were not the only people who readily adapted to modern transportation. Navajos were also frequent rail travelers, in part because of the freedom of movement granted them in their 1868 treaty.[79] Navajos caught trains at Manuelito or Gallup on the Atlantic and Pacific Railroad, which passed just south of their reservation. As early as 1882, Navajos were "in the habit of riding to and fro" on the recently completed A&P line for free.[80] "They are in no manner confined to the limits of their reservation," the Navajo agent observed.[81] Like the Paiutes, Navajos found that the railroads brought new economic ties. Navajos would ride far if they could "secure a better price for anything they may have to sell or if they can make cheap purchases," the agent told the commissioner of Indians affairs in 1886. In fact, the Navajos who lived near a rail line, usually those who lived outside the reservation limits, had an advantage over their competition. It was much less expensive for them to transport their wares to the freight cars. In the 1880s, Navajos were even selling at train stations blankets that were woven to depict trains and advertisements.[82]

Natives readily took advantage of rail travel, especially when they could ride for free, which eventually led to some restrictions on their travel. Complaints from non-Native travelers, usually centered on the appearance of Native passengers, sent them into the baggage cars or the boarding steps for their journeys. White sensibilities were also disturbed because some Paiutes and Shoshones in Nevada and Utah built "squalid wigwams made of poles, brush, and bits of old canvas or army blankets" at the train stations.[83] White American travelers whined that Paiutes expected and received donations from passengers. In 1877, a journalist described Shoshone women and

Three men on the railroad tracks at an unknown stretch in the Southwest, c. 1880s. The Huntington Library, San Marino, California. photCL 215 (88).

children at the Elko, Nevada, station as "repulsive looking creatures" who united "in a guttural cry of 'Muc-ca-muc-ca,' and 'Hungry!' and hold up their grimy hands as the passengers descend."[84] But many women came to train platforms to sell their own products: "trinkets, beaded moccasins, and purses, baskets woven from willows and soap-weed, necklaces of acorns and quartz crystals and agates."[85]

The few complaints from whites aside, agents allowed their Indians to take advantage of rail travel during the last quarter of the nineteenth century. Perhaps because of its affordability and efficiency, agents seemed to encourage Natives to use the railroads on their permitted trips. In one instance, the Cheyenne and Arapaho agent wrote to a freight company for High Wolf and High Chief, two Lakotas visiting from Pine Ridge, to quote a price for railroad transport for them and eight ponies back to Pine Ridge instead of sending them off on horseback for the long journey across the plains.[86] Agents also probably appreciated the directness of rail travel, which might limit the chances of Indians getting behind schedule, straying to unplanned destinations, or generally finding trouble en route.

Convenient and accessible, railroads played a significant part in keeping reservations connected. In the summer of 1890 alone, the railroad station at Billings, Montana, transported Natives between the Crow Reservation and Fort Hall, Fort Berthold, Fort Belknap, and the Nez Perce Reservation. Sometimes an agent could simply provide someone with a written statement of his approval to show to railroad workers, and the person would be allowed to travel. For instance, on a pass addressed the conductor of the Northern Pacific, the Crow agent wrote, "The bearers Hawk and Middle Bear are Gros Ventres Indians and have been on a visit to the Crows. They wish to return to their agency and if you will kindly pass them I will be greatly obliged."[87] The pass given to a group of Crows journeying to Fort Hall in Idaho requested that "the conductor of the NPRR will please pass them over the road."[88] But the railroad companies were not as acquiescent as it may seem. Many of these NPRR Indian passes were intended only as free rides on the flatcars, those "drafty and dangerous open spaces between enclosed passenger cars."[89]

Government Restrictions on Visiting

Intertribal visiting persisted only because Natives demanded it. The US government made efforts to limit intertribal contact at the very beginning of the reservation years, but it proved difficult to control the movements of thousands of Native Americans. Reservation agents far removed from

Washington, DC, could not enforce Indian Affairs' strict policy regarding off-reservation movement. At the ground level, agents had to contend with the resolve of the people. In order to maintain stability on their reserves, agents often obliged those who expressed their dissatisfaction with visiting restraints. When agents refused to oblige, some Natives used the mail to protest directly to the commissioner of Indian affairs. In November 1889, the Yankton headmen Running Bull, Feather-in-the-Ear, White Swan, and three others wrote to the commissioner to complain about the state of affairs at their agency, including their inability to visit other tribes. They argued that when they made their treaty with the government, they were made to agree to "treat as friends all the tribes round about us."[90] Why then, they asked, could they not go and visit their friends? "The Agent won't let us," they wrote. "If we ask him for a pass he won't give us one. If we go of our own will as men do, he telegraphs ahead and has us put in jail as spies." The Yanktons wanted to know why they could not "travel around like white men do!" For government officials, the answer to the Yanktons' question was simple: they were not white men. The Yanktons were colonized people who were told to follow the commands of the US government.

But Native Americans constantly resisted the racist colonial strategies of the reservation system. Many Natives visited distant tribes without permission despite the threats of punishment that might result. Reservation boundaries were permeable. It was impossible for a handful of government employees to limit the movement of hundreds or thousands of Indians. For instance, in 1874, the Pawnee agent expressed how little control he had in stopping Pawnees from visiting Wichitas and Comanches. The only thing he knew about the visit, he told the Wichita agent, was from the Pawnees' "own general statement" that they were leaving "and the fact that they left in opposition to our advice and order."[91] In response to this widespread hitch in the reservation system, that summer, the commissioner of Indian affairs directed agents to make "every effort" to "prevent peaceable Indians leaving the reservation" by informing them that the military held authority off the reservation.[92] If Indians remained on the reserve, they would not have to deal with the military, thus assuring their "safety."

Later in 1874, the commissioner tried again, further modifying Indian Affairs policies regarding what he labeled as the "roaming propensities" of Indians. Agents now had to present Indians with a special permit or written pass if they wanted to leave the reservation and could do so only if it would "benefit" the Indians while not proving "disadvantageous to the discipline of the Indian service."[93] These vague instructions allowed agents to follow their own minds when determining whether a visit was a good idea or not, but the commissioner also emphasized that visiting between reservations that were "widely separated from each other is objectionable." The commissioner was afraid of Indians traveling long distances, which would make "contact with white settlements or mining districts" more frequent. If an agent thought a long-distance visit was necessary, a military force would have to accompany the Indian delegation through areas of white settlement.[94] Without the protections of a travel pass or a military guard, the commissioner thought Indians traveling off the reservation would be "liable to be looked upon and treated as hostile bands." But in the years after this 1874 decree, military escorts were not always used, and thousands of Natives traveled without them, especially in the 1880s, when military escorts were only occasionally used.[95] In the 1880s, for circumstances when escorts were deemed necessary, agents sent Indian policemen, not white troops, to escort visiting parties to their destination.[96] Depending on the agent, Indian police were also involved in directing visiting parties or intercepting trespassers. Some policemen were asked to go to distant reservations to retrieve Indians who traveled without passes.[97]

Indian Affairs struggled to keep Indians on reservations in the 1870s. Because of the limited size of many reservations and the deficiency of government annuities, some groups had to leave their assigned boundaries to hunt and find food (tribes could still have successful bison hunts in the late 1870s).[98] The desire to visit also drew Natives off the reservation. In the Southwest, the Southern Apache Agency reported in 1876 that Chiricahua, Mescalero, Mimbreño, and Mogollon Apaches were "constantly visiting back and forth."[99] That same year up in the northern plains, the Devil's Lake agent complained about the "frequency" and the "interchange of visits" between his Indians, Mandans, Gros Ventres, Chippewas, and "Missouri Sioux."[100] In 1877, the superintendent of Indian affairs in Dakota Territory called intertribal visiting one of "the most serious obstacles to settled habits" and one of his office's "great difficulties."[101] In March of that year, groups of Sisseton Dakotas from the Sisseton Reservation and the Devil's Lake Reservation (now Spirit Lake) and Ojibwes from the Red Lake Reservation visited the Ojibwes at the White Earth Reservation without permission, leading to what the White Earth agent believed was "degrading" dancing, feasting, and gift giving.[102] The agent declared that no more visiting would occur that year, and he refused passes to several Ojibwes who hoped to visit the Sissetons, but some headed to the Sisseton Reservation anyway.[103] The Ojibwes left "very secretly," he admitted to the Sisseton agent, and nothing could be done about it.[104]

The resignation expressed by the White Earth agent was typical. The vastness of reservations and the Indians' unwillingness to make their comings and goings known to agents made visitation difficult to control.[105] In 1879, the Standing Rock agent still called visitation "a constant source of annoyance."[106] Two years after that, because of all the movement between his reservation and Standing Rock, the Devil's Lake agent called the area an interchange station.[107] The US government could not find a remedy. As Northern Cheyennes were coming and going at will between Pine Ridge and Fort Keogh in Montana in 1884, the Pine Ridge agent blamed the excessive travel on a lack of "danger or severe punishment" for being caught without a travel pass.[108] That same week, the acting secretary of the interior instructed the agents at the Lakota agencies (Pine Ridge, Standing Rock, Rosebud, and Cheyenne River) to discontinue rations to those who disregarded "the regulation to remain within the limits of their reservations."[109] The government would attack the stomachs of noncompliant Lakotas, a common tactic of control on all reservations. Nevertheless, three months later, forty Pine Ridge Lakotas went to the Crow Reservation without permission. The Crow agent told them to leave, but they refused until soldiers from Fort Custer arrived. The Crows, in turn, refused to tell the soldiers in which direction the Lakotas had fled, so the Crow agent withheld rations to punish the Crows.[110]

Tribal leaders frequently complained about attempts to halt their freedom to move about and make connections, which Indian agents could not ignore. The commissioner had to admit in 1877 that he did not want to "lay down an absolute rule" that prevented any travel passes, but he wanted "sound discretion" when issuing passes "in cases of known absolute necessity."[111] But he thought that agents like J. M. Haworth at the Kiowa and Comanche Agency were issuing too many passes, which led to reports that Indians were "roaming through the country and doing more or less damage in consequence of the liberties given them." Haworth was told that the policy of the US government was to provide for the Indians on their own reservations and "to have them remain there." But these more defined regulations did not seem to have much effect as Natives continued to move about without asking for permission. Just months after the commissioner again beefed up the rules on visiting, the Cheyenne and Arapaho agent reported that Whirlwind and "quite a number" of Cheyennes went to the Wichita Agency without passes to, he thought, do some horse racing.[112]

Three years later, in 1880, Indian Affairs loosened the off-reservation policy a bit, removing the requirement that agents write to the commissioner for every off-reservation movement.[113] Giving travel passes was up to the "judgement" of the agent, who should give passes to leave the reserve only to Indians who had demonstrated "meritorious conduct and attention to labor." Only visits between distant parties that would bring Indians into white proximity would require special permission from the commissioner, but these types of visits actually became more common in the 1880s. In the summer of 1881, for instance, more than one hundred Northern Cheyennes from Fort Keogh traveled through eastern Montana Territory to visit the Standing Rock Lakotas.[114] At the same time, more than fifty Pine Ridge Oglala Lakotas, including Red Shirt and American Horse, were allowed to travel through eastern Wyoming Territory to visit the Northern Arapahos at the Wind River Reservation for three months.[115] In 1883, Red Cloud and fourteen other Pine Ridge Oglalas visited Arapahos and Shoshones at Wind River for two or three months.[116] In the same year, an enormous party of Southern Cheyennes, 359 people, traveled north through Kansas and Nebraska to visit Northern Cheyennes and Lakotas at Pine Ridge.[117]

Traveling Indians made agents nervous. They regularly assumed that trouble might arise during travel, which would bring more inconvenience to their careers.[118] Butcher, an Arapaho at Wind River, was allowed to visit relatives and friends at the Tongue River Reservation in 1889, but he was given explicit instructions to "travel by a direct route, both in going to and returning, ... abstain from the use of intoxicants, and conduct himself in a quiet, orderly manner on the trip."[119] This is what was expected from traveling Indians: stay out of trouble and mind the rules. Agents also had to worry about protecting traveling Indians from white Americans. In 1887, a group of Utes returning to the Uintah and Ouray Reservation from a visit with Southern Utes in Colorado were instructed by their agent to take an alternate route because people in Colorado had told him that they would "shoot down all Indians that they see across the line of the Reservation."[120] Likewise, the commissioner denied Big Bow, a Kiowa headman, a pass to make a return visit to Pueblo friends in New Mexico in 1881 because of the threat of violence from white settlers there.[121] However, danger from whites had not kept around one hundred Pueblos from visiting the Kiowas and Apaches in Indian Territory the previous winter.[122] Likewise, some Mescalero Apaches made the same visit to the Kiowa, Comanche, and Wichita Reservation from New Mexico (without permission) in October 1882.[123] Mescalero Apaches continued their visits to Indian Territory for years, in some instances with permission.[124]

Of course, some white settlers expressed their dissatisfaction with Native mobility and intertribal visiting. Whites suffered from a fear of any intertribal interactions, a pan-Indian phobia, because they knew the history of intertribal power. The recently suppressed Great Sioux War of 1876–77 had been sustained through close cooperation among multiple bands and tribes. In 1882, the *Boise Statesman*, concerned with Bannocks passing from the Fort Hall Reservation in east Idaho to the Duck Valley Western Shoshone Reservation in west Idaho and north Nevada (and the unfounded rumors of the Bannocks' raiding), argued that the "policy of allowing these Indians to roam off their reservation is liable at any time to breed trouble." There was "no necessity" for these visits according to the paper. "It would be better for the Indians and insure the safety for the white people."[125] Likewise, in 1887, the *Billings Gazette* claimed that allowing Indians to "visit other reservations" had produced "incalculable injury to the white settlers."[126] The "injury" most settlers were worried about was a possible hit to their finances. The Wyoming Stock Growers Association made its own complaints to Wyoming Territory's delegate to Congress, arguing that "the simple presence of wild Indians on the ranges is a detriment and danger to the stock Interest." Stockmen claimed that the "610 Cheyennes, . . . 35 lodges of Crows, many hundreds of Shoshones, . . . and a great number of Sioux from Pine Ridge" whom they believed to be off of their reservations at that moment in 1883 might kill some cows.[127]

While Indian presence was not uncommon in many western towns like Helena in Montana Territory, Rapid City in Dakota Territory, or Lander in Wyoming Territory, traveling Indians still had to be leery of passing near white communities. Racism undoubtedly impacted Native mobility. The *Weekly Missoulian*, for instance, opined in 1879 that it was "better that the two races, . . . red and whites, . . . should be kept apart."[128] But when Native mobility was economically advantageous for whites, fewer complained about it, especially west of the Rockies, where more Natives were integrated into the economy. The Klamath agent complained about the near prohibition of travel, which prevented Indians from interacting with and being employed by whites and thus "earning a living and forming habits of industry."[129] Indians offered settlers cheap labor, after all, but the Klamath agent also believed that close contact with whites would teach Indians "habits, language, [and] modes of thought and civilization." A month later, the acting commissioner of Indian affairs did modify travel policies to the benefit of white business, writing to agents that it was not the "desire or intention" of Indian Affairs "to deprive the Indians of the privilege of selling their products" or "purchasing their supplies."[130] In the pursuit of capitalism, "the same liberty of action should be allowed them that is enjoyed by the whites," he directed.

In most stretches of the plains, however, Native Americans moving about off the reservation still brought out deep-seated fears of an "Indian Outbreak" in paranoid white settlers, often keeping agents on the defensive against unfounded rumors of Indian depredations (typically propagated by newspapers hoping to boost readership).[131] Even a decade after the last Indian war, newspapers continued to report that tribes were up to no good on their intertribal visits. In 1888, the *Idaho World* reported that four Indians from Fort Hall had visited Paiutes in Winnemucca, but because "squaws" had "told the settlers that the Indians meant mischief," it was thought that the visit was made to concoct "some kind" of plan of violence.[132] Settlers left their ranches in panic, according to the newspaper, and the US Cavalry was sent out to the vicinity of Juniper, Idaho, to investigate the bogus claims. Similarly, the sighting of two Southern Utes visiting Lakotas at Pine Ridge in 1887 led to a rumor that they were there "for the purpose of attempting to influence the Sioux to take the war path."[133] The rumored troubles never materialized, of course, but settlers were still concerned by the intertribal activities they heard about.

Despite white demands to keep Natives on the reservations, the Office of Indian Affairs had to balance that public pressure with the Natives' demand that they must be allowed to go off-reservation. Visitation was never banned outright, but some agents did try to put an end to visits by large parties, which agents believed caused the most trouble. In 1885, the new agent at Yankton reported "the displeasure of a good many" after he stopped the practice of visiting, "with great opposition from some of the chiefs and headmen."[134] Some Yanktons inevitably left without their agent's consent. The agent responded by tearing up their ration tickets upon their return, which decreased the number leaving the agency in 1886. But the prohibition did little to stop foreign Indians from visiting Yanktons. During a thirty-day period in the summer of 1886, the Yankton Reservation was visited by about 150 men, women, and children in groups of twenty to sixty. "These visits are prolific evil," the agent demurred. "Indians stop their work to have a general 'good time' with their visiting friends."[135] The visitors danced every night with the Yanktons.

Typical of the US government's colonial strategies, officials discouraged or prevented intertribal visits in an effort to change Native ways of life, particularly to erase customs that seemed abnormal or uncivilized to agents. Agents did not like what they saw as excessive generosity in the tradition of giving gifts to a visiting group. Visitors could expect to receive horses and other fineries from their hosts, which agents viewed as wasteful.[136] Cynical agents saw visitation as a scheme, with visiting groups hoping to profit while "their" Indians lost property and food. They were concerned that the people they administered were being taken advantage of by visiting tribes.[137] Some Natives did make visits primarily to acquire wealth, usually in the form of horses, which were given during dances like the Calumet Dance. In 1880, a group of Omahas admitted that a proposed visit from Otoes might lead to burdensome gift giving. Omahas asked George Merrick, an Omaha who wrote in the Omaha language, to write to an apologetic letter to the Otoes, denying their request to visit, because they had no horses to give away.[138] Agents were not the only ones wary of unwelcome visitors. Omaha letter writers frequently complained of having to give horses to visiting Dakotas or Ho-Chunks. Merrick's letter expressed concern that the Otoes would stay too long and drain the Omahas' limited resources. The letter also reveals the amount of planning that went into intertribal visitation, which would not have been possible without the mail. Because of letter writing, Omahas could relay their thoughts to Otoes before they reached the agency.

While many visits were made in part to acquire material wealth, some groups visited to acquire the necessities for survival. In 1881, forty Paiutes visited Navajos in the northwest corner of the Navajo Reservation and, according to the Navajo agent, came "begging for something to eat as they were in a starving condition, without clothing or moccasins."[139] The Navajos decided to take the Paiutes in because they "used to be friends and have intermarried with your people and yours with ours." But if the Paiutes returned to their "bad life, thieving and murdering," the Navajos warned, "we will hang you." The Navajo agent had to ask the commissioner of Indian affairs if he should encourage the Navajos' "humanitarian purposes." He reasoned that it would be a good "opportunity," while the Paiutes were "suffering," to "make an effort to civilize and reclaim this renegade remnant of savages." A decade earlier, Paiute activist Sarah Winnemucca had protested to the US Army that her people could not acquire enough to feed themselves if they were confined to a barren reservation. "If this is the kind of civilization awaiting us on the reserves," she wrote, "God grant that we may never be compelled to go on one."[140]

Although agents were of mixed opinion about visiting to acquire material things, almost all agents thought that gambling was a problem among visiting tribes. Paiutes and Shoshones regularly gambled together, along with Washoes, sometimes betting on wrestling tournaments that pitted the tribes against each other.[141] Among Plains groups, hand games were a common feature of intertribal visits.[142] These games, which pitted one tribe's shaman against another's, were typically friendly but always competitive and did involve gambling. The Pawnees played games with the Osages, Poncas, Omahas and Otoes, Kiowas, and Arapahos (and they played the moccasin game with the Sac and Fox).[143]

Many officials, perceiving visits to be largely a form of social entertainment, believed that Indians neglected their fields and other responsibilities while visitors were on the reserve. In August 1879, 207 Gros Ventres, Mandans, and Arikaras from Fort Berthold in Montana visited Standing Rock Lakotas in Dakota Territory. They stayed five days and danced, feasted, and exchanged presents while cornfields and hay "were entirely neglected."[144] Several years later, the Standing Rock and Cheyenne River agents approved a Lakota visit to the Crows as a reward for "good conduct and industry," but the Crow agent thought that visiting hindered industry.[145] The Standing Rock agent made efforts to satisfy the Lakotas' request, even writing to the stockmen who owned the lands that the Lakotas would pass through. No objection was raised from them. But the Crow agent refused to welcome the Lakotas, claiming that the Crows had too much work to do "attending to their crops, building fences around their hundreds of allotments, cabins on same, and making root cellars for storage of crops."[146]

Many agents were also afraid that intertribal visitation only encouraged what they thought of as the Indians' "old desire to roam." The US government hoped to take the nomadic habits out of the Indians and make them American domestics; visitation was thought to be the way Indians quenched their inherent desire to move about. But perhaps agents' greatest concerns about visiting had little to do with their nonsensical racial theories. Most agents just did not enjoy dealing with the work that visiting Indians brought. It took time and resources to properly manage visitation. Permission had to be sought through the mail, passes had to be written, and transportation might have to be secured, sometimes through the railroads. With all the movement, agents simply could not keep up, and some travelers were forgotten about. In just one example, Woman Standing Up from Standing Rock visited Fort Peck in 1883. She was supposed to be absent from Standing Rock for just thirty days, but she did not return until 1888. She lived at Fort Peck for five years without the agents' knowledge.[147]

Moreover, the US government could not keep track of every Native man, woman, and child in the West. Throughout the 1880s, there were still hundreds of Native Americans who were not living on a reservation or had never lived on a reservation, even if they were supposed to, especially in areas where white settlers had little interest in living. For instance, throughout late nineteenth and early twentieth centuries, there were more Western Shoshones living off the Western Shoshone Reservation (which was also the home to some Paiutes) than those living on it.[148] After Western Shoshones made it clear that they were not going to move up to Fort Hall in 1884, the US government did little to round up the nonreservation Basin Indians.[149]

In 1890, the Western Shoshone agent reported Paiutes living off-reservation as far northwest as the Jordan Valley in Oregon, more than one hundred miles from the Western Shoshone agency. There were also more than forty Bannocks and Shoshones still living freely in the Goose Creek Mountains around the border between Nevada and Utah Territory. These "Mountain Boys" had never lived on the Fort Hall Reservation, more than two hundred miles away, with the rest of their people.[150]

For many Natives, the limitations on mobility seemed arbitrary. Indian agents, who frequently entered and left these revolving-door positions, had varying opinions about the mobility of those in their charge, which complicated the lives of reservation Natives. Agent W. W. Anderson at the Crow Creek and Lower Brule Agencies believed that if the object of the Office of Indian Affairs was "to make citizens of these Indians," it could not do that "by herding them in spots and not allowing them to come in contact with other people."[151] Some agents, like Anderson, welcomed visits they thought deserving, but most were not so open-minded. There were also some agents who did not want any visitors for any reason.[152] The Crows, for instance, dealt with two very different agents. In 1888, Crow agent E. P. Briscoe refused to give his Indians passes, and he denied multiple requests for visitation from other agencies. Briscoe told the agent at Fort Berthold that visiting Indians only caused problems, which were thwarting his plan to get the tribe "under perfect control.[153] The Fort Belknap agent hoped that Little Chief would be allowed to visit the Crows, but Briscoe would not allow it, reasoning that he wished to keep the Crows "from being excited and 'stirred up' by visitors."[154] In September 1888, a Crow Creek Sioux named Charles LeClaire wrote a letter to Briscoe to ask permission to visit the Crow Indians, but Briscoe denied the visit request. He informed Crow Creek agent Anderson that he did not want any Indian visitors on his agency because his Indians were "quiet and controlled and are kept well in hand" (LeClaire and his party left Crow Creek anyway because Agent Anderson had given LeClaire a pass to the Crow Reservation before he received Briscoe's rejection letter). Briscoe was replaced by W. P. Wyman as agent of the Crows in 1889, and he was not as strict on keeping visiting tribes away.[155]

To make matters more complicated, different tribes were told to follow different regulations. In the decades after the Great Sioux War, the Lakotas got plenty of attention from government policy makers, especially regarding their off-reservation movements. In 1884, the acting secretary of the interior instructed the agents to the Lakotas to not issue anymore passes to Lakotas specifically (and to recall anybody who was off-reservation with a pass).[156] The agents seemed to have ignored those strict instructions. For instance, Bear Heart at Rosebud got a pass to visit Pine Ridge soon thereafter.[157] Unlike most tribes, Navajos had no official restrictions on their movements outside the reservation boundaries because of treaty rights, as the Navajo agent frequently and unenthusiastically explained to the white landowners surrounding Navajo land in the 1880s. Navajos constantly traveled throughout the Four Corners region, frequently on the railroads, visiting Indian and white settlements alike (around Gallup, Albuquerque, Santa Fe, Durango, and even Salt Lake City), largely for economic reasons.[158] After the Southern Ute agent complained of Navajos visiting without his authority in September 1884, the Navajo agent explained that there was nothing he could do; "this privilege" of off-reserve movement was "guaranteed to them in their treaty."[159] A few months later, the Navajo agent had to ask for the release of a Navajo man imprisoned at the San Carlos Reservation who had been arrested for visiting the Apache peoples there without a pass.[160] That same autumn, the Navajo agent told the governor of New Mexico Territory (who had complained about traveling Indians to the commissioner of Indian affairs) that he hoped the Navajos could "be restricted within prescribed limits" because it was "simply impossible for one man to watch over and control them."[161] The agent was afraid, as he told the commanding officer at Fort Lewis in Durango, Colorado, that violence might arise between off-reserve Navajos and annoyed cowboys.[162]

The policies regarding visitation were always fluid, and they seemed to depend on the disposition of the agent in charge. It is not surprising, then, that Indians felt that their rights were being violated arbitrarily when their requests to travel were denied. A new agent at Fort Peck who was trying to curb visiting complained that Indians had seen Fort Peck as "a go-as-you-please Agency."[163] He thought that Assiniboines and Sioux at Fort Peck had "been 'loose' so long" that they saw him as too "severe." But the previous agent at Fort Peck had not believed himself to be lenient on visiting. "These Indians for thousands of years have been nomads," he complained; they would not settle down "as long as the excuse and temptation is before them to visit their relatives at distant agencies."[164] The agent in charge at Fort Berthold in 1883, however, seemed to have a more positive opinion of visitation than the Fort Peck agents. He welcomed 112 Standing Rock Lakotas, believing that their interaction with the Mandans and Hidatsas, former enemies of the Lakotas, would better relations on the northern plains. He also thought, surprisingly, that the visits tended to "strengthen" the Indians' "purpose in adopting the 'white mans ways' in habits of industry, in the pursuit of Agriculture."[165]

The rules regarding visiting were especially arbitrary for the people at Pine Ridge. Pine Ridge's agent H. D. Gallagher knew that the Oglala Lakotas and Northern Cheyennes at his agency enjoyed the freedom to travel and visit other tribes, and he was not as worried about visitation as many of his contemporaries. But by the end of 1889, his opinion would change. Gallagher gave out passes to other reserves for much of 1889. He allowed twenty-five Sissetons to visit his Oglalas at Pine Ridge in May 1889 and did not hesitate to ask J. George Wright, the Rosebud agent, if he would allow seventy-five Oglalas and Cheyennes to visit Rosebud in September 1889 on the invitation of Brulé friends.[166] Granting them the privilege would "make their hearts good by granting passes," Gallagher told Wright.[167] Agent Wright had no objection to a "limited number of deserving Indians" traveling to Rosebud, but he did not want a large group because there was not enough food to support them.[168] Visiting Indians expected "to be 'feasted' while here," Wright explained.

Things changed in September, however. Complying with Wright's request for a smaller party, Gallagher gave out only thirty passes for the visit on September 25, but around two hundred Indians arrived at Rosebud. The Indians held a feast and a dance (reported as being the Omaha Dance).[169] Eight to ten cows were killed to supply the feast, much to the dismay of Wright, who ordered the Pine Ridge Indians to return home without rations. When a Rosebud Indian policeman was sent out to convey the order to the large group, however, Little Hawk detained the policeman and refused to let him go back to the agency headquarters.[170] Additional policemen were sent to the rescue. Bloodshed was avoided only because Little Hawk's brother's rifle jammed, but Wright and his policeman eventually calmed the situation in a council. Nevertheless, the incident soured Gallagher on intertribal visitation. "I sincerely wish the visiting business could be broken up," he wrote to Agent Wright, "and I will be with you in whatever may be undertaken to accomplish it."[171]

Gallagher had given out eighty-four passes to Pine Ridge Indians between September 18, 1889, and October 2, 1889, alone, and many others left the reserve without permission, a volume that eventually grew tiresome for Gallagher. It seemed to him that the Oglalas and Cheyennes were taking advantage of his inclination to issue passes.[172] By June 1890, Gallagher hoped the agent at Rosebud would join him in reducing the number of passes they issued so that "the evil effects resulting from it" would be minimized.[173]

Sometimes the desire to visit was so great that agents would issue passes just to keep those under their charge pleased in an attempt to avoid future difficulties. Agent Eugene White affirmed the problem, writing, "The different tribes are also fond of visiting each other in large numbers, and Agents frequently find it inexpedient to refuse them permission to do so, even if they can see no benefit to be derived from it."[174] Even the less desirable were given passes in order to maintain harmony, but it is clear that some agents chose to be more lenient in regard to visiting for more influential Indians who could make an agent's job more difficult. When Makushto and Yellow Lodge from Standing Rock were caught visiting the Devil's Lake Reservation without permission, their agent asked the Devil's Lake agent to treat them well because Makushto's wife belonged "to one of our best Indian families."[175] The pair would not spend the winter in the Devil's Lake guardhouse.

Most agents used visitation as a reward for Indians who seemed to be progressive and as an incentive for "good conduct."[176] Therefore, some Indians, especially if they were considered "good" Indians by an agent, were allowed to visit or receive visiting family and friends while others were not, often at the whim of an agent.[177] Visits to sick friends and relatives or visits to mourn a death were often given special consideration by agents.[178] Other agents were not so sympathetic. The Fort Berthold agent reported that his Indians were "constantly offering excuses" to get out of work, like wanting to visit a sick relative.[179] The superintendent of Indian affairs in Dakota Territory felt little sympathy for the bereaved, telling the commissioner that a "death in the family is worse than no excuse!"[180] But for the most part, agents gave consent to visits they thought meaningful, like attending to the ill or retrieving stolen or owed horses.[181] Indians living in the Dakotas also found opportunity to visit with other groups during the annual convocation held by the Episcopal Church, mission meetings, and other church-sponsored events at various agencies.[182]

Visiting despite the Restrictions

Agents lacked the authority and manpower to completely rein in Native mobility. For many Indians, a pass was simply a formality that could be ignored, and they constantly traveled without permission. As the struggles of Agents Gallagher and Wright demonstrate, large groups defiantly journeyed off the reservation, even in the late 1880s as agents grew confident in their ability to discourage large visits. Large numbers of Northern Cheyennes from Pine Ridge visited Tongue River in August without authority in the springs of 1889 and 1890, and so did ninety Lakotas sometime in the summer of 1889.[183] Natives in the Great Basin maintained their links with groups outside their region, often without their agents' knowledge. In

January 1884, ten Bannocks from Fort Hall visited Paiutes at Pyramid Lake despite being told not to leave.[184] In 1886, Duck Valley Paiute headman Big Jim visited Fort Hall from the Western Shoshone Reservation without a pass, some 250 miles away, and two white settlers from Silver City, Idaho, complained about the trip to the commissioner of Indian affairs.[185] In the summer of 1885, the Western Shoshone agent, in turn, informed the Fort Hall agent that many Fort Hall Indians visited his reservation without a pass "and it always" ended "in some trouble here."[186]

While many found clear paths to their destinations without bothering to ask permission, others asked for permission to make visits and were then denied by their agents but made their visits anyway.[187] Some agents thought that Indians were taking advantage of their willingness to allow travel.[188] In February 1889, Agent Robert Upshaw began to deny visit requests from Pine Ridge because every time he allowed Pine Ridge Indians to visit Tongue River, too many Indians visited, more than were allowed on the pass.[189]

Likewise, during the summer of 1890, Hollow Horn Bear, the prominent Rosebud Brulé, repeatedly requested passes to Pine Ridge, and Agent Wright finally agreed, but only if he went in a small party of three. Wright threatened to lock up any man traveling without a pass, but Hollow Horn Bear dismissed this warning, and a "large number" accompanied him to Pine Ridge.[190] Wright asked Agent Gallagher (who would soon be dismissed as the Pine Ridge agent) if he would, as "a personal favor," arrest those without passes on their arrival and "put the leaders to cutting wood until ready to return." Wright told Gallagher that Hollow Horn Bear "has always dared you would not do so (I invariably do so and consequently am not much bothered) and I want him to see that you will do so."[191] Hollow Horn Bear went around his agent's authority and wrote to the president, the commissioner, and two members of the Sioux commission to protest, among other things, the restrictions against him. "We are not allowed to visit any where," he complained, "when at our last treaty you promised us that if the treaty was signed we could go when and where we please."[192]

Punishments varied for leaving the reservation without permission. As we have seen, losing rations could be a consequence. Usually the visitors were just sent back home, but a stay in the guardhouse was a common punishment, especially if the visitors refused to go home.[193] Many were willing to travel without a pass and then face the penalties. Increasing the severity of punishment did not work. In fact, it only antagonized reservation populations, which was one of the reasons why agents were still seeing groups as large as four hundred arriving without notice from distant reservations in the late 1880s.[194] Of course, even with stricter rules, agents had to catch the folks leaving the reserve, but they lacked the manpower to patrol the peripheries of their reservations. In 1888, for instance, with Kiowas and Comanches visiting Southern Cheyennes and Arapahos without restraint, the Cheyenne-Arapaho agent proposed sending just ten Indian policemen to patrol on the more-than-one-hundred-mile-long border that divided the reservations.[195] Even with a realistic border-enforcement strategy, many reservation borders were not well defined or, as in the case of the Navajo reserve, were nonexistent. The Navajo borderlines had yet to be surveyed in 1883. As the Navajo agent lamented there was "not a single mark on the ground to indicate where the reservation" was.[196] The agent blamed the problem on lack of funding, which meant that imposing strict reservation boundaries was not always a priority for the Department of the Interior (which housed the Office of Indian Affairs).

To make matters more difficult for agents, some Natives, when denied permission to travel, simply forged passes, letters, and signatures.[197] In another example of Natives using literacy to weaken colonial control, a group of Southern Cheyennes used a forged letter in 1891 to convince their agent that they had permission to visit Comanches.[198] Travelers could also easily alter passes to suit their own plans. In 1886, for instance, the Pine Ridge agent noticed that a pass turned over by some Tongue River Cheyennes seemed to have been altered. Someone had changed the allowed party size from twenty to thirty-five (and they still showed up at Pine Ridge with forty-one people).[199]

Native Americans often sought permission to visit other agencies by writing letters to their agents, the commissioner of Indian affairs, or the agent at the reservation they hoped to visit. Cyrus Matonajin, a half Yankton Dakota, half Brulé Lakota who lived at the Yankton Reservation, wrote to his agent to seek permission to visit his father's side of the family who were Brulés at Rosebud. "I don't want to run off but I want a pass," Matonajin wrote."[200] Crazy Bear, a Pine Ridge Sans Arc Lakota, wrote to the agent at the Crow Reservation, where he intended to visit, rather than his own agent. The Crow agent would not consider the request unless it came from the Pine Ridge agent.[201] Black Eyes, while on a visit to Standing Rock from Fort Peck, wrote to his home agent to ask if he could remain at Standing Rock (his request was denied via return letter).[202] Edwin Phelps at Standing Rock wrote for an acquaintance who wanted to visit his daughter at Cheyenne River (the visit was denied because of winter weather).[203] Spotted Horse, also at Standing Rock, wrote (with the help of John Grass) to his agent hoping to see his mother and sister at Rosebud for the first time in thirteen years. His sister was "very sick," he told the agent. "Wish you give me a pass for 30 days."[204] In 1886, a Red Lake Ojibwe wrote to the Standing Rock agent to inform him that he and thirteen others were about to travel the 650 miles to visit the Hunkpapa Lakotas at Standing Rock. "I often make visits to Indians living on prairies," he wrote.[205] He was already coming to Pine Ridge, with a pass, "to find out what kind of friends I could find."

Other letters demonstrate that some Natives thought asking for permission to travel was unnecessary. Yellow Hair, another writer from Standing Rock, wrote to his agent for a pass to visit the Lower Brule Agency in 1880.[206] Rather than ask for permission to make the trip, Yellow Hair told the agent that he wanted a paper to show why his party was heading to Lower Brule, perhaps to avoid trouble with whites on the trek through Dakota Territory. Similarly, Gray Eagle told his agent that he was going to Cheyenne River to find a horse (he also instructed the agent to tell his wife, who was at the agency, to buy two sacks of potatoes).[207] Likewise, Feather-in-the-Ear asked the secretary of the interior if he could have a horse and a wagon to travel to other agencies, but he did not bother to ask permission to travel. He seems to have assumed that it was his right, in his old age, to visit his friends.[208] These written statements suggest that Natives, when speaking with their agents in person, did not always ask for permission to travel. Rather, they informed their agents that they would be traveling.

Natives made it clear that they were disappointed with any restrictions the US government placed on visitation. In July 1879, Spotted Tail, the Brulé Lakota chief, wrote the secretary of the interior that he was doing everything he was told and had advised his people to stay out of trouble with white people. He wrote that he was trying to be like white people by staying home. But he also was "good hearted" like the white man, and he and his people "like to visit each other as the whites do."[209] Spotted Tail argued, "When you have relatives sick you want to go and see them; so do I." He had sent a young man to Fort Keogh to see his sick sister with a pass from his agent, but the agent there "did not respect it. . . . They shot at him and tried to kill him" because the agent was a military man. "When those people come and visit us we feed them and use them well, and send them back home," he continued. "When any Indian goes there they take his horse away and put him in jail. This will make trouble and I want them to stop it." Spotted Tail could see little reason why his people were not allowed to travel through what had once been their countryside. The interaction with other tribes gave him great pleasure. He said that he "never laughed but once."[210] It was when Lower Brulés visited Rosebud. Spotted Tail's people treated their visitors well, fed them, and gave them 350 horses. Visiting with people from other reservations made Spotted Tail and other Natives happy because it allowed them to interact with like-minded people who were facing the same circumstances.

Native Americans questioned the power of the US government to limit their mobility, which meant much more than living what Indian agents labeled a "nomadic" lifestyle. The Office of Indian Affairs thought that off-reservation mobility and intertribal visits hindered their civilizing efforts, but intertribal connections were made across the West regardless. To counteract discontent, agents had to make concessions to those who wanted to go visiting. The inability to maintain a strict visitation policy in the West demonstrates the influence the Indians held over their agents. Their demands were not always met, but Native men and women certainly pressured agents to bend to their will. And, importantly, many Natives did not bother to ask permission to travel. They wanted to exchange stories and information with their relatives, old allies, or new friends living on distant reserves. But as we will see in the next chapter, the US government put a great deal of effort into suppressing intertribal exchanges that might endanger its authority. Nevertheless, because of Native resistance, intertribal visiting remained an important part of reservation life.

CHAPTER 4

Dangerous Influences

Sequestered but still connected, Native Americans circulated information throughout the West, spurring on intertribal relationships old and new. Unfortunately, US officials believed that some of the ideas spread through those networks might weaken the reservation system. They were especially worried about two vital categories of knowledge spread via intertribal visiting. First, visiting allowed tribal nations to share their experiences dealing with the US government and devise strategies to resist government control. These exchanges gave Natives advantageous knowledge as they negotiated US government demands, often frustrating US officials. The US government considered some ideas to be subversive and limited intertribal contact to prevent their spread.

Second, intertribal visiting spread and reinforced Indigenous religious ideas and practices, even as the US government was attacking those beliefs. Intertribal dancing was the most common purpose for intertribal visits involving large groups in the late nineteenth century. Dancing is still a critical component of intertribal interaction, and before and during the reservation era, intertribal relations were cemented with dancing, which served both social and religious purposes.[1] For nineteenth-century Native Americans, intertribal dancing was more than a physical act. Networking tribes shared religious knowledge, their ever-evolving systems of ritual, and their interrelated constructs of the spiritual world. Unlike Anglo-American Christianity in the same period, Native spirituality was open to acquisition and transformable. Despite Natives' innovations, their forms of religion were seen to be backward, even barbarous, by most white Americans. Reservations were meant to Christianize the Indians, after all, so government officials also tried to limit visiting in order to put a stop to dancing. Despite these restrictions, dancing persisted, and Native leaders exchanged ideas about how to best confront colonial power and reservation life.

Anticolonial Knowledge

Native leaders across the West traveled off-reservation to meet foreign leaders in council, hoping to pool their knowledge, exchange strategies of resistance, and relate their experiences dealing with the US government. Visitors and hosts shared the forced subordination of colonialism, and they often considered ways to mobilize collectively to rebalance power on reservations. Cheyenne River Lakota leaders who hosted an intertribal council in 1883 believed that "the interests of the Indians ... are identical" and that it was "proper" for leaders from different reservations "to meet and talk over matters in which they are all interested."[2] Intertribal meetings could cover a wide variety of common concerns, from the merits of boarding schools to a change of power in Washington, DC, or the intrusion of cattle operations. Leaders struggling to maintain some sense of sovereignty for their people sought information of political value. Intelligence acquired from foreigners could change the course of history for some tribes.

In a critical moment in their history, the Ponca Nation relied on outside information from former adversaries to make decisions about their future. In February 1877, as the US government was pressuring the Poncas to move from Nebraska to Indian Territory to make room for white settlement, Ponca leaders, including Standing Bear, were urged by a group of Pawnees not to consent to the US government's wishes.[3] While on their way to Indian Territory with government officials to take a look at possible sites for their new reservation, the Ponca leaders met with Pawnees who described their present difficulties in Indian Territory and the tremendous disease and death they had suffered since they had been removed from Kansas. They warned the Poncas that it would be the same with them. The Poncas, who had just heard similar testimonies from Osages and Kaws, immediately told their agent in a council (with Pawnees present) that they would no longer look for land in Indian Territory. According to the Pawnee Agency clerk, US officials "blamed the Pawnees for interference" and felt that the Pawnees "had no business to be off their reservation."[4]

Information shared among visiting tribes regularly frustrated the colonial designs of the US government. The Ponca headmen returned home to Nebraska, walking five hundred miles in forty days with little money and only one blanket each to hold back the winter cold.[5] They rejected the US government's favorable description of Indian Territory. Instead, based on information from a foreign tribe, they decided to resist relocation. The Poncas and Pawnees, former rivals who differed considerably, now faced the common enemy of US colonialism.

In the case of the Poncas, however, the US government eventually got its way. Despite their appeals to remain in Nebraska, the Ponca Nation was soon ordered to move to the Quapaw Reservation in Indian Territory in April 1877. Poncas died during the forced removal, and more than one-third of the Ponca population would die by the end of 1878. But the Poncas' plight received national publicity and some sympathy because of the actions of Chief Standing Bear. After the Ponca removal, Standing Bear decided to leave Indian Territory without permission to bury his oldest son on their homelands near the Omaha Agency in Nebraska, which resulted in the arrest and detainment of him and his followers. Standing Bear argued that the US government had no right to arrest and detain him for moving from one place to the next, because he was not acting as a member of the Ponca tribe but as an individual human entitled to the protections of the Constitution. After Standing Bear sued for a writ of habeas corpus in a federal court, a judge determined in the landmark *Standing Bear et al. v. Crook* case that Indians were, in fact, people who had rights that fell under the basic protections of habeas corpus. Because Standing Bear had severed his tribal ties, there was no law that gave the army the right to arrest him.

Although Standing Bear's story convinced many white Americans that Indian Affairs needed reform, the *Standing Bear et al. v. Crook* decision did not make it illegal for the government to arrest tribal members who left their reservations without a pass.[6] In fact, as the trial was underway in May 1879, the Ponca agent asked the Cheyenne-Arapaho agent to look out for a number of Poncas who were on their way to visit the Southern Cheyennes and Southern Arapahos without permission. He instructed the agent to give the arriving Poncas "no aid or comfort." Troops were requested to arrest the Poncas, and while it is not clear that the troops ever confronted the travelers, the request demonstrates the lengths officials went to control the Poncas.[7]

As the Ponca and Pawnee collaboration demonstrates, any idea shared across reservation boundaries that conflicted with US government policies or ideologies—which can be described as anticolonial—could draw the attention of US officials. The Office of Indian Affairs took steps to limit the spread of what it called "nonprogressive" or "demoralizing" thinking. In February 1889, for instance, the commissioner of Indian affairs told the agent at Pine Ridge that he wanted the "least possible intercourse" between Northern Cheyennes at Pine Ridge and Northern Cheyennes at the Tongue River Reservation. If the Pine Ridge Cheyennes were to visit Tongue River, the commissioner reasoned, they would also "in all probability exercise an extremely demoralizing, if not dangerous influence" upon the Tongue River Cheyennes.[8] For the officials at Tongue River, things were going well; the

Cheyennes were "progressing." But there was worry that the constant interaction between the two reservations might bring nonprogressive, traditionalist viewpoints to Tongue River, which would interfere with farming or education.

Officials regularly accused outsiders of trying to disrupt the normal functions of reservation life by introducing disobedient ideas or perspectives intent on decolonization. In 1880, Spotted Tail, the Lakota headman at Rosebud, was accused of sowing discontent at Cheyenne River by inducing a group of Cheyenne River Lakotas, under Bear Thunder and Red Eagle, to leave their reservations without permission. After being caught en route by the Cheyenne River Indian police, Red Eagle agreed to go back to Cheyenne River, but Bear Thunder told the police that he "would not return alive."[9] The police decided to avoid bloodshed and let Bear Thunder continue to Rosebud. Bear Thunder's brother White Ear claimed that Spotted Tail had instructed him to go to Cheyenne River to persuade his families to live at Rosebud, where they could live a better life, keep their guns, and avoid being moved to Indian Territory. Spotted Tail's inducement of disobedience annoyed the commissioner of Indian affairs, who also believed that any notion that Rosebud Indians had it better than Cheyenne River Indians would lead to additional dissatisfaction at Cheyenne River. The commissioner told the Rosebud agent that Spotted Tail's "interference with Indians of other Agencies has a tendency to destroy all discipline, is highly objectionable, and is in violation of the rules" of Indian Affairs.[10]

In 1881, the Standing Rock agent made similar complaints that visitors from Pine Ridge and Rosebud had a "detrimental influence upon the proper management of the Indians of this agency."[11] He thought that the visitors, many of whom, he claimed, were recently released prisoners of war, were inducing Standing Rock Lakotas to leave the place the US government told them to stay and head to Pine Ridge or Rosebud. The visitors informed them that they had "greater privileges," including carrying arms and hunting without restrictions. Coincidentally, the Pine Ridge agent made the same complaints about Standing Rock Indians.[12] In response, the commissioner for a time banned any visits between Standing Rock, Pine Ridge, and Rosebud and approved of "stringent measures" to prevent people from leaving the reserve without permission.[13] "Confine to the reservation if possible," the commissioner telegrammed.[14] It was not possible, however—at least not for long. Eighteen months later, fifty and then three hundred Lakotas from Rosebud traveled defiantly without a pass to Pine Ridge.[15]

Not being able to control the intertribal exchange of ideas made agents nervous, particularly when those ideas seemed to threaten colonial strategies.

As one agent put it, visits to his agency were "calculated to perpetuate sentiments hostile to improvement and civilized life," and Natives did make visits to intentionally subvert the US government's blueprint for their lives.[16] In early 1887, Long Feather (Sihásapa Lakota) and his party from Standing Rock got permission to visit the Oglalas at Pine Ridge and the Brulés at Rosebud, but Long Feather used that visit to contest colonial power. The Rosebud agent claimed (in a letter to the Standing Rock agent) that Long Feather, hiding the intent for his visit, proudly told him about "their achievements in agriculture" at Standing Rock. But when Long Feather met with the Brulés, he told them that he did not have to farm at Standing Rock at all and that those at Rosebud should not either.[17] According to the agent, Long Feather and his party "advised" the Brulés "to come to the agency and put the agent out of the Office."

In response to these "nonprogressive" ideas, the Rosebud agent sent five Indian policemen to remove the Long Feather party from the agency and recommended that the Standing Rock agent put them in the guardhouse upon their arrival home. That same year, the Fort Peck agent, D. O. Cowen, faced similar circumstances. He complained about John Lone Dog, an authorized visitor from Standing Rock, who allegedly told the folks at Fort Peck about all the privileges they were missing out on (including dancing "all the time," "no work," and "plenty of sugar and coffee").[18] Cowen scolded the Standing Rock agent for giving Lone Dog a pass, telling him that visitors had "a tendency to interfere with my design to put this Agency in shape." Cowen had stopped giving out passes altogether, justifying the strict policy as being "wholly for" the Indians' "benefit—in the end."

But in the minds of most Indians, government restrictions on movement and communication were always disadvantageous, especially if their dialogue with other tribal nations was critical of US policies and not in the best interests of the US government. In 1888, Young Man Afraid of His Horses, the influential chief at Pine Ridge, wrote that he wanted to maintain connections with other tribes because those lines of communication were mutually beneficial.[19] He hoped to make another visit to the Crow Reservation in Montana, but the commissioner of Indian affairs deemed his request "inadvisable," which angered him.[20] Young Man Afraid of His Horses had been to the Crow Reservation in the past, and he had relatives living there, but in his last attempt to visit the Crows, he was forced to leave by the Crow agent even though he had a pass from his Pine Ridge agent.[21] In late December 1888, a number of Pine Ridge Indians asked the inspector of annuities, M. W. Day, to write to Gen. George Crook for them. Young Man Afraid of His Horses decided to articulate his quarrel with the US government:

> Is it right to stop us Indians from visiting each other? We ask it because you... made us quit the war path and made us one nation, related to each other. We were at war with one another, you made us stop and be friendly; we now want to keep up this friendship and visit each other so we can talk of things that are of interest, and what is best for our own common welfare.

Young Man Afraid of His Horses believed that in order to secure their future, Natives needed to visit one another to discuss matters that would affect all of them. He also argued that the Oglalas should be able to visit their friends because happiness was a basic right for whites and should be for Indians as well. He continued:

> I want to speak of the future, to talk of making claim for damages, for taking the Black Hills from us so cheaply.... I was appointed Chief of the Ogallalas to watch over and protect them, and I want to look after the welfare of my children in the future. For this I want to visit the Crows and plan with them for the protection of our people; for the white man is crowding us, and will want to crowd us still more.[22]

Young Man Afraid of His Horses wanted to talk with others about getting compensation for the United States' robbing of the Black Hills from his people (the region was retained by Lakotas in the 1868 Fort Laramie Treaty but taken from them in 1876–77 because of a gold rush, leading to the Great Sioux War), an idea that Indian Affairs agents would not support. He also wanted to discuss and "plan" the best strategies to maintain their lands as the "crowding" from whites became more severe. For Young Man Afraid of His Horses, restricting visiting in order to control the flow of information, whether it was anticolonial in nature or not, was unjust and disregarded his people's sovereignty.

Young Man Afraid of His Horses and many others were compelled to visit neighboring reservations to discuss the US government's role in their lives and also to contemplate resistance to legislation, something that worried federal authorities. The Dawes Act and the Dawes Sioux Bill, in particular, were hot topics on reservations in the late 1880s. The Dawes Act required that a majority of a tribe agree to allotment and cession of their lands, which led to debate and division on reservations. Lakota chief Sitting Bull was among those who visited foreign tribes to rally intertribal opposition to the Dawes Act. In 1886, Sitting Bull, who lived at Standing Rock, went to the Crow Reservation, where he met with Crows, a small group from Pine Ridge, and nearly one hundred from Cheyenne River.[23] Most

Crows seemed to favor allotment, but Sitting Bull was able to change the majority opinion at several councils held during his stay. The Crows' agent reported that Sitting Bull's visit had "most pernicious results" and was an "unfortunate occurrence," which convinced him to deny visit requests from various groups in 1886 and 1887.[24] The *Billings Gazette* argued that Sitting Bull's visit "counteracted all that had been done to induce the Crows to settle down and become civilized."[25]

This perceived debacle led to a circular letter that the commissioner of Indian affairs sent to every agency on February 2, 1887, outlining a stricter procedure for intertribal visitation, once again making it necessary that all visitation requests be made through the commissioner (which would be frequently ignored by agents). If the Indians "expect help," the commissioner declared, "they must make an earnest effort to help themselves; this they cannot do while roaming over the country; visiting other Indians; committing depredations and stealing stock."[26] In an editorial titled "The Visiting Reds," the *Billings Gazette* stated that the commissioner's new orders should have prohibited off-reservation movement entirely. "They have room enough to exercise themselves on their own grounds," the editor claimed. "There is no object in letting them straggle over the lines to annoy settlers."[27] A few weeks after the commissioner's instructions, however, a group of twenty-five from Rosebud received permission to visit Pine Ridge under the false pretense that they would be talking about farming with their Oglala friends. But the agent soon learned that the group actually traveled to Pine Ridge so that they could dance, discourage farming, and advance the fight against the Dawes Act.[28]

For agents in the northern plains, the dangers of intertribal visiting seemed even more evident after a Crow named Sword Bearer (or Wraps Up His Tail) challenged government policies (and his agent's authority) by raiding horses on the Blackfeet Reservation in October 1887. Sword Bearer boldly returned home to celebrate his group's success by shooting guns into the air around the Crow Agency buildings. The Crow agent, Henry Williamson, responded to Sword Bearer's defiance by calling in the troops; this sent Sword Bearer and some followers fleeing off the reservation into the Big Horn Mountains, frightening white settlers. As historian Frank Rzeczkowski demonstrates, Sword Bearer was known to be in frequent contact with Northern Cheyennes and Lakotas over the years (he had just been on a visit to Tongue River without permission), and officials were afraid that his rejection of government authority was influenced by or an influencer of some general feeling among Northern Plains tribes. Information moved quickly among tribes, and considering that Brulé Lakotas, who lived four hundred miles from the Crows, were well aware of Sword Bearer's exploits in just a few weeks, there was a fear among agents and officers that an intertribal outbreak of violence was brewing. The Rosebud agent told the commissioner of Indian affairs that "runners have arrived and my Indians are uneasy, traveling from camp to camp and urgently soliciting passes in large bodies to visit other agencies."[29] The Rosebud agent even supposed that Sitting Bull's "incendiary talk" with the Crows the previous year had caused the "trouble," a claim the commissioner was quick to telegram to Sitting Bull's agent.[30]

By mid-October, Sword Bearer, Deaf Bull, and perhaps one hundred other Crows were at Tongue River, visiting Northern Cheyennes, which, of course, alarmed the Tongue River agent. It seems the Crows were there to promote a truth that "this was the Indian's country, the white man had no right to it, and ought to go back whence he came" (as summarized by George Hill, a Crow educated at Carlisle).[31] Lt. Hayden Cole told his general that the Crows were looking for some support but that the Northern Cheyennes had "no sympathy with the Crows" and "did not want to fight the soldier." Unfortunately, Sword Bearer's and Deaf Bull's beliefs led to a violent encounter with troops in early November.[32] Sword Bearer and six other Crows were killed.

The incidents involving Sitting Bull and Sword Bearer proved to officials that persistent communication between reservations was inconvenient for a US government that was trying to propagandize the merits of the Dawes Act.[33] As a result, the commissioner once again mailed out a circular regarding visiting, just eight months after the previous one, this time banning all visits without explicit permission from his office (it allowed leaving the reservation in order to perform labor or services "for the whites").[34] But the commissioner's tougher visitation policy made little difference on the reservations.[35] In fact, just weeks later, Bob Tail Crow, a Crow headman, was invited via correspondence to visit the Nez Perce Reservation in Idaho and, after initially being denied the right, was allowed to go.[36]

Lakotas also continued their off-reservation movement in 1887 and 1888, some still traveling to discuss allotment, even though agents tried to limit intertribal conversations regarding the Dawes Act. John Grass, a headman at Standing Rock, was locked up for trying to visit the Crows to counteract it.[37] But several others, including John Lone Dog, made it to the Crow reserve, and visits among Lakota agencies actually climbed in 1888.[38] Letter writing was key in organizing these visits and councils.[39] The Rosebud agent reported that councils were held at his agency with delegates from every Sioux agency. The Indians thought it "incumbent to council" at Rosebud, and the agent did what he could to prevent it. He sent police to break up the meetings, but if one large council was disrupted by the police, then "two smaller" councils were organized.[40] Of course, Lakotas were encouraged to attend the US government–sanctioned councils held in 1888 and 1889, which gave officials a chance to persuade them to approve the Dawes Sioux Bill. As the Crook Commission implored Lakotas to sign the Sioux Bill in the summer of 1889, Lakota agents were on the lookout for unauthorized visitors. In July 1889, the Cheyenne River agent removed Turning Bear (or Circling Bear) from Standing Rock because he was believed to be an "emissary" of Old Bull, there "to induce my Indians not to sign the new bill."[41]

The commissioner of Indian affairs also did not want Indians from non-Lakota agencies visiting Lakotas while the Crook Commission was working. Fifty Indians (perhaps Mandans or Hidatsas) from Fort Berthold were denied a visit to the Hunkpapa Lakotas at Standing Rock in May 1889 even though the Standing Rock agent welcomed it.[42] Down in Indian Territory, a group of Poncas was denied a visit to the Cheyenne-Arapaho Reservation because the Cheyenne Commission was working there to change minds about allotment. The Cheyenne-Arapaho agent did not want his Indians entertaining the Poncas instead of attending the councils with the commission.[43]

Other agents tried more inventive strategies to limit opposition to allotment. While the Pine Ridge Indians were debating the merits of the Sioux Bill, Agent Gallagher gave a pass to Little Wound (and eight others in his party) to the Wind River Reservation simply to get rid of him for a while. When Gallagher asked for the Wind River agent's permission, he described Little Wound as a "good, peaceable" Indian.[44] But a month later, he confided to the chair of the Crook Commission, whose duty it was to convince at least a majority of the Sioux in the Dakotas to agree to secession and allotment, that Little Wound was "as obstinate as ever."[45] Gallagher wanted him off the reservation so that he would not negatively influence the debate, even misleading a fellow agent to do it. Little Wound knew Gallagher's plan, but he agreed to leave if he was allowed to visit Wind River so that Gallagher "would have a chance to work on his people."[46]

Intertribal Dancing

It is not known why Little Wound was willing to leave Pine Ridge before the momentous vote, but something important must have drawn him to Wind

River. He may have gone to investigate early reports of the Ghost Dance, which had arrived through letters and visiting Utes, Shoshones, Crows, and Arapahos over the previous months.[47] In June 1889, twenty-two Pine Ridge Oglalas came home from a visit with Wind River Arapahos, perhaps carrying the more tangible information of the new dance.[48] In late October 1889, several Pine Ridge Oglalas, along with some Rosebud Brulés, went to Wind River without authorization (which, at that point, had become a habit, according to Gallagher).[49] There was another group, perhaps separate, that was already at the Fort Hall Reservation in Idaho.[50] Months later, Gallagher discovered that the trip was made to learn about a "Great Medicine Man" in Wind River country "who came especially to place the Indians once more in their primitive condition of freedom and independence, surrounding them with immense herds of buffalo and other wild game and bringing such confusion to their white persecutors as would insure the happiness of the Indians for all time to come."[51] The Ghost Dance, which was a religious movement comprising a set of ideas and an innovative (and adaptable) dance, spread because of the intertribal networks established before 1889. Even before the reservation years, religion played an important role in intertribal relationships, and tribes continued to share meaningful ideas and spiritual experiences with foreign groups once they were forced onto reservations.

In the nineteenth century, dances, which were typically intertribal affairs, were significant cultural events where people gathered and exchanged both the material and the spiritual. Dances were expressions of religious meaning but also served social purposes. Religious practices like the Sun Dance or the Omaha Dance were acquired and adapted, and because of the expansion of intertribal communication during the reservation years, these ideas could be shared with distant groups. Dances remained a major motivation for visiting and were often held in order to strengthen intertribal bonds. For federal policy makers, however, dancing only served to remind Indians of their prereservation lives. It was a practice of the past, a "demoralizing influence" that detoured the path of progress. For an agent at Devil's Lake, visiting parties brought dances, and the dances brought out the "paint and feathers," the bodily decorations of the uncivilized.[52] Government officials, missionaries, and reformers included antidancing rhetoric in their civilizing campaigns because dances were the expression and promotion of so-called uncivilized, non-Christian ideas. Like the information spread by Indians in order to subvert colonial control, Indigenous religious concepts were also thought to be damaging to the US government's efforts. But because of their constant contact with foreign groups, tribes discovered and incorporated new religious ideas and dances throughout the 1870s and 1880s.⁵³

The Sun Dance, which was condemned by the US government in the mid-1880s, is a good example of an Indigenous religious rite that was innovated over time because of its intertribal character. The dance was adopted by many of the Northern Plains peoples before the 1800s, and most Plains tribes performed it during the 1800s. It was an earth-renewal ritual, usually held annually, that developed great variety through intertribal exchange. The Sun Dance gathering was a momentous time of the year for Plains people. More than just a single ceremony, the dance was a "public festival" that allowed people to intermingle with relatives and acquaintances from other bands and tribes, to act out visions and share those vision experiences, to witness the power of medicine men, and to participate in giveaway rituals, which distributed material wealth.⁵⁴ According to D. B. Shimkin, the Sun Dance was "a vehicle of intertribal participation" between most Plains Indians during the early 1800s.⁵⁵ Kiowa calendars, for example, recorded their people attending Sun Dances with Dakotas in 1844; Osages in 1849; Comanches, Southern Cheyennes, Southern Arapahos, Osages, and Crows in 1854; Southern Cheyennes in 1867; and Southern Cheyennes and Southern Arapahos in 1868 and 1873.⁵⁶

Natives tried to continue the tradition on the reservations because, for some tribes, the Sun Dance was a demonstration of humility, supplication, and sacrifice before the Great Spirit. The ritual took several days to perform, during which fasting would occur and some men and women (in some tribes) practiced self-torture by pressing skewers, which were attached by string to a center pole, through the skin of their chests or backs.⁵⁷ Uninformed white observers saw it as an especially barbarous event, something that the US government could not allow on the reservations. Although agents tried to draw support from some progressive leaders to end the dances, time and time again, Natives from separate reservations coordinated Sun Dances together.

The Sun Dance became popular throughout the plains long before the reservation era, but some groups farther west, like the Utes, did not acquire the dance until they built connections with Plains groups. As the dance was being suppressed on the eastern reservations in the 1880s, it entered the intermountain region because of intertribal networking and began to flourish in Ute society. It is not known what Utes learned about the Sun Dance during their growing friendship with Oglalas, but in 1890, a Northern Ute named Grant Bullethead learned the ceremony from the Shoshones at the

Wind River Reservation, who had acquired the dance from the Arapahos.[57] The Northern Utes then carried the dance to the Southern Utes. Both groups, according to Marvin Opler, adapted the Sun Dance to "their own needs," "in the light of their own religious experience."[59]

Because of the expansion of intertribal communication during the reservation years, religious ideas and practices like the Sun Dance could be passed to foreign groups. The conditions for the dance's transmission to Ute peoples were not right before the reservation years, when relations with Plains tribes were antagonistic and intertribal exchange was inconsistent.[60] In 1868, Utes captured some Sun Dance medicine dolls belonging to Kiowas (who had lost them to Osages in 1833 and gotten them back in 1835), but Utes did not adopt the Sun Dance for another twenty-two years. Anthropologist Leslie Spier assumed that Utes were not well acquainted with the Sun Dance in 1868, so they did not understand the meaning or significance behind the medicine dolls they captured. But Utes did not have friendly contact with the Kiowas, and they could not acquire knowledge about the Sun Dance from them or the dolls. According to one source, Utes learned more about the dance from a Kiowa man, but he "was soon killed" by Utes.[61] Tribal relations between Utes and Plains tribes were not intimate before Utes began communicating with Plains tribes like the Oglalas in the 1880s. The workings of the Sun Dance, especially the dance songs, were learned by Utes while they were visiting other tribes.[62]

The Sun Dance occurred once a year, but dancing took many forms and served many purposes year-round. As a social norm, intertribal visits involving larger parties required dancing, and agents knew that dancing and visiting were bound together. Even for visits made primarily for social, economic, or political reasons, dancing still played a vital function. But agents took steps to prevent dances from occurring during permitted visits, especially by the mid-1880s. In 1886, for instance, after some Pawnees visited Wichitas with permission but danced without permission, their visitation privileges were taken away.[63]

However, even though agents were instructed by their superiors to curb dancing on reservations, it was rarely outright banned.[64] Natives constantly tried to persuade their agents to allow dancing. Agents sometimes relented, and dances were held with permission in an environment that agents believed they could control. But many Natives organized clandestine dances outside agents' authority. If Indians were caught dancing outlawed dances like the Sun Dance, the "scalp-dance," or the "war-dance," only the courts of Indian offenses (presided over by tribal leaders who were often appointed by the agents) had jurisdiction to punish participants.[65]

Although the US government was able to limit the frequency of dances, tribes like the Southern Cheyennes never stopped intertribal dancing. In the fall of 1889, for instance, more than one hundred Poncas danced with Southern Cheyennes.[66] In May 1890, the Cheyenne chief Whirlwind asked the Cheyenne-Arapaho agent if his people could dance. The agent offered no objection as long as it did not occur within five miles of an agency school. To the chagrin of the agent, around one hundred Kiowas and fifty or so Comanches and Apaches traveled to his agency to join the Cheyenne dance.[67] In the weeks prior, the Cheyenne-Arapaho agent had balked at the idea of a dance on his reservation after he was told that "a large number" of Kiowas were going to visit to join "a big Medicine."[68]

At agencies throughout the West, organized dances often attracted hundreds of Indians from multiple tribes, even after efforts to crack down on the assemblies. Around two hundred Rosebud Brulés visited Pine Ridge to dance in the spring of 1889.[69] A good number from Pine Ridge went to Rosebud without permission to dance later the same year. In September 1890, two hundred Pine Ridge Indians danced at Rosebud (reportedly the Omaha Dance, although it could have been a Ghost Dance).[70] In June 1890, after ration day at Pine Ridge, six or seven hundred Northern Cheyennes and Sioux gathered at White River to dance. The number of dancers was so great that some white settlers near White River and Black Tail and Beaver Creeks (in Nebraska) grew alarmed and left the area in fear of an outbreak of violence (they had heard rumors, but the military saw no reason for fear and concluded that troops were not needed).[71]

Because of the sheer number of Natives who wanted to maintain this critical part of their culture, agents had a difficult time curbing the custom. Some dancing was still allowed at Standing Rock in 1890, an agency controlled by strict Agent James McLaughlin, despite the wishes of the Office of Indian Affairs.[72] McLaughlin confessed to the commissioner that he allowed his Indians to gather for the Grass Dance, but only on Saturdays and without the "wholesale giving away of property."[73] Whenever an Indian gave away "horses, rations, money and clothing" at a dance, the offense was quickly punished. McLaughlin prided himself on being able to end the "pagan practices" of the "'Sun Dance,' 'War Dance,' 'Scalp Dance,' 'Kiss Dance,' 'Buffalo Dance,'" and "Horse Dance" as well as the "'tom-tom' Orchestra" that was heard in "some of the camps." The Omaha or Grass Dance was allowed to continue because it did not have the "objectionable features" of the other dances. It was social in nature. McLaughlin could not think of another "pastime amusement" to substitute for the Omaha Dance, which was needed for the Indians' "recreation and amusement . . . until they become more civilized." Like many agents, McLaughlin had to satisfy the desires of the reservation's populace, but he only allowed dancing that was deemed relatively inoffensive to white sensibilities. He was able to rationalize his toleration of the Omaha Dance by insisting on its harmlessness and by believing that he controlled the practice because he scheduled it. In reality, McLaughlin did not have the power to suppress all dancing without risking all-out opposition.

In the same way that agents had differing policies on visiting, various agents had different opinions about dancing. In 1886, the agent at the Yankton Reservation lamented that he had tried for two years to break up dancing and avoid the visitation from other tribes that came with it, but his predecessor had allowed the Yanktons to build a dance house and hold dances on Saturday nights. Yanktons claimed "the right to continue them," and the agent "utterly failed" in all peaceful means to stop them.[74] "Considering the large number of people who attend these dances," the agent reported in 1885, "and the serious consequences which would result from a forcible ejection from the dance house of the persons in attendance, I have not thought it wise to resort to this means to stop it."[75] In 1887, the Yankton agent jailed and cut the hair of Wakea, "the expert dancer of the tribe," for his "misconduct."[76] The agent prided himself on the effectiveness of the punishment. According to the agent, Wakea seemed to give up dancing and was "living nicely" on a "little farm."

Dancing was tolerated by government employees to keep Indians content, but like the Yankton agent, most tried to discourage the practice. The Cheyenne River agent allowed dances on the Saturday night before ration day, but Natives from Lower Brule and Cheyenne River still held unauthorized dances together.[77] Cheyenne River Miniconjou Lakotas invited Standing Rock Hunkpapa Lakotas to dance at their reservation in May 1890 (the Miniconjou had visited the Hunkpapas the previous winter), but the Standing Rock agent would not allow it. The agent thought that the group of fifty Hunkpapas, headed by Gall (who was considered a leading progressive chief), might leave anyway, but it is not clear if they did.[78]

Some non-Natives were vehemently opposed to any leniency concerning intertribal dancing. In the summer of 1890, a group of Santees visited the Winnebago Reservation in nearby northeast Nebraska, a trip that occurred often. The two tribes danced, and the Santees went home with horses given to them by Ho-Chunks (Winnebagos), a typical gesture among Plains nations. A few months later, a group of Ho-Chunks went to the Santee Reservation to dance, and the Santees gave away some horses in return. Rev. Charles Stroh, of the Episcopal Church at Santee, asked the agent to end the tradition, but the agent did not believe he had the authority to end a religious practice. Alfred Riggs of the Santee Normal School told the commissioner of Indian affairs that the dancing affected the "moral and temporal welfare" of the Indians and that "the better class of Indians" deplored it.[79] Months later, around thirty Sissetons from South Dakota visited the Mille Lac Chippewas (Ojibwe) in Minnesota and initiated a dance. The chairman of the Chippewa Commission complained to the commissioner that the Sissetons were "a worthless set" who had danced and feasted in the fall of 1889 at White Earth and Red Lake and had swindled the Chippewas out of ponies and presents. "The Sioux are crafty, irritating, and worthless, the hospitable Chippewas, generous to a fault will give them their last garment or mouthful of food"; it was, he said, "a begging expedition."[80] The Sisseton agent sent his Indians who were off-reservation a letter, written in Dakota, instructing them to return home at once.[81]

Whites thought that intertribal dancing was a legacy of Indians' superstitious beliefs and did not belong in what they believed was their more advanced Christian world. Missionaries, educators, and government officials saw dancing among students as a step backward in their education. In 1882, two educated Pawnees, Merritt Sherman and Fremont Washburn, joined a larger group of Pawnees led by Nelson Rice on their unauthorized dancing visit to the Cheyenne-Arapaho Reservation. The Pawnee agent lamented that the pair's "example" had the "most pernicious ... influence" on the other Pawnees.[82] Eight years later, an inspector at the Ponca, Pawnee, and Otoe Reservation reported that dancing was still having a negative influence on the schoolchildren. He thought that when the children returned home, "the parents in a few days or weeks undo, presumably by said dances, much good that has been accomplished for the pupils at school." The Pawnee agent agreed with the inspector's recommendation that agents should prohibit persons under the age of twenty-one from dancing.[83] Schools did not accommodate a student's right to dance, because the practice was considered to be incompatible with educational pursuits. Students could be dismissed for dancing, which is what happened to two Yankton students at Saint Paul's School in 1889 because they frequently ran away to join dances.[84]

But not every government official felt the need to eliminate dancing entirely. Some tolerated dancing because they believed the practice would inevitably die a natural death. In 1886, Agent W. W. Anderson, in charge at the Crow Creek and Lower Brule Reservations, reported:

> I have not endeavored to break up the squaw-dance and such other harmless amusements. I like to see happy smiling faces around me,

and want these people to enjoy life in an innocent manner, providing their work is kept up. Every race of people has its amusement, and these should not form the exception. As they gradually get accustomed to work and become more interested in accumulating property, the cruder sports will die out and give place to more enlightened amusements.[85]

Col. J. F. Wade at Camp Schofield, who disagreed with a complaint that some Southern Arapahos were causing a distraction by dancing too close to an Arapaho school, also thought dances were harmless amusement. He told his commanding officer that dancing was "only the Indian method of amusement," similar to "the ball room, theater, saloon, &c., of his more civilized brother."[86] The military found no reason to force the group of Arapahos to stop their dancing, but the policy of Indian Affairs was to outlaw dancing ("the nocturnal orgies, etc.") or any "encamping, congregating, or engaging in any noisy or disorderly conduct" within five miles of a school.[87]

Natives tried to convince the US government that their religion should not be managed by bureaucrats. In May 1889, all the Kiowa headmen asked their agent to obtain permission from the commissioner of Indian affairs to hold their "medicine dance" (Sun Dance) in July. They told the agent that it was their religion, it was how they worshiped the "Great Spirit," but the agent saw "no good results" in their "custom."[88] He called the dancing "demoralizing and disgraceful" and claimed that women had been prostituted and property had been destroyed during past dances.[89] The commissioner denied the request in a letter, which was read to the Kiowas. They insisted that their agent write back, but the agent declined. Other Natives wrote to Washington directly to plead for religious freedom. Oglala Lakota leaders Little Wound, Young Man Afraid of His Horses, and Red Cloud told the president in 1888 that he had shamed them by "stopping" the Lakota ghost lodge rites, which were performed in mourning after the death of a loved one, usually a child, over a period of months. "The Great Father should consider that we are Indians," the leaders wrote.[90]

But the US government did not stop regulating Native religion. There was little concern for the First Amendment rights of Native Americans because they were not US citizens, and policy makers limited Native dancing for the sake of white sensibility. It was not until 1978's American Indian Religious Freedom Act that government interference with the exercise of Indigenous religious belief was deemed illegal by Congress. But back in 1883, Commissioner of Indian Affairs Hiram Price opined that there was "no good reason why an Indian should be permitted to indulge in practices which are alike repugnant to common decency and morality; and the preservation of good order on the reservations demands that some active measures should be taken to discourage and, if possible, put a stop to the demoralizing influence of heathenish rites."[91]

The characteristically intertribal Sun Dance, one of the practices Price singled out, was condemned by the US government for years, but Natives fought to continue the tradition. At the Sioux Agencies, the Sun Dance was an expected and important ritual until the US government used its resources to put an end to it. At least one thousand Brulés from the Lower Brule Agency traveled to the Rosebud Agency to dance in 1879, and nearly four thousand Oglala and Brulé Lakotas met and danced near the Pine Ridge Agency border in 1880.[92] During the 1879 Sun Dance, Oglala leaders tried to demonstrate to white officials how similar their beliefs and rituals were to whites'. At a council with the Pine Ridge agent, Red Cloud said, "This sun dance is a rule of the Great Spirit. On this day we give horses and cloth to the poor to make them rich and happy. We are doing all this for our children, and praying to God for them. You dress up and wash and go to church. My young men for the same reason put on paint."[93] Red Cloud even asked the US government to provide the paint. Likewise, Little Wound tried to reassure whites who were afraid of the Sun Dance, stating that they were simply "dancing [and] praying that nothing bad may happen to the Indians or Whites."

In the summer of 1881, an unauthorized Sun Dance was held at Standing Rock and attracted Lakotas from other agencies.[94] At the same time, down south at Pine Ridge, dozens of non-Indians, including military and agency officials, witnessed another Sun Dance with 3,500 Lakotas from outside agencies gathered. Lakotas, who knew that their religious freedom was in danger, welcomed the whites because they wanted to show the significance of their religion to those who might threaten it, but white minds remained unchanged.[95] An 1882 Sun Dance at Pine Ridge was observed by ethnologist Alice Fletcher, but the Oglalas would not allow her to study other ceremonies, telling her, "The white people do not understand us, they laugh at our sacred things, and they will laugh at these things which they did not know before."[96]

The 1883 Lakota Sun Dance, which attracted a very diverse crowd, brought strong objection from the Rosebud agent, J. George Wright. He reported to the commissioner of Indian affairs that every Sioux agent had given many of their Indians permission to attend the dance at Pine Ridge. The military reported that there were 75 attendees from Pine Ridge, 53 from Standing Rock, 15 from Cheyenne River, and 99 from Lower Brule. There were also hundreds from more distant reservations, including 379 Yanktons, 64 Omahas and Ho-Chunks, and 81 Poncas. All of them had permission to attend. Wright refused to allow Rosebud Brulés to go, but many still went (he had "no means of knowing" how many).[97] He asked the Pine Ridge agent to send them back home, but not a single one was "rounded up." And, to the astonishment of Wright, those who remained at Rosebud organized their own Sun Dance there. Wright claimed that he had "used every persuasion, discouragement, and means in my power" to prevent a Sun Dance at his agency, "but all to no purpose." He had concluded that he "might as well expect to be obeyed in an order for the sun to stand still as in one to suspend or do away with this Sun dance now organized and going on at this agency." Wright blamed the continued normalization of the dance on government officials, pointing to the agents, officers, "staffs and their friends" who would go and watch the Sun Dances as a spectacle.

Because of increasing criticism from worried officials, that summer of 1883 was the last time a Sun Dance was held on a Sioux agency with authorization. Despite strong protest from Lakota leaders, the Department of the Interior ordered an end to the Sun Dance in May 1884.[98] Lakota agents threatened to reduce supplies, farming implements, and food rations to those who Sun Danced and offered benefits to the leaders who agreed not to protest the suppression of the dance, two strategies that successfully ended large Sun Dance ceremonies on those agencies.[99] But Indians living on Rosebud, Standing Rock, Pine Ridge, and other Dakota Territory agencies still held Sun Dances in secret, and some even traveled to other agencies to continue the outlawed ceremony. In August 1888, a Northern Cheyenne named Grasshopper left Pine Ridge with a party of twenty-four others to hold a Sun Dance with the Northern Cheyennes living at the Tongue River Reservation in Montana. Grasshopper was denied permission to leave the agency for such a purpose, but he decided to head to Tongue River anyway. The Pine Ridge agent, H. D. Gallagher, instructed his Indian police lieutenant Fast Horse to catch up with the party and compel them to return home, threatening them with troops if necessary.[100] Troops, in fact, were the ones who had to force Grasshopper's party back to Pine Ridge (Fast Horse's horses had gone lame), but Grasshopper was persistent. He asked Agent Gallagher to write to the Tongue River agent for permission hold a Sun Dance there, but Gallagher convinced Grasshopper that he would never agree to it.[101]

Surprisingly, just months later, in November 1888, Gallagher did allow Grasshopper to visit his mother at Tongue River with his wife and mother-in-law. Gallagher told the Tongue River agent that he was sure Grasshopper would give him no trouble. Grasshopper "has given up the idea of having a dance," Gallagher wrote. "I trust you will feel, like myself, that there would be no impropriety in this visit."[102] Permission for visitation often hinged on the visitors' intentions, and Grasshopper had decided to give the agent a new excuse to visit Tongue River. There is no record of any trouble out of Grasshopper during that November 1888 visit. However, in May 1889, Grasshopper, Roan Bear, and Roan Bear's wife, child, and mother left Pine Ridge for Tongue River in an attempt to lead a Sun Dance.[103] Grasshopper and Roan Bear had repeatedly asked Gallagher if they could visit Oelrichs, a town twenty-five miles from their camp, never mentioning their true purpose for leaving Pine Ridge. Gallagher finally agreed, not realizing that Grasshopper's eventual destination would be Tongue River, which happened to be in the same direction as Oelrichs.

After discovering that Grasshopper had made it all the way to the Tongue River Reservation, Agent Gallagher recommended to the commissioner of Indian affairs that Grasshopper be arrested and jailed. Three cavalry troops were sent to Tongue River to prevent the Sun Dance and preserve the peace, but Grasshopper's party went back to Pine Ridge before the cavalry could intervene.[104] The press reported that Grasshopper had eluded arrest.[105] Frustrated, Brig. Gen. Thomas Ruger urged that agents be instructed to telegraph immediately when Indians left their reserves, including the number that left and their destination. The army had been asked "several times within the past few years" to send troops to capture Tongue River Cheyennes on their way to Pine Ridge but had not been given enough information.[106] In the summer of 1887, around two hundred Pine Ridge Indians were forcibly removed from Tongue River by the military, and it nearly came to blows according to Upshaw.[107]

Grasshopper's 1889 attempt to hold an intertribal Sun Dance among Lakotas, Cheyennes, and Crows at the Tongue River Reservation was covered by the press, which led to false reports that the dance, if held, would "be largely of a military character."[108] Grasshopper's defiance made the US government think twice about Northern Cheyenne mobility, and the commissioner tried to put his foot down regarding visits to and from Tongue River. In July 1889, Upshaw submitted a request to the commissioner for Buffalo Hump (Northern Cheyenne) and other Cheyennes to visit relatives at Pine Ridge.[109] Although Upshaw favorably recommended the visit (and Agent Gallagher did not object), the commissioner denied it because of the recent "disturbances threatened" by Grasshopper to initiate a Sun Dance at Tongue River. "The less intercourse had between the Indians of the two Agencies the better it will be for both," the commissioner responded.[110] The commissioner also denied the request of Red Bird (Northern Cheyenne) and his family from Tongue River to visit Cheyenne River, even though the agents at both agencies approved. The commissioner again cited the disturbances by Grasshopper and his Sun Dance.[111]

Natives living outside the Dakotas also tried to maintain the Sun Dance during the 1880s. In northern Montana Territory, a group of Assiniboines from Fort Belknap went to Fort Peck without permission to participate in a Sun Dance in May 1888. The Fort Belknap agent, worried that the Assiniboines would lose their crops from neglect, asked the Fort Peck agent to send them home as soon as they arrived. The Sun Dance "almost entirely demoralizes our Indians," the Fort Belknap agent wrote, "and they will steal off in spite of all we can do to prevent them."[112] In fact, the Fort Belknap agent struggled to prevent an intertribal Sun Dance on his own reservation that summer. At the same time, a group of Plains Crees living around Fort Assiniboine (about fifty miles west of the Fort Belknap Agency), refugees from southern Alberta who did not belong to any US agency, held their own Sun Dance, which was probably attended by some from Fort Belknap.[113]

The Sun Dance was especially intertribal in character in Indian Territory. During the last quarter of the nineteenth century, it was, according to James Owen Dorsey, "always the custom" for the Southern Cheyennes and Southern Arapahos to attend each other's Sun Dances, "owing to the long intimacy" between the tribes.[114] Unfortunately, Sun Dancing in Indian Territory during the early reservation years became challenging because of the near extinction of bison. A bison bull had to be killed and was used for different purposes in the Sun Dance rite. The Kiowas, for instance, were not able to hold the important dance in 1880, 1882, 1884, or 1886 because they could not locate a bison bull. The 1881 and 1885 dances required weeks of hunting, but a bull was ultimately found (perhaps west of the reservation limits). In 1887, Kiowas, despite being instructed by the US government not to dance, procured a bison bull from a domesticated herd around Clarendon, Texas, sixty miles west of the reservation bounds. The Kiowas on the hunt begged the rancher for a bison, offering several horses for it.[115] Despite not having been offered enough, the rancher, who was afraid the Kiowas would travel too far westward and get into trouble with unfriendly whites, gave them a bull (with a promise from the Kiowas of later payment). Nonetheless, the following two years, the Kiowas' new agent prevented the Sun Dance from being organized.[116]

Back in 1881, a large group of Southern Cheyennes and Arapahos visited the Kiowas to join the Sun Dance officiated by Heap O' Bears. In that instance, the agent tried and failed to use food as a deterrent; he attempted to end the Sun Dance by offering additional rations to those who would leave the dance, but none complied. Instead, the agent relented and actually sent rations and cattle out to the Sun Dance grounds, some sixty miles from the agency office, to feed the hungry participants who could no longer subsist on bison and other game that far from home.

Leading up to that Sun Dance, a Kiowa medicine man named Dátekâñ had spread word that he could bring back the rapidly disappearing bison, which he said had been trapped beneath the ground. He took the name Pá-tépté (Buffalo Bull Coming Out) and erected a medicine tepee at the Sun Dance grounds to prepare the way for the bison. News of Pá-tépté's vision reached Cheyennes, Arapahos, and even some unspecified groups of Sioux. Among the 1,600 Indians at the Kiowa Sun Dance grounds on July 14, there were around 160 Cheyennes (under Little Chief, Little Robe, Bobtail, Jake, and Wild Horse), 44 Arapahos (under Powder Face and Black Coyote), Apaches, and "a few numbers of other tribes."[117] But according to the Cheyenne-Arapaho Reservation interpreter, the Cheyennes were disappointed after the medicine man's promises were unfulfilled. Little Chief, the Northern Cheyenne headman who was living with the Southern Cheyennes at the time, left the Kiowa Reservation "in disgust."[118] Less than a year later, however, Pá-tépté tried again, and a group of Pawnees visited the Kiowa Reservation (without permission) to dance.[119] Not much is known about the Kiowa medicine man's rituals, but his promises were communicated widely enough to attract Cheyennes, Arapahos, Pawnees, and other foreigners to the Kiowa Reservation.

The US government again tried and failed to prevent the Kiowa Sun Dance in 1887. Kiowa chief Lone Wolf and Caddo leader Caddo Jake wrote to the commissioner of Indian affairs to ask him (among other things) not to interfere with their Sun Dance. The commissioner at the time, John D. C. Atkins, the same commissioner who had banned Native languages in government-supported schools, told Lone Wolf and Caddo Jake that their people should not "indulge in any of these customs of your former savage life." Atkins thought that they would "see how foolish" dancing was once they got "farther along" on the path of American-defined civilization. "When you lived by hunting and roaming it was more natural that you should have such customs, but now that the buffalo are gone and you are learning to living by farming and herding and to be like white people," the commissioner maintained, "all such things should be put away." Atkins's ignorant assumptions about Kiowa, Caddo, and other Native cultures were typical of government policy makers in the late nineteenth century. Atkins also incorrectly assumed that the Kiowas would comply with his instructions, but a Kiowa-organized Sun Dance still took place in 1887.

After his orders were ignored, Commissioner Atkins pushed agents to destroy the Sun Dance, and in 1888 the Kiowa agent was willing to prevent unauthorized dancing with the threat of military intervention. Around eighty Kiowas made it to the Cheyenne-Arapaho Reservation to organize a Sun Dance there, but their efforts appear to have failed.[120] In 1889, the new commissioner of Indian affairs instructed the agent to end the Sun Dance, using "all proper means and precautions."[121] Kiowas, along with Southern Cheyennes and Southern Arapahos, were still trying to hold what authorities assumed were Sun Dances in 1890, but the Kiowa agent, who had initially permitted a dance that summer, was directed by the commissioner to use cavalrymen to stop the ceremony.[122] The commissioner argued that the US government did not "wish to force upon" Indians "the white man's religion," but the dances were "very harmful to the young men and prevent them from accepting the white man's way."[123] Rather than risk bloodshed, the Kiowas broke up their Sun Dance lodge on the Washita River.[124] The 1887 gathering was the last-known Kiowa Sun Dance.[125]

Government officials and white missionaries were not the only ones who hoped to silence the religious ideas expressed through dancing. Natives themselves disagreed about the value of dancing, especially the Sun Dance. In August 1886, Richard Davis, a Carlisle-educated Southern Cheyenne who blamed the medicine dances for pulling down his people, reported that the Sun Dance just held by Southern Cheyennes and Southern Arapahos had not been not as "good" as such dances used to be and only six men danced.[126] Davis asked "many of the Indians" why they did not dance, and they told him that it "was getting too old to them." One of the dancers was a returned Carlisle student, which Davis thought showed that man's "weakness." "I was surprised when I saw him," he wrote, "but the rest of the returned boys" were "doing something" to better themselves. Other so-called progressive Indians like Davis believed dancing was a tradition that should be given up. Leonard Tyler (Magpie), an educated Southern Cheyenne and Christian convert, wrote that he and Sam Noble, another Cheyenne, attended two Sun Dances at the Cheyenne-Arapaho Reservation in 1888. Instead of dancing, the men held prayer meetings and sang gospel hymns before they were ordered away by the medicine men.[127]

Some Native leaders sought to eliminate Sun Dancing. In 1882, two Lakotas at Rosebud, headman He Dog and Little Eagle, wrote to George Sword, the captain of the Indian police at Pine Ridge, to tell him to be on the watch for visitors hoping to Sun Dance. "We have made a law requiring all our people to stay at home for our sun dance," they wrote, "and those now absent we want to come back right away to avoid being soldiered on.

Tell this to our people that are with you."¹²⁸ Eagle Hawk, the captain of Indian police at Rosebud, telegraphed Sword three days later to ask him to send home all the Rosebud people who were at Pine Ridge without permission.¹²⁹ Others wrote letters to report dancers to white officials. Big Head wrote to his Standing Rock agent that people were "dancing at night again, very much, here near the Agency and also out there where I live."¹³⁰ He wanted the agent "to put a stop to it by the policemen." At Crow Creek, Hampton graduate Thomas Tuttle told the commissioner of Indian affairs that he was trying his best to convince the "non-progressive" Sioux to stop their dancing. "I also tell the people who dances that they are doing wrong by dancing not try to become civilized," he wrote. "I tell them to send their children to school as after a while they will not need any white people to teach them as their own children can become teachers and they can draw the same salary as a white man."¹³¹ For Tuttle, dancing represented ideas that were incompatible with education and self-sufficiency. But the products of education were used by others to bolster Native religious concepts. Letters coordinated intertribal visits in which dancing took place, and they were used to spread religious ideas like the Ghost Dance.

Federal authorities attacked the "demoralizing influence" of dancing, but Natives compelled their agents to allow the continuation of that important part of their lives. As demonstrated by the Utes' acquisition of the Sun Dance or the spread of Pá-tépté's prophecies, the growing interconnectedness among Native Americans allowed new religious concepts to be acquired and adapted by tribes and individuals during the reservation years. The Omaha Dance, also known as the Grass Dance, was acquired by Plains tribes from the Omahas and others during the 1860s and was disseminated widely in the 1880s. It functioned largely as a social dance, with social gatherings surrounding its performance.¹³² Kiowas were introduced to the Omaha Dance in 1883 by visiting Southern Cheyennes, rather than visiting Omahas, who gifted a large "white man's drum" to the Kiowas to be used in the dance.¹³³ The visiting Cheyennes even chose which Kiowa would lead the dancing, Big Bow, who was given a large eagle-feather bonnet. Kiowas revisited the Omaha Dance on their own the following summer, and it persisted into the twentieth century, demonstrating how important intertribal visiting was to cultural innovation among tribes.

Quite a bit of evidence suggests that the Omaha Dance grew in popularity on the northern plains in 1890, the same year that the Ghost Dance was widely practiced. Omaha Dances were held with regularity at the Rosebud Reservation soon before and after the Ghost Dance arrived.¹³⁴ At the Pine

Ridge Reservation, photographs recorded Omaha Dances (among others) in 1890 and 1891 in front of Indian and white spectators.[135] An Omaha Dance lodge was constructed at the Wounded Knee District at Pine Ridge sometime before December 1890. In 1891, a group of Pine Ridge Indians traveled to Chadron, Nebraska, to buy lumber to build an Omaha Dance lodge.[136] And in 1890, some Tongue River Cheyennes erected their Omaha Dance lodge using lumber issued to them for the purpose of flooring their homes. The dance was allowed at Tongue River because it was "considered peaceable."[137]

Other dances diffused across the plains because of the intense intertribal interactions of the 1880s, including the Crow (or Bird) Dance. The Crow Dance, which may have been similar to the Omaha Dance or a variant of it, made its way through the southern plains, from Poncas and Otoes to Southern Cheyennes and Arapahos and then to Kiowas and others.[138] Southern Arapaho headman Row of Lodges described the use of the drum in the dance as "the voice of the gods of thunder, the voice of the approach of them bringing rain. . . . When we are having this dance, all must pray for rain, so that the harvest may be good and everyone have plenty to eat."[139]

Writing in 1916, anthropologist Clark Wissler noted that the Omaha Dance and "a number of old ceremonies were revived in new forms and associations" beginning in 1890, the same time that the Ghost Dance reached the southern plains.[140] He attributes this phenomenon to the "great period of economic adjustment" that the Natives were experiencing during the 1880s. The Natives' "social ideals and machinery were decidedly out of joint," he discerned, and consequently the "conditions" were met "for the assimilation and diffusion" of revived religious beliefs. According to Wissler, the harsh economic and social conditions that Indians were living through inspired things like the Omaha Dance and the Ghost Dance; "else why should there have been so many other new ceremonies springing into life?" he asked. This opinion, borrowed from anthropologist James Mooney, was popularized by Wissler and his contemporaries and became an accepted understanding of the Ghost Dance. But Wissler did not consider other changes that facilitated the "conditions for the assimilation and diffusion" of dancing, which never disappeared to begin with. Intertribal communication was expanding during the reservation years. Men and women from different tribes were visiting each other in large numbers, creating new relationships, exchanging ideas, and sustaining Native identities. And importantly, by 1890, Native Americans were writing to each other more than ever before, often in a common language, to keep in touch, plan visits, and dispense information. The diffusion of new religious knowledge and practices like the Omaha Dance, Crow Dance, or Ghost Dance among Native groups in the 1880s and 1890s occurred because Native groups had an intertribal network of communication in place. Ideas considered subversive to government policies could be still shared among these increasingly connected communities.

In 1888, Young Man Afraid of His Horses demanded that "the gate" should not be "closed between" the tribes of the west.[141] Three years later, he told a council between his people and government officials,

> We want to live up to the Great Father's words. There are fifty-nine agencies altogether, and the Great Father has asked us all to be one. . . . Indians are all one. . . . These people who came here from the other agencies are of the same blood that we are and want to be one. . . . We want the doors left open so that we may have permission to visit these different agencies if we want to.[142]

Young Man Afraid of His Horses never believed the US government had closed a gate that separated the continent's Indigenous populations. The doors had been "left open," he said. It was his people and their desire to remain connected to one another that kept it that way.

PART III

Communicating the Ghost Dance

CHAPTER 5

"Go and Tell All the Tribes"

After George Bird Grinnell reported that Southern Arapahos, Southern Cheyennes, and Pawnees living in Indian Territory "frequently" received letters about the Ghost Dance from Shoshones, Northern Arapahos, and Sioux living hundreds of miles away, he declared that the Indians' ability to disseminate such ideas was "one of the disadvantages, perhaps, of the Indian education."[1] Literate Natives educated in US government schools used the US Postal Service to spread ideas that most non-Natives considered uncivilized. The originator of the Ghost Dance movement, Wovoka (who was thought by many to be a new Messiah), prophesized the coming of a revived earth, apart from white domination, if Indians danced according to his instructions.

By the time Grinnell made his surprising observation in November 1890, most Native Americans in the country had already heard about the Ghost Dance, and thousands were believers or participants. The years of intertribal interaction, the exchanging of ideas, the adaptations to new concepts, and the understanding that others were facing the same circumstances had all eased intertribal relationships and strengthened the sense of commonality and solidarity among Native Americans. This set the stage for the Ghost Dance to sweep across the West in 1889 and 1890. The speed and scope of the religious movement's spread was unprecedented in Native American history, demonstrating the effectiveness of the intertribal networks established in the 1870s and 1880s. The Ghost Dance introduced new religious ideas, but there was nothing novel about how those ideas were transmitted.

Natives sent letters to inform those living on other reservations that a man in the far West could change their world. Some traveled to distant reserves to spread the news of his message and the instructions for his dance. In turn, Natives investigated the claims that had come through letters and visitors by organizing delegations tasked with finding the source of the dance.

With the help of railroads, many reached Wovoka at the Walker River Reservation in western Nevada. Information was thus sought, gathered, and relayed across a network that spanned the continent. The following chapters will explore in detail how information about the Ghost Dance movement was intentionally transmitted, via all methods of late nineteenth-century transportation and communication, among Paiutes, Hualapais, Shoshones, Bannocks, Utes, Northern and Southern Arapahos, Northern and Southern Cheyennes, Lakotas, Eastern and Western Dakotas, Kiowas, Apaches, Wichitas, Pawnees, Poncas, Crows, Mandans and Hidatsas, Blackfeet, and many others. Tracing the spread of the Ghost Dance movement reveals the extent of these networks, which grew despite colonial efforts to contest the information that flowed through them. Native Americans across the continent were able to inform themselves and others about an important set of ideas that whites deemed anticolonial.

The Point of Origin

Wovoka (also known as Jack Wilson), the intellectual source of the Ghost Dance, was described by white settlers around Mason Valley, Nevada, as an "honest, hard-working Indian."[2] A Northern Paiute born sometime in the late 1850s or early 1860s, he was the son of medicine man Numu-tibo'o (or Tavibo), a follower of the 1870 Ghost Dance prophet Wodziwob, and Tiya, a ranch laborer (a common occupation for Nevada Paiutes). He grew up being regularly employed, fed, and housed by the Wilsons, a prosperous white ranching family. He learned some English and became familiar with Christianity. Wovoka and his wife, Mary (Tumma was her Paiute name), had three daughters who survived childhood, one of whom attended Carson Industrial School when it opened in 1890. Wovoka, like his father, had a reputation as a spiritual man. He became known for his control of the weather after successfully predicting (and producing) rainfall, and by 1887, he gained renown after reportedly performing several miracles. He occasionally experienced visions.[3]

Sometime in 1888 or early 1889, Wovoka was filled with an optimistic belief that God intended to renew the world, to "have it made over again."[4] Wovoka fell into a deep trance while cutting wood in the Pine Grove Mountains and "was taken up to the other world," where he "saw God, with all the people who had died long ago."[5] It was the first of "many times" that God visited to tell him what to do.[6] James Mooney, a non-Native who interviewed Wovoka in 1892 and the first anthropologist to study the Ghost Dance at length, reported that Wovoka believed God had told him to go back and tell his people they must be good and love one another, have no quarreling, and live in peace with the whites; that they must work, and not lie or steal; that they must put away all the old practices that savored of war; that if they faithfully obeyed his instructions they would at last be reunited with their friends in this other world, where there would be no more death or sickness or old age.[7]

God gave him instructions to perform a dance "at intervals, for five consecutive days each time, [and] they would secure this happiness to themselves and hasten the event."[8] It would be Wovoka's mission to teach his people the dance, a modification of the Paiute Round Dance.[9] Wovoka and his Paiute followers cleared an area for dancing and built willow-frame huts to provide shelter during the five days of dancing and praying. For many, the dance itself would become a way to communicate with God and with one's dead relatives. News along local networks drove many surrounding Indians to attend the events, and Wovoka's influence spread throughout the Great Basin. He successfully demonstrated his divine abilities and garnered attention. Some believed he was a new Messiah, although Wovoka would later deny his divinity to white investigators.[10]

James Mooney described the transmission of Wovoka's teachings to the people close to the Paiutes as "nearly" simultaneous. Because of their proximity to Walker River, others quickly learned about Wovoka's dance, including Western Shoshones in Nevada and California, Utes in Utah and southwestern Colorado, Hualapais in Arizona, and Bannocks and Shoshones from the Fort Hall Reservation in Idaho.[11] It seems that some Paiutes acted as emissaries for Wovoka. Hualapais began making trips to Walker River and holding their own Ghost Dances in the spring of 1889 after a Paiute from southern Utah brought the dance to the tribe.[12] They sang their Ghost Dance songs in the Paiute language.[13] Southern Utes were visited by one of Wovoka's emissaries, a Paiute man named Yunitckwo'ov, who taught the tribe the dance. He told them that their ancestors would return within the year (the Utes had traditionally considered the return of the dead to mean access to an ancestor's spiritual guidance, not a physical resurrection), but when the prophecy failed, Southern Utes ceased Yunitckwo'ov's version of the dance and modified it to fit their own cultural systems.[14] In northeastern Utah, Northern Utes at the Uintah and Ouray Agency in Utah sent delegates to investigate Wovoka "soon after" early dances were held at Walker River in January 1889, but it is not clear if an emissary was sent to them.[15] Some Mission Indians in southern California and Pit River Indians in northern California also eventually took up the dance as well.[16]

The swift circulation of Wovoka's beliefs in the intermountain region in early 1889 was reminiscent of the 1870 Ghost Dance movement, which had also originated around Walker River and become popular with groups throughout Nevada, Utah, eastern California, Idaho, and Oregon.[17] The 1870 dance was contained to areas west of the Rockies, but Wovoka's dance and the ideas attached to it were carried across the Continental Divide. Intermountain and Plains Indians were not well connected during the 1870 Ghost Dance, but by 1889, there were long-established relationships among Paiutes, Shoshones, Bannocks, Arapahos, Utes, Cheyennes, Lakotas, and others on both sides of the mountains. Just months after his revelations, news of Wovoka had spread as far as Montana, bringing Plains Indians to Walker River as early as the summer of 1889. Nevada's *Lyon County Times* reported on August 3, 1889, "The Piutes are having the biggest dance ever held in Mason Valley. Representatives of Big Indians are there from Montana, Idaho, Utah, and California. . . . The great weather prophet is said to be a fine looking man, much resembling the late Henry Ward Beecher."[18]

Most Plains Indians who visited Nevada to learn more about Wovoka traveled by rail through the Fort Hall Reservation in Idaho. Because train travel was already an important component of intertribal visitation and communication, moving western Native men and women for years by 1889, news about the dance naturally flowed along the railroads.[19] As mentioned in chapter 3, railroads converged at Fort Hall (see map 1), bridging Indians of the intermountain region from west of the Continental Divide and the Plains peoples from east of the divide. It remained an important node of information during the Ghost Dance's dissemination. James Mooney called the Shoshones and Bannocks at Fort Hall "the chief medium of the doctrine between the tribes west of the mountains and those on the plains."[20] Four rail lines merged at Fort Hall, making it a hub for Indians traveling by rail from all directions, but there were also cultural reasons for the reservation's connectivity. Shoshones are diverse, and their homelands span the Continental Divide. In the 1880s, Shoshones lived at Fort Hall but also in Nevada and Wyoming, positioning them in the worlds of both the Great Basin and the plains.[21] Anthropologist Åke Hultkrantz described Shoshones as "synthesizers and transformers of cultural material derived from both eastern and western sources; their culture is a blend of the two."[22]

Native Americans traveling to spread or acquire information about the Ghost Dance began funneling through Fort Hall in 1889. Around a dozen different tribes passed through Fort Hall during 1890 alone.[23] Some stopped there for an extended time to commune with Bannocks and Shoshones and, according to Mooney, "to procure interpreters from among the Bannock to accompany them to Nevada."[24] From Fort Hall, passengers traveled south down the Union Pacific to Ogden, Utah, then west on the Central Pacific until they reached Wadsworth or Reno, Nevada.

Like other Paiutes, Wovoka himself likely took advantage of the railroad. He traveled extensively in his younger days and used the rails for economic reasons before his revelations. Ed Dyer, Wovoka's non-Native friend and part-time "personal secretary," remembered that the Walker River Paiutes "were in the habit about that time, of making seasonal trips en masse, perched atop the railroad's handy boxcars to northern California for the purpose of picking hops. . . . Young Jack Wilson also travelled to the California hop fields."[25]

The Carson & Colorado Railroad passed right through Wovoka's Walker River Reservation, and it was the line hundreds of Natives took to visit him. Wovoka's Paiute emissaries also made efficient use of the C&C line. California and Nevada newspapers reported that a Paiute traveled west of the Sierra Nevada to the Chico, California, area to exhort the small bands of Western Shoshones there to dance.[26] James Mooney found that some of those Shoshones visited the Paiutes in Nevada to dance as well. Others used the rail to travel to scheduled intertribal Ghost Dances. In 1891, some Hualapais and Chemehuevis came from opposite directions on Atchison, Topeka, and Santa Fe Railway coal cars to meet at a dance site south of the Fort Mojave Reservation (near present-day Needles, California).[27] In northeastern Nevada, newspapers reported that Shoshones and Paiutes were dancing together near the head of the Humboldt River along the railroad line in January 1891. Just as they had for other dances throughout the 1880s, they traveled by train to meet.[28]

Out of the Basin and onto the Plains

The first report of Wovoka to make it out of the Great Basin and onto the Great Plains might have been carried in 1888 by a Northern Arapaho man who was returning home from Nevada, through the Fort Hall Reservation, to Wind River, the closest Plains reservation to Fort Hall.[29] This origin point for the Ghost Dance in the Great Plains was not mentioned by James Mooney in his study, but he did report that a Fort Hall Bannock brought information to the Northern Arapahos and Shoshones at Wind River in "early" 1889. While visiting Paiutes, that unnamed Bannock was told to "go and tell all the tribes" that "the dead people were coming back."[30] According to Dick Washakie, the son of Wind River Shoshone chief Washakie, three Shoshones (named Pawasanga, Warasi, and Waagi) and a Bannock from Fort Hall traveled by rail to Wind River to spread the news and to instruct the people how to dance. "Next year, after having the dance," they said, "the dead will come back, and all the white people will be gone."[31]

Northern Arapahos and Shoshones at Wind River received firsthand knowledge from Wovoka, perhaps for the first time, in the "early spring" of 1889. Sage (Nakash) and Yellow Calf, both Arapahos, and several Shoshones including Täbinshi met Wovoka after a journey, largely by rail, to the Mason Valley in Nevada. The men, who came to believe that Wovoka was a new Messiah, brought home some of the original Paiute Ghost Dance songs.[32] Other Wind River Shoshones, like Tassitsie, would become "so intrigued" by the Ghost Dance that they also made the trip to visit Wovoka.[33] As Sage and Yellow Calf later recalled, they instantly knew that the Paiute wearing white man's clothes whom they came upon in the sagebrush hut in the Mason Valley was the Messiah.

Wovoka gave the men the details of the new dance and instructed them to return to their people "and live in peace, be good, never lie, believe in the Ghost Dance and everything would be fine."[34] Wovoka's identity was proven after the men watched him die and come back to life. "Then he told us he was going to die, go up to the Great Mystery and return with a special message for us," Yellow Calf remembered, "and that is what he did." As Wovoka lay unresponsive, the men could not feel a heartbeat. Sage tickled his nose and Yellow Calf kicked him in the ribs just to make sure he was dead. Once Wovoka revived himself, he claimed that he had been with the Great Mystery and that many of the men's dead friends and relatives told him that they wanted to return to their loved ones and "wanted all our people to live together again, just as they had done before the white man took everything away." The dead wanted Sage and Yellow Calf to believe "this Medicine Man, Wovoka, because he was the messiah, knew what was good, and how to make great things come to pass." If they danced, a "Great Cloud will come and on it will be all the Indians who ever lived, mounted on their war ponies, and all the buffalo, elk, antelope and deer. This Great Cloud will cover over the white man and then everything will be as it always had been." But Wovoka also instructed the men to be peaceful with white men, "not to be too hard" on them, because "he was going to send them to some other place." After Sage and Yellow Calf returned home, they, along with Northern Shoshone headmen Munhavi and Tawunasia, became "promulgators" of the dance at Wind River.[35] Sage eventually sent his knowledge of Wovoka's movement, the dance, and its songs down to the Southern Arapahos in Indian Territory.[36]

Out of western Nevada, through Fort Hall, and onto the Wind River Reservation in Wyoming Territory, information about the Ghost Dance spilled onto the Great Plains in 1889. From Wind River, the already-established networks of written correspondence disseminated that vision faster and farther. By the time Wovoka hoped to spread his vision for the world, intertribal communication had become a normal part of Indian life. Northern Arapahos at Wind River shared their knowledge of Wovoka (which probably came from Sage and Yellow Calf) in letters to their friends and relatives, particularly the Southern Arapahos who lived nine hundred miles southeast in Indian Territory. Sometime in 1889, Southern Arapaho chief Left Hand (the younger) received letters about a "second Jesus" from Wind River.[37] Other Indians at the reservation, including Southern Cheyennes, began receiving similar correspondence in the summer of 1889 from Northern Arapahos at Wind River and from Northern Cheyennes at the Tongue River Reservation in Montana.[38]

Interested in the reports from his northern contacts, Left Hand and other headmen chose Black Coyote, the lieutenant of the agency police, and Washee, a sergeant of the scouts, to investigate and to travel to a mountain where the "second Jesus" reportedly lived. The people at the Cheyenne-Arapaho Reservation were anxious to discover the truth. They raised $200 to pay for Washee and Black Coyote's rail fare north. The railroad made quicker the nine-hundred-mile trip to Wind River, where the two men attempted to gather some details about this new Messiah.[39] While Washee and Black Coyote were on their way, the Northern Arapahos and the Shoshones at Wind River informed the Southern Arapahos via letter that the reports they had received had been "verified."[40] Washee decided to investigate further at the Fort Hall Reservation in Idaho. Black Coyote, who remained at Wind River through April 1890, was fortunate enough to speak with a group of Northern Arapahos, Northern Cheyennes, and several Lakotas from Pine Ridge, Rosebud, and Cheyenne River who had just returned from Mason Valley, where they had spoken with this supposed Messiah directly. They convinced Black Coyote that much of what the letters spoke of was true, and they gave him the instructions they received from Wovoka.

On his return home to the Cheyenne-Arapaho Reservation, Black Coyote conveyed the Messiah's message, his dance, and his songs (that he received indirectly) to the Southern Arapahos and Southern Cheyennes.[41] Some Southern Cheyennes were skeptical of Black Coyote's account, so they decided to send their own Cheyenne investigators, Little Chief and Bark, to question Northern Cheyennes at Pine Ridge and Tongue River about the matter. Later Southern Cheyenne parties, led by White Shield and White Buffalo, respectively, also made trips to Tongue River in August and September 1890.[42]

All the information coming into Indian Territory about Wovoka caught the attention of US government officials in the early months of 1890. In late April, an officer at Fort Reno described what he had heard: that an "Indian Moses" appeared at Wind River and was "prophesizing the destruction of the white people."[43] At the same time, the Cheyenne-Arapaho agent, Charles Ashley, told the Wind River agent, John Fosher, that thanks to the reports "of the coming of the second Jesus" from the Wind River Indians, "much excitement prevails at this agency and much annoyance has been occasioned."[44] Because he wanted to contain "this agitation" from spreading, Ashley denied Fosher's request to allow four Northern Arapahos to visit the Cheyenne-Arapaho Reservation. However, Ashley did say he would consent to the visit if the four Arapaho men wanted to come "simply for the purpose of visiting friends" but not if they had been "prominent" in the Messiah business. This is among the first of agents' attempts to suppress the spread of the Ghost Dance, but visiting was not the only channel of transmission.

While Black Coyote and Washee were away, Southern Arapahos and Southern Cheyennes continued the investigation by sending out letters of inquiry.[45] One of the interpreters at the agency, possibly Paul Boynton (Red Feather), a former student of the Carlisle Indian Industrial School of Cheyenne and Arapaho descent, wrote to the Northern Cheyennes at the Tongue River Reservation in Montana. He wrote (in English),

> Cheyennes and Arapahoes here are greatly excited about a Christ coming among some of the Northern tribes of Indians. The Arapahoes have been getting letters from Northern Arapahoes in regard to it. My friends here wish me to ask what there is about it, and what do you know about it? They sent two of their young men to the Shoshone agency in Idaho a month and a half ago to find out all about it, but those two have not returned yet.[46]

The interpreter at Tongue River replied in part (also in English), "The Indians say Christ is in the mountains, and that he wants all the Indians to come to him. He will put them behind him, and having all the whites before him, will roll the world over on the whites and destroy them. He is a white man."[47]

Portions of these letters were published in a report about this Indian "Saviour" that appeared in newspapers across the country on April 27,

1890. The reporter wondered how this new religion had become so popular among the Indians. "One of the difficult things to explain," he wrote, "is the wide distribution of the story which seems to have been brought out independently at two places, over 1,000 miles apart." The reporter incorrectly assumed that reservations isolated tribes from one another. He did not realize that letters were broadcasting "the story."

Also in April 1890, a large number of Northern Cheyennes gathered at Tongue River to hear the report of the two members of their tribe who were a part of the delegation that Black Coyote encountered at Wind River. Their agent, R. L. Upshaw, was so alarmed by the number of Indians who took their children out of school and left the agency to attend the meeting that he asked for military assistance. According to Upshaw, the returned Cheyennes told their people that the man who claimed to be "the Christ in the flesh" had "a message to all tribes of Indians."[48] Upshaw knew little about "their craze," but he said it was "widely disseminated." His Northern Cheyennes were in communication with the Southern Cheyennes and Arapahos through letters, and he was told by a "half breed Sioux from Pine Ridge" that the news was "'all the talk' among the Indians there."

Kiowas who lived on the Kiowa, Comanche, and Wichita Reservation in Indian Territory may have received their first detailed information about the Messiah at a gathering on the Cheyenne-Arapaho Reservation on May 20, 1890. The Cheyenne-Arapaho agent reported that the intertribal "medicine dances . . . of intense religious excitement" emerged from belief in the new Christ.[49] James Mooney reported that Kiowas learned more about the dance in June after a delegation of twenty men (including Poor Buffalo) was sent to the Cheyenne-Arapaho Reservation to investigate.[50] The Kiowa men brought back some "sacred" red paint (ochre) that Wovoka offered visitors, which was passed among tribes. Inspector for Indian Affairs William Junkin told his hometown newspaper that Kiowas sent investigators all the way to Pine Ridge in May or June, where they believed the Messiah had appeared to the Northern Cheyennes. Junkin thought that not everyone accepted the story that the white man would be swallowed by a flood, so they sent the delegation north to find the truth.[51]

Throughout 1889 and 1890, the dance affected not only the Kiowas, the Southern and Northern divisions of the Cheyennes and Arapahos, and the Paiutes who inaugurated the first dances but also members of more than thirty other tribes including Shoshones, Bannocks, Utes, Mojaves, Hualapais, most bands of the Lakotas, Assiniboines, Gros Ventres, Arikaras, Mandans, Caddos, Wichitas, Comanches, Apaches, Poncas, Pawnees, Otoes, Osages, Kickapoos, and others. The first bits of information that tribes received about the movement were more than just "rumblings" or "rumors." Most of what we know about what Natives knew about the dance, particularly in 1889 and early 1890, comes from the observations and testimonies of white authorities. Unfortunately, the whites who observed the spread of the dance were far removed from the action. Very few whites had any considerable knowledge about the information Natives were receiving. In fact, it took several months for white authorities to even figure out who the new Messiah actually was.[52] Whites finally discovered Wovoka's identity in November 1890, though Lakotas, Arapahos, Shoshones, Cheyennes, and others had been visiting him since 1889.

Natives had enough information to be able to find the Messiah in the sparsely settled, far-off Mason Valley, Nevada, within days of leaving their agencies. For example, one Kickapoo living in northeast Kansas, some 1,500 miles from Mason Valley, received a letter written in English that had an accurate description of the Lakotas' meeting with Wovoka. The newspaper local to the Kansas Kickapoos published its contents, which, among other things, said that Jesus had appeared to Lakotas who had followed "a light in the sky for eighteen days over a country destitute of water," eventually reaching a "secluded place near a mountain."[53] There, inside a grass hut, they saw Jesus, "who told them that he had come once to save the white men," but they had "crucified him," so "this time he had appeared to the Indians." He instructed the Lakotas to "go back and bear the news to other Indians." While incomplete and inaccurate information was undoubtedly transmitted from tribe to tribe, Natives received tangible information about Wovoka from the beginning, and most of the Natives who traveled to Nevada to see Wovoka knew what to expect even before the first "official" delegations were sent out.

Many Native Americans also went to great lengths to find and evaluate evidence, which was an important part of the Ghost Dance's dissemination. Native men and women did not accept questionable information more readily than whites. Only a few years before the dance, after all, Southern Plains tribes had rejected Pá-tépté's well-known prophecies, and Northern Cheyennes did not join in Sword Bearer's rebellion despite his promises. Once news arrived about Wovoka, Natives compiled information through established networks, discerned the legitimacy of reports, and spent money on travel for fact-finding delegations. Some Natives openly criticized the movement, and most who learned about Wovoka never danced. Consequently, the story of the Ghost Dance should not be told simply as peoples' acceptance of a new set of religious beliefs but rather as a complex truth-finding process reliant on communication among diverse nations. Map 3

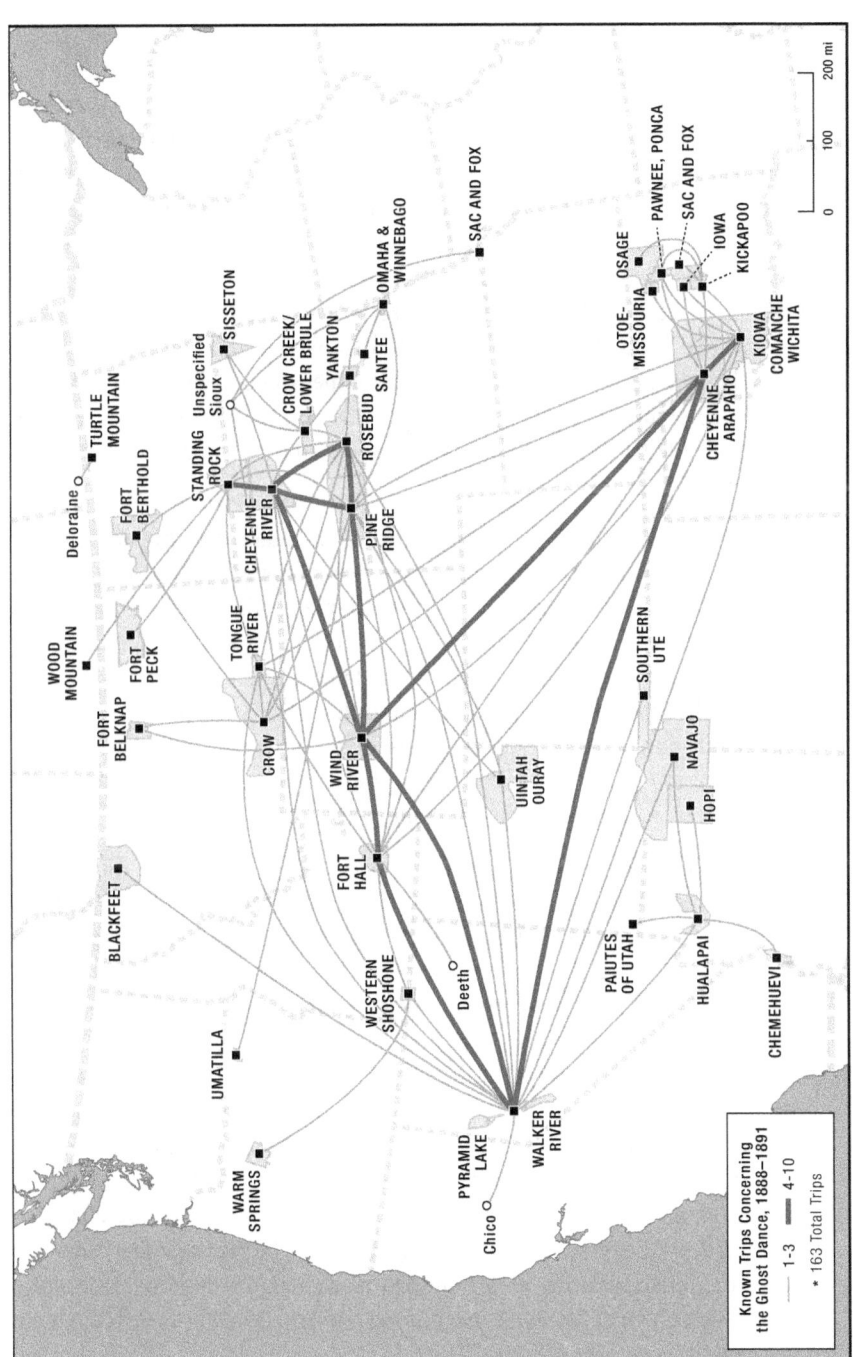

Map 3. Known trips concerning the Ghost Dance, 1888–1891

visualizes the known trips between reservations through 1891 that were a part of this process.[54]

In 1895, Left Hand explained to Alice C. Fletcher, a non-Native anthropologist, why he was attracted to this "new religion" that "sprang up among" Southern Arapahos and Southern Cheyennes. He called it a "sincere" and "earnest" religion.[55] He had "adopted this new faith" and he hoped "that the day is coming when the Indian will have a better religion than many of the white people, who have no reverence for the Maker of Men." Like white Americans, he said, Indians had "a great reverence for the god in whom they believe." But Left Hand thought that whites did not "understand" Native beliefs, perhaps because "the ceremonies of our religion are different from those practiced by the white men." Left Hand described the ceremonies his people had learned from Sage, the Northern Arapaho who had met Wovoka:

> The members who take part in the exercises stand in a ring and each member makes a confession of his wrong doings in the past and weeps before the people and asks the Great Father to have pity on him. There is a land connected with this religion, and at the dance, the members fall in a trance and enter that land where they see their relations. The sky opens and they see into it. There is a prayer and song in which rain is asked for; names are given to persons who enter this new religion. . . . There is a song for the opening of the exercises. . . . The songs were all made by this man, Sage.

Left Hand believed that Sage experienced a revelation much like Wovoka's; he "was taken sick, was about to die, was given up as dead," but "he came back to life, and told the people that he had been to the spirit and was instructed there that he was to return to his people and teach them a new religion that should tell them how to conduct themselves. The people were to abstain from stealing, fighting, lying, and killing. The teachings are to make men good." Row of Lodges, another Southern Arapaho headman, also knew the movement as a peaceful one. While it put them "in mind of our old people," their beliefs were new: "In our former dances, sharp weapons and everything harmful was used; the songs referred to battle; but now all is different. Even the talks are different. Now all the words are changed, and the talk is of advice in peaceful occupation." The message that extended in all directions across the West "taught that a change is coming, and to prepare for that change, we must live a good life and do what is good. A man who does this will get on better."

Into the Dakotas: "A New Religion Came by Letters"

In 1889, Oglala Lakotas and Northern Cheyennes at the Pine Ridge Reservation also began to receive this message in letters from Shoshones and Arapahos at Wind River. But other letters came from their recently established connection with Utes in Utah and other "distant agencies," which relayed information "about the advent" of a "new Messiah."[56] Utes were familiar with the 1870 Ghost Dance movement, and they had plenty of information about the 1890 movement (they were close to Paiutes geographically and linguistically). Northern Utes undoubtedly danced, as mentioned before, but it does not seem to have been especially popular among them.[57] This did not stop them from relaying information about the dance to others, however.

In her history of her people, Lakota Josephine Waggoner wrote that "a new religion came by letters" to the Oglalas at Pine Ridge, who passed it along to other Lakotas.[58] Waggoner, a then nineteen-year-old former Hampton student at Standing Rock of Hunkpapa Lakota and Irish parentage, remembered reading "many letters" coming from both Pine Ridge and Walker River regarding the Ghost Dance. She translated correspondence for Sitting Bull (the Hunkpapa leader), among others, including letters about the new movement.[59] William Selwyn, a literate Yankton employed at the time as postmaster at Pine Ridge, also read some of the letters for the Oglalas and Cheyennes there. "Parties who could not read letters generally brings their letters to me to read for them," Selwyn explained.[60] According to Selwyn, there had been "some talk . . . about the New Messiah" in the fall of 1888 during visits from groups of Utes, Shoshones, Crows, and Arapahos, but the influx of letters from the western tribes in 1889 created "much attention" and convinced the Lakotas at Pine Ridge, Rosebud, and Cheyenne River to investigate the claims. Another source of information for those at Pine Ridge may have come from their visit, probably at Wind River in February or March 1889, to Shoshones who themselves may have received information from Utes.[61]

Intertribal connections brought more knowledge to Lakotas in the summer of 1889 as a Wind River Northern Arapaho traveled east to Pine Ridge, Rosebud, and Cheyenne River. Short Bull, a Brulé Lakota from Rosebud, told a reporter nearly two years later that the visiting Arapaho man had believed that "the buffalo were coming back and that the white people would all be killed" and that the Shoshone chief Washakie at Wind River had more information.[62] Five or six Oglalas, including Good Thunder, went to Wind River to investigate sometime around when the Northern Arapahos arrived. That visit was done "in secret," without the permission of the Pine Ridge or Wind River agents (a common practice; see chapters 3 and 4). According to the captain of the Indian police at Pine Ridge, George Sword, the Oglala party thought they met the "Son of God" on their trip, but it does not seem that they went as far as Nevada. Nevertheless, Sword remembered that Lakotas "all rejoiced and were attracted" to this Ghost Dance in 1889.[63]

In the fall of 1889, Short Bull was given a letter to bring back to the Rosebud "Council house" while on a freight trip to Valentine, Nebraska. The letter, given to him by a "messenger" from "the West," said, "The Father has come."[64] Before the letter was read aloud to the council, "the wind was blowing so furiously," according to Short Bull, "that the whole house was filled dust," but once "the reading of the letter began the wind ceased." This gave Short Bull "confidence," he remembered; he now "had the faith to go" find Wovoka in the West: "I had no belief in it before but now my mind was made up." At the Cheyenne River Reservation, the Miniconjou Lakota (but Oglala-born) Kicking Bear (also Bear that Kicks) received a similar letter from his uncle Spoonhunter, an Oglala married to a Northern Arapaho who lived at Wind River, urging him to come to Wyoming to attend a Ghost Dance.[65] Kicking Bear had a reputation among his people and agency employees as being a rover because he traveled widely in the three years before the Ghost Dance. The Miniconjous at Cheyenne River believed that "he had visited all the Indians in the country," creating connections that served him well in acquiring and circulating knowledge about the dance.[66] He also happened to be Short Bull's brother-in-law. Both men would become dedicated to the Ghost Dance's spread, and both men learned about the movement through letters.

Information came to the Lakotas intentionally, through letters and messengers, and unintentionally, through encounters with those who learned of the dance while traveling through the western reservations. On July 23, 1889, Chasing Crane, a Pine Ridge Oglala, came upon a group of Oglalas hunting deer in the sandhills of northern Nebraska while traveling home from Rosebud. He told the group that God had appeared to the Crows "across the Stony Mountains."[67] Elaine Goodale (later Eastman), a white New Englander who taught school at Pine Ridge, accompanied the hunting party that July. She wrote in her diary that Chasing Crane believed that this God was the same "Savior who once before came upon the earth and was killed by the white people." According to Chasing Crane, this Messiah told the Indians that "he could no longer bear to hear parents crying for their children, dying everywhere of hunger and strange diseases brought by white men. He promised to let down the sky upon all the whites and bring back the buffalo for our use." Goodale wrote that the Oglala hunting party "all listened spellbound" to Chasing Crane's testimony.

During the first half of 1889, the leaders at Cheyenne River held council to discuss the information that had been arriving since 1888, as did the leaders at Rosebud and Pine Ridge. While it is not clear how closely the Lakota leaders at these three agencies coordinated a response to the news, the leaders were in communication. They undoubtedly shared information and deliberated collectively, because a joint investigative delegation made up of representatives from the three agencies was planned in the summer of 1889. The delegation hoped to travel west to Wind River and Fort Hall to gather information on the location of the Messiah so that they could finally speak to him directly. It was a trip that many Lakotas had made before, but it seems few had gone farther west than Fort Hall or the Uintah and Ouray Reservation in Utah.

Lakotas considered the validity of information being sent to them and chose reliable men (but no women) to investigate this new set of beliefs. The Pine Ridge council, made up of Red Cloud, Young Man Afraid of His Horses, Little Wound, American Horse, Big Road, Fire Thunder, and others, asked the experienced Good Thunder to lead the delegation of five to seven other Oglalas. The Rosebud council selected Short Bull, and the Cheyenne River council selected Kicking Bear because of their knowledge and interest in the Messiah. Some Northern Cheyennes, probably from Pine Ridge, and some Northern Arapahos, probably returning to Wind River, also accompanied the Lakotas.[68] The Rosebud council told Short Bull to "be there with a big heart. Do not fail."[69] Short Bull pledged to bring back the Messiah's words even if it took him two years.

Probably sometime in August 1889, Short Bull traveled by horse and buggy to Pine Ridge, where he intended to meet the other delegates. The group had already left Pine Ridge the night before (without their agent's permission), but he caught up with them three days later.[70] The delegates traveled to the Wind River Reservation in Wyoming to visit some Arapahos and talk to Washakie. After staying at Wind River for a week, the delegates made it to Fort Washakie. The agent there, knowing their planned destination, gave them railroad passes.[71] Short Bull and his fellow delegates traveled by rail, stopping at various points due to mechanical problems, deep snow, and socializing opportunities. They finally made it to the Fort Hall Reservation in Idaho and met Bannocks, two Northern Arapahos named Bill Friday and Sitting Bull (the latter would soon be a critical figure in the Ghost Dance in the southern plains), and Porcupine of the Northern Cheyennes.

Porcupine, a forty-one-year-old man from Pine Ridge of both Lakota and Cheyenne parentage who had been on an extended and perhaps unauthorized visit to the Tongue River Reservation, left Montana with two other Northern Cheyennes, Big Beaver and Ridge Walker. Wind River Arapahos were the ones who told Porcupine about Wovoka. They had heard about him from some Shoshones who had visited the Walker River Reservation. The Arapahos told Porcupine that if his people "would listen to this new God he would take away all bad things, and give us all nice things."[72] Porcupine's group traveled without a pass on the Union Pacific Railroad to Fort Bridger in southwest Wyoming Territory, staying two days. Twenty-two years before, Porcupine had helped to tear up track and derail a Union Pacific freight train in Nebraska.[73] Now he took a passenger train, for free, on the same UP line to Fort Hall.

According to Short Bull, more than one hundred Indians, including the Lakota delegations, Porcupine's delegation, and Sitting Bull (the Northern Arapaho), boarded the train at Fort Hall and traveled until they reached Winnemucca, Nevada. They met with Paiutes there, then continued on the Central Pacific Railroad to Wadsworth, where they met the Paiute Captain Dave. Dave loaded them in a wagon, and they traveled farther into the Pyramid Lake Reservation.[74]

The Paiutes at Pyramid Lake told Porcupine that Christ had indeed "appeared on earth again," down at the Walker River Reservation.[75] After several days at Pyramid Lake, Captain Dave's son took the group down to the rail station at Wabuska, where the men hopped on a train on the six-year-old Carson & Colorado Line (free of charge) and rode it until they reached Walker River.[76] What they found astonished them. "It appeared that Christ had sent for me to go there," Porcupine later recalled, "and that was why unconsciously I took my journey. It had been foreordained. Christ had summoned myself and others from all heathen tribes, from two to three or four from each of fifteen or sixteen different tribes. There were more different languages than I ever heard before, and I did not understand any of them. They told me when I arrived that my great father was there also, but did not know who he was."

The Intertribal Gathering at Walker River

The huge gathering at the Walker River Reservation in February and March 1890 was the product of all the information about the movement that was circulating across the West. Wovoka seemed optimistic. That February, he wrote a letter to S. S. Sears, the agent in charge of the Pyramid Lake and Walker River Reservations, hoping that the letter would be forwarded to President Benjamin Harrison. Although a copy of that letter does not survive, a government employee at Walker River told Agent Sears that Jack Wilson, as Wovoka was known, had claimed that he was responsible for the rain storms that had blessed the desolate region that season, and in his letter, he wanted to know if the "government believes in him" and would "acknowledge him as a prophet."[77] According to the employee, there were "at least 200 Indians," not including the women and children, who met in February "in the face of a driving snow storm to see and hear" Jack Wilson and "his wonderful command of the Elements." Those gathered talked "nothing but Jack Wilson and the miracles he performs." Wovoka wanted to "come on the Reservation to farm and guarantees the Indians that if the government gives him permission to come, he will cause lots of rain to fall and they will never lose a crop again."

By March 1890, members from perhaps thirty-four different tribes had gathered at an area designated by Wovoka near Walker River. Despite the influx of foreign Indians at the train depots in western Nevada in the weeks prior, the local papers had yet to learn what was really going on at Walker River. On February 18, 1890, according to a newspaper report, around twenty men from six different tribes, including Bannocks, Shoshones, Blackfeet, and Lakotas, arrived at Reno on a passenger train on their way to Walker River.[78] Major George, a Fort Hall Bannock headman, was among the visitors, but nothing was said by the papers about a Ghost Dance. Perhaps those twenty men were among the thirty-four "reservation Indians from as far east as Dakota" who stopped at Pyramid Lake on their way to Walker River in late February.[79] Paiute leader Johnson Sides told the *Reno Evening Gazette* that the visitors were "anxious to learn all they can relative to the way the Indians are treated by the Government on the Pacific Coast reservations," but nothing was reported about the true purpose of their visit: to learn more about Wovoka.

At the height of the gathering, the Indian police at Walker River estimated 1,600 people were there to wait for Wovoka's next appearance.[80] On the evening of his arrival, Wovoka had his followers demonstrate the dance to the crowd. Before the dance ended, Wovoka, wearing white man's clothes and a pair of moccasins, spoke. "I have sent for you and am very glad to see you," he announced (suggesting that he likely sent out letters of invitation). "I will teach you, too, how to dance a dance, and I want you to dance it."[81] The next day, Porcupine, who "had heard Christ had been crucified," noticed scars on Wovoka's wrist and face, leading him to believe that Wovoka was the man they had heard about. The next morning, Wovoka assembled the people and sat down. Porcupine remembered what he said:

> He said: "I am the man who made everything you see around you. . . . I have been to heaven and seen your dead friends and have seen my own father and mother. In the beginning, after God made the earth, they sent me back to teach the people, and when I came back on earth the people were afraid of me and treated me badly. This is what they did to me (showing his scars). I did not try to defend myself. I found my children were bad, so I went back to heaven and left them. I told them that in so many hundred years I would come back to see my children. At the end of this time I was sent back to try to teach them. My father told me that the earth was getting old and worn out, and the people getting bad, and that I was to renew everything as it used to be, and make it better."
>
> He told us that all of our dead were to be resurrected; that they were all to come back to earth, and that as the earth was too small for them and us, he would do away with heaven, and make the earth itself large enough to contain us all; that we must tell all the people we meet about these things.[82]

Wovoka told them that violence was the wrong approach, that it would be unnecessary because "the earth was to be all good hereafter, and we must all be friends with one another" and "that the whites and the Indians were to be all one people." Porcupine said that Wovoka prophesized that in the fall of 1890, "the youth of all good people would be renewed, so that nobody would be more than 40 years old, and that if they behaved themselves well after this the youth of everyone would be renewed in the spring." If "we were all good," Porcupine recalled, Wovoka "would send people among us who could heal all our wounds and sickness by mere touch, and that we would live forever."

Porcupine's and Short Bull's descriptions of the journey and of Wovoka's message were recorded by Native and white interpreters. In June 1890, Porcupine was arrested at Tongue River (he was deemed to be a "bad influence" because of his knowledge of the Ghost Dance), and he made a statement to the army about his journey, which was translated and recorded.[83] In November 1890, more than four months after making that statement, Porcupine told a council attended by Northern Cheyennes and white officials what Wovoka had told the delegates:

The God was glad that I came to see him. When the Indians were created, they were made bad, but that badness is to be thrown off and they are to be made good. If they listen to him, he will change all their condition and make them good. Everything is now very old and there are now very few Indians. Our dances were bad and the God have given us a new dance. We must not get tired of dancing. Every one must dance, the young and the old, the men and the women the boys and the girls. Four nights in succession we must dance and then on the fifth day. . . . If we dance in this way we will never get tired. If we dance, our gardens will grow nice and we will never get sick or crazy. . . . We must not hate each other. We must love each other. We must love all the world. . . . If the soldiers wont let us dance we must dance any way. We must dance even though the soldiers beat us for it. We must not let the soldiers see the dance. . . . This God said if we lived good lives we would not become poor. . . . Before he went up into Heaven, he said he would come back for the Indians. The Indians must not abuse him when he comes as the whites did, and he will then throw away everything that is bad.[84]

Short Bull recalled that Wovoka told them:

I have sent for you to tell you certain things that you must do. There are two chiefs at your agencies and I want you to help them all you can. Have your people work the ground so they do not get idle, help your agents and get farms this is one chief. The other chief is the church, I want you to help him for he tells you of me; when you get back go to Church. All these churches are mine, if you go to church when you get back, others will do the same. . . . Educate your children, send them to schools.[85]

Short Bull also recognized Wovoka's message of nonviolence. Loving others, farming, sending children to school, and even attending Christian churches were all part of Wovoka's message. Wovoka also predicted that "all nations" would someday (it was not clear when) speak the same language, rather than rely on sign language, and "all over the world one should be like the other and no distinction made." Short Bull and the others listened to Wovoka for five days straight. On the fifth day, Short Bull shook hands with Wovoka, who only told him that "soon there would be no world, after the end of the world those who went to church would see all their relatives that had died. This will be the same all over the world even across the big waters."[86]

While similar, none of the stories of the visiting delegates are exactly the same, and scholars of the Ghost Dance have discussed the differing testimonies.[87] The agent at Fort Hall noticed diverse beliefs regarding the dance among the people living on and visiting his reservation. "The fact is," he told the commissioner of Indian affairs, "scarcely any two tribes" had "the same idea as to exactly what they must do" to bring about Wovoka's prophecies.[88] It is important to remember that Wovoka only spoke his Paiute language and rudimentary English. Anything Porcupine, Short Bull, or other Plains delegates heard came through interpreters or their own understanding of English or sign language. A likely path of communication for the Plains delegates was from Paiute to English and then to sign language.

More important were the "vast cultural differences," as Raymond DeMallie describes them, between Paiutes, Lakotas, and other Plains peoples.[89] Wovoka presented his ideas within his own cultural perspective. There was no unifying "Native religion" that each tribe understood in the same way. A Lakota, Cheyenne, or Arapaho delegate would consider Wovoka's message individually, within the scope of his own traditions.[90] Moreover, Wovoka did not preach a specific doctrine that demanded strict adherence. As DeMallie puts it, "Each man went away from meeting Wovoka with a personal interpretation of the Ghost Dance religion."[91] This nondoctrinal religion allowed individuals to "contribute to the understanding of the totality of the power (*Wakan Tanka* [among Lakotas]) through his own individual experiences," which fell in line with the religious traditions of the Plains groups. Heretics did not exist in the movement, "only believers and nonbelievers." Consistency in doctrine was not a measure of spiritual worth. Individuals had their own experiences and their own understanding of those experiences. Consequently, Short Bull's testimony was different from Kicking Bear's, Porcupine's, and Sitting Bull's, but they all conveyed a similar message.[92] Likewise, letters sent among tribes also expressed the movement outside a western religious framework. While Natives hoped to convey an understanding of the Messiah's message in their letters, they did not expect the written words to be interpreted literally and as the sole message. And for those receiving the letters, they expected to find the variety of interpretations that came from the various authors. The Ghost Dance movement may have originated in the mind of one man, but his ideas were not canonized. There was no Ghost Dance guidebook. As the movement spread from group to group, individual to individual, it could become what the adoptee wanted it to become.

Despite the broad interpretations, networks can homogenize knowledge, and many whites were surprised by the commonality of beliefs among tribes living hundreds of miles apart. They shared the Western Shoshone agent's astonishment that "all the Indians in the country seem to possess practically the same ideas and expect about the same results."[93] Six months earlier, the *Omaha Daily Bee* had offered a similar observation: "It appears that though these Indian tribes are fully 1,000 miles apart they both have the same belief that a savior is soon coming to them and that he will destroy the white people of America."[94] At the Fort Peck Reservation, Agent C. R. A. Scobey found that the Sioux there had a "strong and abiding faith" in the Ghost Dance "as it is propounded at other agencies."[95] They expected the coming of a Messiah in the spring, the resurrection of their dead friends and family, the return of the bison and other game, and, according to the agent, "the destruction of the whites."

Whites were concerned about that last point. Newspapers reported that Indians believed a variety of supernatural calamities would befall white Americans, like a great flood or an earthquake swallowing the white world.[96] Whites focused on the destruction of their race, while Natives only looked toward a transformed earth. While Wovoka himself never told whites that he prophesized the destruction of whites in the West, some Natives may have thought that Wovoka had told them that. Some Natives definitely believed in the supernatural, even cataclysmic, events that would remove the colonizers from their lives.[97] Others, like Sage and Yellow Calf, simply thought that whites would no longer be around on Wovoka's renewed earth. Whatever the process, for whites it would mean a loss of power, and for Natives it would mean freedom from colonial control and the return of their sovereignty and prosperity.

Notably absent in the common current of the delegates' interpretation are any violent ideas. Wovoka always emphasized peace and even taught that some features of the white world were fruitful. He told the people to "educate your children, send them to schools." He relayed to the Lakotas, "Have your people work the ground . . . get farms." Importantly, it may have been typical for a Paiute to have these opinions in the years before the Ghost Dance. According to a newspaper reporting on a Paiute Round Dance gathering in 1888, Paiute elders advised the young "to become farmers; to be truthful, honest, and industrious and sober."[98] Wovoka was rooted in the values of his people. Historian Omer Stewart called Wovoka's message one of "clean living, peaceful adjustment with whites," and "hard work." Michael Hittman thought "the Protestant-type work ethic" was "at the core" of Wovoka's religion.[99] Louis Warren recently argued that Wovoka made "wage work" a "holy commandment, an order from God," even concluding that "work was the path to the glorious salvation that awaited Indians in the afterlife."[100] This might seem like a pro-assimilation message, but Sam Maddra believed that, instead, Wovoka thought that Indians "should take the benefits of white society that are offered, with the knowledge and reassurance that doing so would not make them any less Indian."[101]

It is difficult, however, to generalize how the movement was received by so many different people from so many different cultures.[102] Fundamentally, when relating all the firsthand interpretations presented in this study and others, there is no question that the Ghost Dance was rooted in the belief that you could, with the help of God or a Great Spirit, make the world better by bettering yourself and your people. Southern Arapaho headman Row of Lodges described this optimistic "religion" as asking "God to make our hearts so that they can be good," asking "Him to make our brains good so that we can think good thoughts," asking "Him to make our breath good, so that we can breathe good words."[103] If Indians were "friends with all people, no matter what race, so that good will be done by the Indians," this would "cause others to think of the Father who made all men." For many believers, Wovoka's promises would also decolonize Native life, meaning that the world would be remade in a way that would restore Indigenous autonomy. Although whites might not disappear from the world, colonial control would end, which was not an idea that the US government wanted on reservations.

"The Christ Said We Must Tell It to Everyone"

During the first half of 1890, Native Americans continued to send and receive information about the Messiah in the mail, outside the concern of white officials who still knew little about the Ghost Dance. This correspondence was a critical element of the movement on the plains because it informed those still unfamiliar with the dance while keeping Native communities focused on it. An early letter, published in the February 1890 edition of the *Word Carrier* (the English-language newspaper published alongside *Iapi Oaye* by the Dakota Mission), detailed what an Indian pupil at Santee Normal Training School heard about the Messiah. The editors of the *Word Carrier* published several letters from Native students each month, and no special attention was given to this letter (it was featured on the back page of the paper with the rest of the student letters). It is not clear which reservation the student was from since there were students from all parts of the Dakotas and Nebraska at the school, but the student's account is remarkably in-depth considering it was written weeks *before* the Lakota delegation returned from Nevada. It read in part,

> One day the men gathered . . . and one looked up and saw a black cloud coming, and a man was in the cloud. He came and stood over where the men gathered together. He said many things to them; but I cannot tell you in English, but I will try to do my best to tell you. He said, "I know you people are like little children gathering together and talk. I have seen you from above. It is because of the white men. See what they have done even to me," and he showed his hands and feet, and his side where they stuck him a spear. He told them many things, and said he was going to help them and all the Indians to fight against the white people. And he did many strange things, and gave them some paint, and told them to paint themselves; and when they did, they were like crazy, and after while when they got over, then they as happy as a bird. He said to them to believe all his words, and to believe him.[104]

The student's letter features descriptions of Wovoka that were commonly communicated, including in Porcupine's testimony: his scars of crucifixion, his paint, and his promise to help Native people. There is no mention of a dance, but there is an emphasis on the Messiah helping the "fight against the white people," however the student's use of the phrase is interpreted. It may have meant resistance against colonial control, but, again, violence was not a theme shared by Wovoka himself.

Some may have placed great significance on these Ghost Dance letters. For instance, the *Chadron Democrat* reported in May 1890 that a group of Lakotas at Pine Ridge, perhaps the official delegation, had returned from their visit to the Wind River Mountains in Wyoming with, they claimed, a letter written by Jesus Christ. This letter was given to them as proof of their supernatural experience. It was so powerful, in fact, that the Lakotas told the newspaper that "two white men read the letter and they both died immediately."[105]

The first Lakota delegation did send letters home during their journey to keep their people informed. They claimed that "the Messiah has now come to the world" and there was "no mistake about the advent of the new Messiah."[106] In January 1890, Josephine Waggoner read letters sent by Kicking Bear from Nevada for others at Standing Rock (unfortunately, Kicking Bear's letters do not survive). On January 10, she was asked to go to Thunder Hawk's house to read Kicking Bear's letters, written in the Dakota language, which asked "all the people to stand firm, to keep praying and dancing, for the Messiah would soon be here." Waggoner, however, told those listening that "their new belief was all a mistake."[107] She remembered arguing for an hour and a half and believed that she had "convinced some," including Thunder Hawk, Bear Face, Iron Horn, Crow Feather, "and their bands" that the letters did not contain the truth.

Having inspired debate, these letters created much anticipation for the delegation's return home, in April 1890, after several months away. Sitting Bull, the Northern Arapaho, returned to Wind River, and Porcupine returned to Tongue River. Porcupine called for a gathering where for five days he relayed what Wovoka had told him: "I have returned to my tribe to tell all this. The Christ said we must tell it to every one."[108] Porcupine warned his people to listen to Wovoka's message "for their own good."[109] "It will please the God if we say yes," Porcupine announced. "He told the Indians that they must not quarrel with the whites or kill them. We must dance. If we don't dance we will get crazy and poor."[110] In May 1890, Maj. Henry Carroll reported that the Cheyennes treated Porcupine "with the greatest deference and obedience" during the dances because he "had revelations from the new God."[111] He also found that "unusual mystery" was observed regarding the dance. Whites could get few details about it.

The Lakota delegates did not receive a warm welcome home from their agents, but word of their experiences spread. Short Bull, who was determined to help fulfill Wovoka's prophecies at Rosebud, began to confer with Brulé leaders. But Agent Wright brought Short Bull in and tried to convince him that his belief in the Messiah was foolish and warned him not to continue to spread his stories.[112] Likewise, leaders at Pine Ridge scheduled a council "to organize the new religion," but after William Selwyn informed Agent H. D. Gallagher what the "apostles" were telling the people, the Indian police dispersed the growing crowd. Gallagher was concerned that the gathering would disrupt the early-spring farmwork. The "promoters of the enterprise" (Good Thunder and two others) were "given a good lecture upon the mischief they were doing" and thrown in the guardhouse for two days.[113] Gallagher then met the leaders in council and explained "the silliness of what had been told them."[114] He also put a clamp on visiting, a strategy that would be attempted by other agents in the months to come.[115]

Although some agents, like Gallagher, actively tried to limit the spread of the movement, most did not yet realize how quickly the dance was spreading (a group of Sioux had already told Omahas and Ho-Chunks in eastern Nebraska about it in April 1890), and none of them could predict the extent to which its message would be carried by the mail.[116] By the end of May 1890, white authorities in the Dakotas, Montana, and Indian Territory began noticing the impact of the delegates' return, but most did not think their stories would amount to much, and little was reported specifically about the dance during the next few months.[117] Selwyn wrote that the jailing of the men at Pine Ridge settled things down "for a while."[118] Agent Gallagher did not think "any serious trouble" would come to pass because of the "excitement."[119] He predicted that their belief in the Messiah would shortly pass "from their minds."

Gallagher was, of course, wrong. Information continued to circulate through his and other reservations. In the case of the Pine Ridge Indians, their epistolary connection with Southern Cheyennes and Arapahos sustained the believers' faith of and kept the reservation focused on Wovoka's prophecies. "I see the way they have been corresponding from one agency to another is doing some harm," Selwyn later reported to his agent. "The Cheyennes and Arapahoes at Darlington, Ind. Territory are wild with this excitement. This I come to find out by the reading of some letters while at Pine Ridge."[120] One of these letters sent between the two agencies was obtained by a white missionary, who forwarded a copy to Richard Henry Pratt, the superintendent at the Carlisle Indian Industrial School. The letter was sent by Crooked Nose, a twenty-five-year-old Pine Ridge Cheyenne, to his brother at the Cheyenne-Arapaho Reservation in Indian Territory. Sometime in the summer of 1890, he wrote, "Yes, it is so about Jesus and all Indians talking about it now the heaven, come to save the Indians. . . . It is to far up in sky where he was. It is not half so far where he is now you may come to him and all the Indians Jesus gives some berries some black and some red I ate two."[121]

Another remarkable letter from Pine Ridge in 1890, written in English by Nettie Janis, a twenty-five-year-old woman of Lakota and French-American descent, was a message about the movement to other Lakota "mixed bloods." Janis wrote,

> Now I wish to tell you mixed bloods something. It is in regard to our Father who sits in the west that I wish to speak to you about. The matter now in question is the truth, that is why we joined it. So I wish you to try it and know for yourself, which you will. These are the mixed-bloods who now belong to it. Well I could not name each, but there are 20 or perhaps more who now belong, and that is why I tell you.[122]

Janis not only wanted to spread information about the "Father who sits in the west," she also hoped that others of mixed descent would try the Ghost Dance and know "the truth" for themselves. She wrote that she "individually" believed it "as I know it to be the truth." Before signing her name,

Janis did not close the letter with a phrase typical of Lakota letters (such as "yours truly" or "I shake hands with you"). Instead, she closed with a word in Lakota, *houya*, meaning "to call out" or "calling out," indicating the purpose of her words.

Written exchanges of news between relatives and friends, a common mode of communication by 1890, enabled the remarkable spread of the Ghost Dance movement. Map 4 visualizes the known links of correspondence between reservations regarding the Ghost Dance (demonstrated by surviving documentation).[123] These links represent one or more specific "Ghost Dance letters" that were sent during the peak years of the movement, 1889 through 1894. As we have seen, people living on these reservations were already corresponding with each other before 1889. Perhaps the only connection represented on the map that did not exist before the Ghost Dance is the link of correspondence between the Walker River and Cheyenne-Arapaho Reservations. That new link would persist after 1894.

During the Ghost Dance, it became clear to US officials that Native Americans had command of lines of communication that spanned the continent, which was a dangerous prospect for the government. In June 1890, a brigadier general noticed that knowledge of the Messiah "had quite a wide diffusion and excited much interest amongst a number of tribes."[124] Even those tribes that never danced, like the Potawatomis, learned about it through the mail. The Potawatomis received a letter "from the Sioux to adopt their dance," but according to their agent, none put much thought into it.[125] Nevertheless, an effort was made to inform foreign tribes about the Ghost Dance.

News of the dance reached as far as Hampton, Virginia, by summer of 1890. Robert P. Higheagle wrote from Pine Ridge to Luke Najinhkte that he first learned of the Ghost Dance while away at school at Hampton.[126] Higheagle's progressive father, Martin High Eagle (a Standing Rock Hunkpapa policeman), had sent him an eagle feather in the mail and told him to wear it "in case the troubles predicted should possibly come to pass," but Higheagle's friend advised him to "break up the feather and throw it away," which he did.[127] Other students in the Indian educational system also sent and received letters about the new Messiah while at their boarding schools. Joe Abner, a Southern Cheyenne at the Haskell Institute in Lawrence, Kansas, heard from his people at the Cheyenne-Arapaho Reservation that a Sioux had traveled south to Indian Territory to spread the dance.[128] Another Haskell student got a letter from her father at the Kiowa, Comanche, and Wichita Reservation, four hundred miles away, which told her "not to ridicule the coming of the Indian's Christ, for she knows nothing of the

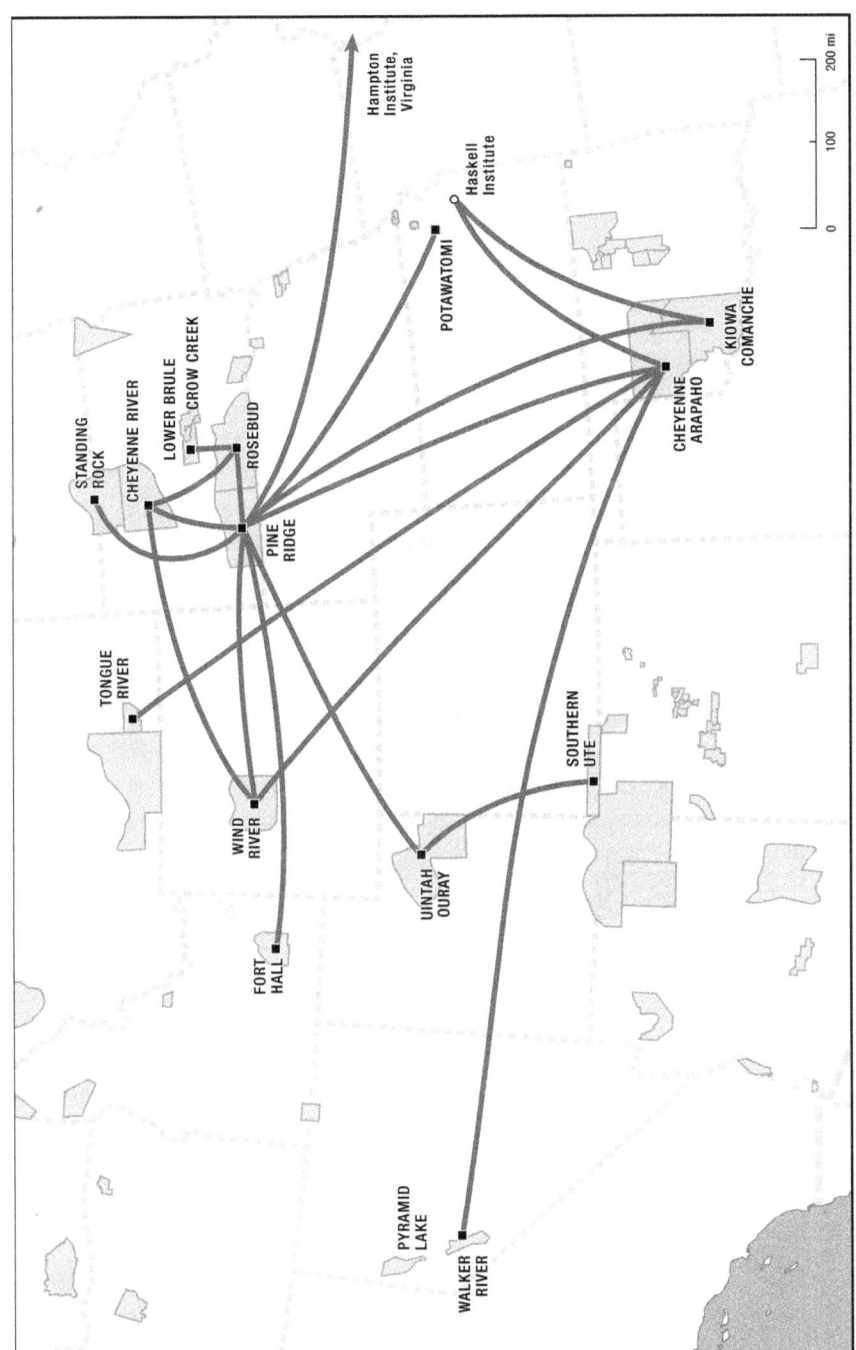

Map 4. Known links of correspondence concerning the Ghost Dance, 1889–1894

wondrous manifestations the Indians have received from Him."[129] Another letter, from an uncle to a nephew, told of the revelations that occurred at Ghost Dances, the trances with dead relatives, and their interviews with the Messiah. The uncle advised his nephew to attend a dance before he judged the truth of the Messiah.

By November 1890, Native-authored letters about the dance had crossed the Atlantic. Several Native men working in Buffalo Bill's Wild West Show in Europe received letters from their friends at Pine Ridge that spoke of the movement. A reporter noted that some, including Rocky Bear, were unconvinced, while others were "inclined to reflect upon the intelligence regarding the Messiah."[130]

Wovoka's ideas, born in western Nevada, became part of a continental, Native-controlled conversation because of the well-established and extensive networks among tribes in the West. It happened quickly because the spans between reservations were bridged by mail and rail, allowing men and women to communicate efficiently across the distances that separated them. Native Americans from many reservations located information about the Ghost Dance, and they discussed it, some defending the movement and others doubting it. There is a written record of these ideas from Natives themselves that shows an optimistic belief that change could be coming. Unfortunately, as the agents' negative responses to the return of the Lakota delegation demonstrate, US officials grew concerned about the attention devoted to Wovoka's message. As we will see in the next chapter, the Office of Indian Affairs would go to great lengths to slow the momentum of the Ghost Dance's spread during the second half of 1890.

CHAPTER 6

Suppressing the Spread

After the first bursts of information about the Ghost Dance hit reservations in the spring of 1890, Native Americans continued to travel to distant reservations, often by rail, to learn more about the dance and to carry it and its purpose to those outside of their own tribes (the post commander at Fort Washakie called them "emissaries of the Indian 'Christ'").[1] A Nevada agent reported thirty-four men of several different tribes who were en route to Wovoka's settlement near Walker Lake in April or May 1890, and another later wrote that Wovoka had attracted "many Indians from abroad, the fame of his preachings expanding in the ratio of distance from point of delivery."[2] But US government agents remained unconcerned about the Ghost Dance until the summer of 1890. Most believed that it was nothing more than a fad, as interest in the dance seemed to have peaked.[3]

During that summer, however, agents in the northern and southern plains and eventually the intermountain region were forced to confront the effects of the Ghost Dance movement, and the US government tried to tighten its restrictions on Native communication. Agents noticed that more people were leaving their reservations without permission, some were dancing more frequently, and interest in the movement was disrupting farmwork. One official believed that the strenuous, persistent dancing had ill effects on Indians' health. He also thought that the dance was only reminding them of their old customs. The US government was "spending large sums of money to wean them away" from these customs, he reasoned, so why should the agents allow the dance to continue?[4] Most important, some agents received inaccurate reports about a rumored uprising somehow tied to the Ghost Dance. Some whites became nervous about all the intertribal interactions and seemingly secret communications relayed among Indians, which was not a new phenomenon, but it became an important factor in the history of the Ghost Dance movement.[5]

Because of these concerns, in the summer and into the fall of 1890, agents tried a variety of approaches to control the Ghost Dance, from moderation to outright suppression. Officials imagined that its spread could be slowed if correspondence was surveilled and visits were further restricted, thus deterring intertribal interactions. But that strategy failed because information about the dance flowed through deep-rooted and flourishing intertribal networks. Native Americans resisted US government interference in their important widespread lines of communication.

Unease about the Ghost Dance among US officials increased in late May 1890 because of the opinion of an influential white settler. A letter from Charles L. Hyde of Pierre, South Dakota, brought new attention to the Ghost Dance and its relationship to Indians' communication and off-reservation movement. Hyde, a large landowner and real estate dealer, informed the secretary of the interior that he had information, gathered from a confidential source, "that the Sioux Indians or a portion of them are secretly planning and arranging for an outbreak in the near future." He said that he did not want to cause alarm, but he suggested keeping watch "on the different bands and using conservative judgement about allowing any of them to leave their respective agencies."[6] Hyde's informant was a Lakota student at the Presbyterian College at Pierre who had received letters about the Messiah, and perhaps this secret outbreak, from his relatives at Pine Ridge.[7] Hyde did not forward the student's correspondence to the secretary, so it is not known exactly what the letters from home contained.[8] Agent Charles McChesney at Cheyenne River told Commissioner of Indian Affairs Thomas Morgan that the letter warned the student "to look out for himself" if the Indians did "break out."[9] Nevertheless, the secretary of the interior passed Hyde's report to the commissioner of Indian affairs. The acting commissioner then called for a report from each of the agents at the Lakota reserves to "take prompt measures to ascertain whether there is any ground for apprehension," but none of the agents thought there was much to Hyde's warning.[10] While the Indians were interested in the new Messiah and his message, there was not any evidence of planned violence.[11] Agent H. D. Gallagher at Pine Ridge said the excitement there would "soon die out without causing trouble."[12] Agent J. George Wright said that most of the Rosebud Indians "scoffed at" the idea of an outbreak.[13]

But Agent Wright also mentioned that "several secret communications" had been passed between the Sioux agencies in the previous months. It is not known if these communications contained any information about the Messiah or why Wright assumed they were meant to be secret.[14] Perhaps he regarded any personal letter between Natives as suspicious if they came from the "nonprogressive Indians" whom he blamed for the communications, those "disgruntled" and "dissatisfied" men who had refused to sign the Sioux Bill the year before. According to Wright, the letters recited the Indians' "grievances against the Government" and urged "their friends to meet them in council at Cheyenne River in the spring, when their future policy, and other matters, would be considered," although he never claimed to have read one of the letters.[15]

Agent Wright's report did not mention anything concerning the Messiah, but it seems likely that these secret communications being passed between Rosebud, Pine Ridge, Cheyenne River, and the other Sioux agencies were, at least in part, about the Ghost Dance. On the same June day as Wright's report, Agent McChesney at Cheyenne River reported that there was "some little excitement among my Indians regarding the coming of the Indian messiah."[16] In addition, a few days after Wright's and McChesney's reports, newspapers reported that some Northern Cheyennes from Tongue River, including one who was made a "high priest" by the Messiah, had just Ghost Danced with the Indians at Rosebud.[17] The newspaper report explained the secrecy the Indians practiced concerning the "new religion." They refused to discuss it with white men; it was "all very mysterious."

In mid-June 1890, white authorities began to suspect that the communications being sent out by Lakotas had a malicious purpose, further tying the Ghost Dance to supposed troublemaking. White settlers around the Tongue River Reservation in Montana grew anxious because some "friendly" Northern Cheyennes told them that messengers had been sent to the Indians at Standing Rock and Pine Ridge "to solicit . . . aid" in a "proposed outbreak."[18] The secretary of the interior suggested that these messengers or "envoys" should be arrested. There was a larger than usual number of Northern Cheyennes roaming about, but the agents at Standing Rock, Pine Ridge, and Tongue River found no occasion for alarm. The trouble began after a white cattleman was supposedly killed by some Cheyennes near the Tongue River Reservation (around Busby, Montana) around the same time that Porcupine assembled a large Ghost Dance at Tongue River. White settlers connected the two events, and the Cheyennes feared retribution, according to the Tongue River agent, R. L. Upshaw. Upshaw was doing what he could to "allay the excitement," he reported, but the "wild stories" being told by both the whites and the Cheyennes made it difficult.[19] An investigation made months later by Brig. Gen. Thomas Ruger suggested that June (and July) visits to Standing Rock from outside Lakotas and Northern Cheyennes were about the Ghost Dance. In fact, they revived interest in the movement there.[20]

Agent Upshaw had the army arrest Porcupine in early June for being a nuisance, but they later released him.[21] Because he was spreading dangerous ideas, Upshaw recommended that Porcupine be placed under surveillance, but if his "delusion" did not die and if he continued to "hold large gatherings to expand and propagate new revelations," Upshaw thought he should be "sent to some other place."[22] Later, though, on the same day that he wrote the letter, Upshaw telegrammed the army to arrest Porcupine once again. Maj. Henry Carroll, however, refused, reporting that the Cheyennes were quiet and had returned to their homes.[23] Major Carroll, anxious to learn exactly what ideas the Cheyennes were discussing, had sent a spy to the camps. William Rowland, of European and Cheyenne ancestry, gathered information under the guise of visiting relatives and even participated in Porcupine's ceremonies, which Rowland claimed involved sprinkling water on people's heads, like a baptism. After three days, Rowland reported back that he did not hear anything about "fighting the whites."[24]

But for some, talk about the Messiah and a planned outbreak went hand in hand. Because of the content of the letters he read for the Oglalas and Northern Cheyennes in the spring of 1890, William Selwyn, the Yankton postmaster at Pine Ridge, expected "a general Indian war" to break out in the spring of 1891.[25] According to Selwyn, Wovoka prophesized that the return of the bison and the removal of the white man would occur in the spring of 1891. Selwyn assumed that some at Pine Ridge were creating "secret plans" over the "last one year or so" in preparation for that prophecy. Secrecy was a part of the movement for the Lakotas; their dance leaders were hesitant to share any information with white authorities.[26] This secrecy created suspicion of communications, and whites distrusted dancers.

Breaking Connections

US officials would continue to use surveillance, spies, and informants to infiltrate Native networks. They also came to realize that letter writing needed to be controlled to halt the progress of the Ghost Dance. "These Indians communicate with each other through the mails to a great extent," complained Charles Adams, the agent at the Kiowa, Comanche, and Wichita Reservation, "and know by these means exactly how things are progressing in the land where this man is now convincing his followers that the white man must go, and that in the near future, nothing but Indians and buffalo will inhabit the earth."[27] Some agents, like Adams, were determined to prevent Indians from reading such communications. So many letters about the Ghost Dance reached the Kiowa, Comanche, and Wichita Reservation that Agent Adams requested the power to censor the Indians' mail. He wanted the postmaster general to instruct the postmaster at Anadarko, Oklahoma, to deliver all mail sent to the Indians into his hands for his "perusal." He thought the Indians were "in an unsettled frame of mind" and that "steps should be taken to avoid future trouble." For Adams, the solution was to prevent his population from communicating with the outside world. He wrote,

> I was, a short while ago, made aware of the contents of a letter written to an Indian Chief, and they were of such a character that he should never have heard them at all. The letter was from one of the Northern Agencies and spoke of the new Christ that has been discovered in that locality, and contained a lot of instructions to these Indians that should never be carried out. Now had this letter fell into my hands originally, he never would have seen or the contents.[28]

But Adams could do little to stop the letters from reaching Native eyes. Several weeks after Adams's request, Maj. Wirt Davis reported that many of the Indians at the Kiowa, Comanche, and Wichita Reservation and at the Cheyenne-Arapaho Reservation could read and write and were receiving letters from friends and relatives at Pine Ridge, Tongue River, and Wind River.[29] At least one illiterate Kiowa man, Bi'ank'i (Eater), who became an influential Ghost Dance "dreamer," sent pictographic letters about the movement and about his own visions to his sons off at Carlisle.[30]

Agent Adams at the Kiowa Reservation was not the only agent who wanted to surveil and censor Indian mail during the dance's spread. The Cheyenne River agent reserved the right to read "all the letters received by Indians" so that he could be "made acquainted with the contents."[31] He thought that the mail was the only way his Indians could obtain information about the troubles outside the reserve.[32] Even the superintendent of Indian schools approved the seizing of letters from students at the Genoa Indian School in Nebraska. He thought the contents of some letters from their friends on the reservations might "be of some value" to Indian Affairs.[33] The superintendent at Genoa promised to send any relevant information (taken from the private letters of his students) to the commissioner.

Agent James McLaughlin at Standing Rock not only made it difficult for Lakotas to receive letters, he also restricted the sending of letters. Lakotas, however, did not take that lying down. In a remarkable letter to the secretary of the interior, Running Antelope, Standing Bear, and Thunder Hawk protested that the post office at the agency was under McLaughlin's control. Some letters were not being sent or received. "To send you these few lines," the men wrote, "we had to run the risk of being imprisoned as we had to steal across the river in the night time."[34] The group traveled to the Vanderbilt Post Office in Campbell County, South Dakota, across the Missouri River from Standing Rock, to mail their letter of complaint because they were "watched night and day." "We understood we had freedom of religion," they wrote, but Agent McLaughlin and his wife were compelling them to become Catholic. "The present Catholic society at this Agency, Mrs. McLaughlin leader, is more dangerous than all the Ghost Dances put together," they maintained. They said agency officials wanted control over the mail because they were "afraid that if the world would know the truth, justice would be done." It is not known what the secretary of the interior made of Running Antelope, Standing Bear, and Thunder Hawk's letter, but McLaughlin was not reprimanded for censoring the mail. US officials wanted to intercept the letters they thought would disrupt their reservations.

Limiting Visits

The US government also tried to curb visitation in order to break intertribal connections and thus stop the Ghost Dance's spread. Agents already knew how hard it was to discourage intertribal dancing, and they learned just how intertribal in character the Ghost Dance was in the spring of 1890. In May, Agent Charles Adams was willing, on behalf of some Kiowas, to ask Agent Charles Ashley at the Cheyenne-Arapaho Reservation if five Kiowas could visit for the purpose of dancing. Neither agent was concerned about the Ghost Dance because neither knew that the Ghost Dance was infiltrating their reservations. Nevertheless, Agent Ashley did not allow the visit because he did not want Kiowa visitors disrupting the farmwork on his reserve.[35] Despite being told that they could not leave their reservation, around 150 Kiowas, Comanches, and Wichitas arrived at the Cheyenne-Arapaho Reservation to dance.[36] To make matters worse for the agents, soon after that illicit visit, Ghost Dances were held on the Kiowa, Comanche, and Wichita Reservation. The Kiowas, Comanches, Wichitas, and Caddos there had learned more about the Ghost Dance while they were with the Cheyennes and Arapahos, with whom Ghost Dancing was well underway.

Native men and women in western Indian Territory had been interacting for years. It was not the first time people from those reservations exchanged beliefs that concerned Indian Affairs, but agents would eventually go to great lengths to stop visits and the flow of information about the Ghost

Dance. Despite his opposition to the large gatherings, Agent Ashley was not entirely against visitation before he realized the Ghost Dance could be a problem. He allowed two Southern Cheyennes to travel to Pine Ridge and Tongue River in June 1890 to investigate the Messiah, perhaps hoping that the men would return with a report discrediting the movement.[37] Dozens of Cheyennes were also given permission to visit the Ponca, Pawnee, and Otoe Reservation in July.[38] Ashley even allowed a Pine Ridge Oglala named High Wolf to stay at the Cheyenne-Arapaho Reservation for an additional thirty days in May.[39] High Wolf knew about the Messiah story, although it is not clear how much information he had. Ashley knew the news was coming to his reserve from the northern tribes, but he saw no harm in High Wolf's presence. High Wolf was allowed to travel throughout Indian Territory to visit other tribes like the Kiowas, possibly spreading information about the dance. A Kiowa named Apiatan accompanied High Wolf home to Pine Ridge in September to determine the validity of Wovoka's claims (which will be discussed in chapter 8).[40]

Agent Adams, too, had learned to permit certain visits in order to please those under his charge, but he would receive quite a lecture from the commissioner of Indian affairs once the Ghost Dance spread to his reservation. According to Agent Adams, the Ghost Dances at the Kiowa, Comanche, and Wichita Reservation in June were quiet, meant to show appreciation to the Messiah, who would restore the bison. Indian Affairs inspector William Junkin counted 2,000–2,500 Indians at a dance (not all participated) two miles west of the agency near the Washita River. The dance site, which was populated for a week, was surrounded by 300 tepees and 150 bowers built from brush.[41] At the height of the dance, Junkin observed, 400 people participated at a time. Men, women, and children danced for hours (with "earnestness and credulity," according to Junkin) until they were exhausted. The "religious feeling" and the dance itself were new to the Kiowas, Junkin discerned. Like all other tribes, the Kiowas danced the Ghost Dance in a circle, with hands clasped, without a drum. But Kiowas and Lakotas were among the few Plains groups that danced around a small tree or pole, which may demonstrate the influence of the Kiowas' visit to the Lakotas at Pine Ridge in May or June 1890.[42]

Agent Adams allowed the dances to continue even though he claimed to know such dancing was prohibited. He did not yet seem to consider the dancing a serious matter. Commissioner of Indian Affairs Thomas Morgan, however, censured Adams for his decision. "To have allowed it . . . was an unpardonable step backward," Commissioner Morgan wrote.[43] Adams defended himself by placing blame on Inspector Junkin, who had convinced him to permit the dance.⁴⁴ Junkin said he had allowed the dance for a few reasons, primarily because "it would have required a regiment of soldiers" to tell the Kiowas no. Junkin was also convinced by the argument of Kiowa chief Big Tree, who beseeched Junkin and Adams at a council on June 24, 1890 (held to discuss a variety of issues), to let his people keep dancing:

> We have always had different roads. The Great Spirit when he created us gave us forms of worship; the whites one, the reds another. We worship in the form of dancing; you worship in the form of prayer. We are not responsible for our different ways. As the reds have their way to worship a god, so have the whites theirs. They do not like ours and instead of scolding us when they are angry, as they think they do, they scold the Great Spirit. Last summer we thought it our duty to have one of these dances or forms of worship; the privilege was denied and we accepted the denial. We want to worship this summer. There is nothing bad in it. We believe in it and we want your help. Any orders from the department we are ready to comply with, but when we want a favor it seems as though we cannot get it.⁴⁵

Big Tree was not a Ghost Dancer, but he could not accept the US government's unreasonable attacks on Kiowa beliefs.⁴⁶ He saw little difference between his religion and the so-called modern religion of the whites. Commissioner Morgan, dismissive of Big Tree's reasoning, told Big Tree and other Kiowa, Comanche, and Plains Apache headmen in a letter that he did not "wish to force upon them the white man's religion" but that they could not dance; "it is now prohibited" because dancing was "very harmful to the young men and prevent them from accepting the white man's way, and becoming prosperous."⁴⁷ But Junkin wrote that his "heart melted" after hearing the Kiowas' plea, and he gave them permission to hold their dance "upon condition that nothing bad or cruel would be practiced."⁴⁸ Besides, Junkin thought, the Kiowas would stop dancing soon enough once their delegations returned from the North with evidence that the "new Christ" was really "a myth or humbug."

In mid-July, however, Agent Adams tried to put a stop to a dance planned by Kiowas, Comanches, and Apaches. Commissioner Morgan received a telegram purportedly from Joshua Given, an ordained Kiowa who had been educated at eastern boarding schools, asking his permission to allow the dance (it was not sent by Given but by imposters hoping to use his credibility).⁴⁹ Morgan, who was more concerned about a possible Sun Dance than the Ghost Dance, replied with his own telegram: "The dance among the Kiowas is positively prohibited."⁵⁰ On July 20, Agent Adams asked for troops to prevent the dancing. The Kiowas, Comanches, and Plains Apaches were "determined to hold their medicine dance," he telegrammed, and he did not think he could stop them alone.[51] "Nearly all of the Indians throughout the country are greatly exercised," Adams had told the commissioner four days earlier. "This man whom they call Jesus, sometime ago made his appearance at one of the northern agencies, and the report, probably greatly exaggerated, reached these Indians in a short while, and most of them believed."[52] A party of soldiers from Fort Sill was sent to the Kiowa Agency (Anadarko, Indian Territory) to prevent the dance, which they did without a hint of violence. But the Kiowas were disappointed. They believed that Inspector Junkin had promised them the privilege.[53]

Dancing also took hold at the neighboring Cheyenne-Arapaho Reservation. The Northern Arapaho Sitting Bull (mentioned in the previous chapter and not to be confused with the Lakota chief) became the leading proponent of the Ghost Dance there. In June 1890, Sitting Bull, who was living at the Wind River Reservation, sought permission to transfer south to the Cheyenne-Arapaho Reservation. The Wind River agent agreed to ask the Cheyenne-Arapaho agent, Charles Ashley, if the transfer could happen. However, Ashley learned that Sitting Bull had gained prominence, being "one of the Indians who claims to have seen Christ," and he did not want "further . . . agitation" at his reservation.[54] Ashley heard that his Indians were expecting a visitor from Wind River who could "verify the reports received by them," and he believed Sitting Bull was that man. He denied Sitting Bull's transfer, but the Wind River agent convinced Ashley that Sitting Bull would be no trouble for just a short visit. Surprisingly, after Sitting Bull spent several weeks visiting, Ashley granted his transfer request, calling him "an inoffensive man," despite his growing prominence as a man who had "an interview with Christ."[55] Sitting Bull must have made a good impression.

A lieutenant at Fort Sill called Sitting Bull "the most graceful sign talker" that he had ever met in the Southwest, which allowed him to communicate effectively between the peoples of the Great Basin and the northern and southern plains. Sitting Bull told the lieutenant that much of what had been said about him was not true, one of the many times Ghost Dancers disputed information whites had about the dance. Sitting Bull did not think that he saw Jesus alive, only a man who Jesus had "'helped' or inspired," who told him that persevering in the dance would "cause sickness and death to disappear."[56] By December 1890, Maj. Wirt Davis was calling Sitting Bull "an apostle like St. Paul" who was "preaching the doctrine" off the Cheyenne-Arapaho Reservation to Kiowas, Apaches, Wichitas, and others in Indian Territory.[57]

The Ghost Dance continued to spread quickly throughout Indian Territory despite government efforts to limit intertribal visiting. Most camps at the Cheyenne-Arapaho Reservation were holding dances two to three times each week during that summer of 1890.[58] In September, Southern Cheyenne runners invited all Kiowas, Comanches, Apaches, Wichitas, and probably others in Indian Territory to their reservation. Agent Ashley sent an urgent telegram to the Kiowa agent, asking him to "use all possible means to prevent" his Indians from leaving.[59] Nevertheless, around three thousand Southern Cheyennes, Southern Arapahos, Kiowas, Caddos, Wichitas, and others gathered in September 1890 to dance under Sitting Bull's direction or to witness the event.

Dancing and illicit off-reservation movement persisted after that gathering (according to Col. J. F. Wade, Southern Cheyennes were "good-natured" and "well-disposed" throughout the summer and fall).[60] Pawnees, Poncas, and Caddos sought information about the dance from Southern Cheyennes, Southern Arapahos, and Kiowas. A delegation of Poncas, Iowas, and Missourias returned to their people from a visit to the Cheyenne-Arapaho Reservation in late November and began dancing soon after.[61] Poncas visited Cheyennes again in order to learn more about the dance, and Caddos became more interested.[62] Caddos, including Frank Whitebead and Hadibuh, visited the Cheyenne-Arapaho Reservation to find out more, and on December 15, they had a "grand dance" before the winter season set in.[63] The Caddos brought the dance home and composed Ghost Dance songs in their own language. In early December, a large group of Kiowas and Comanches joined the Cheyennes at their reservation for dancing.[64] Later that month, a newspaper reported that the Kiowa men White Cloud, Hatch-e-she, and Running Bear were in Guthrie, Indian Territory, a new town along the rail line, "to invite some friends and their legal advisers" to a Ghost Dance, but all the Indians there were "friendly and peaceful."[65] Iowas, Missourias, Kickapoos, Cheyennes, Arapahos, and three Lakota "runners" were at the dance, but White Cloud decided to cut the dance short on the second day, perhaps under pressure to do so.[66]

Some agents were worried that their Indians would be contaminated with Ghost Dance ideology from foreign Indians; others were not.[67] Some agents, especially those in Indian Territory, allowed the Indians under their charge to travel to other agencies to learn more about the dance, often fully aware of the purpose of the visits. White Shield, a Southern Cheyenne, was given permission to visit the Tongue River Reservation in August 1890 to investigate. Another Southern Cheyenne named White Buffalo, a former Carlisle student, made the same trip in September.[68] White Elk, a Pawnee, was given a ten-day pass to the Kiowa, Comanche, and Wichita Reservation in late October.[69] While it is impossible to know the purpose of his trip, White Elk surely brought some knowledge of the dance back to the Pawnees. He was a Ghost Dancer at one point in his life, and he devised a Ghost Dance hand game after a vision experience.[70]

Some US officials were confident that if people saw and heard Wovoka or other Ghost Dance apostles themselves, they would not believe their claims. John Mayhugh, a former Western Shoshone agent, advised the commissioner of Indian affairs to allow an expected delegation from "most of the tribes north and northeast" to visits Paiutes in Nevada in November 1890.[71] Mayhugh believed that tribes were seeking "the truth of the Prophecy" and these visits would convince them that Wovoka was not a Messiah. Of course, not every person who encountered Wovoka, Kicking Bear, Sitting Bull, or other influential Ghost Dancers in person thought they were telling the truth.

Eventually, most agents realized that visitation only encouraged the dance's spread.[72] Down in Arizona, Indian Affairs ordered Paiutes to stop visiting Hualapais after a visit from a Ghost Dance emissary named Panamite. Susquatama (Hualapai Charley), a progressive Hualapai leader, asked a judge in Kingman to inform the military about Panamite's "inhuman" dances, which compelled women and children to "dance until they are exhausted and nearly dead" four and five nights in a row.[73] According to the judge, the purpose of the dance was to cause "hurricanes and storms to destroy" white people and the Hualapais who did not participate in the dancing. The commissioner of Indian affairs considered the contact between Paiutes and Hualapais to be so dangerous that he asked the Paiute agent and agents in the vicinity to "repress" their dancing "by any proper means at your command."[74] Weeks later, an Arizona newspaper reported that trouble from the Hualapais was not anticipated but warned that there was "no doubt" that they were "in direct communication with all the tribes" north of Arizona, as if that were a dangerous thing.[75] On December 10, a group of Mohave County, Arizona, citizens petitioned the governor of Arizona for protection from the Hualapai Ghost Dancers, whom they claimed had become "impertinent and ugly" after they "contracted" the "Messiah Craze."[76] But nothing close to an outbreak took place in Arizona even though newspaper suggested the possibility in early 1891.[77]

Other agents west of the Rockies noticed a sharp rise in intertribal activity in the fall of 1890. Newspapers reported that dances were "more frequent than ever" in Nevada, with hundreds at the gatherings.[78] The agent at the Western Shoshone Reservation in northeastern Nevada, William Plumb, reported "so many strangers" coming around, groups from Warm Springs in Oregon and Fort Hall in Idaho and off-reservation Paiutes and Shoshones from Nevada.[79] By December 1890, Agent Plumb reported that Ghost Dancing was well underway. Some of the Shoshones there were "crazed with a religious fervor," and "all of the excitement" there was "caused by visiting Indians from other tribes."[80] Plumb allowed the planned dances to continue occurring one week in each month as long as the visitors were "peaceable and orderly." He told the commissioner of Indian affairs that if the Indians decided not to follow his orders, he "would be powerless" to enforce them because they had guns and he and his Indian police did not have enough. He asked for more guns "in case of emergency," but he also believed that the Ghost Dance was losing ground there. Compared to the dance the month before, there were half as many participants, and the nonbelievers ridiculed the dancers. But he also thought the dancing might rebound if it received "a fresh impetus from outside sources."

Combating the Spread on the Northern Plains

Intertribal visiting also circulated the dance in the northern plains. Movement continued between Wind River, Tongue River, and the Lakota agencies (Pine Ridge, Rosebud, Cheyenne River, and Standing Rock) in the summer and fall of 1890. A group of Pine Ridge Northern Cheyennes visited the Arapahos at Wind River in August 1890, for instance, and in October, some Wind River Northern Arapahos visited the Northern Cheyennes at Tongue River.[81] At one point, the Northern Arapahos assured the army officers at Fort Washakie (on the Wind River Reserve) that Pine Ridge Oglalas were visiting to impart their agricultural knowledge, not to share information about the dance (this was probably a lie; the Northern Arapahos did not want to damage the relationships they had taken pains to cultivate with the officers).[82]

Agents in South Dakota continued to arrest influential emissaries of the dance, hoping that time in the guardhouse might convince illicit travelers to stay home. Kicking Bear from Cheyenne River (who had kinship ties at Wind River), for instance, became a nuisance for a few agents there and was eventually arrested because of his desire to impart knowledge about the dance to other reservations. The new agent at Pine Ridge, D. F. Royer, blamed Kicking Bear for spreading the dance at his agency in August 1890.[83] According to George Sword, the captain of the Indian police at Pine Ridge, Kicking Bear brought more information about the dance back to Pine Ridge sometime after a trip to Wind River that summer. Sword recalled that Kicking Bear spent time with the Northern Arapahos shortly after the Pine Ridge agent arrested Good Thunder on their return from Nevada. While at Wind River, Kicking Bear watched the Northern Arapahos dance and learned their methods, once again making the Arapahos a primary source of Ghost Dance knowledge for Indians from the northern and southern plains.[84] Historian Jeffrey Ostler suspects that Kicking Bear returned to Pine Ridge in August "with a strong argument for continuing the dances even in the face of government opposition."[85] Kicking Bear knew that the Pine Ridge agent wanted to suppress the movement, but he propagated the dance anyway.

Kicking Bear's continued exploits show the believers' determination to spread the dance and ignore the barriers put up by the US government. He returned home and, sometime between August 1890 and early October 1890, instructed dancers at the Cheyenne River Reservation camps of Miniconjou leaders Hump (also of Cheyenne descent) and Big Foot (Spotted Elk). But in early October, he made his way without authorization to Standing Rock at the invitation of Sitting Bull (the Hunkpapa Lakota) and demonstrated the dance there. The dancing lasted several days.[86] In defiance of his agent, James McLaughlin, Sitting Bull had directed six men to slip off the reservation to find Kicking Bear at Cheyenne River and invite him to Standing Rock. In response, McLaughlin ordered Kicking Bear arrested and sent off the reservation, but the Indian police, "fearing the power of Kicking Bear's 'medicine,'" did not expel him. A few days later, however, Kicking Bear willingly returned to Cheyenne River (after Sitting Bull promised McLaughlin that his visitors would leave), but Kicking Bear continued to travel without regard for US government authority.[87] He would later head down to Pine Ridge and Rosebud, leaving Low Dog to lead the dancing at Cherry Creek on the Cheyenne River Reservation.[88]

Kicking Bear was not the only believer in the North who hoped to travel to other reservations that summer. In August 1890, a group of more than thirty Lakotas (including four women and an unknown number of children) from both Cheyenne River and Rosebud, led by the Miniconjou Touch the Clouds and the Brulé High Hawk, were twice denied permission to visit the Crow Reservation.[89] High Hawk was known by an army officer as "the leader of the dances," so officials would not allow his party to go to the Crows. It seems that some Indians believed that the Messiah or his prophet lived somewhere near the Crow Reservation in Montana. According to Joshua Given, a group of Kiowas wanted to visit the Crows in August 1890 (after a visit with the Sioux) because they thought this.[90] That inaccurate piece of information, that the Messiah might be in Montana, was carried

Kicking Bear and Young Man Afraid of His Horses at Pine Ridge, January 1891.
Denver Public Library, Western History Collection, X-31367.

to other agencies like Pine Ridge in August and September 1890.⁹¹ Groups from the Nez Perce (late July), Fort Belknap (August), Fort Berthold (September), Tongue River (September, without permission), and Pine Ridge (late October) Reservations all visited Crows in Montana in the summer and early autumn.⁹² Groups of Crows visited Fort Berthold in July and

Wind River in August.[93] Bad Belly's party of Crows was allowed to visit Pine Ridge and Rosebud in August for a period of sixty days.[94] Bad Belly, however, did not return to the Crow Reservation. Instead, he became a Ghost Dancer and a "teacher or spreader of the Messiah craze," traveling around for the next several years.[95] The agents' decision to grant Bad Belly's visit backfired.

In November, Crazy Bear at Pine Ridge also sought permission to visit the Crows, but he wrote directly to the Crows' agent, who told Crazy Bear that he had to submit his request to his own agent.[96] In early December, Young Man Afraid of His Horses and forty-three other Pine Ridge Oglalas visited the Crows (something Young Man Afraid of His Horses did regularly, see chapters 3 and 4) and camped four miles from the agency. The Crow agent was concerned that the Oglalas were "talking up this Messiah Craze and are talking something of dancing 'Ghost-dances.'"[97] He asked the commanding officer at Fort Custer to remove Young Man Afraid of His Horses and his people immediately. Even though Young Man Afraid of His Horses never appeared to be a Ghost Dance supporter, their presence there was "no good," according to the agent. "The Crow would be more content and better satisfied without the presence of such people."

For an agent who wanted to keep information about the Ghost Dance off his reservation, he made a sensible decision. After all, by September 1890, perhaps one-quarter to one-third of the Lakotas at Pine Ridge, Rosebud, Cheyenne River, and Standing Rock were dance participants or believers or were seeking to learn more about the movement. One missionary at Rosebud estimated that 10 percent were dancing at Standing Rock, 15 percent at Cheyenne River, 30 percent at Rosebud, and 40 percent at Pine Ridge.[98] Jeffrey Ostler estimates that 4,000–5,000 Lakotas were "involved" in the Ghost Dance (there were around 18,000 Lakotas on the reservations).[99] At one dance along White Clay Creek at Pine Ridge, just eighteen miles north of agency headquarters, 2,000 had gathered (including spectators).[100] Perhaps because of the surge in dancing, Lakota agents grew increasingly nervous in late summer, and one agent tried, without success, to use the Indian police to break up dancing.[101]

As summer turned to autumn, amid the growing interest in the dance at the Lakota reservations, agents also continued to struggle to curb communication. Agent McLaughlin at Standing Rock thought the Ghost Dance movement had been "engrafted" to his reservation by letters and visits from Pine Ridge and Rosebud, reporting a surge of Ghost Dance belief among the Hunkpapas in October 1890.[102] The agent at the Fort Berthold Reservation, more than one hundred miles north of Standing Rock, reported that many Mandans, Hidatsas, and Arikaras were "more or less affected" by the information transmitted to them by Lakotas.[103] This information was "undoubtedly" carried to Indians in Canada.

Just south of Standing Rock, the Cheyenne River agent, Perain Palmer, reported on the last day of October 1890 that Indians were coming from other agencies "to be initiated into the Ghost dance."[104] So many were coming that the rations at the camp were quickly exhausted, which led some to kill the agency's cattle to feed the dancers. The agency police watched the Ghost Dancing camps along the Cheyenne River closely to prevent the poaching, although some police joined the Ghost Dancers. Palmer persuaded some "influential Indians from some of the Christian camps," and Narcisse Narcelle, a man of French and Native descent married to a Lakota and employed as an agency farmer, to travel to the dancing camps in an effort to convince the dancers to stop.[105]

But Agent Palmer could do little to stop the flow of information about the dance from entering his agency. He thought that if he could remove Hump, the prominent Miniconjou whom he considered the "chief medicine man of the Ghost dance," and the other leaders from the area, the "craze so great among these wild Indians" would quickly die out. If that was not possible, Agent Palmer believed he could manage the "temper" of the Indians if "no new apostles" came to Cheyenne River.[106] Palmer soon put his police and employees on the task of watching out for any visiting apostles, but it was no use.[107] On November 10, an exasperated Palmer told the commissioner that the Indians were coming to his reserve "from other agencies at will and go from this to other agencies, the Police have no longer any control of these dancers." Around four hundred were dancing at the Cherry Creek camp, "quite a number" of which were "Christian Indians." When told that Indian Affairs was displeased with their actions, the dancers replied that they were displeased with Indian Affairs. They would not stop dancing, and perhaps because of their defiance, Agent Palmer thought that the dancing "hostiles" from all the Sioux agencies were coordinating a joint "outbreak."[108]

The Escalation

Officials saw that the connections were energizing the Ghost Dance. According to a report from Brig. Gen. Thomas Ruger, all the dancing at Cheyenne River would have ended "had not the excitement been fed by Indians coming from other agencies, Pine Ridge and Rosebud in particular."[109] Ruger thought the agent had lost control: "He is not now able to stop the dancing." Eventually, troops were sent to South Dakota to stop the dancing. But rather than sending troops to Cheyenne River, Ruger recommended sending troops to Pine Ridge, "where principally the excitement started amongst the Sioux and from which it is fed by emissaries to other reservations." Pine Ridge was thought to be the main hub.

Unfortunately, Pine Ridge had gotten a new agent, D. F. Royer, in October, just as the dance was attracting more attention. He was a medical doctor, teacher, and newspaper editor, but most important, Royer was a Republican. The 1888 presidential election of Republican Benjamin Harrison led to Royer's spoils appointment. The more competent but Catholic Democrat, Hugh D. Gallagher was released from his duties, and the inexperienced Royer, who had little firsthand knowledge of Native Americans, took charge at Pine Ridge. Royer proved to be a disaster; his ignorance and timidity caused him to send reports to the commissioner of Indian affairs that were misinformed and exaggerated.[110] In early November 1890, he reported that hundreds of Oglalas were dancing at Pine Ridge.[111] Little Wound was made "high priest over all the ghost dances," and he refused to end the dances.[112] Royer continually asked for permission to leave Pine Ridge for a visit to Washington so he could convey the severity of the situation in person, a request that was always denied.[113] Some accused him of wanting to leave out of fear. On November 13, Royer claimed that a large number of dancers, perhaps two hundred, were armed and ready to fight after he had tried to arrest a man for killing agency cattle. He requested troops in a November 18 telegram to the commissioner of Indian affairs: "Indians are dancing in the snow and are wild and crazy.... We need protection, and we need it now. The leaders should be arrested and confined in some military post until the matter is quieted."[114]

Because of Royer's alarm as well as the reports of dissent at other Lakota agencies, an inaccurate interpretation of the Lakota dance as a threat to civilian life, and the secretary of the interior's concern, President Harrison decided that the Ghost Dance deserved the government's complete attention.[115] Commissioner Morgan told the secretary of the interior that the situation at Pine Ridge was "very critical," and because of Royer's reports, he believed that an "outbreak" might be imminent.[116] This created fear that the Ghost Dance could instigate rebellion on any reservation, especially if the "emissaries" were left unchecked. Even though it was clear that a minority of the Lakotas seemed disobedient, the military was eventually tasked by the Department of the Interior to manage the situation. Troops from Fort Robinson under the command of Gen. John Brooke were ordered to Pine Ridge and Rosebud.[117] Several companies were also stationed along the

Cheyenne River, and Fort Sully, Fort Bennett, and Fort Meade were garrisoned, shielding the white settlements surrounding the Badlands with soldiers. Agents were told to cooperate with the military, and a reassured Royer wrote a business associate that "the red skins are red hot but we are going to . . . bring them to terms so they will comply with law and order."[118] By November 20, nearly three thousand soldiers were ready to suppress any Indian threat, a turn of events that made Lakotas nervous.

After troops arrived, hundreds of Lakotas, believers and nonbelievers alike, left their camps in fear. Nonbelievers and some dancers sought refuge at the agency headquarters. A large group of Rosebud Brulés, perhaps two thousand, fled to the northern outskirts of Pine Ridge at Cuny Table in the Badlands, a camp that the military later called the Stronghold.[119] Short Bull (who thought the soldiers were coming to Rosebud to kill him) and his followers were among those who camped there, refusing to give up the dance. Around fifty Rosebud Brulés went to the Cheyenne River Reservation and remained there until April 1891.[120] Two Strike first heard about the troops' arrival while at a trader's store; he put his "women and children into wagons and got on our ponies and left our homes."[121] Pine Ridge officials ordered whites and Indians to head to agency headquarters for their own protection from roaming "hostiles." Some of these hostiles took advantage of the homes left empty, rummaging for supplies and intentionally damaging nonbelievers' property.

Quarantine

Measures were designed to stop the dancing at the Lakota agencies, but they had little success. Directed by the commissioner of Indian affairs, agents tried to prevent the Indians under their charge from having contact with Indians from other agencies. On November 22, 1890, the acting commissioner sent a circular letter to every agency office in the West. Because it was "very important in view of the tendency of such excitement to spread and obtain a general hold upon the Indians," he ordered agents to keep his office advised on their "condition of affairs" regarding the Ghost Dance.[122] Officials saw the dance as a contagion that needed to be quarantined to the already-affected areas. In response to the commissioner's orders, Agent George Steel would not allow some Gros Ventres from Fort Belknap, Montana, to visit the Blackfeet Reservation. He did not want his reservation "infected in any way" with the Ghost Dance.[123] It would "not be for the good of the soul, but for evil," Steel told Agent A. O. Simmons at Fort Belknap;

there needed to be "as little visiting as possible at present" between reservations. The connections among the tribes needed to be severed.

Although agents assumed that their tribes would begin dancing if they obtained information about the dance, that was not the case. There was little interest in the dance at the Blackfeet Reservation in Montana, for instance, but Blackfeet knew about it. Not only had Blackfeet visited Wovoka's Walker River Reservation, they were also connected to sources of information about the dance's progress at other reservations, and they knew about the troops being sent to Pine Ridge and Rosebud. Strangely, Agent Steel believed that Blackfeet knew "too little in regard to religion to have any knowledge of the second coming of Christ."[124] But like other agents, Steel was worried that the Blackfeet could become interested in the dance if they received more information about it. He asked officials visiting his reservation to keep quiet because any inquiry or talk of the dance might have "injurious effect instead of good."[125] "It is a very easy matter to agitate the minds of the Indians," Steel declared, which compelled him to remain vague when several Blackfeet asked him about the Ghost Dance.[126] Perhaps he did not understand that Blackfeet like William Jackson, who was literate, received information about the dance from white pen pals like George Bird Grinnell among other printed sources.[127]

Agent Simmons at the Fort Belknap Reservation eventually took similar precautions to limit intertribal contact. He thought it would be wise to use a cavalry company to "restrain" the outbreak of the dance by capturing "renegades" and the traveling "emissaries" of the movement. On November 21, he telegraphed the commanding officer at nearby Fort Assiniboine to report that the Messiah craze was "very strong" at his agency and "nearly all" were "affected."[128] The dancers prepared "quietly" and kept their actions "secret." But only eight days later, Simmons presented a calmer assessment of the situation to the commissioner of Indian affairs. He reported that many of the Gros Ventres and Assiniboines at Fort Belknap had been "attacked" by "the Messiah craze" but it was of a "light nature."[129] There was no threat of violence. But he noted that the "craze" was brought to the people by a Gros Ventres man formerly of Fort Belknap who had been living with the Northern Arapahos at Wind River. The man returned to his friends and family at Fort Belknap with news of the Messiah, and some received it "with unquestioning faith."[130]

Farther south, the agent at Rosebud, J. George Wright, also refused to allow suspected Ghost Dance leaders to visit other reservations. Crow Dog and Two Strike repeatedly asked to visit Pine Ridge but were denied each time. Nevertheless, the two Brulé Lakotas ignored the threat of punishment and went to Pine Ridge while Agent Wright was away from the agency.[131] A special agent in charge in Wright's absence had apparently given Crow Dog and Two Strike the permission they needed.[132] Wright blamed this visit for the later coordination in mid-November 1890 between the Ghost Dancers at Rosebud and those at Pine Ridge.

Agents at other South Dakota agencies were also troubled with increasing off-reservation traffic driven by the Ghost Dance. In November, the Cheyenne River agent reported to the army that delegates from the Sisseton Reservation were at Cheyenne River while a group of fifteen families from the Lower Brule Reservation headed to Cheyenne River without permission.[133] Days later, Agent A. P. Dixon, in charge at the Crow Creek and Lower Brule Reservations, arrested three Ghost Dance "leaders from other reservations" but discharged them after the men promised "good behavior."[134] Agent Dixon realized that the movement between reservations was causing headaches for all the Sioux agents, the Lakotas' and the Dakotas' alike. He refused to issue or accept any new travel passes. A week later, after a small band of his Brulés began dancing near Rosebud, Dixon had its leaders arrested, recalled all his Indians who were off the reservation with passes, and sent all visitors home.[135] Seventeen were arrested "for participating in the 'Ghost Dance' and for endeavoring to induce others to engage therein . . . for disturbing the peace and mental attitudes of the Indians of that reserve," and "for a general disobedience of orders of the Agent in charge of said reservation."[136]

The Yankton agent had the same strategy to "prevent visitors from the western agencies . . . and to restrain the Indians from this agency from going abroad."[137] Nevertheless, dancers were still able to pass through their reservation borders. The *Omaha Daily Bee* reported that the vigilance of the agency authorities could do little to stop the "emissaries of the Messiah."[138] A party of Yanktons who were "worked into a state of extreme excitement" were headed to the Lower Brule Reservation, passing directly through Chamberlain, South Dakota on wagons led by fifteen or twenty teams of horses. Kuwapi, a Rosebud Brulé, was arrested in November at the White Swan community on the Yankton Reservation for "teaching the Ghost Dance and preaching the doctrine of the New Indian Messiah."[139] At Tongue River, the Northern Cheyenne Porcupine had been threatened with arrest by the temporary authority there, special agent J. A. Cooper, if he continued to lead dances.[140] Porcupine had also told Cooper that he did not believe Wovoka, but Porcupine later admitted that he only said that to avoid being put in prison. Porcupine believed that the dance would "make friends between the whites and Indians," but he knew that the federal officials did not have the same belief.[141] Big Foot (Spotted Elk) at Cheyenne River had similar misgivings under the threat of punishment. He told Agent Perain Palmer in late October 1890 that he was "only leading or advising with a view to thoroughly investigate" the Ghost Dance, not promote it.

But by late November 1890, following the arrival of troops south at Pine Ridge, forbidden travel continued, and Agent Palmer's reports to the Indian Office sounded dire. There were some Standing Rock and Pine Ridge Indians there with the Cheyenne River dancers. "They have their runners all over from different agencies," he recorded in his private notes.[142] Palmer also noted that Big Foot's dances had "influenced many Christian Indians to dance." The Ghost Dancers were disobedient; Big Foot, Hump, and other leaders were unwilling to talk to the agent or the agency farmers; and it was thought that Big Foot had his people preparing for war. Some of the nondancers told Palmer that the dancers wanted to fight soon.[143] To make matters worse, Palmer thought he had positive evidence that "the best make of guns" were being sold to the dancers by white merchants.[144] Little No Heart, a progressive chief, asked Palmer via letter to assign more than one policeman to the dancing camp at the mouth of the Moreau River.[145]

Reports at Cheyenne River began to sound more optimistic for a time. Narcisse Narcelle was able to convince 482 dancers (including 26 from the Standing Rock Agency) to leave their camps and go to the agency headquarters, where many surrendered their guns. According to Agent Palmer, Hump was "induced to turn against the dancers," and those who came in to the agency were "quiet and orderly," and they "expressed their regrets for the trouble they caused."[146] But Big Foot, who was called a "bad man" by a frustrated general, refused to come in.[147] He and his nearly one hundred men could not be persuaded to stop dancing. On December 12, Narcelle reported to Agent Palmer that the dancing at Cherry Creek was not letting up. The camp had "just got the news" that the Pine Ridge and Rosebud Indians had "left their Agencies and gone west."[148] According to Narcelle, the dancers were excited about it. Special Agent James Cooper at Pine Ridge told the agent at the Fort Berthold Reservation of the "serious trouble" there, it looked "very much as though bloodshed will ultimately be the result here."[149]

Throughout November and December, men and women who refused to stop dancing at Cheyenne River were arrested.[150] White Buffalo Man, who had come to dance from Standing Rock, was among them. He was taken to Fort Pierre and placed under guard. While he was with the state attorney, he was able to write a letter (or have a letter written) in English to his nephew Sitting Bull (the Hunkpapa Lakota headman) at Standing Rock. In those weeks, Sitting Bull was reportedly corresponding with folks at all the Lakota reservations and reservations in Wyoming, Indian Territory, and Canada ("assisted . . . by a large number of his tribe . . . who have been educated").[151] It seems White Buffalo Man's letter was never delivered to Sitting Bull, mostly likely at the instruction of the Standing Rock agent James McLaughlin, who was censuring the mail there. White Buffalo Man wrote:

> I understand that my rashens are stoped, and I am now under guard by the soldiers, and that they are talking of sending me off somewhere. They wanted me to stop the dance, and I did not do it, so I understand that is what it is all done for. Will you let me know why they are doing me this way. If you can stop the action taken against me I will take it a great favor. Respectfully White Buffaloman.[152]

White Buffalo Man knew that he had been arrested for dancing, but he could not understand why. For him, the Ghost Dance was harmless, and the US government misunderstood the movement.

Another letter intercepted at the Standing Rock Agency office (postmarked at Pine Ridge on December 7, 1890) came from Spotted Mountain Sheep and was intended to be read by his brother-in-law Kills Standing and Luke Najinhkte. Spotted Mountain Sheep told the Standing Rock men that there were twenty companies of soldiers at Pine Ridge. "We thought of fighting them," he wrote, "but gave it up until the spring. Then is the time we decided on fighting."[153] Spotted Mountain Sheep exaggerated the number of Brulés (10,100 lodges) that arrived from Rosebud to support the dance. For Agent McLaughlin, this letter that he stole was evidence of a conspiracy among the Lakotas. McLaughlin, like other agents, did not want information about a possible uprising sent to his reservation. Agents McLaughlin, Palmer, and Royer all thought that the culmination of the Ghost Dance, with its prophecy of a changed world, would be an "Indian outbreak." But Spotted Mountain Sheep's letter and his thoughts on "fighting" were a response to the unnecessary military presence on his reservation, not a product of Wovoka's message or the meaning of the Ghost Dance as Lakotas understood it.

US government officials tried to stop the spread of the movement by controlling the flow of information, but they never understood the ideas Native Americans were communicating. Moreover, Native Americans were persistent in their desire to leave their reservations and learn more about the dance, spread information about it, and practice it. They remained mobile during a time with the tightest colonial restrictions on intertribal visiting and corresponding. The US government grew frustrated with its lack of control, officials resorted to calling the military to reestablish order, and the country's attention turned to the Ghost Dance. As we will see in the next chapter, Native Americans from across North America, believers and nonbelievers alike, responded by communicating their thoughts within a continental network.

CHAPTER 7

The Ghost Dance in a Continental Network

Although thousands of Native Americans participated in the Ghost Dance, the majority of those who heard Wovoka's message did not dance. But most of the people living at Walker River; Pyramid Lake; Western Shoshone; Fort Hall; Wind River; Tongue River; Pine Ridge; Rosebud; Standing Rock; Cheyenne River; Crow Creek; Yankton; Crow; Fort Berthold; Fort Belknap; Fort Peck; Santee; Omaha and Winnebago; Cheyenne-Arapaho; Kiowa, Comanche, and Wichita; Pawnee and Ponca; Caddo; Hualapai; Uintah and Ouray; Southern Ute; and other reservations did learn about the movement. The Ghost Dance became a common purpose for the diverse Native American groups of the West—a purpose not solely to propagate the movement, which many did, but simply to inform others about it, regardless of tribal bonds or kinship. Because it was such an important set of ideas, it was crucial for many Native Americans, whether they thought these ideas were true or not, to learn more and communicate their views to both Natives and non-Natives.

Thus, Native Americans shrewdly used literacy not only to spread the movement but also to make sense of the information surrounding it. A Native-led dialogue about the Ghost Dance spanned the continent. Some wrote to promote Wovoka's instructions to live a good, peaceful life; to love one another; and to work hard, while others wrote to criticize the new Messiah's claims and to convince other Natives not to participate in the dancing. Some wrote to better inform America's non-Native population about the realities of the movement and the escalating situation at the Lakota agencies. Others chose to defend their religion in letters to whites and to the American press.

Natives also used non-Native sources to stay informed about the dance and the US government's responses to it. Newspapers were eagerly printing sensational reports on the "Messiah Craze," as it became known. The dancers at the Cherry Creek camp at Cheyenne River, which the US government thought to be full of hostiles, regularly sent "educated Indians" to Pierre to buy newspapers to discover the latest news.¹ From Standing Rock, Agent McLaughlin told Commissioner Morgan in November 1890, "There are now so many of our Indians who speak English and read the newspapers that current news is soon known to them."² Officials noticed that English literacy seemed to be giving Indians an unforeseen advantage in strategizing against agency and military tactics to end the Ghost Dance. Newspapers throughout the country reported on November 18, 1890, that Gen. Nelson Miles was hesitant to release troop movements to the press because Indians were reading about them in the newspapers and adjusting accordingly. "Anything I might say would be telegraphed all over the country and tomorrow would be in the Indian camps," Gen. Miles told the reporter. "I have nothing to say now beyond the fact that there is reason for grave apprehensions of trouble with the Indians on the plains."³ Miles was reticent with the press for a reason; he ordered troops onto Pine Ridge and Rosebud on November 19.⁴

After their arrival, the army hoped to be able to weed out the "hostile" Ghost Dancing Indians from the "friendlies" and stop them from moving around, but it proved difficult.⁵ Frederic Remington, who was emerging as America's great artist of Western themes, reported in *Harper's Weekly* that the military still did not anticipate the Indians' ability to read. Lakotas were able to gather intelligence by glancing at a front page of a newspaper. "The thing that is most remarkable about this concentration of troops," Remington observed, "is that the white people of the country read it in the evening papers, and with the first rays of tomorrow's sun the Ogallalas, the Cheyennes, and the Sitting Bull people will see it with their own eyes."⁶ Remington wondered, "Why did not the white people know it before?" "The reason is this," he wrote:

> Not until late years could the Indians read English, but now the school-boys and squaw men can, and I have picked up copies of the New York and Chicago papers on the counters of an Indian trader's store, where a room was full of Indians, three or four of whom could probably read as well as most men. The cause of the secrecy is at once apparent.... In these days a military officer has to conduct his operations as secretly in Indian war as he would in a civilized case.⁷

It was surprising to learn that the colonized were using the strategies of colonization (assimilation-driven education) against the colonizers. Remington proposed that an Omaha paper should print misinformation about troop numbers to trick the hostiles into rushing into an unwinnable battle. "That paper would be on the counter in a trader's store inside of a day and a half, and the Ogallalas in all probability, would be scampering over the plains on the way to meet the northern Cheyennes and join issue with Uncle Sam's troops," he guessed.

But Natives did not believe everything they read in the papers. They knew reports were typically inaccurate. A few weeks after the troops arrived, an "Indian spy" named Ghost Horse reported to the *Chicago Tribune* (in a story titled, "Hostiles Are Well Posted") that the Indians at the Cherry Creek camp who were reading newspapers from Pierre laughed "heartily when they heard of the great alarm everywhere. . . . It seemed to strengthen their belief that the Messiah was coming and that the whites were becoming afraid and getting ready to die off or flee and leave the lands to the Indians."[8] Historians have studied how the press shaped the national perception of the "Messiah craze" and created white anxiety that led to events like the Wounded Knee tragedy, but little has been said about the Native reaction to the sensationalization of their beliefs.[9] Beginning in the summer of 1890 and peaking that fall, newspapers printed plenty of false rumors of Indian outbreaks and violence, some that prompted fear in the white populations surrounding reservations. Reporters often printed outright lies to dramatize their papers' coverage.

Some Natives were afraid of the effect the press was having on white minds as early as June 1890. Frank Locke, a twenty-four-year-old Brulé at Rosebud, wrote that his people were afraid that their "friends in East will hear the report of the outbreak of the Rosebud which will be a story."[10] Locke said this outbreak was only "a little confusion" between the Indians and the Indian police about a man who ran away from the guardhouse. Everything was quiet at Rosebud, according to Locke, but they were "afraid that newsman will make too big a picture . . . that might excite our friends." By December 1890, Locke's fears were realized. He blamed the newspapers, which were heavily invested in the "Messiah craze," for the troubles at the South Dakota agencies. Locke believed the reporters intentionally frightened the public because they were only interested in getting paid.[11] Edgar Fire Thunder at Pine Ridge reported in late November that there was little worry there; only "some of the Indians had Ghost Dance, but think they will stop now."[12] A "good many soldiers" had arrived because "the newspapers told that the Indians wanted to fight white men." He wrote, "That's all a mistake." Frank Twiss, also at Pine Ridge, blamed the newspapers as well.[13] Two Strike and Little Wound, both dance leaders, told the *Omaha Daily Bee* that they did not appreciate how they were being portrayed in the newspapers as bad people. They were simply practicing their religion.[14]

Natives also combated the glorified colonial narrative that filled newspapers across America. An Indian named John Daylight (Masse-Hadjo) wrote a letter to the *Chicago Tribune* defending the Ghost Dance movement.[15] Responding to an editor who mocked the movement, Daylight presented a blistering critique of American Christianity, accusing whites of hypocrisy and cruelty. From the Quapaw Mission in Indian Territory, he wrote:

> You say: "If the United States army would kill a thousand or so of the dancing Indians there would be no more trouble." I judge by the above language you are a "Christian" and are disposed to do all in your power to advance the cause of Christ. You are doubtless a worshiper of the white man's Savior, but are unwilling that the Indians should have a "Messiah" of their own. The Indians have never taken kindly to the Christian religion as preached and practiced by the whites. Do you know why this is the case? Because the Good Father of all has given us a better religion—a religion that is all good and no bad, a religion that is adapted to our wants. . . . The code of morals as practiced by the white race will not compare with the morals of the Indians. . . . If our Messiah does come we shall not try to force you into our belief. We will never burn innocent women at the stake or pull men to pieces with horses because they refuse to join in our ghost dances. . . . You are anxious to get hold of our Messiah so you can put him in irons. This you may do—in fact you may crucify him as you did that other one, but you cannot convert the Indians to the Christian religion until you contaminate them with the blood of the white man.

Daylight believed that the Indians' religion was superior to the white man's because it was peaceful and uncorrupted. It was "adapted" to the Indians' "wants." Daylight's letter was reprinted in papers throughout the country; the *Sacramento Daily* said it ranked with the "speeches of Tecumseh, Phillip, Black Hawk and Logan" for its "pathos and satire and rhetorical eloquence."[16] The letter was also featured in Sophia Alice Callahan's 1891 novel *Wynema, A Child of the Forest*, the first novel written by a woman of Native American descent. Callahan used "Old" Masse Hadjo's letter to present a Native's perspective in the aftermath of Wounded Knee and to demonstrate the usefulness of Native literacy.[17]

Men and women at the Cheyenne-Arapaho and Kiowa, Comanche, and Wichita Reservations also stayed informed by reading the papers.[18] After the Wounded Knee Massacre in late December 1890, Lt. Hugh Lennox Scott was worried that the information in the papers—the "stories about the arming of the settlers in Oklahoma and Texas and the disarming of the

Indians, the fighting with the Sioux"—might "excite" the Indians in Oklahoma more than they already were.[19] He noted that the papers were read at the Kiowa, Comanche, and Wichita Reservation by the former students of eastern boarding schools. At those boarding schools, pupils received news from letters, their teachers, and newspapers. In fact, soon after Wounded Knee, the superintendent at White's Institute in Indiana reported that his students were "anxious about the action and fate of their people in the present Indian trouble."[20]

It seems some Native groups received the bulk of their information about the movement through newspaper accounts. The Nez Perces' agent claimed that, as far as he knew, "no emissaries of the faith" had visited his reserve in Idaho by late November 1890, but the Nez Perces were learning about the "craze" from the papers, just like he was.[21] Newspapers allowed tribes outside South Dakota to follow the troubles the Lakotas were having with the US government in late 1890. A couple of Ute chiefs in Utah told their agent that they had heard the Lakota news from the papers but they could not understand "what it all meant."[22] The agent did not think the chiefs had much interest in the Ghost Dance, but he told the commissioner that if "emissaries from the hostile tribes" made it to the Uintah Agency, the people there might show interest. The Tongue River agent did not notice any Ghost Dancing in November 1890, but he reported that the Indians were "fully informed on the disturbances existing elsewhere."[23] The Yankton, Wind River, and Fort Belknap agents had similar reports.[24] A Sac and Fox council purportedly laughed at an article that falsely claimed they were dancing.[25]

Some learned of false newspaper reports through letters from other tribes. In June 1890, the Southern Utes in Colorado (Buckskin Charley, Ignacio, and others) informed the Northern Utes at the Uintah and Ouray Agency in Utah that they had learned of reports that the Utes intended to make trouble with white settlers. Of course, the reports were not true, and the Northern Utes responded with shock. They replied to their southern brethren:

> We feel bad that a report has been circulated that we want to fight and make trouble. We have not thought of such a thing, we the same as you want to be at peace with all, we are farming and attending to our cattle and horses and do not want trouble.... We all of us want peace and do not like it when we are reported as making trouble, we are friends of all the whites about here and are getting along well.[26]

Six months later, in December, the Northern Utes wrote to Sevaro of the Southern Utes that the "Sioux trouble" was "too far away for us to pay attention to it, their affairs should not bother us."[27]

For some Natives, combating false reports of outbreak was a constant struggle. As the press converged on Pine Ridge and Rosebud in November 1890 and white authorities and settlers grew nervous, reports of angry, conniving Indians were widespread. In late November, Dr. Charles Eastman, a Santee Dakota physician employed at Pine Ridge, tried his best to dispel rumors of outbreak there. He wrote to Frank Wood, a white Bostonian who was an Indian rights advocate, that there was no danger of violence and that nearly all the Indians were willing to give up the Ghost Dance (only Little Wound and thirty families were out dancing). He was treating the sick among the Ghost Dancers just the same as the nonbelievers.[28] Red Cloud told Eastman that he thought the dance would "melt away like a spring snow."[29] Likewise, John Tiokasin, a former Hampton Institute student at Standing Rock, reported to his former school on December 2 that there were "not more than a hundred Indians who have believed in the new Christ" and that the people were "all right" and "quiet."[30] "I heard that the white people are talking about," he wrote, "saying that Indians want to fight, but I say that the Indians do not want to fight." Tiokasin suspected that the whites who talked "about fighting . . . are fooling themselves or maybe they afraid of Indians."

Native leaders in Nevada also had to write letters to assure the whites near them that their people were not planning for an outbreak of violence. Newspapers like the *Walker Lake Bulletin* and the *Nevada State Journal* stirred the fears of settlers by reporting exaggerated rumors of imminent violence. The US Army did not occupy the territory in great numbers in Nevada like it did on the Great Plains. It would only take a few hundred Indians, the *Nevada State Journal* warned, to "lay waste hundreds of homes and massacre their occupants before relief could reach them."[31] Responding to white fears, the Shoshone headman Captain John offered to help defend the residents of Nye County in the rare event of an attack from another tribe.[32]

Other Indians were worried that federal officials might receive inaccurate information that their people were growing antagonistic. Wolf Chief, a Mandan at the Fort Berthold Reservation who wrote to officials frequently, wanted President Harrison and Commissioner Morgan to know that the Mandans and Gros Ventres were "good people"; they did not want to fight the white man or the Sioux. "We are a good friend to the Whites," Wolf Chief assured them. "We very few Indians and we are very Poor."[33] When

Wolf Chief heard that Sitting Bull (the Lakota) "want to fight white mans," he thought it was "very foolish." The Mandans and Gros Ventres were struggling to find enough to eat that winter. They did not know what they would do for food. Wolf Chief seemed to be worried that their rations might be held back because of the events at Pine Ridge and Rosebud. He assured the president that they had no part in it. They were not "dangerous tribes."

Quanah Parker, a Comanche headman at the Kiowa, Comanche, and Wichita Reservation, had to denounce a newspaper that reported his involvement in the dance with the other Sitting Bull (the Northern Arapaho) and his desire to incite "various tribes to mischief." Parker told the editor that it was all a "fabrication" and sardonically replied:

> I will state for the benefit of the anxious public, that I have not attended any ghost dances with the Cheyenne, nor have I been to visit my red brother of the North (Sitting Bull), or know any more about the Indian on the Cheyenne reservation or in Sitting Bull's tribe, except what I am told, than if they were on the other side of the big water, and will say that but few of the Comanche Indians pay any attention to the Messiah craze, and those who do are crazy. Some of the Kiowa are taking the craze, but I don't know to what extent, and as for inciting various tribes to mischief, it would be like a crazy man to even think of such a thing with the little handful of warriors that all the tribes could combine and turn out.[34]

Even the Kiowas who were Ghost Dancing were worried that the Lakota troubles were causing bad publicity for the movement. The Kiowa agent reported to the commissioner that Kiowas, most of whom were still "faithful believers," were "behaving themselves remarkably well considering the conduct of their brethren in other parts of the country . . . and the pressure brought to bear upon them by sensational reports and bad advice, which they, no doubt receive from the North."[35] Some Kiowas told Lieutenant Scott that the Lakotas were always "too excitable."[36] They wondered why the Lakotas did not just wait until the "change is made," meaning the time when Wovoka's prophecy of a new world would come about. It would all happen; it would "be all right without fighting." Rather than make war, Scott stated that Kiowas believed "their prophet wants them to live at peace with all men."

Believers, Nonbelievers, and the Uncertain

Other white observers interpreted the Ghost Dance differently than Lieutenant Scott, who had a talent for empathy. Some newspapers, like the

Omaha Daily Bee, attributed the wide dissemination of the Ghost Dance to the superstitious and naive nature of Indians. "It is easy to believe," the paper commented, "that the prophecy has been passed around among all the tribes of the northwest . . . being generally accepted as a true forecast of what is come to pass."[37] But, of course, not everyone who heard the Messiah's story became a believer. Many white Americans assumed that the Indians' inherent naivete ensured the success of the Ghost Dance movement. It was thought that skepticism was not a part of their uncivilized minds and that Indians accepted religious ideas without reasoning and short of evidence. One reporter proclaimed that "no stronger proselyting power is possessed by any people or class in the world than that of Indian over Indian."[38] They were too trusting of their own kind, he thought, and they believed what they heard.

Indians did, in fact, investigate and criticize the movement, and in the process, they helped spread information about it. Sometime in 1890, Abe Somers, a twenty-two-year-old Southern Cheyenne who had spent five years at Carlisle, visited the Northern Cheyennes at the Tongue River Reservation in Montana for an extended period. He became a trusted interpreter for the Northerners.[39] Somers's cousin Ridge Walker had accompanied Porcupine and Big Beaver on their journey to see Wovoka in early 1890. The three Northern Arapahos, and Porcupine most prominently, became teachers of the Ghost Dance at Tongue River. Even though Somers was doubtful about what he heard about the Ghost Dance from Ridge Walker and Porcupine, he still relayed their explanation of the movement south to the Cheyenne-Arapaho Reservation in Indian Territory. But before he returned home to the Cheyenne-Arapaho Reservation, Somers made a stop at the Haskell Institute in Lawrence, Kansas, in February 1891, where he told what he had learned about the Ghost Dance to students from several tribes, including Henry Dawson North (Henry Shave Head), a Southern Arapaho. At the request of the Haskell superintendent, Somers also made a written statement that the students, and perhaps other Natives, could read. Still doubting the legitimacy of the dance, he wrote:

> Dear Friends, one and all: Don't force your and others' minds on this letter, but resist it and keep your minds from it. I simply want to tell you just what I learned from Mr. Porcupine, Big Beaver, and I am sorry to say from one of them, a cousin of mine, Ridge Walker, son of Beaver Claws. I expect many of you are wishing to know, and perhaps many of you have already heard about it. I have met them face to face, and have questioned them personally when I met them; and

so I learned from them some of their Messiah ideas. I try to make an account of just what I have learned from these three persons.[40]

Next, Somers recounted Porcupine's narrative of his experience with "the Messiah" at Walker Lake, which is very similar to Porcupine's other recorded testimonies. According to Somers, Porcupine claimed that Wovoka said the earth was "getting old and worn out, and the people getting bad" and that he was going "to renew everything as it used to be, and make it better." The "youth of everyone would be renewed in the spring," the dead would be "resurrected," and the earth would be made large enough to contain "us all." Porcupine told Somers that Wovoka condemned fighting, saying it was "bad and we must keep from it" and that "the earth was to be all good hereafter; that we must be friends with one another." Wovoka told them that they "must tell all the people we meet about these things."

Somers wrote that there were "many other things wonderful" that he could not describe, but he did not believe them. "Please don't follow the ideas of that man," Somers pleaded. "He is not the Christ. No man in the world can see God at any time. Even the angels of God cannot."[41] Somers was not a proponent of the dance, but he communicated its meaning to others; he was a relay, and some found truth in the message. Richard Pratt, superintendent at Carlisle, once told Standing Elk, a Northern Cheyenne headman at Pine Ridge, that he was glad that Cheyennes listened to Abe Somers, because his "knowledge of the English language" would "continue to be a great help your people."[42] Somers, in fact, did what he could to help his people using literacy, but probably not in the way Pratt had hoped.

James Murie, a Hampton graduate of both Pawnee and white descent who became an important ethnologist, also had a complicated experience with the Ghost Dance. He took part in the dances at the Pawnee Reservation in late 1891 and wrote to the Pawnee agent about it, explaining his participation. The letter demonstrates the need some felt to experience the dance before judging its significance. It also places us in the mind of a Pawnee man who had a deep connection to white culture but also needed to be a part of his people's community. He wrote,

> No doubt what you have heard is that I took part in the dance—understand not that I believed in it, but that I was curious to find out what good there was in it, and if it was wrong.... I just go into it myself and find out. I was with them 3 days, and it had no effect on my mind or physical power, nor my will power. I saw while with them that those who are weak minded were effected.... All through the dancing they are told to have one mind upon Christ and the deceased

Ghost relation. Major I am glad to say that I found some good true hearts who only put their trust in our God and his son, Christ. They would not put their whole trust and faith in this unknown God.[43]

Murie continued, telling his agent he had tried to convince some that there was only one true God, offering his opinion on the dance's psychological powers of mesmerism and concluding that he wanted to go dance again in order to learn more.[44] He asked the agent to save his letters so that he could "make a report of it to some newspaper."[45]

While information about the movement reached thousands of Native Americans, not all of them were convinced. In fact, the large majority of those who learned about the Ghost Dance movement did not become devoted dancers. Moreover, some neighboring tribal nations received the same information from the same sources, but they responded to it in different ways. For instance, there were believers among the Brulé Lakotas at the Lower Brule Reservation, but there were few believers among the Dakotas at the Crow Creek Reservation, which was just east across the Missouri River.[46] Crow Creek Dakotas had also heard about the dance from Oglalas, Rosebud Brulés, and Miniconjous, just like their neighbors had, but most at Crow Creek did not want to take part in the dance, despite being in "constant communication" with the other Sioux groups.[47] Acquiring knowledge about the movement did not guarantee full acceptance of it. And although it is impossible to gauge thousands of Native people's acceptance of the movement's ideas, it is clear that many were skeptics, and they used the same methods of communication to investigate and express their concerns.

Even though most Lakotas did not dance, troops nonetheless arrived at the Lakota Agencies in late November 1890 because of the dancing. As we saw in the last chapter, tensions rose dramatically between the Ghost Dancers and the US government. Natives throughout the West, both believers and nonbelievers, felt it. Some Natives tried to convince others not to instigate conflict. A group of Northern Arapahos under Black Coal at Wind River sent word to other tribes that they were "peaceful" and wanted "all," both Native and white, "to keep the peace."[48] While some messengers were sent out to impart a message of peace, it seems other Natives tried to stop the dancing altogether. According to one newspaper report from Indian Territory, the Iowas received many Cheyenne, Arapaho, and Creek visitors and "two messengers from the Sioux" who would "do all in their power to allay, as far as possible, the Messiah craze."[49] It is not known why those messengers wanted the Iowas to stop believing, but their visits occurred as troops were gathering at Pine Ridge and Rosebud to prevent an outbreak. Some

Natives were afraid of the consequences that the dance's persistence might bring. Luther Standing Bear, a Lakota schoolteacher at Rosebud, warned others not to dance because he believed the US government would stop them with force.[50]

Some dancers sent letters to warn other dancers of possible violence against them. Letters from Northern Cheyennes at Pine Ridge to Southern Cheyennes in Indian Territory reported the threat of troops and their decision to stop dancing. Because of the information provided by their northern relatives, Southern Cheyennes knew that the government was threatening to use force to end the dance. The same might happen at their reservation. An army officer reported that Southern Cheyennes lost enthusiasm for the dance following those letters, but it was not nearly the end of the movement among them; they just took a more cautious approach.[51]

Lakota Believers and Nonbelievers

Division grew at the Lakota agencies between the believers and the nonbelievers. Some nonbelievers, worried that continued dancing would only provoke a harsh reaction from the US government, began telling federal authorities what they thought was happening at the Lakota reservations. In late October, the progressive leaders at Rosebud, including Swift Bear, Hollow Horn Bear, Sky Bull, Pretty Eagle, and He Dog, wrote the president, saying that many of their people were "crazy and excited over the new religion which has come among us."[52] "On this account," they continued, "and our being hungry—our young men are feeling very bad, and think the Government is trying to starve us to death." The men urged the president to send the rations and beef that had been promised not only to prevent starvation but also to stymie the popularity of the Ghost Dance. American Horse, Fast Thunder, Spotted Horse, and other progressives at Pine Ridge made a similar argument to their agent in late November.[53] George Sword, the Oglala captain of the US Indian police at Pine Ridge, wrote Commissioner Morgan that some of the head chiefs allowed their people to Ghost Dance, but he did not think that was the "right way to worship."[54] The dancers were told to stop, but "they never listen," and Sword was "getting tired of it."

At Standing Rock, Thomas Ashley, a twenty-three-year-old Hampton graduate, was disappointed that the Ghost Dance was affecting his people. "I am sorry to say some of us do not use all our education," he wrote to his agent. "Oh father help me through this trouble so that I may live happy in this dark world and work for my Father which is in heaven."[55] Even Ashley's wife had gone "back on old way" and was wearing traditional Lakota clothing. Sam White Bird at the Lower Brule Reservation wrote a commentary in a November issue of *Iapi Oaye*, the Dakota-language paper printed by the Dakota Mission, titled "Messiya Itonsni" (the lie of the Messiah, or the false prophet).[56] He understood the Ghost Dance to be the product of the devil (*wakha sica*) and his false prophet. White Bird hoped that his people would stop believing the lie and reminded them that the Bible warned that false prophets only led to destruction.

Some Lakota dancers, however, blamed nonbelieving progressives for intentionally misrepresenting the Ghost Dance as a possibly violent militant movement to their agents with the hope that dancing would be suppressed. Issowonie, an Oglala, told Short Bull that his own people's lies about the dance "caused the soldiers to come here." Crow Dog, the infamous Brulé murderer of Spotted Tail, blamed the interpreters at Rosebud for lying to the agent, telling him "that the Ghost Dance was really a war dance."[57] According to these men, progressives helped convince the US government that the Lakota Ghost Dance was not just a harmless religious movement but one that would lead to trouble. Relations between the dancers and the nonbelievers fell apart in November. Elaine Goodale saw many families divided over the movement, "and feeling was intense." After the troops arrived, some dancers vandalized the abandoned homes of progressives at Pine Ridge and Rosebud, destroying farming tools and stealing horses and cattle.[58] Swift Bear, a progressive Brulé chief who sought shelter at Fort Randall, did not want to come into the agency for his rations, fearing retribution from dancers (and US soldiers).[59]

American Horse wrote to his non-Native friend James Landy in Cincinnati on two occasions to tell him that some Rosebud Indians, upset about the troops, had severely damaged his and others' houses at Pine Ridge, stolen thirty-four of his horses, and killed all of his cattle. They also shot at a large photo of American Horse that Landy had given him, which was hanging on the wall; one bullet was sent through his forehead, another through the heart.[60] American Horse believed that he had "many enemies" because he had "the idea to lead my people toward civilization." He was not discouraged by the damage to his property, but, he confessed to Landy, "at times the position is a very unpleasant one among the Indians."[61] He thought some of the nonprogressives hated him enough to shoot him "if they should have an opportunity." He wrote, "If these Indian should kill me remember I shall die for a good cause."

Ideological differences divided Lakotas that fall. Ring Thunder, a Brulé headman at Rosebud who did not believe in the dance, was sent by his agent to counsel with the dancers at Black Pipe Creek to try to convince them to stop. But the dancers would not listen to Ring Thunder, and they called him a fool. According to Ring Thunder's letter to his former agent Lebbeus Foster Spencer, they told him that if he joined them, he "would never have any more pain or sorrow," but if he "followed after the ways of the white men," his "path would be hard and full of trouble."[62] But Ring Thunder told the dancers that he had once been "one of their bravest warriors," but he no longer wanted to fight; his heart was "not with them." Ring Thunder wrote that "the ways of the white man seem hard at times," but if the government would give them back their beef and rations, all would be well with them.

Other Lakotas wrote to whites to explain why they were not dancing. Good Voice, a progressive Brulé leader from Rosebud, wrote Spencer that he did not join the Ghost Dancers because he believed in the "good people of the Church and the good Book that tell us there is only one God and that God dont like bad people." He was "not going to be foolish and join the Dancers."[63] Little Soldier, a Hunkpapa Lakota, expressed regret for joining dances in a letter to his agent. But now his heart was "good"; he would follow his "own judgement" and the advice of his uncle Gray Eagle, the Great Spirit, the Great Father, and the agent "and be happy."[64]

Dancers at the "hostile" Lakota camps in the Badlands also remained in contact with the outside world via letters. Lebbeus Foster Spencer corresponded with several leaders who defended the dance, including Two Strike. Foster found it difficult to get his letters to those in the "hostile camp," like Gray Eagle Tail (the Brulé, not to be confused with Gray Eagle), Brave Eagle, Big Turkey, and others, but at least one of Two Strike's letters got through.[65] A former Carlisle student named Raymond Stewart was described as Little Wound's personal secretary, penning letters and translating for the chief (see chapter 8).[66] Also, on November 22, three days after troops arrived at Pine Ridge, Little Wound wrote to Agent Royer (with the help of John Sweeney, teacher at the No. 8 Day School at Pine Ridge) from the Badlands. He said that his people would not stop dancing even though the troops were on their way. "What are they coming for?" he asked. "We have done nothing." He continued:

> Our dance is a religious dance and we are going to dance until Spring, If we find then that Christ does not appear we will stop dancing, but in the mean time troops or no troops, we shall start our dance on this creek in the morning.... I have also been told that you intended to stop our rations and annuities; Well for my part I don't care the little rations we receive do not amount to anything but Dr. Royer if such is the case please send me word so that my people and myself will be saved the trouble of going to the Agency.[67]

Sweeney told Royer that he thought Little Wound would "continue to dance until he is stopped by force."[68] Five days later, however, Little Wound and Big Road yielded without violence. But Kicking Bull and Short Bull were still in the Badlands, Big Foot remained uncooperative, and Two Strike's camp was on Wounded Knee Creek.

Over the course of the next month, agency officials and the military attempted to quell the Ghost Dancing at these holdout dancing camps. Agents forwarded lists of the men they thought were most responsible for the trouble and whom they thought should be arrested (Royer at Pine Ridge had by far the longest list). Eventually, after thorough negotiations between dancers, progressives, and white authorities, all would be forced to come into Pine Ridge to surrender. On December 6, E. G. Bettelyoun, an Oglala assistant clerk and former student at the Lincoln Institute in Philadelphia, described the atmosphere at Pine Ridge to his former teacher: "All the Indians of this Agency have quieted down. It is the Indians of Rosebud reservation that are making all the trouble now. They have been making good many depredations and are afraid to come to the Agency for fear that the troops will make them prisoners. I think it will be settled peaceably if they come in. . . . I think all the papers are making it worse then it is."[69]

Miscommunication and Wounded Knee

Despite Bettelyoun's optimism, the atmosphere at the Lakota agencies took a turn for the worse after the death of Sitting Bull (the Hunkpapa Lakota) at the hands of the Standing Rock Indian police on December 16, 1890, just a week after Quanah Parker, the Kiowa dancers, and Wolf Chief expressed their displeasure with the Lakotas. Sitting Bull refused to instruct his people to stop Ghost Dancing, a decision that angered his agent, James McLaughlin, who was already frustrated with Sitting Bull's role in some of the illicit visitation that was occurring. In late November, Sitting Bull was told by others at Standing Rock that McLaughlin would arrest him and send him to Indian Territory if his people did not stop dancing. Sitting Bull sent a letter to McLaughlin to ask if that was true. With help from a literate acquaintance, Sitting Bull argued that his people's beliefs and their prayers were harmless. Although Sitting Bull wrote that he prayed to God and danced, he still was unsure about the legitimacy of the Ghost Dance.[70] On December 11, 1890, he wrote again to McLaughlin to express his disappointment with the US government's stance on the Ghost Dance. He questioned McLaughlin's power to suppress freedom of religion and the basic right of prayer: "So all the Indians Pray to god for life & try to find out good

Road & do noting wrong. In they life: This is what we want & Pray to god but you did not bleaven us—So you must not say anything about our Pray: because did not Say nothing about your Pray. because you pray to god: So we all Indians, while: we both Pray only one god to make us."[71] Sitting Bull also said that he knew what was being written in the newspapers about him and the Ghost Dance, particularly what McLaughlin was reporting. Sitting Bull's argument was similar to Big Tree's "different roads" argument (see chapter 6). He did not understand how the government could stop a man from finding a "good road" through prayer. It was a different form of prayer from the white man's, but they were both praying to God.

Because the letter was written in broken English, it might have been difficult for McLaughlin to understand everything Sitting Bull hoped to communicate, but Sitting Bull's main arguments were clear. The most consequential communication barrier between the men was cultural. McLaughlin was unconvinced because his truth was incompatible with Sitting Bull's. His heart did not melt like Inspector Junkin's did after hearing Big Tree's plea. McLaughlin did not consider that the Ghost Dance was a viable form of religion. For him, the Ghost Dance was an "absurd craze," but for Sitting Bull, it was a way to communicate with God. McLaughlin told Sitting Bull that he did not know what would happen to his people if they continued to dance in "open violation of the department regulations," but it would not be allowed to continue much longer.[72] Although McLaughlin never told Sitting Bull that the army wanted him arrested, he warned him not to visit any other agencies.

McLaughlin received Sitting Bull's letter on December 12 at 6 p.m. On that same day, the post commander at Fort Yates instructed McLaughlin to arrest Sitting Bull as part of the US government's effort to curb the Ghost Dance. McLaughlin replied to Sitting Bull's letter the next day, December 13, calling himself Sitting Bull's friend (which was a lie; McLaughlin deeply disliked Sitting Bull). He claimed that the US government was Sitting Bull's "true friend"; after all, there was "no other government in the civilized world that would have treated a conquered foe so humanly."[73] On December 14, police lieutenant Bull Head reported to McLaughlin that Sitting Bull would soon head to Pine Ridge with or without permission, which made McLaughlin hasten the arrest (he had planned it for December 20, ration day). At his own cabin, Sitting Bull and seven of his followers were killed during the arrest attempt.[74] Bull Head and seven policemen also died. Skirmishes between the Indian police and members of Sitting Bull's stunned band broke out immediately following the incident. The military tried to control the situation, but it only grew worse.[75] Nearly five hundred men and women from Standing Rock fled their reservation out of fear and frustration.

Lakotas immediately took to the pen to send and receive information about the critical developments. On the day Sitting Bull was killed, December 15, Chiefs John Grass and Gall at Standing Rock wrote to Agent McLaughlin, unsure about what was happening and worried about both the soldiers and the Ghost Dancers. "We stay in our places for hold our school Boys & Girl teachers," they assured their agent. "Please send us 10 guns & send a note & tell us what we going to do."[76] The next day, Louis Breast at Cheyenne River wrote his agent that some of Sitting Bull's camp had arrived on his land from Standing Rock that morning, and he was worried what they might do.[77] Claude Bow at Standing Rock wrote his former superintendent at the Hampton Institute, updating him about Sitting Bull and asking him to "tell the Indian students don't be scare about it."[78] Indians from other reservations wrote to get information about the crisis from officials. Pawnee Tom at the Pawnee Reservation down in Indian Territory wrote to Agent McLaughlin at Standing Rock to learn "all about the fighting with Sitting Bull and how it commenced."[79]

Agents were concerned about the Lakotas heading off their reservations and were not sure where they might go or what they would do. Some from Sitting Bull's camp ended up at Big Foot's Miniconjou Ghost Dancing camp at Cherry Creek on the Cheyenne River Reservation; others made it to the dancing camps in the Badlands with Kicking Bear and Short Bull. The sight of traveling Indians frightened white settlers, especially the residents of Cheyenne City who abandoned their town after Narcisse Narcelle warned them of certain danger.[80] Members of the 12th Infantry were sent out to prevent Hunkpapas from joining Big Foot's camp and the camps in the Badlands. They surrounded Big Foot's camp, and with Hump serving as the mediator, the soldiers tried to persuade Big Foot's people to return to Cheyenne River. Some surrendered to the army; others stayed with Big Foot.[81] Big Foot, sick with pneumonia, was told to give up or be attacked. He was afraid that the army would attack no matter what he did. In two weeks' time, more than two hundred of Big Foot's band would be massacred by soldiers at Wounded Knee Creek on the Pine Ridge Reservation.

Before the horrors at Wounded Knee, Oglala leaders from Pine Ridge sent letters urging the holdouts in the Badlands to come in peacefully.[82] They wrote to Big Foot, asking him to come into Pine Ridge to discuss the situation. According to Hump, Big Foot initially thought the letters were invitations to come to Pine Ridge to fight.[83] But a particular letter from Red Cloud, No Water, Big Road, and several others made it obvious that these "overtures" to Big Foot's camp were trying to convince the dancers to "join with the friendly Indians and help make peace."[84] According to Joseph Horn Cloud, this letter finally convinced Big Foot to go to Pine Ridge. Dewey Beard (Iron Hail), a Miniconjou Lakota Ghost Dancer who was twenty-two years old at the time, later recalled that the letter read, "My Dear Friend Chief Big Foot. Whenever you receive this letter I want you to come at once. Whenever you come to our reservation a fire is going to be started and I want you to come and help us to put it out and make a peace. Whenever you come among us to make a peace we will give you 100 head of horses."[85] Big Foot agreed and replied to the Pine Ridge headmen with a letter of his own (one that Dewey Beard did not see).

These communications gave hope that the crisis might end peacefully, but Lakotas still expressed a great deal of concern in their personal letters during the last days of the year, particularly about the conduct of the US soldiers. On December 26, 1890, Sky Bull, a Brulé headman at Rosebud, wrote to his former agent Lebbeus Foster Spencer to tell him about the "trouble" at his old reservation with the hope of some assistance.[86] Sky Bull blamed both the hostiles and the soldiers for the disorder there. Short Bull, Two Strike, and Crow Dog had "made many of our young men foolish and taken them away," he wrote. But Sky Bull also told Spencer that the recently arrived soldiers "spoil our girls." "Wont you tell the Great Father about it?" he asked. "Many of the Indians think the Great Father has sent his children to starve us. I do not believe that for we now get the rations Genl Harney promised us."[87] Two days later, and one day before the Wounded Knee Massacre at Pine Ridge, Pretty Eagle, also a Rosebud headman, wrote (with the help of John Stephen Lance) to Spencer that they did not "want to any trouble here in this country." "My friend will you help us?" he asked. "Short Bull makes run off half of my people, this the reason I want to hear some word from the Great Father about it. No will you help me, I wish you would help me all you can."[88]

Sky Bull and Pretty Eagle did not join Short Bull, but they were both worried about the trouble that might arise because of the Ghost Dance. In another letter to Spencer, sent in the days after Wounded Knee, Sky Bull, Pretty Eagle, and He Dog wanted their apologies conveyed to President Harrison on behalf of their people. The headmen wanted to let the president to know that the Rosebud Brulés who had run off to Pine Ridge with their families did so because they were afraid of the soldiers who had arrived at the agency. The men also hoped that the president could help them reopen the schools at Rosebud. They trusted Spencer, their former agent, to pass their concerns on to Washington.[89]

As 1890 drew to cold end, it seemed that trouble would be avoided, but some expected things to get worse after the snow melted.[90] On Christmas Day, William Courtis, the postmaster at Rosebud, said he expected "hell in the spring, unless a large force of troops remain in the field."[91] Unfortunately, because of that large force of troops, hell came before the year's end. On December 29, Big Foot's Miniconjou band headed toward Pine Ridge to surrender, but they were confronted en route by the 7th Calvary, who had been ordered to disarm the people before they reached the agency. The Miniconjous, already afraid of military retribution, accepted disarmament, but a shot was fired during the tense process, and soldiers began firing into the crowd of men, women, and children. Soldiers chased the fleeing people, shooting many in the back, while machine guns positioned atop a hill blasted round after round. The official army report counted 176 Lakotas dead, but the actual number was undoubtedly higher.[92]

Just as they did after Sitting Bull's death, Lakotas immediately wrote letters relaying news about the massacre at Pine Ridge.[93] And like white Americans, Natives read about the massacre in the papers, but their reactions were much more empathetic than most whites'. Lakotas had "been treated shamefully," John Half Iron (Santee) wrote to Herbert Welsh of the Indian Rights Association.[94] He continued,

> The officer of the war took all their guns and than shot into them with two Hotchkiss man women and children. My friend I don't like that at all, and would like to know what you think about it. This is what I think. The Indians are ignorant and poor, But some whites are mean to them, they tries to take away what little they have. And when they took it all away from them they treat them poorly.

Following the massacre, agents ordered Indian police, agency employees, and the "friendly" Indian populations to be on the watch for roaming hostiles and any "rumors of strangers." Ghost Dancers who had surrendered at Pine Ridge fled back to the Badlands, some committing depredations along the way. Out of fear and anger, cattle were killed or stolen for food, homes of progressives and mixed-bloods were vandalized, and one schoolhouse at Pine Ridge was burned.[95] Skirmishes between the hostiles and soldiers lasted for a few weeks. The Lakota reservations were temporarily handed over to military control, and officers replaced agents as the decision makers. Rumors of a united Lakota outbreak persisted.[96]

By the end of January, however, most of the Ghost Dancing "hostiles" had peacefully returned to Pine Ridge. Social dancing, like the Omaha Dance, began again at Pine Ridge at least as early as January 3.[97] There was still concern that Lakota dancers might once again cause trouble, however, and a number of Lakota and Cheyenne Ghost Dance leaders were sent to a prison for several months to keep them off the reservations until the belief (of some) that the earth would be renewed in the spring of 1891 was proven wrong.[98]

US officials also tried to control the narrative regarding the massacre, lying in at least one instance to Indians congregated at Cheyenne River about why women and children had been killed. Capt. Joseph Henry Hurst told the crowd that the barrage from the Hotchkiss and Gatling guns were intended for the five hundred hostile Brulés coming up Wounded Knee Creek toward the shooting, not the women and children fleeing for their lives; this was not true.[99] The army would not admit the nature of the slaughter for fear of inspiring more resentment.

Agents also remained concerned about the influence of traveling Indians and the information they might spread. At Cheyenne River, the agent had his district farmers watch the camps to make sure that the nondancing families and the "Christian camps" were not "disturbed" by the "hostiles" and to prevent Indians from passing from one camp to another. All were told to stay at their homes and to send away any visitors. The Cheyenne River Indian police had the enormous task of traversing the reservation, often riding 120 miles without resting, to carry messages between an agency employee at the last Ghost Dancing camp and the troops. Those at the Cherry Creek camp at Cheyenne River eventually pledged their loyalty to the US government in April 1891 and asked for a boarding school to replace the day schools on the agency. They appointed a "committee," as the Cheyenne River agent called it, "to send word" of their decisions "to other agencies," probably by letter.[100]

During that spring, some Lakotas hoped to convince authorities and other tribes, using the written word, that their people would not cause any more trouble despite the rumors that said otherwise. Two Strike, the Rosebud Brulé headman and proponent of the dance who had led several hundred Brulés and Oglalas into the Badlands and established a camp there with Short Bull and Kicking Bear in late November 1890, surrendered his "hostile" party in January 1891. In April, Two Strike replied (with the help of an army officer) to a letter from Richard Pratt, the Carlisle superintendent, who asked Two Strike if any mischief was planned for the spring. Two Strike denied any intentions for trouble and gave his version of events the previous fall and winter. He said that his party of dancers "did not have anything to do" with Wounded Knee, but it had given them "a lesson."[101] He argued, "We did not want to fight in the first place but somebody called for troops," placing the blame on a rash decision by the US government. "All we think about now is to farm," he claimed.

Letters allowed Lakotas to navigate the stories that spun in newspapers and on the reservations after Wounded Knee. Two Strike received letters from Indians at the Lower Brule Reservation and from "a young man from Standing Rock," asking about the rumors of additional trouble. He told them that the Rosebud Brulés "were not going to make any more trouble and they must not pay attention to such talk. This talk gives me much trouble and I do not like it."[102]

Other Lakota believers expressed their disappointment, writing that the true nature of their religion was never understood by whites and their US government. A group of Lakota headmen, who were about to head off as part of a delegation to Washington, DC, agreed to speak with the *Washington Evening Star* in late January. They knew the newspaper was published in the nation's capital and hoped that politicians would read their side of the story. Big Road told the reporter that many Americans did not understand the movement "because the truth had not been told" to them. He wanted the paper's readers to understand that

> most of the Indians here belong to the church; we have many church house. This dance was like religion; it was religion. Those who brought the dance here from the west said that to dance was the same as going to church. White people pray because they want to go to heaven. Indians want to go to heaven, too, so they prayed. . . . We danced and prayed that we might live forever; that everything we planted might grow up to give us plenty and happiness. . . . The Messiah told us to send our children to school, to work on our farms all the time and to do the best we could. He also told us not to drop our church. . . . We never prayed for anything but happiness. We did not pray that the white people should be all killed. . . . All the dance trouble here was caused by Agent Royer and his policemen telling stories about us that were not true.[103]

Little Wound agreed with Big Road's assessment: "Many lies have been told about some of the Indians who were in the dance." These men thought the government's decision to use the military was based on bad intelligence. Their dancing was not a security threat—they were not praying to have the white race destroyed—they were only dancing and praying so that they might "live forever," just like white Christians. Big Road was doing what

Wovoka had told the Lakota delegates nearly twelve months before: "Send our children to school . . . work on our farms . . . go to church," and pray for "happiness."

In the months leading up to Wounded Knee, Native Americans had great success communicating that message among themselves, but many believers and nonbelievers were frustrated that white Americans refused to understand the Ghost Dance. As much as Natives tried to enter the national dialogue with their letters to whites and their interviews with the press, most Americans did not care to listen. As a letter received soon after the Wounded Knee Massacre by an army officer at Pine Ridge from a cousin back in Michigan makes clear, many Americans still agreed with "the old adage" that "the only good Indian is a dead one."[104] "If I were in command," the officer's cousin bragged, "there would be more good injuns."

Wounded Knee was not the end of the Ghost Dance. Just four days after the massacre, Wovoka received a visit from more groups of foreign Indians (Kiowas, Arapahos, Bannocks, and Lakotas), as he would for years to come.[105] Letters concerning the movement continued to be sent. As we will see in the next chapter, intertribal communication kept the movement alive, and dancing reached new peaks on several reservations in 1891. Natives were forced to defend the movement's ideas well into the 1890s. Row of Lodges, the Southern Arapaho headman, told a white anthropologist in 1895 that his people were afraid that there would be more "false reports about this dance and that the Department would stop it," but "this religion teaches the Indians to have respect to white men, and to do no hurt to anyone. The trouble generally has come from the white people, and not from the Indians."[107] Row of Lodges wanted the anthropologist to use his interview to better explain what the Ghost Dance was to those who believed in its benefits. "I want you to write and tell me what the people think of it," he said, hopeful that non-Natives could make sense of the movement.

CHAPTER 8

Continuing the Movement

Despite the massacre on Lakota land, Native American mobility and communication continued. Between eighty and one hundred Natives are known to have visited Wovoka during the first half of 1891 alone, sustaining the connections that linked the plains to the Great Basin.[1] But in the weeks following Wounded Knee, whites who had settled near reservations, having read the sensationalized reporting out of Pine Ridge, worried about uprisings of angry Indians. They were alarmed by any intertribal collaboration. A Nevada paper reported that Bannocks in Idaho were "closely allied" with Paiutes and were "in constant communication with each other, with a probability of massing forces shortly."[2] Nervous settlers wanted the ongoing intertribal dances in Nevada to end. The *Reno Gazette*, noting the eight hundred Indians Ghost Dancing near the rail line passing through Deeth, Nevada, recommended in January 1891 that Nevadans should "be prepared to resent the first insult the Indians offer, and annihilate the whole tribe."[3] The *Elko Independent* recommended a more humane strategy, arguing that it "was wrong" for the railroad companies to allow "Indians to ride on the trains at this time, as without that means of conveyance they could not possibly assemble in such multitudes on so short notice."[4] Without the railroads, the newspaper reasoned, the Indians could not come together.

Despite the threats from settlers, Native Americans kept seeking information, and many kept dancing, but agents ramped up their efforts to stop the transmission of information among groups, believing that their interactions were a threat to US government authority. Agents were more determined to eliminate the movement, using different and sometimes tougher tactics to limit visiting and letter writing regarding the dance. There were also Native American critics of the Ghost Dance who thought the movement was not a significant one or that Wovoka was a fraud. Some Natives even believed that the dance was dangerous, and others urged the US government to do more to stop it. Nevertheless, the Ghost Dance persisted into the 1890s because of intertribal interaction and because of the many who challenged US colonial authority by refusing to give up their freedoms of speech, religion, and mobility.

The amount of movement among tribes had been obvious before the Wounded Knee Massacre. On a ration day in mid-December 1890, at least twenty-seven Cheyenne River Lakotas were off at other agencies, such as Rosebud, Pine Ridge, and Standing Rock, without permission.[5] "Strolling Indians," a white reporter explained, were "constantly moving from band to band within the limits of each tribes to make distant pilgrimages to visit other tribes."[6] After Wounded Knee, another reporter criticized the Lakota agencies for not creating a "system of the strictest surveillance" that would have prevented the "hostile spies" from "constantly" visiting those who had not been affected by the dance.[7] It "should have been inaugurated weeks ago," the reporter wrote. Lakota agents failed in that regard before Wounded Knee, but they claimed to be even more concerned about the information that visiting Indians might bring to their reserves in early 1891. "The importance of stopping visits at this time has been fully appreciated," the Rosebud agent assured the commissioner, "and every means in my power has and is being used to effectually stop such."[8] Agents thought that a network between the nonprogressive elements had enabled their coordination during the previous winter, and they knew that visitors and letters were the primary conduits of communication.[9]

But intertribal corresponding could not be reined in, and it was vital in the Ghost Dance's persistence. In early 1891, a captain in the 9th Infantry reported that there was correspondence between the "disappointed Indians at different agencies" who did not trust the promises made by the US government after Wounded Knee. One of these letters, written in Dakota, was acquired by an interpreter at the Rosebud Agency for $100. It was sent from Bad Water in Rump at Pine Ridge to his relative White Back at Rosebud in March 1891. It read in part, "Lately there is a man died and come to life again and he say he has been to Indian Nation of Ghosts and tells us: dead Indian Nation all coming home. The Indian Ghost tell him, come after his War Bonnet; the Indian gave him his War Bonnet and he died again. He tells us he prepared every day before he died again. This man is Ogallalla man—that is the one who makes the prediction."[10] Bad Water in Rump relayed the information his people received from Cheyennes to White Back and his people at Rosebud. He believed that an Oglala Lakota prophet was keeping the dance alive for the sake of the "Indian Nation" and that a large gathering of all tribes would take place in the Black Hills in the summer. It would be a pan-Indian undertaking.

In another letter, Many Eagles (or Plenty Eagles), an Oglala living at Pine Ridge, wrote to his sister on March 5, 1891, advising her to believe in the dance:

> I would like to inform you of something. It is in regard to the dance which created a commotion up there. It is the truth and will surely come to pass. . . . Now you must use every effort to come in possession of some Eagle's-down, and have them in readiness. From the time the grass starts you must be on the lookout and when a thunder storm comes you must attach them to your hair. Take care that you heed what I say. These five camps of Ogalallas who have inlisted in the US Army. It is a plot amongst the people, for the sole purpose of arming themselves. Try to get arrows, at least. That is all I have to say.[11]

According to Many Eagles, the eagle down would protect her from a flood that would submerge the nonbelievers (similar to the eagle feather that Robert Higheagle received from his father at Standing Rock; see chapter 6). It is not clear if Many Eagles's sister ever saw his warning; the letter somehow made it into the possession of Agent McLaughlin at Standing Rock, who seized incoming mail to curtail the dance's spread. McLaughlin was probably concerned about Many Eagles's belief that Oglalas were enlisting in order to get their hands on guns. It is clear, however, that even though Native networks were attacked and dancing was restricted at the Lakota agencies, the belief in the promise of the dance remained.

But believers were not the only ones who continued to spread information about the Ghost Dance. Nonbelievers and skeptics relayed news about the movement to friends and family regarding what it meant and what the US government was doing to stop it. Lawrence Industrious (Blihica), an eighteen-year-old former Hampton student at Pine Ridge, for instance, did not seem to be a dancer, but while answering his cousin's questions about the state of affairs at Pine Ridge, he transmitted news that dancing might be revived in the spring of 1891. He told his cousin (One Bull at Standing Rock, the adopted son of Sitting Bull) to bear in mind that Kicking Bear would possibly be allowed to dance again.[12] "Keep your ears open this way I say this to you on the quiet," he advised. It is not clear how many letters passed in and out of the Lakota agencies in the weeks after the Wounded Knee Massacre, because many had to be sent "on the quiet" to make it to their destinations. These surviving letters were all confiscated by the Office of Indian Affairs.

Dancing despite Suppression

On several reservations, the Ghost Dance actually peaked in 1891 and 1892. One thousand dancers were reported among Wichitas, Caddos, Delawares, and Kichais at one gathering in Indian Territory in February 1891.[13] At the Ponca, Pawnee, and Otoe Reservation, large dances were held in November 1891 through January 1892 and endured in some form for years. A Pawnee named Frank White had become a disciple of Sitting Bull (the Northern Arapaho) while participating in a Ghost Dance at the Kiowa, Comanche, and Wichita Reservation with Wichitas, Caddos, and three hundred Pawnees in the late summer of 1891. White convinced Pawnee leadership that the dance was compatible with their traditions and instructed Pawnees in the dance and its songs.[14] Pawnees and Poncas were able to organize at least three large dances led by White without their agent's knowledge, something the secretary of the interior thought "unpardonable."[15] But Pawnee agent J. M. Wood was not fully at fault, and while he blamed much of the business on exaggerated press reports, Pawnees and Poncas were careful not to advertise their intentions to dance. In fact, Agent Wood had written a letter directly to Frank White, ordering him to leave the reservation (and return to the Wichitas, where he had been living for the past three to four years).[16] White ignored the order and stayed on the reservation, but Agent Wood did not want to aggravate the situation. He told Commissioner Morgan that whatever dance the Pawnees were doing, they "had best be left alone as opposition breeds trouble."[17] According to Wood, the Ghost Dance was "harmless" despite what newspapers were writing about the movement. It was the "spreading of such falsehoods that do more than all else to retard the true advancement of the Indian," especially considering that "a great many of the Indians who are educated read the daily papers and then tell the other Indians" about false reports, "which makes the Indians dissatisfied."

A few weeks later, in January 1892, Frank White and the Pawnee dancers told Agent Wood that their dance was "their way to worship Christ"; they "believed the Indian religion and the white man's religion was the same."[18] They wanted to be left alone. They would quit dancing when it was time to work, and they believed that Christ would soon come and save the "Indians and whites." Pressured by the commissioner to end the dancing, Agent Wood told the dancers that it was not necessary to dance to "worship God in the heart," and he again instructed Frank White to leave the Pawnees. But none of the Pawnees promised that the dancing would stop, and a few said they would die before they would stop. The dance was so popular among Pawnees that the Indian police refused to help prevent it. White planned a dance with Otoes in late March, but Agent Wood, now tired of White's disobedience, had White arrested. White was charged with insurrection and sent to a federal prison in Wichita, Kansas, but was released after he agreed to never participate in the Ghost Dance again. Despite his pledge, White still tried to maintain his spiritual influence among the dancers before his death in 1893, but he was superseded by others who visited Sitting Bull (the Arapaho) at the Cheyenne-Arapaho Reservation, returning with what they called a more authentic vision of the dance.

Stacy Matlock, a young Pawnee man and a Carlisle graduate, wrote in 1892 that when he returned to the Pawnee Reservation, he attended "great and surprising . . . gatherings every day."[19] Ghost Dancing friends told him "that it was not very long when the time will come when we will see our old relatives who died many years ago." They said Matlock had to throw away his "citizen clothes" and put on his "Indian clothes," but he told them that he "was too old to believe such a thing," and he kept his clothes on. Even though Matlock paid no mind, the Ghost Dance persisted at the Pawnee Reservation well into the twentieth century. Pawnees practiced secrecy to avoid trouble with the agent. Dances were held in remote areas, sometimes in deep snow. The dancing was done quietly; they softened their voices, and as one Pawnee remembered, they "began to hide around to do it."

Belief also persisted among Lakotas and Northern Cheyennes in South Dakota. At the Rosebud Reservation, a group under Black Moon and Little Thunder was dancing in secret in March 1891. They were worried about the repercussions from the US government and from their own people. Little Thunder's son received more than thirty visions, during which he said he could see Short Bull (who was being punished in a federal prison at the time). He saw "Christ" seven times, and the Christ told him that another world was coming soon.[20]

Some whites figured that if the dance stuck around, it would eventually lead to more trouble, and any communication among Indian groups continued to be seen by whites with apprehension. Officials who still associated the Ghost Dance with militancy tried to piece together the Lakotas' secret plans. Some imagined that a grand pan-Indian conspiracy was being built through intertribal communications. In late February 1891, for instance, an agent of the Indian Rights Association, Rev. William Cleveland, reported, based on his investigation, that there was little doubt that prominent Lakotas were planning hostilities for the upcoming spring.[21] He was told by Soldier Star, a scout of both European and Lakota descent, that around June 1890, Red Cloud, No Water, and He Dog at the Pine Ridge Reservation received a letter (written in Dakota) from Sitting Bull at the Standing Rock

Reservation. Soldier Star read the letter to the men, which stated (according to Cleveland's report), "My friends I have formed a purpose today, and will tell it to you plainly. I can to-day no longer endure the way in which the whites make me suffer. I send this thought to you from house to house. . . . Next spring we will all meet at the Hill-in-the-woods."[22] The chain letter was meant to be forwarded to Big Foot at the Cheyenne River Reservation then to Big Mane at the Lower Brule Reservation then to Two Strike and on to Short Bull at Rosebud and then to No Water, Red Cloud, American Horse, and Young Man Afraid of His Horses at Pine Ridge.

Soldier Star supposed that if Sitting Bull had not been killed, plans for a spring outbreak would have been "fully matured" by February 1891. Despite Soldier Star's belief, there was no malicious plan or hostile strategy in the letter. There was only a vague proposal to meet. But Cleveland agreed with Soldier Star, and he told the Indian Rights Association that "all Indian communications on similar subjects" were purposefully vague, written "in the blind manner," and had to be read between the lines. Their letters, of course, were being confiscated before delivery. Cleveland also claimed that Afraid of Bear at Pine Ridge, the brother of George Sword, received a letter from some Crows in Montana who wanted to know when "the fighting with the whites" was to begin at Pine Ridge. The Crows supposedly pledged they would begin fighting "up here at the same time."

The officials' suspicions made it to the press, which further sensationalized them. Reports out of South Dakota in March 1891 warned that the Rosebud Indians were preparing for an outbreak, using "secret conferences."[23] The dissatisfied Brulés were supposedly planning to meet up with the Crows and Cheyennes in Wyoming to raid white settlements. There was nothing to the reports, but Indian Affairs became concerned about possible trouble that could spring up on the Lakota reserves nonetheless.[24] On March 17, the acting agent at Pine Ridge, Capt. Charles Penny, reported to his superiors that more troops were needed there to suppress a growing "hostile element."[25] He hoped that additional troops would allow him to better surveil suspects.

White suspicion, which lasted for months and even years after Wounded Knee, lived on because the Ghost Dance did not die the natural death that many expected. Agents throughout the West continued to chase down rumors of Ghost Dancing. They assumed that communication between tribes, secret or otherwise, could carry plans for dancing. Captain Penny believed that some Oglalas wanted to resume their Ghost Dancing and were "privately and among themselves in secret councils" preparing for war in the spring. Much of Penny's intelligence on the matter came from the personal letters written and received by the hostile Lakota "prisoners of war" who were then held at Fort Meade, South Dakota. The commanding officer forwarded all the POWs' letters directly to Penny so that he could read them first and use his "discretion in regard to the propriety of delivery."[26] In fact, some of the letters written by the relatives of the prisoners indicated that the Ghost Dance was "still going on or about to commence."[27] Soon after, an Indian scout named Charles Whitebull reported that Pine Ridge Indians had received letters from other Indians "out west" who said that "they would help them if they broke out."[28] Whitebull's findings were forwarded to the agent at Pine Ridge, and while his concerns never amounted to anything, Penny associated Ghost Dancing with continued outright dissent.

Besides the troublesome correspondence, Penny also had trouble with illicit visiting. He told the Rosebud agent for a second time that "quite a number" of his Indians were still coming to Pine Ridge without passes. The Rosebud agent admitted that Indians could leave Rosebud "without being detected."[29] Penny had already arrested three of the visitors, William Red Deer and two other Brulés, for "going about the country . . . spreading rumors and gossip not consistent with peace and good order."[30] Red Deer was held at the agency guardhouse in late May, five months after Wounded Knee, because of the information he carried.

But threat of punishment was not enough to curb the visiting. According to Penny, the Indians at Pine Ridge were in a "state of uneasiness and evinced a disposition to leave the Agency and wander about in search of gossip and news." He thought this indicated that the people wanted to resume the "Messiah craze, the ghost dancing and consequent trouble." In October 1891, Agent Penny reported that he was constantly being pressured to grant passes for hunting in Utah, Montana, and Colorado, which made him suspect that those Indians, who were thought to be nonprogressives, really wanted to "search for, and bring back, news of the Messiah."[31] There were indications that dancing was occurring in seclusion at night, and rumors were swirling from unknown sources.

The agent found it "impossible" to find reliable information about the secret doings of the people at Pine Ridge. Desperate to secure "definite information," Penny asked the commissioner to allow him to spend no less than fifty dollars a month as a "secret service fund" that would allow him "to ascertain definitely, and secretly, exactly what is going on all over the reservation." Penny seems to have put his intelligence funding to use. Days later, he received a letter from a headman who probably had not been a Ghost Dancer, reporting that there was no Ghost Dancing going on at Pine Ridge's Medicine Root District.[32] Months later, however, an employee at

Pine Ridge reported that Ghost Dancing had resumed at the White Clay District. To curb the dance, Agent Penny would stem the spread of information, recommending that the Indians who were on his reservation without permission be sent back to their "legal homes."[33]

Officials outside South Dakota also blamed intertribal interaction for the ongoing dancing. At the Western Shoshone Reservation in Nevada, the agent felt that the "craze" was "losing ground" in December 1890, but visiting Indians from other tribes and reservations were keeping up the excitement.[34] The agent had "no hope of breaking up their dances altogether"; he only hoped he could control them. John Mayhugh, the former Western Shoshone agent, also noticed the surge in visitors coming to Nevada in early January 1891. He wrote to President Harrison that there had been an "unusual number of dances," which were caused by the "visiting delegations of Indians from several tribes," especially from the Fort Hall Reservation.[35]

The connections among tribes also continued to worry some in the far western plains. An army scout, Frank Grouard, heard from a friend at the Wind River Reservation that visiting Cheyennes believed the Lakotas were sending delegates to other reservations, "trying to get all the tribes to go into a general outbreak." Grouard believed that Lakota runners had been sent out to all the tribes as far west as the Blackfeet in Montana, contacting others (Cheyennes, Crows, Gros Ventres, and Mandans among them) about a joint outbreak. Some Lakotas were supposedly going to resist government control whether others joined them or not. "All of this is being kept very quiet," Grouard insisted. Only his friends offered the intelligence that there was "no doubt about the attempt to arrange for an outbreak." All the Lakota agents, however, denied that their Lakotas had sent out runners, each reporting that they had been limiting visitation to only deserving Indians and Indian police.

Trying to stop visiting was one thing, but stopping vast correspondence was another. In May, Agent Wright at Rosebud heard reports that "many letters" were being received by Indians from other agencies.[36] That same month, Agent Penny at Pine Ridge got hold of a letter that a Rosebud man visiting the Crow Creek Reservation sent to his brother, an army interpreter at Pine Ridge. A copy of that letter no longer exists, and its contents are not known, but it was deemed important enough to be sent to the acting agent at Rosebud in case he wanted to have the letter writer arrested. As is evident by this and the imprisonment of Red Deer, agents were willing to jail those who spread information that was deemed dangerous.[37] They believed that communications among Lakotas had contributed to the "hostilities" of the past winter.

Even into 1892, rumors of secret letters propagating the Ghost Dance reached the agents at the South Dakota reserves. Agent McLaughlin at Standing Rock still blamed the "fairy tales" about the revival of the Ghost Dance at his reserve on the "numerous letters" received from Pine Ridge that were being circulated at his agency.[38] McLaughlin recommended stopping "to some extent the carrying of messages and circulation of rumors among the tribe detrimental to the general good," although he offered no strategy to limit the communication. He was worried the "nonprogressive" minority might exert an unwarranted influence over the majority because of the letters. Whether these letters were about the Ghost Dance or not, agents were on the lookout for intertribal communication because they knew it weakened the control they thought they had on Native life.

Native Critics of the Movement

There were still many Natives who wanted to learn more about the Ghost Dance after Wounded Knee. Investigations went on, and a variety of conclusions about Wovoka were reached, including the opinion that the man was a fraud. There were also nonbelievers who tried to distance themselves from the dancers throughout 1891. Soon after Wounded Knee, Henry Kendall (Pueblo) assured his former superintendent at Carlisle, Richard Pratt, that he opposed the Ghost Dancing that had reached Pueblos in New Mexico Territory.[39] Some Indians even used the mail to condemn Indian Affairs for not doing enough to end the Ghost Dance. A group of twenty-nine former Hampton students from the Crow Creek and Lower Brule Reservations asked their agent, through a petition, to suppress dancing "of any class" because it was a "hindrance to their and our progress toward civilization."[40] Lewis Miller, a Southern Arapaho at the Haskell Institute, was so concerned about the continuation of the dance at the Cheyenne-Arapaho Reservation that he wrote a letter to President Harrison, asking for troops to stop the dance. Miller wrote that the agent's lack of concern about the movement allowed the dances to persist.[41] Likewise, Swift Bird at Cheyenne River wrote to his agent to ask him to replace the lieutenant of police there because he had not tried to prevent the dancers from going to Pine Ridge the previous autumn.[42]

Some Indian leaders, in an effort to retain good relations, wrote to federal officials after Wounded Knee to make it clear that they were not dancing. The Shoshone chief Washakie at Wind River assured the president and Commissioner Morgan that they had "always been the friends of the white men," never giving the "Chiefs at Washington any trouble at all." His people did "not know why" Lakotas were "so foolish as to want to fight with the people."⁴³ Likewise, Black Coal's Northern Arapahos, who had been trying to convince Indian Affairs to give them an agency separate from the one they shared with the Shoshones at Wind River, were quick to tell the secretary of the interior that they would not harbor any "malcontents" or allow anything wrong in their camps.⁴⁴ The group knew that their campaign for their own reserve could be ruined if the US government thought they were a source of Ghost Dance trouble. Black Coal, who, according to James Mooney, had suspicions about the dance from the beginning, sent his own delegation, partly by rail, to see Wovoka in late 1890, and they concluded that the movement was disingenuous upon their return to Wind River in early 1891. However, those Northern Arapahos outside Black Coal's influence, such as the followers of Sharp Nose, continued to believe in the dance.⁴⁵ The Wind River agent reported that they were led by a "few fanatics" but were not insubordinate or ill-tempered.⁴⁶

Some Natives continued to be conflicted about the Ghost Dance. It was complicated for them because they saw aspects of the movement that were both good and bad. Henry Dawson North, a Southern Arapaho student at Haskell, attended Ghost Dances in the fall of 1891 after his return to the Cheyenne-Arapaho Reservation. In early 1892, North's former superintendent at Haskell, Charles Meserve, asked North to write down what he knew about the dance in Oklahoma. North admitted that he had learned "a little about it" from Sitting Bull, the Northern Arapaho proponent of the dance. The movement had "always seemed" to him "a good step in way of making Indians religious.... Their former ways of trying to be wonderful medicine men are put aside."⁴⁷ According to North, Sitting Bull explained to the dancers that the white race would not "be banished or sent away," only that "the Indians of all tribes" would live in a "separate place, as has been in the past." The dance did not "mean harm"; it did not "try to make a fuss." Despite its value, North still hoped that the dancing would end. He could not understand why some dancers starved themselves or how the "foolish" ones claimed to see their dead relatives. And he thought Sitting Bull and the "fore-runner," as they called the Messiah, were probably trying to profit from the movement.

Unlike North, there were others who concluded that the Ghost Dance was entirely fraudulent. The most effective Native critic of Wovoka was a Kiowa man named Apiatan (Wooden Lance). Because of his investigation and testimony, many Kiowas rejected the dance in February 1891. Back in September 1890, Apiatan had journeyed to the northern reservations (partly by rail) to examine the validity of the Ghost Dance and sit face-to-face with

Wovoka. His agent, Charles Adams, eventually encouraged the trip, believing that Apiatan's investigation would prove the Messiah a fraud. Apiatan was not a headman (it seems even Agent Adams did not know much about him), and his plan to visit Wovoka was not revealed to government officials until after he had already made it to Pine Ridge. The Pine Ridge agent did not object to the visit, and the commissioner of Indian affairs allowed it because he was told that Apiatan was only planning to visit his relatives.[48]

James Mooney described Apiatan as a downtrodden, grieving man who had recently lost a child and who hoped to be able to see the departed in a vision initiated by Wovoka. Apiatan convinced Kiowa headmen to fund his efforts, which would clearly answer the questions about Wovoka's legitimacy. Most Kiowas, anxious to find more tangible evidence of Wovoka, went to the agency to see Apiatan off, an event that is recorded on a Kiowa calendar along with his return five months later.[49] After staying at Pine Ridge and securing permission to travel to the Wind River Reservation, Apiatan took the Union Pacific west.[50] Writing from Saint Stephen's Mission in Fremont County, Wyoming, presumably with the help of a priest, Apiatan let his friends back home know how his trip was going and asked that some more money be sent to him so he could travel farther to the Fort Hall Reservation in Idaho. He also wrote about the new connections he made with Lakotas, Arapahos, and Shoshones and their interest in the Kiowa Nation:

> After I left home my first visit was to the Sioux Reservation at Pine Ridge Dakota. I found everything good, and all the people very kind. My Second visit was to the Arapahoe + Shoshone reservation [Wind River] and I have the pleasure of shaking hands with all the people who were also very kind to me.... My only desire's to get along with all the parties and see all the different Indian tribes I can.... Although I am a stranger to all these people, they are all glad to see me, and treat me very kindly both Whites and Indians.... When you get this letter I hope you will write to me at once and give me all the news you can about our home, as nothing can give me more pleasure.... Chief Black Coal ... wishes to shake hands with our people in the Indian Territory.[51]

The agent at Wind River, John Fosher, asked Apiatan upon his arrival if he came there to investigate the "second coming of Christ." For reasons unknown, Apiatan told Fosher that he had not, but he still asked permission to continue farther west to the Fort Hall Reservation. Fosher informed Agent Adams back at the Kiowa Reservation that Apiatan was at Wind River and that he wanted an extension on his pass.[52] Agent Adams asked Fosher to extend it and admitted that Apiatan was indeed seeking out the Messiah. The investigation could "do no possible harm," Adams explained.[53]

Apiatan made it to Fort Hall, and the agent there allowed two Bannock men to guide him to Mason Valley in Nevada to see Wovoka.[54] On the day before Christmas 1890, Apiatan's party, now made up of five men, arrived at the Nevada Agency and was "treated Royally" with a "Big Eat" and new clothes.[55] Before they visited Wovoka's home near the Walker River Reservation, Nevada agent C. C. Warner passed along Apiatan's message to the Kiowas. Apiatan wanted his father and friends to know about the letter right away so that they could send him news from home (which "they were anxious to hear"). Apiatan said the Paiutes were glad they had come; they treated them kindly, and he felt that the Kiowas and the Paiutes were "like brothers." He promised to send a report about Wovoka (Jack Wilson) as soon as he could. Agent Warner sent Apiatan to Walker River with a letter that would ensure his good treatment upon arrival. In the *Daily Nevada State Journal*, Agent Warner called the members of Apiatan's party "intelligent" Indians who "fully understood the import of their important mission."[56]

Unfortunately, Apiatan was disappointed by his meeting with Wovoka, which took place sometime in the first half of January 1891.[57] He had expected Wovoka to be all the things that were said about him, a man with powerful medicine. He hoped that Wovoka, being omniscient, would already know why he was there, but he did not. He thought he would be able to understand the Kiowa language, but a Shoshone had to interpret. Apiatan found Wovoka in his bed, covered with a blanket, singing to himself, looking like an ordinary man, a little demoralized.

Wovoka did not, however, deny being the man Apiatan was looking for. Apiatan asked if he could see his dead relatives, his recently deceased child especially, but Wovoka told him there were none to see. Also, Wovoka did not have the scars of crucifixion, like some said he would have, and Apiatan concluded there was nothing divine about Wovoka.[58] The meeting took place in the days after the Wounded Knee Massacre, and Wovoka, probably devastated about the events in South Dakota, told Apiatan that Lakotas had distorted the things he had told them. Wovoka told Apiatan that he had better go home and tell his people to quit the dancing before they also got into trouble.[59]

Agent Warner said the Kiowa visitors looked "upon the 'Messiah' as a great 'humbug'" and would report as much when they got home.[60] In fact, Apiatan and his guides expressed their disappointment to the Bannocks and Shoshones at Fort Hall.[61] The bad news was also sent via letter to the Kiowa Reservation. Apiatan wrote, in part, "I am leaving here in three days to go to Pine Ridge Agency to tell the Sioux what I saw and heard in Nevada where the great Indian Prophet lives, and where I went to see along with other Indians. We found him to be an immense fraud who has been imposing on the credulity of the ignorant.... His game is all up."[62] It was a letter that Indian Affairs wanted Kiowas to read. On February 10, at least six days after receiving Apiatan's letter, Agent Adams replied, "Dear Friend: I ... was especially glad to know that you have lost all confidence in the so called Messiah. Your people were glad to hear from you and believe what you say. Now I think it is about time for you to return home and get ready for summer work on the farm, so I will look for you shortly. Your people all send love."[63] Agent Adams told the commissioner of Indian affairs that he believed the dance was "a bad thing ... physically, morally, and financially."[64] Adams tried to deprive Kiowa, Caddo, and Wichita dancers of certain privileges, which followers of Sitting Bull (the Arapaho) resented but Adams thought effective.[65]

Apiatan's letters home discouraged many Kiowa dancers. James Mooney claimed he was present when a letter sent by Apiatan (while he was at Fort Hall, which would have predated the letter from Saint Stephen's) was read to Kiowas by Apiatan's sister Laura Dunmoi, a former Carlisle student. Mooney said the crowd was divided; some felt "that the ground had been taken from under them," while others stayed faithful.[66] Although many Kiowa dancers stopped dancing because of the letters, others persisted because they knew Apiatan's letter came to them through two white men. Moreover, Apiatan's January 26 letter did not offer any details about why he had reached his conclusions. And the dancers knew Apiatan spoke little English (the letter must have been transcribed by a translator), so they decided to wait until Apiatan's return before changing their minds. Lieutenant Scott reported that even though "a number" of Kiowas put aside "the doctrine of the new earth," they hoped to continue the dances as a way to worship the "'Christ' who is in heaven" and "to pray to him for what they need."[67] They still held a large dance before Apiatan's return.

After five months absent, Apiatan arrived home in February 1891 (the Fort Hall agent had helped Apiatan raise some money to get him there).[68] Apiatan's personal testimony and recommendation to end the dances would greatly reduce the popularity of the movement among Kiowas. Hundreds of Indians attended a scheduled council on February 19 in which Apiatan recounted his journey and confronted Sitting Bull, the Northern Arapaho who had spent weeks propagating the movement in Indian Territory. Agent Adams called for the council, knowing that Apiatan would influence a good percentage of the Kiowas. However, Sitting Bull also claimed to have met

Wovoka in 1890, and his story was much different from Apiatan's. It proved to be a monumental debate and an important event in Kiowa history.

Sitting Bull held a lot of influence with the southern tribes. Incredibly, in late January 1891, a month after Wounded Knee, Charles Ashley, the Cheyenne-Arapaho agent, allowed Sitting Bull to visit the Wichitas and Caddos, unconcerned about his influence as "a teacher of this faith."[69] Laura Tatum, a Wichita, and Thomas Wooster, a Caddo, traveled from the Kiowa, Comanche, and Wichita Reservation to Agent Ashley's office, at least fifty miles, to ask him if Sitting Bull could come to their homes. Ashley told their agent that Sitting Bull was a "good Indian," that he had "no trouble with him," and that he did not object to the visit.

At the February 19, 1891, council, Apiatan challenged Sitting Bull's beliefs. Every word of the debates was translated into English, Kiowa, Comanche, Caddo, Wichita, and Arapaho—a slow process according to James Mooney, who attended the gathering. Agent Adams and different headmen asked Apiatan about his experience before Sitting Bull was given the chance to defend himself. Apiatan accused Sitting Bull of deceiving Indian Territory for economic gain. He had been given horses and other gifts by believers, which had been a point of controversy among skeptical Kiowas.[70] In fact, back in late December, James Deere (a Kiowa critic of the dance) had written a letter to his agent to report that his people were giving Sitting Bull too many horses and cattle, so much so that "the Cheyenne medicine man" had gotten "rich in stock since they been dancing."[71] Sitting Bull was making the Kiowas "very poor" because he told them they should "do away with their cattle and hogs" because "Jesus is coming." During the council, Sitting Bull defended himself by saying that he never asked for anything and would return everything if asked (Apiatan reminded him that Kiowas would never take back what had been given).

Some who attended the council remembered it as one of the worst days in Kiowa history.[72] Many more Kiowas were persuaded by Apiatan's arguments. They had heard the testimonies of those who had met Wovoka before, from both Black Coyote and Sitting Bull, but Apiatan's was perhaps the first firsthand story that denied the truth of the movement. It was reported that the commissioner planned to send several thousand copies of Apiatan's story to all the dancers in the West.[73]

Although most (but not all) Kiowas accepted Apiatan's version, Caddos and Wichitas continued to dance at the reservation. And in the years that followed, particularly 1894 and 1895, Kiowas did experience periodic revivals of the Ghost Dance and its songs, even into the twentieth century.[74] In the fall of 1895, the new Kiowa agent asked the US Army to help the Indian police break up the dances led by Afraid of Bears, but it was ineffective.[75] Afraid of Bears, who was blind, entered trances and claimed to speak with Jesus, who told him that whites were their adversaries because they had "hemmed them in a small reservation."[76] Afraid of Bears believed that Jesus wanted Kiowas to dance and that Jesus had "a good home above where is plenty of land and buffaloes and no white people." Afraid of Bears undoubtedly kept Wovoka's message alive, and the US government struggled to do anything about it.[77]

Apiatan, on the other hand, was given a silver medal because of his "services to the Government" during the "Messiah craze."[78] Indian Affairs spent much more, $500, on the construction of a house for Apiatan because of his influence "in persuading his people of the falsity of the rumors of the coming of the 'New Christ.'"[79] In 1930, the US government spent another $500 painting and repairing the house for the then seventy-three-year-old Apiatan, citing his service during the Ghost Dance.[80]

Another Investigation from the Southern Plains

In July 1891, Fort Hall hosted a new delegation from the South, this time Southern Arapahos from the Cheyenne-Arapaho Reservation.[81] Casper Edson, a former Carlisle student, joined two other Southern Arapahos, Little Raven and Red Wolf, on their own self-funded investigative mission similar to Apiatan's.[82] They left with permission, but under the guise of visiting friends and relatives at the Wind River Reservation in Wyoming, not telling their agent the true purpose of the trip.[83] Their agent, Charles Ashley, was glad to allow Edson the opportunity; after all, he was employed at the Arapaho Agency school and was considered "one of the brightest and best of the returned students." He had returned home from Carlisle in November 1890. Little Raven and Red Wolf were two "of the best of the uneducated Indian young men." The Carlisle school paper, the *Indian Helper*, once described Edson as "one of our earnest, thoughtful students" and was sure the he would "do well in whatever he finds to do, whether it be upon the reservation or away from it."[84] But unlike Apiatan's journey, Edson's would give more credence to Wovoka's dance.

A previous delegation from the Cheyenne-Arapaho Reservation led by Frank Tall Bull, the captain of the Southern Cheyenne police, had visited Wovoka in early 1891.[85] The Southern Arapaho scout Arnold Woolworth (Bagugi or Big Boy), another former Carlisle student, interpreted for the group, which included an unknown woman.[86] They participated in a Ghost Dance with the Paiutes under the direction of Wovoka and brought home balls of Wovoka's sacred red ochre (which was mined near his home and was used to make paint). Not much else is known about Tall Bull's journey, but Casper Edson's group decided to head north soon after their return. Some Cheyennes and Arapahos were dancing "day and night" on their reservation in early 1891, with around 165 attending in late January.[87]

Edson, Little Raven, and Red Wolf traveled by trail from Darlington (near present-day El Reno, Oklahoma) to the Fort Hall Reservation, where they met a group of English-speaking Shoshones and Bannocks at the Pocatello train station. After becoming acquainted, they were led to the house of Tighee, a Bannock chief, at Fort Hall and joined them in a council that lasted all day. The men lied to the white officials at Fort Hall, telling them that they were "traveling for pleasure to the Pacific Coast" and that it was only by accident that they met the Shoshones and Bannocks at Pocatello. Lt. W. H. Johnston, who happened to be a recruiting officer, was instructed to give the trio a tent and rations, but he would only do so after Edson, who spoke fluent English, agreed to help "induce" Fort Hall Indians to enlist in the army.[88]

Edson, Little Raven, and Red Wolf stayed at Lieutenant Johnston's camp for five days and visited Tighee's house occasionally. "They seemed very intelligent," Johnston observed, "yet talked only with the wildest and most ignorant Bannocks; avoiding the more progressive Shoshones."[89] On July 28, the men told Johnston that they were going to board a northbound train to Montana, but Johnston saw them hiding in a baggage car that was heading south with other Indians in traditional dress. The lieutenant tried to speak to the men, but they ignored him. Confused, Lieutenant Johnston questioned those who made contact with the men and discovered that they really were on their way to the Walker River Reservation to meet Wovoka. They had stopped at Fort Hall, intending to meet some Crows to travel the rest of the way with. The Fort Hall agent, S. G. Fisher, wrote to the Arapahos' agent as well as the Nevada agent, C. C. Warner, to inform them.

Agent Warner reported that the group arrived there, in Elko, Nevada, on August 1 and that Edson told him that the men were on a vacation, wanting to see that part of the country. Warner gave them passes to Walker River and asked the Central Pacific Railroad to give them passes back east, all the way to Ogden, Utah, when they were ready to leave. Warner did all this before he knew that the "sole mission" of the Southern Arapahos was to see Wovoka. He later acknowledged that he would not have permitted them to go to Walker River if he had known.[90]

Nevertheless, Edson, Little Raven, and Red Wolf took a C&C express train on August 10 to Mason Valley, where they reportedly found Wovoka pitching hay for a wage.[91] Two other Southern Arapahos, Black Coyote, a policeman, and Grant Left Hand, the son of Chief Left Hand and one of the first students at Carlisle, and two Southern Cheyennes, Black Sharp Nose and Standing Bull, were also at that meeting, probably as members of Edson's delegation.[92] Black Coyote, who had brought instructions for the dance to the Southern Arapahos after he made an earlier trip to the Northern Arapahos at Wind River, told Mooney that Wovoka demonstrated his power after he waved eagle feathers over his empty hat. Inside, Black Coyote "saw the whole world."

Casper Edson and Grant Left Hand interpreted and, on the spot, wrote down in English what Wovoka told them. Edson brought that written message home to the Cheyenne-Arapaho Reservation, confirming the truth of the movement while relaying Wovoka's instructions east. Anthropologist James Mooney was eventually able to read this message—he called it the "Messiah Letter"—even though Wovoka explicitly told the men not to show his words to a white man. Black Sharp Nose trusted Mooney enough to show him the letter because Mooney himself had visited Wovoka in January 1892. Historians can only wonder what other letters were kept secret, but Edson's transcript remains. The letter instructed, "When you get home you make dance."[93] On the reverse side of the "Messiah Letter," Black Sharp Nose's daughter rewrote Edson's transcript into clearer English; Mooney called this the "Cheyenne version":

> You must dance four nights and one day time. You will take bath in the morning before you go to yours homes, for every body, and give you all the same as this. Jackson Wilson likes you all, he is glad to get good many things. His heart satting fully of gladness, after you get home, I will give you a good cloud and give you chance to make you feel good. I give you a good spirit, and give you all good paint, I want you people to come here again, want them in three months any tribe of you from there. . . . Grandfather, said, when they were die never cry, no hurt any body, do any harm for it, not to fight. Be a good behave always. I will give a satisfaction in your life. This young man is a good father and mother. Do not tell the white people about this, Juses is on the ground, he just like cloud. Every body is a live again. I don't know when he will be here, may be will be this fall or in spring. When it happen it may be this. There will be no sickness and return to young again. Do not refuse to work for white man or do not make any trouble with them until you leave them. When the earth shakes do not be afraid it will not hurt you. I want you to make dance for six weeks. Eat and wash good clean yourselves.[94]

Wovoka's message had to be written down in English because there was no written form of the Cheyenne or Arapaho languages. The message was carried from Wovoka's lips, through an interpreter who understood Paiute and Arapaho, to Casper Edson, who translated the translator's words into written English.

Following Edson and Grant Left Hand's return to Indian Territory and their delivery of the Wovoka's message, Southern Cheyennes and Southern Arapahos tried to convince the authorities that the Ghost Dance was harmless so that it could continue. In December 1891, Southern Arapaho headman Row of Lodges told Agent Charles Ashley that their ceremony was a prayer to the Great Spirit "to make them a better people and teach them the ways of the white man, they might grow to be a prosperous, happy and powerful people; that the songs they sang were similar, in sentiment, to those sung by the Indian children in school" (referring to church hymns).[95] Suspicious of Row of Lodges's claim, Ashley asked "the educated young Indians of the tribe" if that was the purpose of their Ghost Dancing. They said that it was.

Because of Row of Lodges's description, Ashley, who had done his fair share to suppress the Ghost Dance, reported to the commissioner of Indian affairs that the Ghost Dance, as practiced by the Southern Arapahos, was "a long step in the direction of true religion, as compared with their former customs of worship." It resembled the religion that Agent Ashley recognized, something closer, in his mind, to Christianity. Row of Lodges did believe in one God; he said that the Ghost Dance "may differ from other religions; it is good for it teaches there is but one father."[96] The efforts by Edson, Row of Lodges, and other Cheyennes and Arapahos to communicate the purpose of the movement finally got through to Agent Ashley. In his opinion, the Ghost Dance's ideas promoted progressive ways and did not "interfere with their industrial pursuits to any considerable extent." Ashley told James Mooney that he saw "no particular harm" in the Ghost Dance and that he "never interfered with it excepting in the working season."[97] Even some of the Arapahos at the Seger Colony, founded by missionaries, were dancing in late 1891, and other groups of Cheyennes and Arapahos visited Wovoka in January and October 1892.[98]

"When First Our Father Came, I Prayed to Him"

Casper Edson, by all accounts a standout at Carlisle, used written English to encourage belief in Wovoka's message. Native Americans used so-called modern means to acquire and disseminate ideas about the Ghost Dance, but most white Americans saw nothing modern, or civilized, in the movement. There was a long-held misconception that the Ghost Dance movement was opposed to all elements of American modernity, which masked the innovative ways in which the dance was spread. In November 1890, the *New York Times*, covering the "Indian Messiah Delusion," reported that the Ghost Dance appealed to Indians who saw themselves as belonging to the same "red" race, "particularly to those who oppose civilized life." "Never has unadulterated native Americanism been carried further," the reporter declared.[99] Whites thought the Ghost Dance movement was incompatible with American modernity; it was "native Americanism," not Americanism.

The success of the Ghost Dance also convinced many whites, even some who identified themselves as "friends of the Indian," that Indians were simply too different, or too inferior, to become civilized in the American sense of the word. At the 1891 Lake Mohonk Conference, an event organized annually by whites to discuss Indian education and rights, Merril Gates, the president of the conference and of Amherst College, expressed his pessimism in the aftermath of the Wounded Knee Massacre, saying that the event was a "disaster" that made clear the dangers of "savagery." But according to Gates, the savagery was the Ghost Dance, not the slaughter of innocents at Wounded Knee. It was a "superstitious" movement, the antithesis of modernity, that only a simple-minded person could believe in. He claimed that for somebody "brought up in the atmosphere of Christian civilization to enter the consciousness of the savage at such a time is almost as impossible as it is for us to get behind the great, blue limpid eyes of the ox as he chews his cud in the pasture, and know how the world looks to him."[100] Those who were civilized, like himself, could not comprehend the mind of a Ghost Dancer just as a white man cannot understand what is going on in the mind of an animal.

But what about those Indians who had spent years within the artifice of a Christianizing, civilizing school? Were they immune to the "savagery" of the Ghost Dance? Casper Edson used what he learned in a school that existed to eradicate Indianness to propagate religious ideas that embodied Indianness. Belief or doubt in the Ghost Dance movement did not always hinge on an Indian's level of white education. Apiatan, the Kiowa who denounced the movement, was not educated like Edson was.

Some educated Indians who were deemed to be civilized by white observers became Ghost Dancers nonetheless. Paul Boynton, a Southern

Casper Edson in 1888 *(left)* and Apiatan and his wife sometime in the 1890s. Smithsonian Institution, National Anthropological Archives, NAA 74176, PL 81–12 06894700, and The Huntington Library, San Marino, California, photCL 161.

Arapaho (of Cheyenne and Arapaho descent), who was described as a "proficient" typesetter and a "good penman," was a clerk at the Cheyenne-Arapaho Reservation in 1890 and 1891. He had attended Carlisle off and on from 1880 to 1889. A white missionary named John Seger saw Boynton at the agency in December 1890 or January 1891 and reflected on how much Boynton had changed while at Carlisle. He had once been a boy with long hair, dressed in "Indian costume"; now he sat with pen in hand at his own desk in the agency office. Seger saw that Boynton's "knowledge of the English language" made him a good fit to be a clerk. Seger's observations led him to believe that Boynton and the other students there were "trying to exterminate the Indians within themselves by leading industrious lives."[101] But Seger did not know that Boynton and some other boarding school returnees were actively involved in the Ghost Dance on the reservation. In fact, Boynton, as a member of a Presbyterian church, had joined a Comanche peyote society in 1884 and was an active peyotist for years to come.[102] He experienced the Ghost Dance like many others; he once fell into a trance and talked with his dead brother. Boynton wrote a song about the encounter in Arapaho, which Mooney translated:

> When first our father came—Ahe'ey'!
> When first our father came—Ahe'ey'!
> I prayed to him, I prayed to him—
> My relative, my relative—
> He'yahe'eye'![103]

Boynton, like most Indian students, never met white expectations for education.[104] Indian students gathered knowledge and learned how to read and write, but they never intended to "exterminate the Indians within themselves." Educators' rhetoric never became reality. While students negotiated their changing worlds in ways whites deemed "civilized," many still envisioned their futures through the lens of Indigenous spirituality.

By 1890, there were thousands of educated Natives living on western reservations, but officials were concerned that graduates of the US government's most prominent Indian schools, Carlisle and Hampton in particular, might be using their education to help promote the Ghost Dance.[105] A government inquiry was made, spurred by an American public concerned with the effectiveness of those tax-funded schools. In the midst of the Ghost Dance troubles in the fall of 1890, Congress was preparing to give attention to a new Indian appropriation bill, and the commissioner of Indian affairs, Thomas Morgan, hoped to determine where additional funds should be directed.[106] There was a concerted effort by educators and the US government to cover up the fact that some Ghost Dancers decided to use their education to broadcast Wovoka's message to Native and white audiences across the continent.[107]

Some, like Casper Edson and Grant Left Hand, are known to have played critical roles in the dissemination of the movement. Smith Curley, a Southern Arapaho who was said to be a "Carlisle boy" (although no record of his attendance, or much of his life, exists), was called Sitting Bull's (the Arapaho's) "lieutenant" by Lt. Hugh Lennox Scott.[108] It is not clear what role a lieutenant might serve for Sitting Bull—he may have served as an interpreter and letter writer—but Scott thought it was an important one. In early January 1891, Scott obtained five Arapaho "Messiah songs" from a "Carlisle boy," probably Curley.[109] Another former Carlisle student, Raymond Stewart (White Bull), a Rosebud Brulé, played the important role as Short Bull's "private secretary" while Short Bull, Kicking Bear, and their followers were dancing in the Badlands in late November and December 1890, according to William C. Courtis, the postmaster at Rosebud.[110] Courtis hoped that Stewart would one day "furnish us with a History of the Sioux Rebellion of 1890," but Stewart never wrote his side of the story, and Stewart's letters written for Short Bull have not survived. Stewart was not the only former boarding school student from Rosebud or Pine Ridge who was involved with the so-called hostiles who fled to the Badlands. Edgar White Horse, Arthur Two Strike, Plenty Living Bear (Plenty Horses, son of Living Bear), Julia Walking Crane, Clayton Brave, Edward Star, George Little Wound, Mack Kutepi, Robert White Cow Killer, Isaac Bear, and Howard Goes Flying were officially identified, though certainly more involved themselves with the Ghost Dance to some degree.[111]

Although agents knew that educated Indians were among the Ghost Dancers, Indian educators, especially Pratt, tried to deny their former students' involvement. Newspaper reports surfaced that former eastern boarding school students were among the "hostiles" who refused to come to the agency and surrender after Wounded Knee (under the headline "They Turned Ghost Dancers").[112] Commissioner Morgan had called education "the medium through which the rising generation of Indians are to be brought into fraternal and harmonious relationship with their white fellow-citizens," but it seemed that education was being used to generate dissent against white authority.[113]

By the end of 1891, however, educators and officials had effectively shifted the narrative and convinced most Americans that educated Indians had nothing to do with the Ghost Dance's success.[114] Like Carlisle, the Hampton Institute eventually proclaimed that its educated pupils resisted the dance. Their conversion "received its test in the ghost craze of '91 and came out victorious; light and truth had triumphed over darkness and superstition."[115] Herbert Welsh, head of the Indian Rights Association, was worried that Congress would soon reduce Indian appropriations by $2 million, which would destroy Indian schools.[116] But he argued that Indian education actually saved the US government money; it was the "cheapest as well as the only humane and honest solution" to the Indian problem. The "Indian uprising" of 1890–91 was caused by "the ignorance and savagery of those Sioux Indians who we had left without education" (along with "other dangerous elements" like "hunger, spoil-system Agents, etc."). If the Indians were better educated, Welsh reasoned, then they would no longer believe in superstitious religions and they would not resist the US government.[117] It was an effective sleight of hand by Welsh; he placed blame for the Ghost Dance on the politicians who opposed funding for Indian education while concealing the involvement of educated Indians. The schools remained funded.

In 1891, the *Journal of American Folklore* published an assessment of the Ghost Dance by ethnologist Alice C. Fletcher, one of earliest scholarly publications about the movement. Fletcher inaccurately reported that the "craze" was "confined almost exclusively to the uneducated."[118] If it was not for the "non-progressive and turbulent elements," she thought, the "progressive and educated part of the people" would have killed the movement. While ignoring the efforts of former students to propagate the dance, educators also did not mention the literate young men and women, like Josephine Waggoner or Abe Somers, who remained skeptical of Wovoka but helped others send and receive information about him. Despite evidence to the contrary, educated Indians were left out of the narrative of the Ghost Dance, as was the modern means of its dissemination. Like most of her contemporaries, Fletcher detached the elevating effects of education from the "craze," but many Natives used literacy to foster their culture, not destroy it. The education by the colonizers did not always eradicate one's spiritualism or one's opposition to American colonialism. Native Americans understood that the new forms of communication taught at schools could spread their ideas on a mass scale, bringing them closer together.

Lines of Communication Well Established

Because of the results of the so-called Messiah craze at Pine Ridge, whites continued to fear the dissension that Native communication might create on western reservations. In February 1893, the Associated Press reported troubles at Pine Ridge after the murder of three white men at a beef contractor's camp on the reserve. The article suggested that further trouble might be imminent, perhaps even an outbreak, and former agent Valentine McGillycuddy told a reporter that talk of the Messiah was still common at Pine Ridge, as if those two developments were connected. But "the most significant" sign of trouble, according to the Associated Press, was "the fact that there has been communication between the various Indian tribes all during the past year of a secret and apparently important nature."[119] There was even a "line of communication well established and constantly used between Indian Territory and British America." Because of this network, "the Indians all along the line understand that the other bands are kept posted." Nothing violent came out of these reports, of course, but they demonstrate the suspicion whites held about any associations among the tribes of the West. Intertribal networks only grew in the 1890s, and the message of the Ghost Dance persisted through those connections, which worried Indian Affairs.

As the Ghost Dance carried on year after year, eventually into the new century, the US government continued to attack the communication that sustained it.[120] The need to control anticolonial information drove some agents to create outlandish plans of surveillance and espionage. Crow agent J. W. Watson crafted a convoluted plan in early 1895 to discover what Crows knew about the Ghost Dance and what information was being shared with their former rivals, the Lakotas. Watson had become worried about the work of Bad Belly, the Ghost Dance proponent who had received permission to visit Pine Ridge and Rosebud back in August 1890 (see chapter 6) but never returned to the Crow Reservation permanently. Bad Belly had been teaching and spreading the movement for several years, traveling around so much that the Agent Watson could not track him down. His beliefs had "taken some slight hold on the Crows, but not to amount to anything worth considering seriously."[121] But Watson wanted to know if Bad Belly's teachings and influence were "widespread or spread to any extent at all outside of the Reservation." He proposed to Agent Penny at Pine Ridge that a group of Crows should be allowed to visit the Oglalas at Pine Ridge. While there, Watson suspected that the Crows and Oglalas would discuss "the Messiah matter," and they might even talk about Bad Belly and his teachings. The Pine Ridge police would (in theory) later ascertain, by questioning the Oglalas, "pretty accurately how far, if at all," the Oglalas "were affected in this Ghost Dance and 'Messiah' matter" and whether or not "the Messiah craze has spread any or is likely to spread." It is not known how successful Watson's plan turned out to be, but it is clear that Watson knew that the Ghost Dance was disseminated through intertribal networks, and he went to great lengths to try to silence it.

Wovoka, in the years following his revelation, received letters from distant Indian groups in "considerable numbers."[122] Ed A. Dyer, who operated a general store in Mason Valley, frequently translated and answered these letters. Dyer stated that many were from Grant Left Hand and postmarked Darlington, Oklahoma, home of the Cheyenne-Arapaho Reservation. Left Hand seemed to be a "scribe for most of the Indian Nations" as he invariably sought invitations for others to see Wovoka. He also requested multiple sacred items from Wovoka, who made a habit of sending visiting delegates back with balls of red ochre, magpie feathers, rabbit furs, and other religious tokens. This led others to want balls of red ochre of their own, and Wovoka obliged, sending and usually selling the paint balls, magpie feathers, and items of his worn clothing, particularly shirts and hats. Just as Sears Roebuck was ramping up its mail order business, Wovoka was selling a great many "Texas Plaza Hats" for twenty dollars apiece and shipping them 1,500 miles through the United States Postal Service. The "Father," as the letters addressed him, received all kinds of gifts of "Indian finery": moccasins, vests, gloves, shirts, pants, and headdresses, particularly from Bannocks in

Idaho. Wovoka, with the aid of Dyer, would reply with gratitude and most likely a word or two about his dance.[123]

However, Wovoka, for a time, responded to these letters with unusual secrecy. He would sneak into Dyer's grocery store at night, have the letters read to him, and have Dyer prepare the proper packages in response.[124] In the fall of 1892, Agent C. C. Warner at the Nevada Agency grew concerned with claims from the press that Wovoka was having "an evil influence" on the Indians who visited him.[125] The *Silver State* reported that Wovoka had sent "emissaries" to Fort Hall, "urging them to inaugurate ghost dances and prepare for war this spring."[126] According to the newspaper, some Bannocks at Fort Hall were also angry with Wovoka because they thought he was stirring up trouble with whites. Agent Warner was "fearful of its results abroad."[127] Wovoka knew the negative attention his activities were drawing.[128]

Because of the antagonism toward the dance and the perception among whites that the movement was militant, it is no surprise that Wovoka and many believers were cautious in the years after Wounded Knee. When James Mooney visited the Northern Arapahos at Wind River in 1892, the agent told him that the Indians were no longer dancing because of his efforts to curtail it. The agency clerk and interpreter even took Mooney out to a camp to talk with some Arapahos "over a pipe and a cup of coffee," and all of the men "were so ignorant" about the Ghost Dance "that they wanted to know what it meant."[129] But later that night, as Mooney traveled to another camp with the interpreter, they heard "the familiar cadence of the ghost songs." The interpreter, Henry Reed (of Cheyenne, Arapaho, and European descent), who had been asked by his agent to "spy" on Mooney, finally admitted to Mooney, "Yes, they are dancing the Ghost dance. That's something I have never reported, and I never will. It is their religion and they have a right to it."[130]

The Wind River agent would have tried to end the Ghost Dancing had Reed told him about it—he thought the Ghost Dance was "dangerous"—but the agent could not ban dancing outright. In fact, as James Mooney's trip to Wind River was winding down, Shoshones and Arapahos received permission from the agent to hold their annual Sun Dance, violating Indian Affairs policy. Like other agents, he believed that "the Indians had to have some amusements," but in truth, he could do little to suppress all dancing. This inability of the US government to curtail dancing was a trend that James Mooney observed at several reservations in 1892. He claimed that "not a single agent on any important reservation" even pretended to enforce Indian Affairs' total prohibition on dancing.[131] Because they did not have the power to enforce Indian Affairs policies, agents had to compromise and attack what they considered to be the lesser of two evils—ban the Ghost Dance, but allow the Sun Dance. Unlike the Wind River agent, the Kiowa agent, George Day, decided to keep suppressing the Sun Dance while turning a blind eye to Ghost Dancing, which was going on within earshot of the agent and Mooney during their conversation. Soon after, Mooney saw Day allowing "a large party" of Southern Cheyennes and Southern Arapahos to visit Kiowas to dance the "pony dances" for "several weeks."[132]

Even more remarkably, according to Mooney, Day also joined Kiowas in one of their dances and "went through the motions and songs as well as he was able and urgently called upon several of the head chiefs to join him." The commissioner of Indian affairs would have relieved Agent Day of his duties had he known, but the commissioner was not the one trying to control and transform hundreds of unwilling Indians at the ground level. The following year, 1894, the folks at the Kiowa, Comanche, and Wichita Reservation got a new acting agent, who ordered that Ghost Dancing stop, but the dancers refused and had a dance anyway.[133] There were *several thousand* participants from "all the surrounding tribes."[134]

Among Native Americans, after the Wounded Knee Massacre, the Ghost Dance continued to be practiced by believers, investigated by the uncertain, and disputed by critics. Indian agents were given the task of policing the beliefs of colonized people, which was impossible. Not only did agents not understand Native American beliefs, they could do little to prevent Indians from thinking about and discussing those ideas collectively. What does this say about the relationship of power between the US government and the tribal nations of the West in the late nineteenth century? Despite colonization, it is clear that Native Americans were not powerless, in part because they were able to control their avenues of exchange. As Crow agent J. W. Watson observed, strong connections were created among distant nations, even among once bitter enemies, and those nations shared information that they thought could be mutually beneficial. If the designs of the US government's reservation system had worked, groups like the Crows and Oglalas or the Kiowas and Southern Cheyennes would not have been able to communicate such things. But Native men and women remained mobile and exchanged ideas and information, giving them additional control over their own lives.

Conclusion

Belief in the Ghost Dance and its practice persisted into the 1900s, even spreading farther into Canada along intertribal connections.[1] In 1902, the dance was brought to the Sioux Wahpeton Reserve at Round Plain (near Prince Albert, Saskatchewan) by an Assiniboine named Fred Robinson, who had recently learned about Wovoka's movement from Kicking Bear, who was still a Lakota proponent of the dance.[2] Wovoka received letters from Fred Robinson and R. W. Medicine in Saskatchewan (at what was the then called Moose Wood Reserve, now the Whitecap Dakota Reservation). In a surviving letter from 1909, Fred Robinson asked Wovoka (known to them as Jack Wilson) for three cans of red ochre and for help improving the lives of his people. "I am telling them about the news," he wrote. "I am telling every day what they ought to do father will you help me with the heart of the people? . . . How can it be done to grow one church or prayer? . . . Help me that I want the people on earth to think and go into the road of life." Wovoka's responses do not survive, but Robinson received his paint. He wrote Wovoka six more times that year and visited him in 1910.[3] Anthropologist Grace Dangberg collected fourteen other surviving letters written by eleven different men and one woman from a variety of tribal nations between 1908 and 1911.[4]

Fred Robinson's efforts to incorporate Ghost Dance teachings in the community at Prince Albert, Saskatchewan, were successful. Wovoka's message was interpreted by Sissetons at Prince Albert as the importance of leading "a clean, honest life," which would reunite a "believer" with their "loved ones after death" but not bring the dead back to life.[5] Ghost Dancing around Prince Albert among Sissetons (and perhaps Plains Crees) continued "strong" until 1922, and some dancing lasted until around 1950, but the "ethical code" of the movement endured in the community.[6]

Jack Wilson (Wovoka) on the set of the silent film *The Thundering Herd* in 1924 near Mulner Lake, California. Behind him stand Northern Arapahos *(left to right)* Charlie Whiteman, Rising Buffalo, Red Pipe, Woman Dress, Chief Lodge, Night Horse, Painted Wolf, Many Tipi Poles, and Goes in Lodge. Smithsonian Institution, National Anthropological Archives, NAA SPC 003068.00.

Ghost Dancing also persisted in the southern plains, and many Ghost Dancers became or were already adherents of the peyote religion (which was officially incorporated as the Native American Church in 1918). Peyotism also spread through intertribal connections, moving slowly out of Mexico and Texas into Indian Territory in the 1870s and 1880s through Carrizos, Lipan, Mescalero, and Plains Apaches; Kiowas; and Comanches (with the help of folks already mentioned in this study, Quanah Parker and Paul Boynton, among them).[7] In the Southern Plains, peyote began to be used as a sacrament in sacred ceremonies, and it was fused with a system of Christian ethics. Because of the great connectivity in Indian Territory, peyotism diffused and evolved rapidly in the 1890s among Southern Arapahos, Southern Cheyennes, Comanches, Kiowas, Pawnees, Poncas, Otoes, Wichitas, Caddos, Delawares, and Quapaws in far northeast Indian Territory.

Some in Indian Territory, including Kiowas, practiced peyotism alongside the Ghost Dance.[8] Frank White, the Pawnee Ghost Dance leader, may have encountered peyotism and the Ghost Dance during the same visit to the Comanches and Wichitas.[9] Peyote roadmen, like Ghost Dancer John Wilson (Caddo), carried the peyote buttons, their ceremonies, and their ethical teachings (decency, clean living, and industriousness) to other groups. Railroad expansion also expanded peyotism with rail lines heading to the Mexican American peyote fields in South Texas.[10] Boxes filled with lightweight peyote were shipped up to Indian Territory through the US Postal Service. By the end of the first decade of the twentieth century, peyotists were practicing across the North American West.

Like the Ghost Dance, Sun Dance, and other Indigenous religious concepts, the US government did what it could to prevent the propagation of the peyote religious complex, but the Native American Church is now the largest pan-Indian religious organization in the United States. The Ghost Dance as a practice, however, did not survive US government attacks. In 1915, a new agent at the Kiowa Reservation finally ended Ghost Dancing there. He told Ghost Dancers that they would lose their per capita payments if they held their planned weeklong dance.[11] Apiatan, still denouncing the Ghost Dance, wrote a letter of support for the new agent to the commissioner of Indian affairs, while Afraid of Bears, still leading Ghost Dances, argued that they prayed "to the same savior and the Father, who made the heaven and earth," as white people.[12] Chief Big Tree, who was a Christian and a peyotist, also beautifully argued for religious liberty, just as he had done during the 1890 dancing (see chapter 6). Some Kiowas danced when they wanted to anyway, joined by visiting Southern Cheyennes, so the Kiowa agent withheld the per capita money from seventy-nine Kiowas because of unauthorized dancing, effectively ending the Ghost Dance there. In order to get the money owed to them, the dancers would have to sign an affidavit promising to never hold the Ghost Dance or gift dances again. Most of them refused to sign, including Red Buffalo, who had been a Ghost Dancer since the 1890s and whom the Red Buffalo Hall at the Kiowa Tribal Complex in Carnegie, Oklahoma, is named after. Kiowas gather there for powwows with visiting nations from across the continent.[13]

The Ghost Dance and the peyote religion—their ideas and all the news and information surrounding them—were only a small fraction of what was exchanged among Native Americans living on reservations before the twentieth century. Below is a portion of a letter that reveals what typical correspondence between separated relatives looked like in the 1890s. In the Dakota language, John Kills Swimming (Nuwan Kte or Anuwakte) at Pine Ridge penned a few lines to his cousin Frank White Belly (Tezi Ska) living on a different reservation on August 10, 1896:

> This day I will write you this letter. I will tell you how we are. We all have been very well, except that High Thunder Wind is dead and I have felt badly, but I feel better now, and, therefore I write you this letter. He died sometime ago therefore you may have heard it before this. It occurred about June 18th. There was a general good time during the Fourth of July. Cousin you got a sister-in-law on the 18th of May; and another one on July 8th. I still live with her, friend, and it is always pleasant. Cousin, I write this while I came to town although I am here for a trip.... A council was held and I just came out of it when I write this. Cousin, it is just eight days hence when there will be some good time—it will be issue time. Cousin, now tell me how you are. Cousin, how are my aunt and Kills-young? Tell me.... Now it is your turn to tell me some news. When you see this write me one very soon. I shake your hands with a happy heart.[14]

Kills Swimming wanted to relay bad news about a death and good news about two marriages. He told White Belly that he was doing "very well," that his community had a good Fourth of July, and that he wanted to know how his cousin and aunt were doing. This is only one of thousands of letters sent and received by western Natives during a quarter century that brought enormous change to their lives. John Kills Swimming and most Native Americans in the West were living as colonized people on reservations, but they did express themselves outside the dominion of white America. Even illiterate men and women, perhaps of the older generation, continued to take part in this great exchange. One Indian agent reported that his office had written three hundred letters for Indians "to friends on distant reservations, even to points in Canada," in a single year.[15]

But, as this study has shown, Natives were not given complete freedom to communicate. Sometimes communication among Indigenous men and women did not align with colonial policies or strategies. When the US government saw such anticolonial information passed from reservation to reservation, there were often attempts to suppress it. In 1892, Tall Bull (Lakota) was ordered to be arrested after he wrote letters to Hump (at Cheyenne River) and Running Antelope (at Standing Rock), inviting them to come to Pine Ridge to join his people in a "strike for their rights of which they had so long been deprived."[16] Tall Bull, who had already ignored US government authority by moving from Cheyenne River to Pine Ridge without permission, was pushing for united defiance, perhaps a plan to fight for their freedom of religion, which was not tolerated by the Office of Indian Affairs.

For Native Americans, imparting information meant to weaken US government control through letters or during visits was an effort toward decolonization. Before the twentieth century, western Natives fought effectively to decolonize their lives—to diminish US government interference—by sharing their ideas with other colonized people. Lakota letter writers urged others to join the movement against the Dawes Severalty Act, Pawnees advised Ponca leaders to fight their relocation to Indian Territory, and Utes acquired the Sun Dance from their new Plains friends as that important ritual was being attacked by US Indian agents. Anticolonial communications often led to anticolonial actions.

And, as we have seen in this study, intertribal relationships were often nurtured through a common opposition to the colonial policies of the Office of Indian Affairs. The Ghost Dance, deemed to be anticolonial by many US authorities, continued to be a common cause among tribes years after it began. In 1894, two Shoshone leaders at Fort Hall, James Bollard and Joe Wheeler, wrote to Kicking Bear, the Lakota Ghost Dance proponent, to maintain a connection with the Lakotas who had recently visited their reservation and to urge their friends to continue to fight for their way of life.[17] The Pine Ridge agent obtained the letter and forwarded it to the commissioner of Indian affairs because he "had no doubt" that "its real meaning" was to "revive the Ghost Dancing" at Pine Ridge. It read,

> We the undersigned chiefs and head men of the Shoshone and Bannock tribe of Indians, hereby write you our appreciation of the visit of your people to our Reservation. You people have seen with their own eyes what we are doing out here in the west. We still have all our old customs, providing such dances and sports do not in any way interfere with our work etc. We believe there is time for everything in this world—time for work, time for dancing and pleasure, and time for sleep. We understand that out in your country, all old Indian games customs are abolished. We fail to see the humanity and justice in abolishing all our time immemorial pastimes and forms of worship. We see no harm in indulging in worshipping the Great Spirit in our old way, and also see no harm in our old games and sports, long

as they do not interfere with our work. We earnestly hope you shall explain to your Agent and prove to him there is no evil in your customs of worship and dances etc.[18]

The leaders reminded the Lakotas what Shoshones had accomplished at Fort Hall and urged Lakotas to try to keep their "customs of worship and dances" from being abolished. James Bollard and Joe Wheeler, who cared about the experiences of other tribes, hoped Lakotas would challenge government authority and convince their agents that there was "no evil" in their religion. Whether the Shoshone leaders were promoting the Ghost Dance or not, it was a letter of activism with an optimistic certainty that relationships among tribes could benefit all Native peoples.

Native Americans acquired literacy and made it their own, aggressively seeking to connect with others off-reservation. Intertribal visitation, a right that tribal nations fought to keep, also allowed tribes without a previous relationship to forge new bonds and enabled those with a history of conflict to make peace. Before the Ghost Dance and peyotism swept into the plains, a web of interconnectedness had formed among the tribes of the West. Despite US government control, reservations were bridged together by mail and rail. As Natives faced the consequences of US colonialism—the constraints, the population loss, and the destitution—they communicated with a purpose: not only to stay in touch, but also to keep their cultures alive, make political and religious change, and preserve some sense of power over their own lives.

Intertribal connections continued to grow in the 1890s. The brutal reaction of the army at Wounded Knee did not subdue Lakotas' ability to move about. They continued to travel long distances to share fellowship with Shoshones, Utes, Southern Cheyennes, Arapahos, and others, usually on the railroads.[19] Paiutes continued to use the Carson & Colorado Railroad to travel through the Great Basin, to the aggravation of their agent.[20] They continued to send letters to other nations to plan visits and "talk together and have a good time."[21] Pueblos continued to journey the five hundred miles through the rancher-filled Texas Panhandle to trade with the Plains Apaches, Comanches, and Kiowas in Indian Territory.[22] Southern Cheyennes and Southern Arapahos continued to value the visits with their neighbors in Indian Territory, giving and accepting ponies, blankets, and other valuables. In 1897, their agent complained, exactly as other agents had the previous quarter century, that "tribal visiting serves no good purpose."[23] Visiting "should be prohibited at all agencies," he suggested, "since it exercises a retarding influence on all progress and keeps old customs that ought to be abrogated," but he found no solutions. Like the people under his charge, the agent saw intertribal interaction as an act of decolonization that preserved Indigenous ways of life. On these visits, Cheyenne and Arapaho men, women, and children kept talking about the things that mattered to them outside colonial control.

Other Southern Plains nations continued to travel north and west, over the Great Divide, to meet with foreign tribes who were becoming increasingly familiar. In 1893, five Kiowa men, Little Bow, Big Bow, White Wind, Lance Bear, and Poor Buffalo, visited the Northern Utes at the Uintah and Ouray Reservation in Utah, around one thousand miles from their home near Anadarko, Indian Territory. They spent their nights visiting different camps, communing with as many Utes as they could. The Uintah agent noticed that a "great many" Utes traveled to the agency headquarters to meet the "guests of the tribe." While at the headquarters, the Kiowas took the opportunity to write home to let their people know that they were fine. A Ute headman named Catoomp enclosed his own message in the envelope to the Kiowas back in Indian Territory. He wrote,

> Our old beloved Chief Ouray told us to be friendly with all the Indians, we are happy to see these our Indian brethren among us, they are strangers to us. . . . This is an Indian Reservation like all the other reservations, any Indian can come here, and we will be glad to see him. We are all one people now. . . . It is better than before when we were always at war with different tribes.[24]

Catoomp saw Indians as "all one people," living under the same circumstances. If the definition of a community is a group that interacts and shares ideas and ways of life, then western Native Americans were building a pan-Indian community in the early reservation years. It was (and still is) an extraordinarily diverse community, but all of its members faced a common, unyielding challenge, hoping for a similar outcome. Because of the rise of communication among tribal nations, Native Americans could discuss the circumstances that tied them to one another. Meaningful ideas, like the ones originating on a reservation in Nevada, could be transmitted to every reservation in the West because a community actively spread those ideas. This book has argued that the US government failed, despite its expensive efforts, to contain Native Americans both geographically and intellectually during the late nineteenth century. From the very beginning of the reservation years, Native Americans kept fighting US government power, kept pushing for change, and kept creating connections amongst themselves.

Abbreviations

ARCIA	*Annual Report of the Commissioner of Indian Affairs*
BAE	Records of the Bureau of American Ethnology
Bancroft	Bancroft Library, University of California, Berkeley
CIA	Commissioner of Indian Affairs
GBGP	George Bird Grinnell Papers, Yale University Library
GRBIA	General Records of the Bureau of Indian Affairs
Huntington	The Huntington Library, San Marino, California
IRAP	*Indian Rights Association Papers, 1864–1973*, Historical Society of Pennsylvania
LFSP	Lebbeus Foster Spencer Papers, History Colorado
LSCIAPR	*Letters Sent to the Office of Indian Affairs by the Pine Ridge Agency 1875–1914*, Microfilm Publication M1282 (Washington, DC: National Archives, 1985)
NAA	National Anthropological Archives, Smithsonian Institution, Washington, DC
NFR	Navaho Agency Field Records, MSS P-D 105 FILM
RBAE	Records of the Bureau of American Ethnology
RBIA	Records of the Bureau of Indian Affairs
RG	Record Group, National Archives and Records Administration
RHPP	Richard Henry Pratt Papers, MSS S-1174, Yale Collection of Western Americana, Beinecke Library
SC	Records of the Bureau of Indian Affairs, Special Cases, 1821–1907
THRP	Thomas Howard Ruger Papers, Yale Collection of Western Americana, Beinecke Rare Book and Manuscript Library

WHC	Western History Collections, University of Oklahoma Libraries
WSCC	Walter Stanley Campbell Collection, Western History Collections, University of Oklahoma Library
YCWA	Yale Collection of Western Americana, Beinecke Rare Book and Manuscript Library

Notes

Introduction

1. Walker, *The Indian Question*, 92.
2. Ibid., 78–79.
3. Ibid.
4. Eastman, "The Ghost Dance War," 26.
5. Little Wound et al. to Cleveland, Dec. 10, 1888, RG 75.19.85, Sent, Box 54.
6. See Rockwell, *Indian Affairs and the Administrative State in the Nineteenth Century*; White, *It's Your Misfortune and None of My Own*, 85–118.
7. I have documented evidence of these trips from a variety of sources, mostly from letters written by Indian agents in US government agency archives; see map 2 along with note 3 in chapter 3 for more on these trips. Also see table 5 for precise numbers for the Lakota reservations.
8. For examples of the complex interactions among tribal nations before the mid-1870s, see Blakeslee, "The Plains Interband Trade System"; Bray, "Lone Horn's Peace"; DeMallie, "Sioux before 1850"; Ewers, "The Indian Trade of the Upper Missouri"; Fowler, *Arapahoe Politics*; Hämäläinen, *Comanche Empire*; Reid, *The Sea is My Country*; Rzeczkowski, "The Crow Indians and the Bozeman Trail"; Shimkin, "Dynamics of Recent Wind River Shoshone History"; Spier, "The Sun Dance of the Plains Indians"; Stands in Timber, *Cheyenne Memories*; Swagerty, "Indian Trade in the Trans-Mississippi West to 1870."
9. *ARCIA*, 1889, 496–514. The *Annual Report of the Commissioner of Indian Affairs* detailed the state of the office and the state of Indians under government care. The commissioner presented a compilation of reports from Indian agents throughout the country who gave their testimony (with appropriate statistics) on the state of agriculture, industry, health, economy, crime, religion, and education (which was often given the most attention). Each report was specific to each reservation or tribe.
10. *ARCIA*, 1880. Unfortunately, the total population of those tribal nations decreased from 80,513 in 1880 to 65,402 in 1890.

11. Stewart, *Peyote Religion*, 63–64. The name and administration of the Kiowa, Comanche, and Wichita Reservation (the home of Kiowas, Comanches, Wichitas, Apaches, and Caddos) changed over time. The Kiowa-Comanche Agency (also known as the Kiowa-Comanche-Apache Agency) and the Wichita-Caddo Agency were consolidated in 1878.
12. Fortunately, this is not the only study to recognize the permeability of reservation boundaries. Frank Rzeckzkowski's *Uniting the Tribes* demonstrates the ways Crows interacted with other Northern Plains peoples before and during the reservation era, a time of "exceptional cultural and social vitality." In fact, Rzeckzkowski places great interest in visitation among the Crows and others, finding that this intertribal contact had "covert—and sometimes overt—political dimensions"; see Rzeckzkowski, *Uniting the Tribes*, 12.
13. Running Antelope et al. to Sec. of Int., March 20, 1891, *James McLaughlin Papers*, Roll 2.
14. *New York Times*, Nov. 16, 1890.
15. *New York Herald*, Nov. 23, 1890, reprinted Grinnell, "Account of the Northern Cheyennes."
16. Grinnell to Dunbar, Nov. 22, 1890, GBGP, MS 1388, Box 2 (Reel 3), Manuscripts and Archives; Grinnell to Fannin, Nov. 22, 1890, GBGP, MS 1388, Box 2, Reel 3; Grinnell to Jackson, Dec. 1, 1890, GBGP, MS 1388, Box 2 (Reel 3).
17. *New York Times*, Nov. 16, 1890.
18. *New York Herald*, Nov. 23, 1890.
19. Among the many studies on the Ghost Dance, see Mooney, *Ghost-Dance*; Hittman, *Wovoka and the Ghost Dance*; Warren, *God's Red Son*; Andersson, *The Lakota Ghost Dance*; Andersson, *A Whirlwind Passed through Our Country*; Maddra, *Hostiles?*; Ostler, *The Plains Sioux and U.S. Colonialism*; Thornton, *We Shall Live Again*. For the 1870 Ghost Dance, see Du Bois, *The 1870 Ghost Dance*; Hittman, "The 1870 Ghost Dance at the Walker River Reservation"; Smoak, *Ghost Dances and Identity*, 113–51.
20. For other scholars who have looked at the dance after Wounded Knee, see Clow, "The Lakota Ghost Dance after 1890"; Andersson, *A Whirlwind Passed through Our Country;* Hitman, *Wovoka*; Kehoe, "The Ghost Dance Religion in Saskatchewan"; Kracht, "The Kiowa Ghost Dance."
21. While letters and other texts written by Native Americans living on the reservations of the plains and Great Basin in the last quarter of the nineteenth century are relatively scarce, this is not evidence that few were writing letters. Compared to the non-Native population of the United States (62,947,714 in 1890, 88 percent of which could read—compared with 43 percent of African Americans), the dwindling Native populations

(220,314 by 1889) left behind far fewer letters than whites for future historians to find. However, thousands of Native Americans, around 15 percent of those living on western reservations (outside the so-called Five Civilized Tribes), could read in English or a Native language in some capacity by the end of the 1880s. (It is not known how many could write. Only 144,523 Indians were counted for reading, and 21,756 were deemed able to read.) See *ARCIA*, 1890.

22. In addition, most of the Native-authored texts that have been preserved in government, university, and institutional archives were written in English because that was the language of the whites who received the letters, the same whites who controlled the archives.
23. The ethnologist James Owen Dorsey was able to collect 238 letters written in the Native language Ȼegiha by and for Omaha and Ponca men and women. The letters, many of which are private correspondence, were written between 1872 and 1889. More than one hundred of those letters were published with Dorsey's *The Ȼegiha Language*, and the rest were published in 1891's *Omaha and Ponka Letters*. These are still the largest collections of Native letter writing ever printed.
24. Letters quoted in this study are presented as closely as possible to the original; no grammar or punctuation is corrected, and "*sic*" is not used. Necessary corrections are made in the notes.
25. For insight on the difficulties of interpreting Native written material, see DeMallie, "These Have No Ears"; Parks, "Plains Indian Native Literatures."
26. The transcriber or translator always inserted his or her voice into the text to some degree, whether he or she was Native or white.
27. Little Wound et al. to Cleveland, Dec. 10, 1888, RG 75.19.85, Sent, Box 54.
28. "Letter from the Secretary of the Interior in Relation to the Affairs of the Indians at the Pine Ridge and Rosebud Reservations in South Dakota," March 16, 1892, Ex. Doc. No. 58, *Executive Documents of the Senate of the United States for the First Session of the Fifty-Second Congress, 1891–'92*, 42–43.

Chapter 1

1. "1895 Council with the Cheyennes & Arapahos," THRP, MSS S-2699, Box 4.
2. Taylor, "Indian Lingua Francas"; Leap, *American Indian English*, 151–56; Mallery, "Sign Language among North American Indians"; Meadows, ed., *Through Indian Sign Language*; Davis, *Hand Talk*; Lang, *Making Wawa*.

3. Dakota Presbytery Council, *The Dakota Mission*, 17; Spack, *America's Second Tongue*, 49.
4. Greene, ed., *The Year the Stars Fell*, 2–3.
5. Mallery, "Picture Writing."
6. Maximillian, *Travels in the Interior of North America*, 352.
7. "Translation of a Picto-Graphic Letter Reporting the Routes and Incidents of a Crow Indian Hunting Party," Walter Scribner Schuyler Papers, WS 71, Huntington.
8. Lookingbill, *War Dance at Fort Marion*; the prisoners were taken during the Red River War, which was fought between the US Army and resistant bands of Comanches, Southern Cheyennes, Arapahos, and Kiowas. Prisoners famously created volumes of "ledger art" (drawings and paintings made in ledger or accounting books); see Szabo, *Art from Fort Marion*.
9. White Buffalo Head to Minimic, 1877 (undated), MS 30,740, NAA.
10. *Bradford (VT) Opinion*, Oct. 13, 1877.
11. Mallery, "Picture Writing," 363–364.
12. Pratt to CIA, Dec. 31, 1889, RHPP, Box 10–16; Pratt to Mallery, May 6, 1891, RHPP, Box 10–18.
13. Graber, *The Gods of Indian Country*, 200.
14. Stevenson, "Calling Badger and the Symbols of the Spirit," 89–92.
15. Ibid., 90.
16. Ibid., 92.
17. Fletcher, "A Phonetic Alphabet," 299. The Sac and Fox developed their script as early as 1800, which also came in use with the Kickapoos and Potawatomies; see Walker, "Native American Writing Systems," 156–62.
18. Agent to Fletcher, Aug. 1885, Alice Fletcher Papers, MS 4558, Series 1, Box 1, NAA. The Ho-Chunk phonetic alphabet (Hoocąk) borrowed seventeen English letters (thirteen consonants and four vowels) and created two new symbols; see Walker, "The Winnebago Syllabary and the Generative Model."
19. Ibid.
20. Josephy, *The Nez Perce Indians*, 185–86.
21. Parks and Rankin, "Siouan Languages," 110. A language primer was printed for the Poncas in 1873.
22. Kreis, *Lakota, Black Robes*, 4–5.
23. *Iapi Oaye* (Greenwood, SD), March 1876, 12, quoted in Renville, *A Thrilling Narrative of Indian Captivity*, 8.
24. *ARCIA*, 1851, 437–38. The Red Lake Mission reported that all twenty-one of the Ojibwe students could read and write in English and Ojibwe.
25. See Canku, *The Dakota Prisoner of War Letters*.
26. Meyer, *History of the Santee*, 136–37.
27. *Journal of the Rev. S. D. Hinman*, Jan. 24, 1869.

28. In 1870, the Jesuit Pierre-Jean De Smet baptized more than four hundred Sioux along the Missouri River. In 1875, the Episcopal Church sent missionaries to Lakotas being held by the army at Pine Ridge and Rosebud. In 1876, Catholic missionaries, who were the most active in the Dakotas, established the first lasting mission at the Standing Rock Agency. See Ostler, *The Plains Sioux*, 56–57.
29. Bray, "Lakota Statesmen and the Horse Creek Treaty of 1851," 157.
30. The Medicine Lodge Treaty of 1867 surrendered tribal territories in the southern plains for much smaller reservation lands (agencies). The US government's goal was to keep the tribes on their reservations within Indian Territory and out of the way of white settlement. See Mann, *Cheyenne and Arapaho Education*, 10–11.
31. DeMallie, "Yankton and Yanktonai," 780. "Agencies" were what the US government called their administrative bodies on Indian lands or on reservations. The "agency" was also the government's headquarters or their collection of offices on a reservation. Over time, the term "Indian agency" was often used synonymously with "Indian reservation." US government correspondence and records referred to the reservations they administered as "agencies."
32. *ARCIA*, 1872, 263.
33. *ARCIA*, 1874, 238.
34. *ARCIA*, 1881, 1–8.
35. Mann, *Cheyenne and Arapaho Education*, 25–26, 29–33.
36. Wetherill to Wife, March 7, 1873, in Gillmor and Wetherill, *Traders to the Navajos*, 5; Battey to Battey, Oct. 5, 1873, Thomas Battey Papers, HM 61142, Huntington.
37. Cutler, "Lawrie Tatum and the Kiowa Agency: 1869–1873," 237–38.
38. Fear-Segal, *White Man's Club*, 8.
39. *ARCIA*, 1875; Hagan, "19th Century Indian Education Programs," 99.
40. *ARCIA*, 1875.
41. Mann, *Cheyenne and Arapaho Education*, 25–26, 29–33.
42. "Council with the Cheyennes and Arapahos of Oklahoma, Washington, March 21, 1895," THRP, MSS S-2699, Box 4.
43. Prucha, *American Indian Policy in Crisis*, 3–71.
44. *ARCIA*, 1868, 43.
45. Ibid.
46. Quoted in Spack, *America's Second Tongue*, 18–19.
47. Ibid.
48. *ARCIA*, 1892, p. 41. Data do not include amounts provided for by treaty agreements. For a look at the US government's own assessment of Indian education in the late 1880s, see Fletcher, *Indian Education and Civilization*.

49. Prucha, *The Great Father*, 687–715.
50. *ARCIA*, 1887, xxi.
51. *ARCIA*, 1886, xxiii.
52. For a look at English-only at the Genoa School, see Goodburn, "Literacy Practices at the Genoa Industrial Indian School."
53. Nineteenth-century Lakotas read and wrote in the written Dakota dialect, which is easily understood by Lakotas, because a Dakota writing system was developed first.
54. DeMallie, "Santee," 773; Spack, *American's Second Tongue*, 33–35. For a look at the English-only debate after the mandate, see CIA to Sterling, July 24, 1890, RG 75.19.85, Rec'd from OIA, Box 9; Wood to Pawnee Supt., May 1, 1890, RG 75.19.77, Reel 17; *Indian Helper* (Carlisle, PA), Sept. 2, 1887; *Indian Helper*, Sept. 30, 1890; *Indian Helper*, Nov. 11, 1887; *Indian Helper*, Nov. 18, 1890; *Indian Helper*, Feb. 20, 1891; Pratt to Pierson, Nov. 22, 1890, RHPP, Box 10.
55. *ARCIA*, 1890, 268.
56. Gallagher to CIA, January 27, 1890, *LSCIAPR*, Reel 10; Riggs to R. McChesney, Sept. 24, 1888, RG 75.19.11, Box 569; Palmer to McLaughlin, Oct. 6, 1890, RG 75.19.113, Rec'd, Box 33; Penny to Supt. White's Institute, May 15, 1891, RG 75.19.85, Sent, Box 54; Penny to Supt. Genoa, March 29, 1891, RG 75.19.85, Sent, Box 54; Supt. Immaculate Conception to Wright, Nov. 18, 1889, RG 75.19.96, Rec'd, Box 5; PR telegram to CIA, Feb. 10, 11, 1891, *LSCIAPR*; Ashley to CIA, Feb. 20, 1891, RG 75.19.10, Sent, Reel 32; St. Paul's to Simmons, Oct. 10, 1889, RG 75.19.30, Rec'd 1877–1915, Box 2.
57. Sioux Indians to Harrison, Oct. 23, 1890, RG 75.4, Rec'd, 33608, Box 674; Blackfeet to CIA, Dec. 15, 1890, RG 75.4, Rec'd, 40165, Box 690; Medicine Bull to CIA, Feb. 12, 1891, RG 75.4, Rec'd, 5562, Box 704; Jenkins to CIA, March 1890, *Registers of Letters Received*, P2186, Reel 34, 8100; Huntley to CIA, Dec. 1, 1890, RG 75.4, Rec'd, 38133, Box 685; Wolf Chief to CIA, Aug. 10, 1889, RG 75.4, Rec'd, 23002, Box 545; CIA to Wolf Chief, Sept. 14, 1889, RG 75.4, Sent, Law and Land; Wolf Chief to CIA, Nov. 5, 1889, RG 75.4, Rec'd, 33401, Box 572; Lone Wolf and White Wolf to CIA, Jan. 15, 1889, RG 75.4, Rec'd, 1003, Box 497. At least one letter sent in 1890 was opposed to the construction of new schools; see Gros Ventres and Assiniboines to Sec. Int., June 27, 1890, RG 75.4, Rec'd, 23002, Box 645.
58. Adams, *Education for Extinction*, 209–22, 244–52. For examples of agents' methods to send or keep children in school, see Alonzo to CIA, Nov. 12, 1889, RG 75.4, Rec'd, 33317, Box 571; Wyman to CIA, March 17, 1890, RG 75.19.21, Sent, Box 3; CIA Circular 14780, Nov. 21, 1888, RG 75.19.18, Decimal Files, Box 159; CIA to Stollsteimer, Feb. 29, 1888, RG

75.19.18, Decimal Files, Box 159; CIA to Bartholomew, March 13, 1890, RG 75.19.18, Decimal Files, Box 159; CIA to McChesney, March 25, 1886, RG 75.19.11, Box 249; CIA to Lillibridge, Oct. 18, 1892, RG 75.19.11, Box 569; CIA to McLaughlin, Sep. 19, 1890, RG 75.19.113, Rec'd, Box 34; Ashley to Vestal, Feb. 5, 1890, RG 75.19.10, Sent, Reel 32; Adams to White Wolf, Aug. 22, 1890, RG 75.19.50, Sent, Reel 18; "A Right Move," *Indian Helper*, Aug. 1, 1890.
59. CIA to McLaughlin, Feb. 21, 1882, RG 75.19.113, Rec'd, Box 27. A teacher at the Hampton Institute asked the Standing Rock agent if agents could use "rations as a leverage" in "uplifting the Indians" and wondered if Congress could get involved; see Brown to McLaughlin, Jan. (undated) 1883, RG 75.19.113, Rec'd, Box 29.
60. CIA to McLaughlin, Nov. 2, 1883, RG 75.19.113, Rec'd, Box 28.
61. Pugh to McGillycuddy, Sept. 29, 1884, RG 75.19.85, Rec'd, Box 27.
62. Ostler, *The Plains Sioux*, 159.
63. Cheyennes and Arapahos to CIA, Nov. 28, 1888, RG 75.4, Rec'd, 29627, Box 492; Bland to CIA, July 30, 1890, RG 75.4, Rec'd, 23452, Box 646; Weldon to CIA, Aug. 7, 1890, RG 75.4, Rec'd, 24695, Box 649.
64. Pratt telegram to CIA, Jan. 3, 1890, RG 75.4, Rec'd, 204, Box 583; Pratt telegram to CIA, Jan. 2, 1890, RG 75.4, Rec'd, 205, Box 583; Simmons to CIA, March 13, 1890, RG 75.4, Rec'd, 8476, Box 605; Goodale to CIA, July 15, 1890, RG 75.4, Rec'd, 22027, Box 643; Wyman to CIA, June 18, 1890, RG 75.19.21, Misc. Sent, Box 3; Wyman to CIA, March 17, 1890, RG 75.19.21, Misc. Sent, Box 3; St. Paul's to Simmons, Dec. 18, 1889, RG 75.19.30, Rec'd, Box 2; Scobey to CIA, May 13, 1891, RG 75.19.35, Sent to CIA, Box 34; Wright to CIA, March 24, 1890, RG 75.19.96, Sent, Vol. 18; CIA to Swan, April 15, 1885, RG 75.19.11, Box 570; CIA to McLaughlin, Sept. 19, 1890, RG 75.19.113, Rec'd, Box 34; Ashley to CIA, Feb. 20, 1891, RG 75.19.10, Sent, Reel 32; Adams to Supt., May 10, 1890, RG 75.19.50, Sent, Reel 18; Wood to CIA, Oct. 27, 1890, RG 75.19.77, Reel 17.
65. *ARCIA*, 1884, 45.
66. Gallagher to CIA, May 1, 1890, *LSCIAPR*, Reel 10; Goodale to CIA, October 11, 1890, RG 75.4, Rec'd, 32124, Box 671.
67. Plumb to CIA, July 15, 1890, RG 75.19.132, Box 372.
68. Pratt, *Battlefield and Classroom*, 116–90; Fear-Segal, *White Man's Club*, 2–26.
69. Glancy, *Fort Marion Prisoners*, 78, 95–97.
70. Pratt, *Battlefield and Classroom*, 190–229; Adams, *Education for Extinction*, 30–59. See also Eastman, *Pratt, the Red Man's Moses*. The Hampton Institute was led by Gen. Samuel C. Armstrong. A program for Native American students at Hampton began in 1878. Seventeen of the

Fort Marion prisoners went to Hampton after their release, and a handful of others found spots at other schools.
71. Fear-Segal and Rose, eds., *Carlisle Indian Industrial School*.
72. Mann, *Cheyenne and Arapaho Education*, 50–51.
73. Ibid., 52.
74. Ibid., 53–54, 56–57.
75. Pratt to Unamson, March 15, 1887, RHPP, Box 10–12.
76. *Arizona Weekly*, April 23, 1882.
77. Hyde, *A Sioux Chronicle*, 51–57; *ARCIA*, 1880, 45.
78. Fear-Segal and Rose, eds., *Carlisle Indian Industrial School*; Adams, *Education for Extinction*.
79. Hoxie, *The Final Promise*; Ellis, *To Change Them Forever*; Child, *Boarding School Seasons*; Katanski, *Learning to Write "Indian"*; Mann, *Cheyenne and Arapaho Education*; Fear-Segal, *White Man's Club*; Cahill, *Federal Fathers and Mothers*; Kreis, *Lakota, Black Robes, and Holy Women*; Prucha, *The Churches and the Indian Schools*; Bell, "Telling Stories out of School"; Coleman, *American Indian Children at School*; Lomawaima, *They Called It Prairie Light*.
80. Spack, *America's Second Tongue*. Spack shows that Native people took ownership of English "and shaped it to accommodate new and powerful forms of expression." See also Morgan, *The Bearer of This Letter*; Konkle, "Indian Literacy, U.S. Colonialism, and Literary Criticism."
81. *ARCIA*, 1873–1892. Curriculum and teaching methods at Indian schools varied greatly until the mid-1880s, when the US government put a greater emphasis on standard practices. Most schools devoted a large portion of instruction time to industrial education. See Adams, *Education for Extinction*. For a detailed look at language instruction, see Spack, *America's Second Tongue*, 45–109.
82. *ARCIA*, 1880, 30.
83. Ibid., 36, 40, 45.
84. Pratt to Whirlwind, Feb. 11, 1885, RHPP, Box 10–10.
85. *ARCIA*, 1887, 19, 26.
86. Steell to CIA, Nov. 1, 1890, RG 75.4, Rec'd, 34529, Box 676.
87. "Monthly Report Western Shoshone Day School, June 30, 1885," RG 75.19.132, Box 362B.
88. *ARCIA*, 1889. The Office of Indian Affairs did not count those who had the ability to write in most years, nor did their statistics measure competency. Agents did not give their Indians exams to gauge their abilities. They only counted subjectively, often estimating or trusting the opinions of teachers or the Indians themselves; see Pine Ridge School Reports, 1882–1936, RG 75.19.85, Box 1112. Because dozens of agents

with hundreds of employees gathered the annual statistics, it is difficult to ascertain exactly what "can read" meant. It does seem, however, that Indian Affairs considered the accuracy of its annual census and corresponding statistics important. Although the commissioner admitted that it was difficult to get accurate statistics in 1887, agents and teachers were continually urged to report "reliable" stats; see *ARCIA*, 1887, xxxvii; Gallagher to Teachers, Feb. 20, 1890, RG 75.19.85, Sent, Box 54; Gallagher to Superintendents and Teachers, RG 75.19.85, Sent, Box 54; CIA to Tully, July 2, 1892, RG 75.19.117, Rec'd 1890–1924, Box 5. In 1892, the acting commissioner questioned the accuracy of the Western Shoshone agent's statistics because of the "remarkable increase" in English speakers "in so short a time," among other non-education-related discrepancies; see Acting CIA to Plumb, July 2, 1892, RG 75.19.132, Box 385A. The agent reported 250 English-speaking Shoshones in 1889 and 440 in 1891.

89. *ARCIA*, 1880.
90. *ARCIA*, 1890.
91. A modification of the Dakota alphabet system for the Lakota dialect was published in 1939 by Rev. Eugene Buechel, *A Grammar of Lakota*. See also White Hat, *Reading and Writing the Lakota Language*.
92. Harrington, *Vocabulary of the Kiowa Language*; Petter, *English-Cheyenne Dictionary*; Kroeber, "The Bannock and Shoshone Languages."
93. *ARCIA*, 1886, 396.
94. *ARCIA*, 1892.
95. Ibid.; *ARCIA*, 1882.
96. Enoch, *The Jesuit Mission to the Lakota Sioux*, 22.
97. Olson, *Red Cloud and the Sioux Problem*, 268.
98. Hehaka Najin to McLaughlin, Oct. 28, 1884, *James McLaughlin Papers*, Reel 2.
99. Hare to McLaughlin, Nov. 16, 1884, RG 75.19.113, Rec'd, Box 29.
100. *Southern Workman* (Hampton, VA), Feb. 1883, 19; Adams, *Education for Extinction*, 248.
101. *Southern Workman*, Aug. 1880, 85.
102. *Southern Workman*, March 1891, 166–67.
103. Zadoka to Hall, March 15, 1887, RG 75.19.50, Reel 90.
104. White Swan to Dawes, Aug. 8, 1890, RG 75.4, Rec'd, 25905, Box 652.
105. *Greenwood County (KS) Republican*, May 6, 1891.
106. "1895 Council with the Cheyennes & Arapahos," THRP, MSS S-2699, Box 4.
107. McLaughlin to Commanding Officer Ft. Randall, Nov. 21, 1881, Standing Rock Letterpress Copybook, MSS S-3052.

108. Agent to Chiefs, Sept. 29, 1886, Navaho Agency Field Records, MSS P-D 105 FILM, Vol. 10, Bancroft; Battey to Battey, Dec. 10, 1873, Thomas Battey Papers, HM 61144, Huntington; Bent to Miles, Nov. 10, 1876, RG 75.19.10, Sent, Reel 51.
109. Wright to CIA, Jan. 2, 1891, RG 75.19.96, Sent, Vol. 20; Wright to CIA, Jan. 23, 1891, RG 75.19.96, Sent, Vol. 20; Adams to White Wolf, Aug. 22, 1890, RG 75.19.50, Sent, Reel 18.
110. Running Bull et al. to CIA, Nov. 6, 1889, RG 75.4, Rec'd, 33002, Box 571; White, *Service on the Indian Reservations*, 312–16.
111. *Greenwood County Republican*, May 6, 1891.
112. Pratt to Whirlwind et al., Nov. 27, 1886, RHPP, Box 10–12.
113. "Council with Cheyennes and Arapahos, March 20, 1895," THRP, MSS S-2699, Box 4.
114. Proceedings of Indian Council Held at Sun Dance, June 1, 1879, RG 75.19.85, Sent, Box 52.
115. Ostler, *The Plains Sioux*, 123.
116. Collins, "A Short Autobiography," reproduced in Vestal, *New Sources of Indian History*, 61–62.
117. Vestal, *New Sources of Indian History*, 273–74.
118. Ibid., 274.
119. Ahern to Campbell, July 12, 1929, Walter S. Campbell Collection, Box 107, Folder 4, WHC.
120. Dennis to McLaughlin, Sept. 12, 1887, RG 75.19.113, Rec'd, Box 31; Dennis to McLaughlin, Oct. 20, 1887, RG 75.19.113, Rec'd, Box 31.
121. *ARCIA*, 1879, 20.
122. *Daily Press and Dakotaian* (Yankton, SD), May 23, 1879.
123. American Horse to Landy, April 30, 1880, American Horse Papers, MSS S-903, YCWA.
124. American Horse to Landy, Dec. 8, 1880, American Horse Papers, MSS S-903, YCWA.
125. Littlefield, *American Indian and Alaska Native Newspapers*, 151–56. For a history of newspapers and the Five Civilized Tribes, see Littlefield, xi–xxiii.
126. DeMallie, ed., *The Sixth Grandfather*, 8; Spack, *America's Second Tongue*, 50.
127. Littlefield, *American Indian and Alaska Native Newspapers*, xxv.
128. Ibid., xxviii–xxix; Fear-Segal, "Eyes in the Text," 123–45. For testimonies from Native readers on their fondness for the Carlisle paper, the *Indian Helper*, see *Indian Helper*, March 2, 1888; June 8, 1888; Oct. 5, 1888; March 22, 1889; April 19, 1889; April 26, 1889; May 24, 1889; June 28, 1889; Nov. 28, 1890.
129. *Indian Helper*, April 18, 1890. Jacqueline Emery argues that few "realize just how influential student-run newspapers . . . were in helping to

form and sustain a cross-tribal community at the turn of the twentieth century"; see Emery, "Writing against Erasure," 195.
130. *Indian Helper*, June 20, 1890. One of those copies went to E. D. Prescott, the postmaster at Wounded Knee Creek at the Pine Ridge Agency; see *Indian Helper*, Nov. 29, 1889.
131. "Cheyenne Transporter," Oklahoma Historical Society's *Gateway to Oklahoma History*, https://gateway.okhistory.org/explore/collections/DARLIN/.
132. Quoted in Vizenor, *The People Named the Chippewa*, 78.
133. For an example, see Rahn, "Young Eyewitnesses to History," 112–15.
134. *Harper's Weekly*, Dec. 6, 1890.
135. Standing Rock Agent Telegram to Editor *Bismarck (ND) Tribune*, Aug. 26, 1881, Standing Rock Letterpress Copybook, MSS S-3052, YCWA.
136. Stevick to Stevick, (undated) 1891, RHPP, Box 18.
137. White Bird et al. to W. H. Wills & Co., Dec. 30, 1889, RG 75.4, Rec'd, 1456, Box 498; W. H. Wills & Co. to Maxwell, Jan. 15, 1890, RG 75.4, Rec'd, 1456, Box 486.
138. Omahas to Tibbles, Aug. 22, 1879, in Dorsey, *Omaha and Ponka Letters*, 20–33.
139. Dorsey, *Omaha and Ponka Letters*, 37–41. It is not known if the *Cincinnati (OH) Commercial Tribune* published the letter.
140. For a thorough study, see Blevins, "The Postal West."
141. Fuller, *The American Mail*, 73–74, 103. For a look at the expansion of the post before the Civil War, see Henkin, *The Postal Age*; Johns, *Spreading the News*.
142. *United States Postal Guide*, vol. 11, no. 1, 6; *Annual Report of the Postmaster General of the United States*, 1870–1889, compiled in Helbock, *United States Post Offices*, vols. 1–2 (2001), made digitally available by Cameron Blevins, "Data: Geography of the Post," http://www.cameronblevins.org/postal-data/.
143. *Annual Report of the Postal Master General of the United States*, 1890, 198. Natives were employed as mail carriers; see *ARCIA*, 1886, 242; White Shield to Post Office, May 28, 1879, RG 75.19.10, Box 472. The earliest documented play written by a Native American was *The Indian Mail Carrier* by the Seneca Gowongo Mohawk, copyright 1889 and 1892; see Rebhorn, *Pioneer Performances*, 6–11; Cheyfitz, ed., *The Columbia Guide to American Indian Literatures*.
144. Brice, *Reminiscences of Ten Years Experience on the Western Plains*, 12–14, 20.
145. Pine Ridge had a post office at the agency headquarters and at trader stores at Wounded Knee Creek and Kyle. The Cheyenne-Arapaho Reservation had post offices at Darlington, Cantonment, and Fort Reno. The

Kiowa-Comanche-Wichita Reservation had post offices at Anadarko and Fort Sill.
146. *Daily Press Dakotaian* (Yankton, SD), April 26, 1876. US government statistics show that 293 of 744 Santees at the Santee Agency could read in that year; see *ARCIA*, 1877, 296.
147. Howell to Howell, March 11, 1876, Howell Family Papers, Box 8, HM 67064, Huntington. The clerk, George Howell, regularly translated written English for illiterate Pawnees.
148. Plumb to CIA, Nov. 15, 1890, RG 75.19.132, Box 386.
149. Aug Achin, a Pueblo, shipped a loaf of bread from New Mexico to Carlisle, Pennsylvania, in 1887; see *Indian Helper*, Dec. 23, 1887; "Aug Achin," RG 75.20.3, Carlisle, Entry 1327, Box 58, Card 2909.
150. Penny to Ashley, July 7, 1891, RG 75.19.85, Sent, Box 55; Ashley to Penny, July 20, 1891, RG 75.19.85, Rec'd, Box 28.
151. Dorsey, *The Ȼegiha Language*, 722. Dorsey translated the Omaha word "'i-amádi" (meaning "where they carry them on their back") as "mail-bag."
152. Clark to Pine Ridge Agent, Aug. 15, 1880, RG 75.19.85, Rec'd, Box 26.
153. *Annual Report of the Postal Master General of the United States*, 1890, 28.
154. Bisnett, a seventeen-year-old Oglala girl, told R. H. Pratt in a letter that she would write more often if she lived closer to the agency post office; see Bisnett to Pratt, June 24, 1890, RG 75.4, Rec'd, 21249, Box 640. Others had difficulty getting to their mail because of geography and the weather; see "Letter from C. W. H.," *Word Carrier* (Greenwood, SD), April 1890.
155. Anderson to CIA, March 20, 1888, RG 75.4, Rec'd, 7973, Box 30.
156. Standing Bear, *My People, the Sioux*, 234–35.
157. Just before Standing Bear's request, Pine Ridge did have a Native postmaster, a Yankton named William Selwyn, at least according to James Mooney; see Mooney, *Ghost-Dance Religion*, 819. Several scholars have called Selwyn a postmaster because of Mooney.
158. Dorsey, *Omaha and Ponka Letters*, 32.
159. Barker to CIA, March 12, 1891, *Registers of Letters Received*, P2186, Roll 44, Letter 10318; Little Wound et al. to Cleveland, Dec. 10, 1888, RG 75.19.85, Sent, Box 54; Fine to Pratt, June 21, 1890, RG 75.4, Rec'd, 18284, Box 632; Running Bull et al. to CIA, Nov. 6, 1889, RG 75.4, Rec'd, 33002, Box 571; Two Strike and High Hawk to Manderson, Nov. 20, 1889, RG 75.4, Rec'd, 34692, Box 575; Testimony of High Hawk et al., April 26, 1890, RG 75.4, Rec'd, 13660, Box 619; Hollow Horn Bear to Harrison, CIA, Sept. 13, 1890, RG 75.4, Rec'd, 29579, Box 664; Rosebud Indians to CIA, Oct. 23, 1890, RG 75.4, Rec'd, 33608, Box 674; Fisherman to CIA, Jan. 21, 1890, RG 75.4, Rec'd, 2490, Box 589; Swift Horse to Agent,

Jan. 29, 1890, RG 75.4, Rec'd, 3958, Box 592; Anderson to CIA, Feb. 5, 1890, RG 75.4, Rec'd, 3958, Box 688; Clark to CIA, Feb. 2, 1891, RG 75.4, Rec'd, 5983, Box 704; White Ghost and Truth Teller to CIA, April 1, 1890, *Registers of Letters Received*, P2186, Roll 39, Letter 15739; White Swan et al. to CIA, June 9, 1890, RG 75.4, Rec'd, 18265, Box 632.

160. Anonymous to Sec. Int., (undated) 1890, RG 75.4, Rec'd, 23611, Box 647.
161. Onion to Pratt, June 8, 1890, RG 75.4, Rec'd, 18556, Box 633; Red Wolf to Pratt, June 16, 1890, RG 75.4, Rec'd, 21249, Box 640; Saketopa to McLaughlin, Jan. 3, 1888, *McLaughlin Papers*, Roll 2; Conroy to CIA, Aug. 5, 1890, RG 75.4, Rec'd, 24626, Box 649; Plenty Living Bear to Pratt, June 29, 1890, RG 75.4, Rec'd, 20195, Box 637; Pretty Scalp to CIA, Sept. 1, 1890, RG 75.4, Rec'd, 27654, Box 658; Eagle Feather to CIA, Jan. 20, 1891, RG 75.4, Rec'd, 6842 (with 8742), Box 710; Little Elk to Pratt, June 14, 1890, RG 75.4, Rec'd, 20195, Box 637; Tuttle to CIA, (undated) 1890, RG 75.4, Rec'd, 13928, Box 619.
162. Running Bull et al. to CIA, Nov. 6, 1889, RG 75.4, Rec'd, 33002, Box 571; Yanktons to Foster, undated 1890, RG 75.4, Rec'd, 37633, Box 684; Swift Bird to Palmer, Nov. 20, 1891, RG 75.19.11, Box 570; Cloud Chief et al. to CIA, Dec. 4, 1890, RG 75.4, Rec'd, 38384, Box 685; Cloud Chief et al. to CIA, Dec. 4, 1890, RG 75.4, Rec'd, 38384, Box 685; Grindstone and Little Eagle to CIA, July 31, 1890, RG 75.4, Rec'd, 24201, Box 648; CIA to McLaughlin, Aug. 9, 1890, RG 75.4, Sent, Accounts, Book 114; Lone Wolf and White Wolf to CIA, Jan. 15, 1889, RG 75.4, Rec'd, 1003, Box 497; Noheart to Palmer, Nov. 5, 1890, RG 75.19.11, Box 570; Sissetons to CIA, Jan. 31, 1890, RG 75.4, Rec'd, 8207, Box 604.
163. Fast Horse to Miller, Jan. 15, 1890, RG 75.4, Rec'd, 2921, Box 590.
164. Wolf Chief to CIA, Dec. 21, 1889, RG 75.4, Rec'd, 37274, Box 582.
165. Selwyn to CIA, Feb. 6, 1891, RG 75.4, Rec'd, 6060, Box 704; Gage, "Intertribal Communication," 120–21.
166. Running Bull et al. to CIA, Nov. 6, 1889, RG 75.4, Rec'd, 33002, Box 571.
167. Chon-za-nin-ga to CIA, April 14, 1889, RG 75.4, Rec'd, 10379, Box 515; Wolf Chief to CIA, Jan. 26, 1889, RG 75.4, Rec'd, 2948, Box 500; Lip to Welsh, Dec. 4, 1889, RG 75.4, Rec'd, 113, Box 583; Quickbear to Welsh, Dec. 4, 1889, RG 75.4, Rec'd, 113, Box 583; Hollow Horn Bear to Harrison, CIA, Sept. 13, 1890, RG 75.4, Rec'd, 29579, Box 664; Lip to CIA, Oct. 12, 1890, RG 75.4, Rec'd, 32874, Box 672; Lip to Sec. Int., Oct. 12, 1890, RG 75.4, Rec'd, 32740, Box 672; Boughter, *Betraying the Omaha Nation*, 136.
168. Star to J. Wright, March 22, 1883, RG 75.19.96, Rec'd, Box 5.
169. Kash-y-pas to McLaughlin, April 19, 1881, *McLaughlin Papers*, Reel 2; Crow Creek Indians to Arthur, April 15, 1882, RG 75.4, Rec'd, 36332, Box 579; Buford to Teller, Aug. 4, 1884, RG 75.19.63, Sent, Box 4.

170. Rosebud Indians to CIA, April 20, 1889, RG 75.4, Rec'd, 11010, Box 516; Arapahos to CIA, Aug. 30, 1889, RG 75.4, Rec'd, 25344, Box 552; Whittlesey to CIA, March 7, 1890, *Registers of Letters Received*, P2186, Roll 39, 7053; Winnebago to CIA, Nov. 14, 1889, RG 75.4, Rec'd, 33390, Box 572; Standing Buffalo to CIA, Oct. 2, 1890, *Registers of Letters Received*, P2186, Roll 42, 30866; Tobacco Eater to CIA, Feb. 26, 1891, RG 75.4, Rec'd, 8469, Box 710; Tobacco Eater to Sec. Int., Feb. 6, 1891, RG 75.4, Rec'd, 8605, Box 710; Tobacco Eater to Sec. Int., Feb. 25, 1891, RG 75.4, Rec'd, 8605, Box 710; Copy of Cheyennes to Procter, Feb. 10, 1891, RG 75.4, Rec'd, 10003, Box 714.
171. Brulés to CIA, Sept. 16, 1890, RG 75.4, Rec'd, 29157, Box 663; Pappan to CIA, May 29, 1889, RG 75.4, Rec'd, 15120, Box 526.
172. Wolf Chief to Cleveland, Dec. 1888, RG 75.4, Rec'd, 30060, Box 492; Wolf Chief to CIA, Dec. 8, 1890, RG 75.4, Rec'd, 39465, Box 688; Wolf Chief to CIA, Feb. 17, 1891, RG 75.4, Rec'd, 7158, Box 707; Pazi to IRA, May 28, 1889, *IRAP*, Roll 15; Chattle-kon-kee et al. to CIA, June 9, 1890, RG 75.4, Rec'd, 18248, Box 632; Spotted Bear to Swan, April 29, 1885, RG 75.19.11, Box 569; *ARCIA*, 1891, 192–93; Crow Indians to CIA, Nov. 12, 1889, RG 75.19.21, Sent, Box 2; M. P. Wyman to CIA, Sept. 30, 1890, *Registers of Letters Received*, P2186, Roll 42, 30877; Sissetons to CIA, Dec. 2, 1890, RG 75.4, Rec'd, 37601, Box 684; Red Cloud to CIA, Feb. 4, 1891, RG 75.4, Rec'd, 5556, Box 704; White Swan to McLaughlin, Oct. 14, 1891, RG 75.19.113, Rec'd, Box 34.
173. Martin to Waldron, Nov. 21, 1890, RG 75.19.113, Rec'd, Box 33; Noheart to Palmer, Nov. 5, 1890, RG 75.19.11, Box 570; Wolf Chief to CIA, Feb. 21, 1890, RG 75.4, Rec'd, 6439, Box 705; Bearface to McLaughlin, Aug. 28, 1888, *McLaughlin Papers*, Roll 2.
174. Feather in the Ear to CIA, July 25, 1890, RG 75.4, Rec'd, 22983, Box 652; Little Chief to CIA, March 19, 1890, RG 75.4, Rec'd, 9581, Box 608; Big Road to Welsh, Feb. 28, 1891, *IRAP*, Roll 17; Pratt to Big Tree, July 18, 1889, RG 75.4, Rec'd, 22093, Box 543; Myers to CIA, Aug. 5, 1889, RG 75.4, Rec'd, 22093, Box 543; CIA to Gallagher, April 12, 1890, RG 75.19.85, Rec'd from OIA, Box 9; Fast Horse et al. to CIA, March 5, 1890, *Registers of Letters Received*, P2186, Roll 39, 9083; Big Horse to Pratt, June 8, 1890, RG 75.4, Rec'd, 18556, Box 633; Greasy Horn to CIA, Aug. 28, 1890, RG 75.4, Rec'd, 26015, Box 653.
175. Big Road to Pratt, June 9, 1890, RG 75.4, Rec'd, 20195, Box 637.
176. Running Bull and Lightning Iron to IRA, May 27, 1889, *IRAP*, Roll 15; CIA to Gallagher, July 22, 1890, RG 75.19.85, Rec'd from OIA, Box 9; Red Cloud to CIA, May 30, 1890, RG 75.4, Rec'd, 17061, Box 628; Kiowa Indians to CIA, Dec. 5, 1890, RG 75.4, Rec'd, 38273, Box 685; Adams to CIA, Dec. 6, 1890, RG 75.4, Rec'd, 38273, Box 685; Yanktons to CIA,

Dec. 17, 1890, RG 75.4, Rec'd, 40370, Box 690; Under Bull et al. to CIA, Sept. 20, 1888, RG 75.19.30, Gen. Corres., Box 1.
177. Wolf Chief to CIA, Feb. 2, 1891, RG 75.4, Rec'd, 4820, Box 702; Wolf Chief to CIA, May 18, 1889, RG 75.4, Rec'd, 13918, Box 523.
178. Half Iron to IRA, Feb. 28, 1891, *IRAP*, Reel 15.
179. Wright to CIA, Jan. 23, 1891, RG 75.19.96, Sent, Vol. 20.
180. Standing Buffalo to CIA, July 3, 1890, RG 75.4, Rec'd, 20525, Box 638.
181. White Eagle to CIA, May 6, 1889, RG 75.4, Rec'd, 13082, Box 521.
182. Cloud Chief et al. to CIA, Dec. 4, 1890, RG 75.4, Rec'd, 38384, Box 685.
183. *ARCIA*, 1883, 59; Dorsey, *Omaha and Ponka Letters*, 44. Gahige wanted to hear "the true account" of Red Cloud's words after Heqaka-mani's visit with the Oglala Sioux. *ARCIA*, 1883, 59.
184. Feather-in-the-Ear to Sec. Int., July 25, 1890, 22983, RG 75.4, Rec'd, Box 645.
185. Ibid.
186. Copy of Carroll to Post Adj. Ft. Custer, May 24, 1889, 156XX (illegible), RG 75.4, Rec'd, Box 527.

Chapter 2

1. Clerk to Pratt, May 31, 1890, RG 75.19.50, Reel 18; DeKnight to Adams, April 21, 1890, RG 75.19.50, Reel 91; *ARCIA*, 1883, 226; Adams, *Education for Extinction*, 249.
2. *ARCIA*, 1883, 167, 169.
3. Woods to CIA, May 16, 1890, RG 75.19.77, Reel 17.
4. *ARCIA*, 1887, 267.
5. Roberts to Reverend, March 22, 1875, Mary D. Burnham Papers, MSS S-2157, Box 1, YCWA.
6. Pratt to McGillycuddy, Dec. 16, 1879, RG 75.19.85, Rec'd, Box 26. Pratt, superintendent at Carlisle, wrote that these messages would "periodically keep the parents informed upon those points most likely to concern them."
7. See Pratt to McGillycuddy, May 6, 1882, RG 75.19.85, Rec'd, Box 26. During summer vacation, Carlisle students were not required to write home, but they were urged to do so; see Pratt to Hunt, RG 75.19.50, Reel 90.
8. Bales to Crow Creek Agent, Aug. 2, 1886, RG 75.19.20, Box 21; Bales to Kiowa Agent, Sept. 2, 1886, RG 75.19.50, Reel 93.
9. Conkling to Father, Sept. 30, 1889, RG 75.19.50, Reel 93. ("I want you to [*write*] a letter to me.")
10. *Indian Helper* (Carlisle, PA), March 9, 1888; *Indian Helper*, Feb. 22, 1889; *Indian Helper*, Feb. 8, 1889; *Indian Helper*, Feb. 8, 1889; *Indian*

Helper, June 21, 1889; Pratt to Gallagher, Dec. 2, 1889, RG 75.19.85, Sent, Box 54.
11. McGillycuddy to Pratt, May 15, 1882, RG 75.19.85, Sent, Box 52.
12. *ARCIA*, 1887, 163. For other examples of letters from worried parents, see Otaakadi to Armstrong, Jan. 3, 1890, RG 75.19.113, Rec'd, Box 34; Rulean to CIA, May 12, 1890, RG 75.4, Rec'd, 14827, Box 622.
13. *Indian Helper*, Feb. 2, 1889.
14. McKassey to McKassey, Jan. 1, 1883, John O. Dorsey Papers, MS 4800 [247]; Wankicun to McLaughlin, Jan. 14, 1890, RG 75.19.113, Rec'd, Box 34; *Twenty-Two Years' Work*, 467–68; Pretty Scalp to CIA, Sept. 1, 1890, RG 75.4, Rec'd, 27654, Box 658; Smith to CIA, Nov. 2, 1890, RG 75.4, Rec'd, 33932, Box 675.
15. Lane to Friend, Oct. (date illegible) 1889, RG 75.19.50, Reel 92.
16. Friend to Giving, Nov. 7, 1889, RG 75.19.50, Reel 92.
17. *Indian Helper*, March 3, 1888.
18. Ibid.
19. *Indian Helper*, March 9, 1888; *Indian Helper*, June 27, 1890; *Indian Helper*, Aug. 1, 1890.
20. Brave Bull to Daughter, Jan. 4, 1880, in Adams, *Education for Extinction*, 252.
21. Swift Bear to Rainwater and White Woman, April 17, 1880, *ARCIA*, 1880, 306; Adams, *Education for Extinction*, 249.
22. Dorsey, *Omaha and Ponka Letters*, 90.
23. Torlino to Torlino, Dec. 5, 1884, RG 75.19.63, Sent, Box 5. Tom Torlino was the subject of perhaps the most well-known "before-and-after" photographs produced by Carlisle. See "Tom Torlino," RG 75.20.3, Series 1327, Box 18, Folder 872, accessible at Carlisle Indian School Digital Resource Center, http://carlisleindian.dickinson.edu/student_files/tom-torlino-student-file.
24. Bobtail to Son, Dec. 15, 1879, in Adams, *Education for Extinction*, 249.
25. *ARCIA*, 1880, 184.
26. Ibid., 185.
27. Ibid.
28. Ibid.
29. Tall Sun, the Southern Cheyenne chief of the Indian police at the Cheyenne-Arapaho Reservation, wrote to Carl Matches at Carlisle, telling him to come home so that he could attend the Sun Dance in the spring of 1885. With his typical disdain for Native culture, Carlisle superintendent Richard H. Pratt replied to Tall Sun with a scathing letter that denied Tall Sun's request, writing, "A Cheyenne who is on the Police force and is in favor of such things ought to be discharged. If you are not ashamed of yourself, I am ashamed of you"; see Pratt to Tall Sun, March 5, 1885,

RHPP, MSS S-1174, Box 10–10. Pratt was typically cordial, even kind, to parents because in its early years, his school's survival depended on parents' willingness to send children there.
30. *Indian Helper*, Oct. 14, 1887.
31. Pratt to Slow Bull, March 29, 1886, RHPP, MSS S-1174, Box 10–11.
32. Pratt to William H. Ward, Feb. 11, 1888, RHPP, MSS S-1174, Box 10–14.
33. In 1890, Pratt answered the concerns of the chaplain at the Mount Vernon Barracks in Alabama, where a number of Apaches had been held as prisoners since 1887. The prisoners were receiving letters from Carlisle students, and the chaplain had some unknown concern about them. Pratt told him that he should act as postmaster and the officer in charge should "manage just how that should be done." Pratt recommended, "There is more or less of discipline connected with it, and he being responsible should control." While Pratt did not explicitly discuss restricting the prisoners' incoming mail, it seems that was what he was referring to; see Pratt to Rev. W. Pierson, Nov. 22, 1890, RHPP, MSS S-1174, Box 10–17.
34. Pratt to Rev. Cook, Feb. 16, 1892, RHPP, MSS S-1174, Box 10–20. Fannie died on March 7, 1892, not long after this exchange; see "Fannie Charging Shield," RG 75.20.3, Series 1329, Box 4, accessible at Carlisle Indian School Digital Resource Center, http://carlisleindian.dickinson.edu.
35. Gallagher to Pratt, Feb. 26, 1890, RG 75.19.85, Sent, Box 54; Penny to Pratt, May 20, 1891, RG 75.19.85, Sent, Box 54; Penny to Supt. Lincoln Institute, Aug. 6, 1891, RG 75.19.85, Sent, Box 55; Penny to Supt. Lincoln Inst., Aug. 6, 1891, RG 75.19.85, Sent, Box 55; Ashley to Pratt, June 14, 1890, RG 75.19.10, Reel 33; Ashley to Pratt, June 14, 1890, RG 75.19.10, Reel 32; Ashley to Pratt, June 14, 1890, RG 75.19.10, Reel 33; Penny to Pratt, May (date illegible) 1891, RG 75.19.85, Sent, Box 54; Penny to Pratt, May (undated) 1891, RG 75.19.85, Sent, Box 54.
36. Cheyenne-Arapaho Agent to Supt. Haskell, Jan. (undated) 1889, RG 75.19.10, Reel 31.
37. Gallagher to Pratt, Feb. 28, 1890, RG 75.19.85, Sent, Box 54; Penny to Supt. Genoa, Aug. 20, 1891, RG 75.19.85, Sent, Box 55; Ashley to Supt. Haskell Institute, Oct. 31, 1890, RG 75.19.10, Reel 32.
38. Pratt to Blue Tomahawk, Jan. 19, 1889, RHPP, MSS S-1174, Box 10.
39. Dennis Blue Tomahawk's gravestone at the Carlisle Indian School cemetery records his death on January 19, 1880, but Pratt's letter to Blue Tomahawk regarding Dennis's illness was sent in January 1881.
40. Pratt to Young Man Afraid of His Horses, March 17, 1888, RHPP, MSS S-1174, Box 10–17.
41. Springers to R. H. Pratt, Nov. 20, 1883, Alice Fletcher Papers, MS 4558, Series 1, Box 1, NAA.

42. Mother to McLaughlin, Feb. 5, 1889, RG 75.19.113, Rec'd, Box 32.
43. Penny to Supt. St. Francis Xavier's, May 21, 1891, RG 75.19.85, Sent, Box 9.
44. Ahatone to Adams, June 2, 1891, RG 75.19.50, Reel 91; Ahatone and Rush to Adams, June 6, 1892, RG 75.19.50, Reel 91; Jackson to Adams, June 2, 1891, RG 75.19.50, Reel 91; Moore to Adams, RG 75.19.50, Reel 92. Some wrote hoping to be enrolled at a school; see Harrel to Tyler, Nov. 25, 1889, RG 75.4, Rec'd, 34070, Box 573; Boswell to CIA, Oct. 14, 1889, RG 75.4, Rec'd, 29620, Box 562; Supt. Lincoln Institute to CIA, Oct. 28, 1889, RG 75.4, Rec'd, 30584, Box 565; Pratt to CIA, Nov. 4, 1889, RG 75.4, Rec'd, 31687, Box 567; Adams, *Education for Extinction*, 236–38.
45. Baker to CIA, April 3, 1889, *Registers of Letters Received*, P2186, Roll 34, 8618; Walker to CIA, April 3, 1889, *Registers of Letters Received*, P2186, Roll 34, 8619; Star to CIA, May 1, 1890, *Registers of Letters Received*, P2186, Roll 40, 15485; Little Beaver to Robinson, Dec. 10, 1888, RG 75.4, Rec'd, 30575, Box 493; Miller and Redwolf to CIA, Feb. 18, 1890, RG 75.4, Rec'd, 5728, Box 597; Pine Ridge Agent to Longwell, May 19, 1891, RG 75.19.85, Sent, Box 54; Ikinicapi to CIA, Dec. 6, 1888, RG 75.4, Rec'd, 30013, Box 492; Ikinicapi to CIA, Jan. 4, 1889, RG 75.4, Rec'd, 398, Box 496; Weston to CIA, Jan. 3, 1890, RG 75.4, Rec'd, 433, Box 583; Patterson to CIA, Sept. 6, 1890, RG 75.4, Rec'd, 27725, Box 658; Snake to CIA, March 21, 1890, RG 75.4, Rec'd, 8886, Box 606.
46. Babby to CIA, March 27, 1889, *Registers of Letters Received*, P2186, Roll 34, 8326; Gallagher to CIA, April 6, 1889, *Registers of Letters Received*, P2186, Roll 34, 9175; Pine Ridge Agent to Two Elks, Dec. 2, 1891, RG 75.19.85, Sent, Box 55; Ashley to Pratt, Oct. 26, 1890, RG 75.19.10, Reel 32; Bobb to Meserve, Dec. 19, 1892, RG 75.19.50, Reel 92; Garneaux to CIA, Aug. 13, 1889, RG 75.4, Rec'd, 23175, Box 546.
47. Hyde, *A Sioux Chronicle*, 168; Hyde, *Spotted Tail's Folk*, 343.
48. Long Pumpkin to CIA, Oct. 22, 1890, RG 75.4, Rec'd, 33019, Box 673.
49. Unknown Student to Kiowa Agent, Nov. 1892, RG 75.19.50, Reel 92; Inkanish to Kiowa Agent, July 8, 1891, RG 75.19.50, Reel 91.
50. Lonewolf to Myers, July 18, 1889, RG 75.19.50, Reel 91; Inknaish to Adams, May 13, 1890, RG 75.19.50, Reel 91.
51. *Indian Helper*, Jan. 18, 1889; *Indian Helper*, Feb. 22, 1889; *Indian Helper*, March 29, 1889; McHenry Cox to Wright, March 7, 1891, RG 75.19.96, Rec'd, Box 5.
52. Running With to Armstrong, March 29, 1888, RG 75.19.113, Rec'd, Box 31.
53. Hairy Chin to McLaughlin, Aug. 20, 1889, RG 75.19.113, Rec'd, Box 32.
54. Pee Shee Dwin and Blandin to Richards, March 1, 1874, RG 75.19.50, Reel 39.

55. Dorsey, *Omaha and Ponka Letters*, 117.
56. Ibid., 111.
57. Ibid., 121.
58. Dorsey, *The Cegiha Language*, 476, 485. Others made similar expressions to absent loved ones. An Omaha man wrote: "When I do not see you I am poor, but when I see you I am not poor. Since you departed my heart has been sad."
59. Pendleton to Little Medicine, Oct. 7, 1878, "From Warrior to Saint," Oklahoma State University Library Digital Collections, https://dc.library.okstate.edu/digital/collection/oaker. After being imprisoned at Fort Marion from 1874 to 1878, Pendleton went to study Episcopal theology in Syracuse. His wife joined him there in 1879, but she died in 1880; see Kueteman, "He Goes First," 2006.
60. *Indian Helper*, Sept. 31, 1888.
61. Culbertson to McLaughlin, Nov. 27, 1888, RG 75.19.113, Rec'd, Box 32.
62. For the identity of Red Cow, see *Chicago Tribune*, March 1, 1889, 2; *Inter Ocean* (Chicago), March 4, 1889, 4. The *New York Times* reported that "for some unexplained reason," Red Cow was given the name Picket Pin by Bill Cody in 1887; see *New York Times*, Feb. 17, 1889, 1. Red Cow, aka Picket Pin, worked on the Buffalo Bill Wild West Show, was in Europe in 1889, and may have been with the 1890 European tour when this letter was written. Miss Pte Sa may have been a woman called Susie Picket Pin who died in 1932.
63. Take Way From Crow to White Cow and Hobbles, March 1, 1890, MS 1748, NAA. The letter was obtained by Edgar Mearns, who gave it to Walter Hough, who worked for the Smithsonian. The letter proved difficult to translate for the Bureau of American Ethnology (Francis LaFlesche could not). It was eventually translated in late 1915 by Joseph Black Spotted Horse (from Rosebud), who read it aloud in Lakota while an interpreter named Louis Bordeaux transcribed it in English. Bordeaux transcribed the name of the sister-in-law as "Miss. White-cow," but I believe the proper translation should be Miss. Red Cow ("pte sa" or "pté šá," not "pté ská").
64. *Journal of the Sixth Annual Session of the General Council of Indian Territory*, 61. More than one hundred Pawnees were killed by some Oglala and Brulé Lakotas at Massacre Canyon in 1873 while the Pawnees were hunting bison in southwest Nebraska; see Blaine, "Pa-Re-Su A-Ri-Ra-Ke," 342–58.
65. Sun Chief et al. to Wichita Agency, Nov. 12, 1874, 75.19.50, Reel 40.
66. Pawnees had served as guides and scouts since the 1850s against their old Lakota, Cheyenne, and Arapaho enemies. For more on Pawnee Scouts, see van de Logt, *War Party in Blue*.

67. Howell to Howell, Jan. 21, 1877, Howell Family Papers, Box 10, MSS HM 67113–67164, Huntington.
68. Howell to Howell, Feb. 4, 1877, Howell Family Papers, Box 10, MSS HM 67113–67164, Huntington.
69. *Black Hills Weekly Pioneer* (Deadwood, SD), March 6, 1880.
70. Ibid.
71. *ARCIA*, 1879, 22.
72. Pawnee Woman to Cheyenne-Arapaho Agent, July 24, 1881, RG 75.19.10, Reel 22.
73. Lynde to McLaughlin, May 22, 1881, *James McLaughlin Papers*, Reel 2.
74. Black Hawk to McLaughlin, Nov. 26, 1891, RG 75.19.113, Rec'd, Box 34.
75. For more on the Paiutes and the Winnemuccas, see Zanjani, *Sarah Winnemucca*; Canfield, *Sarah Winnemucca of the Northern Paiutes*.
76. *Pioche (NV) Record*, March 26, 1881.
77. Carpenter and Sorisio, eds., *The Newspaper Warrior*.
78. See West, *The Last Indian War*; Greene, *Beyond Bear's Paw*.
79. Lawyer to McLaughlin, Aug. 18, 1883, RG 75.19.113, Rec'd, Box 29. The agent's reply is unknown, and we do not know how many Nez Perces were at Standing Rock (most likely no more than a few), but we do know that a Shoshone-Bannock named Steps (or No Feet), who had become an adopted Nez Perce after being taken captive (and losing his feet to frostbite), traveled with Sitting Bull from Canada to Fort Buford in 1881 and then to Standing Rock; see Sprague, *Standing Rock Sioux*, 57. For more on Lawyer, see Lewis, "Leadership in the Native Tradition."
80. Arnold to Cheyenne River Agent, Oct. 18, 1888, RG 75.19.11, Box 249.
81. Dorsey, *Omaha and Ponka Letters*, 69. Parentheses added by Dorsey in his translation.
82. Spotted Tail Jr.'s Last Will and Testament, LFSP, MSS 596. Whirlwind Soldier got his buffalo shield, Thunder Hawk his headdress, Big Turkey his bear claw necklace, Sky Bull his bonnet of eagle feathers, High Bear his porcupine scalp shirt, and Running Antelope his Omaha Dance outfit.
83. Gallagher to McLaughlin, June 3, 1890, RG 75.19.85, Sent, Box 54.
84. Eastman, "A Hasty Conclusion," 192–99. While at Standing Rock, Luke Shield wrote to a former teacher: "This is not good place to live. No church on Sunday, and I never see any of the boys I know. Indians here all too wild. Dance all the time. . . . I saw one girl yesterday. She like me very much and maybe I marry her. What think?"
85. These letters are accessible because the Southern Ute agent kept them with the rest of the agency's official correspondence and records (something that most Indian agents did not do—the letters written by the Southern Utes in reply do not survive). The early letters from the Northern Utes were composed by their agent, who simply transmitted the thoughts

of a Ute leader or leaders in the third person (the letters begin with "Sapparrano wishes me to express" or "wants me to write . . . to tell your Indians"), rather than transcribing the Ute's words in the first person. But after 1886, most of the letters were written by Utes themselves or by a Native or non-Native interpreter or transcriber.

86. Uintah and Ouray Agent to Southern Ute Agent, Dec. 22, 1886, RG 75.19.18, Decimal Files, Box 2; Chepeta to Ignacio, March 8, 1890, RG 75.19.18, Decimal Files, Box 1; Charley et al. to Ignacio et al., March 8, 1890, RG 75.19.18, Decimal Files, Box 2 (both letters have the same handwriting). Chepeta to Buckskin Charley et al., March 8, 1890; Northern Ute to Buckskin Charley and other Utes, May 10, 1890; Northern Ute to Buckskin Charley et al., June 7, 1890; Shawanaux to Buckskin Charley et al., June 21, 1890; Shavanaux to Buckskin Charley et al., July 4, 1890, all in RG 75.19.18, Decimal Files, Box 2.
87. Sapporrano et al. to Buckskin Charley et al., March 19, 1887, RG 75.19.18, Decimal Files, Box 2.
88. Elk, Ignacio, and Johnson Smith to Buckskin Charley et al., Nov. 1, 1890, RG 75.19.18, Decimal Files, Box 2.
89. Rooriguts to Southern Ute Agent, Aug. 8, 1891, RG 75.19.18, Decimal Files, Box 2.
90. Rooriguts to Southern Ute Agent, Feb. 16, 1891, RG 75.19.18, Decimal Files, Box 2.
91. Ostler, *The Plains Sioux*, 54.
92. Lakotas were also separated from the Eastern and Western Dakotas living in Dakota Territory and Nebraska at the Santee, Yankton, and Sisseton (Lake Traverse) Reservations. I define communication among the Lakota bands as "intertribal" for the sake of consistency even though Lakotas saw themselves as part of a larger Lakota tribe with distinct and largely independent bands. They were certainly divided by the reservation system. Today, Lakota bands are politically independent of each other and are federally recognized as different tribes (Oglala Sioux Tribe, Rosebud Sioux Tribe, Cheyenne River Sioux Tribe, Lower Brule Sioux Tribe, and Standing Rock Sioux Tribe).
93. See Rosebud to McGillycuddy, (undated) 1880, RG 75.19.85, Rec'd, Box 26.
94. Crazy Elk to McGillycuddy, May 24, 1880, RG 75.19.85, Rec'd, Box 26.
95. Charging Eagle to Three Bear, May 7, 1880, RG 75.19.85, Rec'd, Box 26.
96. Swan to McLaughlin, June 2, 1885, RG 75.19.113, Rec'd, Box 30.
97. Old Strikes the Ree to Yankton Agent, Nov. 19, 1880, RG 75.19.113, Rec'd, Box 26. To complete a transfer, agents would have to drop an individual from their agency rolls and transfer the individual's enrollment to a new agency.

98. Dorsey, *The Ȼegiha Language*, 720.
99. Dorsey, *Omaha and Ponka Letters*, 74–75. Parentheses added by Dorsey in his translation.
100. Ibid., 80.
101. Ibid., 69.
102. Dorsey, *The Ȼegiha Language*, 480. Older Omaha men commonly addressed younger Omahas as "my grandchild," even outside of kinship. These two men may have not been genetically related; see Dorsey, *The Ȼegiha Language*, 505.
103. See McGinnis, *Counting Coup and Cutting Horses*.
104. McGrady, *Living with Strangers*, 14.
105. Ross, *The Red River Settlement*, 325.
106. Ibid., 326–28.
107. Ibid., 328–30.
108. McGrady, *Living with Strangers*, 14.
109. Gillmor and Wetherill, *Traders to the Navajos*, 8; Burns, *A History of the Osage People*, 312.
110. *New York Times*, May 24, 1873.
111. Vanderwerth, ed., *Indian Oratory*, 223–24.
112. McLaughlin to Kauffman, Jan. 29, 1884, RG 75.19.113, Sent to CIA, Box 1.
113. For more on intertribal conflict on the northern plains before the 1870s, see White, "The Winning of the West"; Ewers, "Intertribal Warfare."
114. Kauffman to McLaughlin, Feb. 1, 1883, RG 75.19.113, Rec'd, Box 29.
115. Horse Roads et al. to Young Man Afraid, (undated) 1880, RG 75.19.85, Rec'd, Box 26.
116. McGillycuddy to CIA, Nov. 22, 1879, RG 75.19.86, Sent, Box 3. *ARCIA*, 1890, 53. There were 905 Northern Cheyennes at Tongue River in 1889–90; see *ARCIA*, 1890, 133.
117. More than ninety Cheyennes remained at Pine Ridge in 1891; see *ARCIA*, 1891, 287.
118. Porter to Par-Thee, Feb. 9, 1871, RG 75.19.10, Reel 22; *ARCIA*, 1891, 291.
119. *Sioux City (IA) Journal*, Oct. 30, 1878.
120. Shim-a-raff to Snake Pete, Aug. 6, 1891, RG 75.19.18, Decimal Files, Box 2; Dorsey, *The Ȼegiha Language*, 730.
121. Ibid., 732. Dorsey translated the Omaha word "zéȼiȼaí" (which means "they prescribe for you") as "vaccination."
122. Ibid., 476.
123. Ibid., 497.
124. Ibid., 502.
125. Ibid., 486, 491.
126. Typescript excerpts from the unpublished memoirs of Philip Faribault Wells, "95 Years among the Indians of the Northwest," WSCC, Box 117.

127. Baird, "Sketches of the Indian Campaigns of General Nelson A. Miles, U.S. Army," George William Baird Papers, MSS S-878 B163, YCWA.
128. Victor, *Our Centennial Indian War*, 85.
129. Ibid., 85–87.
130. Sitting Bull to Rosebud Agent, Nov. 24, 1882, RG 75.19.96, Rec'd, Box 4.
131. Sitting Bull to Standing Rock, (undated) 1883, RG 75.19.113, Rec'd, Box 29.
132. Dorsey, *Omaha and Ponka Letters*, 64.
133. Paul, *The Nebraska Indian Wars Reader*, 164. Spotted Tail wrote to General George Crook during the Great Sioux War in 1877.
134. Welsh to McLaughlin, Feb. 2, 1886, RG 75.19.113, Rec'd, Box 30.
135. McLaughlin to CIA, Feb. 23, 1888, RG 75.19.113, Sent to CIA, Box 2. Later in the spring of 1888, the Indian Rights Association, which supported the bill, began distributing among Lakotas the Dawes Sioux Bill translated into their language so that more people could understand it; see Harrison to McLaughlin, April 23, 1888, RG 75.19.113, Sent to CIA, Box 2.
136. Asay to CIA, May 11, 1889, RG 75.4, Rec'd, 13851, Box 523. The trader could not obtain a copy of the letter to send to the commissioner.
137. Parker to CIA, Sept. 13, 1889, RG 75.4, Rec'd, 26149, Box 554. Six weeks earlier, the secretary of the interior had asked the commissioner of Indian affairs to do what he could to limit the influence of Red Cloud and to recognize American Horse "as the chief of the Sioux," see Sec. Int. to CIA, July 1, 1889, RG 75.4, Rec'd, 17191, Box 531. Even those who were in favor of allotment could express their opinions to members of other tribes. In 1889, an Omaha man wrote to a Ponca friend, "We Indians in all parts of the country will become citizen: although we are not white people by birth, we know that only when we imitate the white men in working can we hope to prosper continually"; see Dorsey, *Omaha and Ponka Letters*, 115.
138. Even those who were visiting Pine Ridge wrote letters to Red Cloud. In 1891, a number of Lakotas from surrounding reserves asked the Oglala "permission to remain" at Pine Ridge through letters to Red Cloud; see *Executive Documents of the Senate of the United States for the First Session of the Fifty-Second Congress*, 50.
139. McLaughlin to CIA, Nov. 15, 1881, Standing Rock Letterpress Copybook, MSS S-3052, YCWA.
140. For some speculation on how Red Cloud acquired the samurai sword, see Bleed, "Indians and Japanese Swords on the North Plains Frontier," 112–15.
141. *Inter Ocean*, April 28, 1877; Red Cloud to Grinnell, June 22, 1886, Joseph and Hilda Grinnell Papers, MSS 73/25 c, Bancroft.
142. *Harrisburg (PA) Independent*, July 16, 1878.

143. *Black Hills Times*, Oct. 6, 1880; *Salt Lake (UT) Herald*, Aug. 27, 1882.
144. *Bozeman (MT) Weekly*, July 1, 1885.
145. McGillycuddy to CIA, Aug. 20, 1882, RG 75.19.85, Sent, Box 52; Acting Agent to Sumner, (undated) 1882, RG 75.19.85, Sent, Box 52; McGillycuddy to CIA, Aug. 22, 1882, RG 75.19.85, Rec'd, Box 27. For more, see Ostler, *The Plains Sioux*, 203–5.
146. Dorsey to Powell, Sept. 1, 1879, NAA, RBAE, Box 67.
147. Schwoch, *Wired into Nature*, 15, 28, 156–57.
148. CIA to John Cook, June 20, 1881, RG 75.19.96, Rec'd, Box 3. By 1890, Pine Ridge had a Native telegraph operator, E. G. Bettelyoun, who was hired as an assistant clerk; see Gallagher to CIA, March 25, 1890, *LSCIAPR*, Reel 10.
149. Anonymous telegram to American Horse, March 31, 1882, RG 75.19.96, Rec'd, Box 4; Billy telegram to Robideaux, April 4, 1882, RG 75.19.96, Rec'd, Box 4; Stranger Horse telegram to Adams, June 6, 1882, RG 75.19.96, Rec'd, Box 4.
150. Two Strike telegram to White Blanket, Aug. 18, 1882, RG 75.19.96, Rec'd, Box 4.
151. Yellow Breast to Lightning Bear, (undated) 1882, RG 75.19.96, Rec'd, Box 4.
152. Thunder Hawk telegram to No Flesh, May 8, 1882, RG 75.19.96, Rec'd, Box 4.
153. Thunder Hawk telegram to Edwards, May 19, 1882, RG 75.19.96, Rec'd, Box 4; *Black Hills Daily Times*, March 6, 1882; Andreas, *Andreas' Historical Atlas of Dakota*.
154. Brave Bull to McGillycuddy, May (undated), 1882, RG 75.19.96, Rec'd, Box 4.
155. Crazy in the Lodge et al. to Spotted Tail, Feb. 21, 1882, RG 75.19.96, Rec'd, Box 4.
156. Spotted Tail to Swift Bear et al., Feb. 21, 1882, RG 75.19.96, Rec'd, Box 4.
157. Dorsey, *The Ȼegiha Language*, 486–87.

Chapter 3

1. *Reno (NV) Evening Gazette*, April 28, 1882.
2. *News Reporter* (Dayton, NV), Feb. 24, 1887; *Reno Evening Gazette*, Jan. 3, 1889. In fact, while visiting Bannocks and Shoshones at the Fort Hall Reserve in Idaho Territory in 1888, Sides saw Nez Perce and Lemhi Indians join in a "grand dance," their first at Fort Hall in quite some time. Sides was an informant of sorts for the *Reno Evening Gazette*; see "The

Rise, Fall, and Redemption of Johnson Sides," in Kelly, *Emerson's Wife*, 161–68.
3. This map visualizes the known trips between reservations from the beginning of 1880 through the end of 1890 (reservation boundaries changed dramatically in the 1880s—this map represents reservation lines circa 1890). I know there were many more trips between reservations in this period than the map visualizes, but these are the ones I can document with certainty. Most of this documentation comes from the reservation records held in regional National Archives. Because of the limitation of reservation records and because of the limitations of my own research, this map cannot be a comprehensive visualization of all the West's intertribal connections. There are blank spots in the Pacific Northwest, in California, and around several other reservations because of these limitations. All reservation records are incomplete (missing or damaged—for instance, there is very little surviving from Fort Hall or Wind River in this period) and no agent kept ongoing logs of visits to/from his agency (although I have found such records for white visitors). The documents that I have gathered that give evidence of trips between reservations are mostly letters between agents that describe the movement between their reservations and there are some travel passes preserved. Some reservation records are much more complete than others—which can skew the map—it might appear that people on one reservation were visiting much more than those on another reservation. Also, I have documented that at least 37 percent of these trips were made without permission, but I also know that there must have been many more unauthorized visits that agents did not know or care to know about. Moreover, this is a map of "trips"—I cannot call all of these "visits," even though most all of this movement is visitation (visiting friends, family; traveling delegations; traveling to dance, trade, socialize, etc.). Agents usually did not mention specific reasons why visits were made. There are a couple categories of "trips" that I have mapped that might not have been a "normal" visit, such as traveling to another reservation to recover a lost or stolen horse.
4. Half Iron to Welsh, Dec. 16, 1889, *IRAP*, Reel 15.
5. Little Wound et al. to Cleveland, Dec. 10, 1888, RG 75.19.85, Sent, Box 54.
6. White, *Service on the Indian Reservations*, 161.
7. Bell to Southern Ute Agent, Sept. 13, 1886, RG 75.19.18, Decimal Files, Box 1. Acting Agent Bell of Pine Ridge asked the agent at the Southern Ute Agency to send the Oglalas home if they reached his agency, but it is not clear if the Oglalas made it there.
8. Bell to Wind River Agent, Aug. 30, 1886, RG 75.19.85, Sent, Box 54.
9. Wind River Agent to Bell, Sept. 3, 1886, RG 75.19.85, Rec'd, Box 27; Wind River Agent to Bell, Sept. 4, 1886, RG 75.19.85, Rec'd, Box 27; Bell

to Southern Ute Agent, Sept. 13, 1886, RG 75.19.18, Decimal Files, Box 2; Bell to Wind River Agent, Sept. 13, 1886, RG 75.19.85, Sent, Box 54; Southern Ute Agent to Bell, Sept. 18, 1886, RG 75.19.85, Rec'd, Box 27. The Pine Ridge acting agent thought that Jack's party was headed to the Southern Ute Agency in southwest Colorado, not the Uintah and Ouray Agency in northeast Utah. Perhaps the Southern Ute Agency was Jack's ultimate destination.

10. White, *Service on the Indian Reservations*, 161–62.
11. Sowawick to Ignacio, May 7, 1887, RG 75.19.18, Decimal Files, Box 2. At least fifty-seven letters were sent from the Uintah and Ouray Utes in Utah to the Southern Utes in southwest Colorado between 1883 and 1893. Agents wrote the letters for the Utes during the first few years, but it is not always clear who transcribed the letters in later years.
12. Gallagher to Uintah Agent, May 21, 1888, RG 75.19.85, Sent, Box 54; Chaffe to Asst. Adj. Gen., May 24, 1889, RG 75.4, Rec'd, 15595, Box 527; Catoup to Buckskin Charley, Feb. 1, 1890, RG 75.19.18, Decimal Files, Box 2; *Townsend (MT) Tranchant*, Oct. 10, 1888, as reported by the *Northwest Tribune* (Stevensville, MT); Copy of Brig. Gen. Ruger to Asst. Adj. Gen. Div. Missouri, May 10, 1889, RG 75.4, Rec'd, 13580, Box 522; Gallagher to Byrnes, June 3, 1889, RG 75.19.85, Sent, Box 54; Gallagher to Uintah Agent, July (undated), 1889, RG 75.19.85, Sent, Box 54.
13. Selwyn to Foster, Nov. 25, 1890, RG 75.4, Special Case 188, Box 199.
14. Marcisco to Buckskin Charley, March 10, 1890, RG 75.19.18, Decimal Files, Box 2; Marcisco to Buckskin Charley, March 15, 1890, RG 75.19.18, Decimal Files, Box 2. It is not clear why Red Cloud wanted the Utes to meet him at Wind River; the letter is missing, but the request was made around the same time a delegation of Lakotas from Pine Ridge and Rosebud returned home from a journey west to find information on the Ghost Dance. See Gallagher to Wind River Agent, June 30, 1890, RG 75.19.85, Sent, Box 54; Copy of Tilford telegram to Asst. Adj. Gen., July 25, 1890, RG 75.4, Rec'd, 24858, Box 650; Copy of Tilford telegram to Asst. Adj. Gen., Aug. 21, 1890, RG 75.4, Rec'd, 26879, Box 655; Acting CIA to Royer, Sept. 5, 1890, RG 75.19.85, Rec'd from OIA, Box 9; Fosher to Gallagher, Sept. 29, 1890, RG 75.19.85, Rec'd, Box 27.
15. Byrnes telegram to CIA, Aug. 19, 1889, RG 75.4, Rec'd, 23195, Box 546; Berry to Hunt, March 21, 1882, RG 75.19.50, Reel 40.
16. Agent Byrnes telegraph to CIA, August 19, 1889, RG 75.4, Rec'd, 23195, Box 546. The party of Lakotas went from Pine Ridge to Wind River, then to Uintah, back to Wind River, and finally home to Pine Ridge.
17. Ewers, "Intertribal Warfare," 397–410; White, "The Winning of the West," 319–43; "Interview with Washakie," MS 34 C1, Bancroft.

18. Troth to Darlington, Feb. 28, 1871, RG 75.19.10, Reel 22; Mooney, "Calendar History of the Kiowa Indians," 333–34.
19. Mooney, "Calendar History of the Kiowa Indians," 143–45, 333–34. Mooney believed that the 1871–72 Pawnee visit with the Kiowas should have been recorded by the Kiowa calendar as 1872–73, but it is probable that the Pawnees visited in both 1871–72 and 1872–73 (evident in the 1871 Jacob Troth letter cited in note 18).
20. Tatum to Miles, Jan. 28, 1873, RG 75.19.10, Reel 22.
21. Travel Pass, June 30, 1882, RG 75.19.63, Sent, Box 3.
22. Youngkin, "Hostile and Friendly," 410.
23. *ARCIA*, 1870, 210; *ARCIA*, 1879, 30.
24. See "Calendar by Good Voice Hawk, 1822–1912," RG 75.19.35, Series 13, Box 109; Rzeczkowski, *Uniting the Tribes*, 21–47; Williamson to Allen, Sept. 9, 1886, RG 75.19.21, Sent, Box 3; Williamson to Baldwin, Nov. 17, 1886, RG 75.19.21, Sent, Box 3; Williamson to Heth, Oct. 28, 1886, RG 75.19.21, Sent, Box 3; Williamson to Cowan, Feb. 26, 1887, RG 75.19.21, Sent, Box 3; Williamson to Baldwin, Feb. 26, 1887, RG 75.19.21, Sent, Box 3.
25. McGillycuddy to Carpenter, Mar. 16, 1885, RG 75.19.85, Sent, Box 53; Hoxie, *Parading through History*, 140. Blackfeet (Southern Piikani)/Crow relations took a turn in 1887 after men from both sides raided each other's horses.
26. Carroll to Fields, June 7, 1887, RG 75.19.30, Rec'd, Box 2. For more on the Blackfoot Confederacy, see Hungry Wolf, *The Ways of My Grandmothers*; Dempsey, *The Vengeful Wife*.
27. See Charging Crow, "History of the Lakotas as Told by Alex Charging Crow," in Adee Dodge Papers, WA MSS S-2701 Series III, Box 40, YCWA; Rzeczkowski, *Uniting the Tribes*, 79–103; Bray, "Lone Horn's Peace," 28–47.
28. McLaughlin to CIA, July 31, 1886, RG 75.19.113, Sent to CIA, Box 2.
29. Charging Crow, "History of the Lakotas as Told by Alex Charging Crow," 98.
30. Grinnell to Kuhns, Jan. 4, 1890, GBGP, MS 1388, Box 1 (Reel 2).
31. Grinnell to Kuhns, Feb. 28, 1890, GBGP, MS 1388, Box 1 (Reel 2). For more on Massacre Canyon, see Riley, "The Battle of Massacre Canyon."
32. Grinnell to Harry Kuhns, Jan. 4, 1890, GBGP, MS 1388, Box 2 (Reel 3).
33. *Reno Evening Gazette*, May 24, 1888; *Reno Evening Gazette*, May 28, 1888.
34. *Reno Evening Gazette*, May 28, 1888.
35. *Pioche (NV) Record*, June 3, 1882.
36. Dorsey, *Omaha and Ponka Letters*, 44.

37. Ibid., 481, 482; Dorsey, *The Ȼegiha Language*, 475–76, 490, 494, 513, 518, 519, 522.
38. Dorsey, *The Ȼegiha Language*, 482.
39. Dorsey, *Omaha and Ponka Letters*, 115.
40. Dorsey, *The Ȼegiha Language*, 712–14, 731.
41. Howell to Howell, Sept. 18, 1876, Howell Family Papers, Box 9, HM 67091, Huntington.
42. Howell to Howell, Aug. 9, 1876, Howell Family Papers, Box 9, HM 67087, Huntington.
43. Howell to Howell, Feb. 25, 1877, Howell Family Papers, Box 10, HM 67119, Huntington.
44. Lesser, *The Pawnee Ghost Dance Hand Game*, 150–51. This Kiowa visit must have occurred before 1883, which was the year Evarts began his ten-year stay at Carlisle. Lesser guessed it must have occurred before 1880. It is also likely that it occurred after 1875, the year most Pawnees relocated to Indian Territory.
45. Battey, *The Life and Adventures of a Quaker among the Indians*, 130–31.
46. Ibid., 131–32.
47. Howell to Howell, Aug. 7, 1876, Howell Family Papers, Box 9, HM 67087, Huntington.
48. Ibid., 133. Battey's understanding of the end of that dance is as follows: The Pawnee men threw their "war implements upon the ground with such force, in case of tomahawk or hatchet . . . then with gestures of covering it up, they would go away leaving it to lie there; thus imitating that, though they had been foolish, and fought, they now rejoiced in the beams of peace, and hoped that the red men everywhere might live in peace with one another."
49. *ARCIA*, 1872, 214.
50. Stover, *American Railroads*, 83.
51. Fuller, *The American Mail*, 73–74, 103.
52. Lubetkin, *Jay Cooke's Gamble*.
53. Fellman, *Citizen Sherman*, 264.
54. *ARCIA*, 1872, 15.
55. Brown, *Hear That Lonesome Whistle Blow*, 85–93, 101, 205, 217. Railroad companies began promoting tourism in the West in the early 1870s, leading to the creation of Yellowstone National Park; see Gordon, *Passage to Union*, 155, 243.
56. Adams, *Education for Extinction*, 248.
57. Viola, *Diplomats in Buckskins*.
58. An 1879 report described Shoshones and Paiutes arriving in Winnemucca for a "fandango" on rail cars, on horseback, and afoot; see *Reno Evening Gazette*, Aug. 19, 1879.

59. *Reno Evening Gazette*, June 19, 1883. Natchez (the son of Paiute chief Winnemucca) told (in English) a crowd, including whites, that they wanted to live in peace with whites but that they "detested reservations."
60. *Morning Appeal* (Carson City, NV), Sept. 2, 1887.
61. *Reno Evening Gazette*, May 1, 1888.
62. *Reno Evening Gazette*, Jan. 3, 1889.
63. Mooney, *Ghost-Dance Religion*, 807. D. B. Shimkin described the Wind River Shoshones as adaptable people who traveled widely; see Shimkin, "Dynamics of Recent Wind River Shoshone History." Unfortunately, the Fort Hall and Wind River Agencies' records from the nineteenth century are fairly incomplete.
64. The Pocatello station was nearest to Fort Hall; see Waite, *The Railroad at Pocatello*.
65. Howard, "A Phenomenal Scout," *Youth's Companion*, Oct. 15, 1891, in Stanton G. Fisher Papers, MS106, Folder 15, Idaho State Historical Society.
66. Farr, "Going Buffalo," 35.
67. Sharon to Sec. Int., April 22, 1880; CIA to Sharon, May 13, 1880; Spencer to Yerington, May 24, 1880; all in Carson & Colorado Railroad Company Records, MS P-G 232, Bancroft.
68. Waite, *The Railroad at Pocatello*, 7, 9, 12. The Utah & Northern only had a two-hundred-foot-wide right-of-way. The Utah & Northern merged with the Oregon Short Line and other Union Pacific subsidiaries in 1889, forming the Oregon Short Line & Utah Northern Railway Company (OSL&UN). The line south of Pocatello was narrow gauge until 1890.
69. Link, "The Iron Horse in Indian Country," 187–88; Rzeczkowski, *Uniting the Tribes*, 85; Armstrong to Ainslie, Feb. 20, 1884, RG 75.19.21, Sent, Box 1.
70. Due, "The Carson and Colorado Railroad," 260. Paiutes were worried that the railroad would lead to increased competition for their already limited natural resources; see Johnson, *Walker River Paiutes*, 60.
71. Myrick, *Railroads of Nevada and Eastern California*, 179. The C&C stretched along western Nevada down to Owens Lake in eastern California. It was built between 1880 and 1883 and in 1890. Paiutes used the route on trips between the Pyramid Lake and Walker River Reservations. It was the route most Indians took on their visits to Wovoka, the intellectual source of the 1889 Ghost Dance.
72. *Reno Evening Gazette*, July 27, 1880.
73. *Record-Union* (Sacramento, CA), Aug. 19, 1891; Dyer, "Wizardry," Special Collections, University of Nevada Libraries, Reno, transcribed in Hittman, *Wovoka*, 247–55.
74. *Reno Evening Gazette*, Aug. 23, 1887. By 1891, prominent Paiute Johnson Sides complained that the Central Pacific was charging too much for

its trips to the hops fields around Sacramento. A few weeks later, two hundred Paiutes jumped into empty boxcars on a freight train to avoid the fare; see *Weekly Gazette and Stockman* (Virginia City, NV)), Aug. 6, 1891; *Reno Evening Gazette*, Aug. 22, 1891.

75. *Reno Evening Gazette*, June 28, 1890.
76. Reinhardt, ed., *Out West on the Overland Trail*, 118.
77. *Reno Evening Gazette*, Nov. 22, 1887. For more on the Paiutes' shifting economic world, see Warren, *God's Red Son*, 82–90.
78. See correspondence in boxes 250 and 314, RG 75.19.129.
79. Navajo agents in the 1880s interpreted Articles 9 and 13 of the 1868 Treaty as giving Navajos the right to travel to areas contiguous to the reservation for economic purposes; see discussion on page 106 in this text; Eastman to CIA, Oct. 14, 1882, RG 75.19.63, Sent, Box 3. See also "Treaty between the United States Government and the Navajo Indians Signed at Fort Sumner, New Mexico Territory on June 1, 1868," National Archives Catalog, https://catalog.archives.gov/id/6173067.
80. Eastman to Smith, March 20, 1882, RG 75.19.63, Sent, Box 3. The Navajo agent complained that because of the railroad, Navajos were "connected with the Saloons at Gallup and vicinity."
81. Bowman to CIA, Feb. 22, 1886, NFR, Vol. 9, Bancroft.
82. Gordon, *Passage to Union*, 308.
83. *Harper's Weekly*, March 22, 1890.
84. Reinhardt, ed., *Out West on the Overland Trail*, 113. For more on the particular disdain white Americans have had for Great Basin Natives, see Blackhawk, *Violence over the Land*, 267–93.
85. *Harper's Weekly*, March 22, 1890.
86. Ashley to Atwood, May 31, 1890, RG 75.19.10, Reel 32. The price of transporting the travelers' ponies was also a consideration for agents and the railroads; see Blake to Gifford, July 3, 1884, RG 75.19.21, Sent, Box 3.
87. Railroad Pass for Hawk and Middle Bear, Nov. 11, 1889, RG 75.19.21, Sent, Box 4. For a look at the understanding between the Crow Agency and the NPRR, see Williamson to Holbrook, July 8, 1886, RG 75.19.21, Sent, Box 3.
88. Railroad Pass for Fish High Up and Charges through the Crowd, Aug. 30, RG 75.19.21, Sent, Box 4.
89. Schwantes and Ronda, *The West the Railroads Made*, 101.
90. Running Bull et al. to CIA, Nov. 6, 1889, RG 75.4, Rec'd, 33002, Box 571.
91. Burgess to Richards, Feb. 11, 1874, RG 75.19.50, Reel 40.
92. Hoag to Haworth, Aug. 25, 1874, RG 75.19.50, Reel 40.
93. CIA Circular, Dec. 17, 1874, RG 75.19.50, Reel 40.

94. This policy was modified to include Indian police escorts in 1878 as Indian police forces were being established on reservations; see CIA Circular, Dec. 23, 1878, RG 75.19.113, Rec'd, Box 26.
95. For more on military escorts in the early 1870s for Flatheads, Pend d'Oreilles, Kootenais, Spokanes, and other Indigenous groups in the northern plains, northern Rockies, and western plateau, see Farr, "Going Buffalo."
96. Royer to Wyman, Nov. 3, 1890, RG 75.19.85, Sent, Box 54; Travel Pass, Nov. 1, 1890, RG 75.19.77, Reel 17; Blackfeet Agent to Ft. Belknap Agent, Nov. 29, 1890, RG 75.19.3, Sent, Box 6.
97. Waugh to McLaughlin, Sept. 18, 1890, RG 75.19.113, Rec'd, Box 34.
98. Farr, "Going Buffalo," 33–43.
99. *ARCIA*, 1876, 112–13.
100. Ibid., 25.
101. *ARCIA*, 1877, 50. Also at the same time, two hundred Lakotas from Standing Rock were allowed to visit the Cheyenne River Reservation; see CIA telegram to Stephen, RG 75.19.113, Rec'd, Box 27.
102. Stowe to CIA, March 20, 1877, White Earth Letter Book, 1876–1877, MSS S-3097, YCWA. The White Earth agent claimed that the conduct of the Sissetons alarmed all the white settlers around White Earth as well as those living in the areas that they passed through. The Sissetons ignored the White Earth agent's instructions to leave, so the agent paid at least sixteen white settlers (mostly from Detroit Lakes, Minnesota) to help his four employees escort the Sissetons off the reservation; see also pages 472–89 in White Earth Letter Book, 1876–1877, MSS S-3097, YCWA.
103. Stowe to Hart, May 11, 1877; Stowe to Hamilton, May 20, 1877, both in White Earth Letter Book, 1876–1877, MSS S-3097, YCWA.
104. Stowe to Hamilton, June 25, 1877, White Earth Letter Book, 1876–1877, MSS S-3097, YCWA.
105. If an agent agreed to allow one of "his" Indians to visit another agency, the agent was supposed to ask both the commissioner of Indian affairs and the agent at the intended destination. Most agents did not bother the commissioner with every visit request, even if they allowed the visit to occur. In the late 1880s, there were many more of the agent-to-agent requests than the trio of agent-to-agent-to-commissioner requests.
106. *ARCIA*, 1879, 48.
107. Cramsie to McLaughlin, Oct. 21, 1882, RG 75.19.113, Rec'd, Box 28.
108. McGillycuddy to Pancoast, July 10, 1884, RG 75.19.85, Sent, Box 53.
109. Acting CIA to McLaughlin, July 15, 1884, RG 75.19.113, Rec'd, Box 29. Some agents also had a policy of refusing rations to visiting tribes; see Cowen to Fields, Oct. 22, 1888, RG 75.19.30, Rec'd, Box 2.

110. *Deseret Evening News* (Salt Lake City, UT), Oct. 10, 1884.
111. CIA to Nicholson, Aug. 14, 1877, RG 75.19.50, Reel 40.
112. Miles to Richards, July 24, 1877, RG 75.19.50, Reel 40.
113. CIA Circular, March 10, 1880, RG 75.19.113, Rec'd, Box 26.
114. Stephan telegram to CIA, Aug. 11, 1881, Standing Rock Letterpress, 1881, MSS S-3052, YCWA.
115. Travel Pass, Aug. 5, 1881, RG 75.19.85, Sent, Box 52.
116. Travel Pass, July 16, 1883, RG 75.19.85, Sent, Box 54; *Black Hills Times*, Aug. 18, 1883. In 1885, another seventy-five from Pine Ridge got approval to be at Wind River for two months, and fifty others headed to the Crow reserve for two months (both with Indian police escorts); see Travel Pass for Little Wound, Sept. 8, 1885; Travel Pass for Young Man Afraid, Sept. 8, 1885, both in RG 75.19.85, Sent, Box 53.
117. Pine Ridge Clerk to McGillycuddy, Sept. 18, 1883, RG 75.19.85, Sent, Box 53.
118. Officials blamed the troubles among Lakotas in the 1870s on their roaming habits; see Youngkin, "'Hostile and Friendly,'" 402–21.
119. CIA to Fosher, Sept. 7, 1889, RG 75.4, Sent. In a few instances, agents were afraid that visits might contribute to the spread of disease. In 1884, the Blackfoot agent reported that Blackfeet had contracted a disease while visiting in Canada; see Blackfoot Agent to CIA, Jan. 1, 1884, RG 75.19.3, Sent, Box 3. In 1885, the Blackfoot agent was worried about a smallpox breakout among Indians in the region because "members of the different tribes are constantly visiting each other"; see Blackfoot Agent to CIA, July 8, 1885, RG 75.19.3, Official Sent, Box 1. The Pawnee, Ponca, and Otoe agent blamed the transmission of syphilis to the Otoes on a band of visiting Omahas in the winter of 1886; see *ARCIA*, 1887, 87. In 1889, agents at the Lakota Agencies temporarily stopped issuing passes because of a scarlet fever outbreak in Bismarck; see Anderson to McLaughlin, March 8, 1889, RG 75.19.113, Rec'd, Box 32. Indians were also worried about visits leading to the spread of disease. In 1881, leaders at the Sisseton Reservation learned that there might be smallpox at the Crow Creek Reservation, and they asked that no visitors be allowed from there; see Sisseton Agent to Dougherty, May 2, 1881, RG 75.19.20, Rec'd, Box 3.
120. Byrnes to Stollsteimer, Sept. 9, 1887, Aug. 8, 1887, RG 75.19.18, Decimal Files, Box 1. The Utes made it home safely; see Byrnes to Stollsteimer, Sept. 16, 1887, RG 75.19.18, Decimal Files, Box 1.
121. CIA to Hunt, Sept. 5, 1881, RG 75.19.50, Reel 40. At least two Kiowas, Timyda and Zamigeat, received permission to visit New Mexico in 1889; see CIA to Myers, Jan. 22, 1889, RG 75.19.50, Reel 40; W. D. Myers, Nov. 3, 1888, RG 75.19.50, Reel 40.

122. Mooney, "Calendar History of the Kiowa Indians," 347.
123. Hunt to Mescalero Agent, Oct. 19, 1882, RG 75.19.50, Reel 12; CIA telegram to Hunt, Oct. 28, 1882, RG 75.19.50, Reel 39.
124. Mescalero Agent to Hall, June 16, 1887, RG 75.19.50, Reel 40.
125. *Boise (ID) Statesman*, May 20, 1882; *Wood River Times* (Hailey, ID), May 23, 1882.
126. *Billings Gazette*, March 26, 1887. The movement of Crows, Lakotas, and other groups had been, according to the editorial, "more severely felt in Montana than in any other part of the Northwest."
127. Davis to Post, Feb. 14, 1883, RG 75.19.85, Rec'd, Box 26.
128. *Weekly Missoulian* (Missoula, MT), April 25, 1879, cited in Farr, "Going Buffalo," 39.
129. Klamath Agent to Kiowa-Comanche-Wichita Agent, Feb. 6, 1880, RG 75.19.50, Reel 40.
130. CIA Circular, March 10, 1880, RG 75.19.113, Rec'd, Box 26.
131. Muncy telegram to Dyer, July 8, 1885; Dyer telegram to Muncy, July 8, 1885, both in RG 75.19.10, Reel 22.
132. *Idaho World*, June 22, 1888.
133. *Black Hills Journal*, Aug. 26, 1887.
134. *ARCIA*, 1885, 62.
135. *ARCIA*, 1886, 94.
136. Wyman to Agents at Pine Ridge and Rosebud, July 19, 1890, RG 75.19.21, Sent, Box 4; Wyman to Simmons, May 10, 180, RG 75.19.30, Rec'd, Box 2; *ARCIA*, 1876, 25.
137. Ashley to Wood, June 24, 1890, RG 75.19.10, Reel 32; Ashley to Wood, March 9, 1890, RG 75.19.10, Reel 32.
138. Dorsey, *Omaha and Ponka Letters*, 77.
139. Eastman to CIA, Sept. 27, 1881, RG 75.19.63, Sent, Box 3.
140. Winnemucca to Douglas, April 4, 1870, reproduced in Winnemucca, *A Century of Dishonor*, 396.
141. *The Times* (Philadelphia, PA), Dec. 23, 1883; *Reno Gazette-Journal*, Aug. 6, 1887, Nov. 10, 1887.
142. Kracht, *Religious Revitalization among the Kiowas*, 79–82.
143. Lesser, *The Pawnee Ghost Dance Hand Game*, 149.
144. *ARCIA*, 1879, 49.
145. McLaughlin to CIA, July 31, 1886, RG 75.19.113, Sent to CIA, Box 2; McChesney to McLaughlin, Aug. 9, 1886, RG 75.19.113, Rec'd, Box 30. Lakotas from Cheyenne River, who were in constant communication with Standing Rock Lakotas, heard about the visit and wanted to go along.
146. Williamson to McLaughlin, Sept. 7, 1886, RG 75.19.113, Rec'd, Box 30. The acting commissioner of Indian affairs deemed the visit "inadvisable"

and refused permission; see CIA to McLaughlin, Aug. 31, 1886, RG 75.19.113, Rec'd, Box 30.
147. Cowen to McLaughlin, May 30, 1888, RG 75.19.113, Rec'd, Box 32.
148. In 1889, there were nearly 3,300 Indians reported "wandering" in Nevada off the Western Shoshone Reservation, while just 477 lived on the reservation; see *ARCIA*, 1889, 506.
149. Crum, *The Road on which We Came*, 43–48, 72.
150. Plumb to Fisher, May 17, 1890, RG 75.19.132, Box 372.
151. Anderson to Kinney, June 26, 1888, RG 75.19.20, Sent, Box 2; Anderson to Briscoe, Sept. 19, 1888, RG 75.19.20, Sent, Box 2.
152. Edwin Fields, agent at Fort Belknap, believed that the "best interest of the Indians are served by requiring them to live within the limits of their reservation," but he never prohibited all visitations; see Fields to Reed, May 25, 1889, RG 75.19.30, Sent 1880–1927, Box 1.
153. Briscoe to Jones, Sept. 14, 1888, RG 75.19.21, Sent, Box 4.
154. Briscoe to Fields, Sept. 22, 1888; Briscoe to Fields, Sept. 14, 1888, both in RG 75.19.21, Sent, Box 4; Fields to Briscoe, Sept. 17, 1888, RG 75.19.30, Sent 1880–1927, Box 1; Briscoe to Anderson, Sept. 24, 1888, RG 75.19.21, Sent, Box 4; Briscoe to Anderson, Sept. 14, 1888, RG 75.19.21, Sent, Box 4; Briscoe to Comm. Officer Ft. McKinney, Sept. 24, 1888, RG 75.19.21, Sent, Box 4; Briscoe to Upshaw, Sept. 25, 1888, RG 75.19.21, Sent, Box 4.
155. Wyman to Upshaw, Oct. 23, 1889, RG 75.19.21, Sent, Box 4.
156. Acting CIA to McLaughlin, July 15, 1884, RG 75.19.113, Rec'd, Box 29.
157. W. J. to McGillycuddy, Aug. 7, 1884, RG 75.19.85, Rec'd, Box 27.
158. Travel Pass to Salt Lake, Aug. 9, 1886, NFR, Vol. 10, Bancroft.
159. Bowman to Patton, Sept. 6, 1884, RG 75.19.63, Sent, Box 4. The Navajo agent cited section 9 of the 1868 treaty.
160. Bowman to Woodgate, Dec. 8, 1884, NFR, Vol. 6, Bancroft.
161. Bowman to CIA, Oct. 18, 1884; Bowman to Sheldon, Oct. 18, 1884, both in NFR, Vol. 6, Bancroft.
162. Bowman to Comm. Officer Ft. Lewis, Nov. 18, 1884, NFR, Vol. 6, Bancroft. This concern for safety explains the thirteen passes the agent provided for Navajo travelers between October and December 1884, which asked "Americans" to treat pass holders with "respect and fair treatment"; see Travel Pass, Oct. 9, 1884, NFR, Vol. 6, Bancroft.
163. Cowen to McLaughlin, June 30, 1887, RG 75.19.113, Rec'd, Box 31.
164. *ARCIA*, 1886, 184. The agent grew so frustrated with not being able to control his Indians' movements that he recommended breaking up the remote Wolf Point Subagency and moving the Indians living there to other agencies. His Gros Ventres visited Fort Berthold and the Yanktonais visited Standing Rock so frequently that the agent thought it best that they be permanently moved to those respective reservations.

165. Kauffman to McLaughlin, Feb. 1, 1883, RG 75.19.113, Rec'd, Box 29.
166. Gallagher to Sisseton Agent, May 3, 1889, RG 75.19.85, Sent, Box 54.
167. Gallagher to Wright, Sept. 16, 1889, RG 75.19.85, Sent, Box 54.
168. Wright to Gallagher, Sept. 21, 1889, RG 75.4, Rec'd, Box 559, 28215.
169. Ibid.; Cartwright to Wright, Oct. 1, 1889, RG 75.4, Rec'd, 28215, Box 559.
170. Parker to CIA, Oct. 1, 1889, RG 75.4, Rec'd, 28215, Box 559. It seems that it was the Brulé Little Hawk of Rosebud, the nephew of Crazy Horse and son of Two Strike, not the Oglala Little Hawk, headman of the Hunkpatila band and uncle of Crazy Horse, but it is not certain.
171. Gallagher to Wright, Oct. 2, 1889, 75.19.96, Rec'd, Box 5. A similar episode had occurred in the previous spring of 1889; see Gallagher to Upshaw, Aug. 31, 1889, RG 75.19.85, Sent, Box 54.
172. Gallagher to Wyman, Nov. 1, 1889, RG 75.19.85, Sent, Box 54; Wyman to Gallagher, Nov. 10, 1889, RG 75.19.21, Sent, Box 4; Wyman to Gallagher, Nov. 10, 1889, RG 75.19.21, Sent, Box 4; McChesney to Gallagher, Dec. 14, 1889, RG 75.19.85, Rec'd, Box 27.
173. Gallagher to Wright, June 12, 1890, RG 75.19.85, Sent, Box 54.
174. White, *Service on the Indian Reservations*, 160.
175. McLaughlin to Stephan, Dec. 29, 1879, RG 75.19.113, Rec'd, Box 26.
176. Woods to Adams, Oct. 15, 1890, RG 75.19.50, Reel 40.
177. Anderson to CIA, Sept. 9, 1889, RG 75.4, Rec'd, 25973, Box 553; Fosher to CIA, March 15, 1890, RG 75.4, Rec'd, Box 606, 8748.
178. Adams to Ashley, May 19, 1890, RG 75.19.50, Reel 18; Dixon to McLaughlin, Oct. 31, 1890, RG 75.19.113, Rec'd, Box 34.
179. *ARCIA*, 1885, 30.
180. *ARCIA*, 1877, 50.
181. *ARCIA*, 1886, 75, 94.
182. Gallagher to Sisseton Agent, June 13, 1888, RG 75.19.85, Sent, Box 54; Clark to Spencer, Sept. 10, 1889, LFSP, MSS 596; Sterling to Gallagher, Aug. 8, 1890, *LSCIAPR*, Reel 10; Wyman to Bandini, Nov. 25, 1890, RG 75.19.21, Sent, Box 5; Dakota Mission to McLaughlin, Sept. 9, 1890, RG 75.19.113, Rec'd, Box 34; Foster to CIA, Nov. 29, 1890, RG 75.4, Rec'd, Letter 37463, Box 683.
183. Gallagher to Upshaw, August (undated) 1889, RG 75.19.85, Sent, Box 54; Upshaw to Carroll, April 21, 1890, RG 75.4, Rec'd, 19493, Box 635; *Rapid City (SD) Journal*, April 25, 1890. The number of Cheyennes traveling between Tongue River and Pine Ridge was a constant problem for the agents, and soldiers were often responsible for chasing them down. In April 1890, the army recommended that the Pine Ridge Cheyennes be allowed to live with their Tongue River brethren, but that did not happen until October 1891.
184. *Reno Evening Gazette*, Jan. 21, 1884.

185. CIA to Scott, Aug. 30, 1886, RG 75.19.132, Box 385A.
186. Mayhugh to Cook, July 14, 1885, RG 75.19.132, Box 372.
187. Adams to Ashley, May 7, 9, 12, 1890, RG 75.19.50, Reel 18; Ashley to Adams, May 20, 1890, RG 75.19.10, Reel 32.
188. Wright to Kusick, Jan. 2, 1891, RG 75.19.96, Sent, Vol. 20; Kusick to Wright, Jan. 10, 1891, RG 75.19.96, Rec'd, Box 5.
189. Gallagher to Upshaw, Jan. 9, 1889, RG 75.4, Rec'd, Letter 3787, Box 502.
190. Wright to Gallagher, Aug. 24, 1890, RG 75.19.85, Rec'd, Box 27.
191. Ibid. Threats of cutting wood or a temporary jailing were the harshest punishments the agents would impose.
192. Hollow Horn Bear to the President, CIA, Sept. 13, 1890, RG 75.4, Rec'd, 29579, Box 664.
193. McChesney to Wright, April 14, 1890, Rec'd, Box 5; Wright to Gallagher, July 7, 1890, RG 75.19.85, Rec'd, Box 27; Gallagher to Anderson, May 28, 1888, RG 75.19.85, Sent, Box 54; Gallagher to Wright, July 8, 1890, RG 75.19.85, Sent, Box 54. Some Indians went to other reservations to escape punishment for other offenses; see Gallagher to Wright, June 12, 1890, RG 75.19.85, Sent, Box 54; Scobey to McLaughlin, July 6, 1890, RG 75.19.113, Rec'd, Box 33; Scobey to Ft. Belknap Agent, Aug. 28, 1890, RBIA RG 75.19.30, Rec'd, Box 2.
194. *ARCIA*, 1888, 93.
195. Williams to White, March 17, 1888; Williams to White, Dec. 26, 1887, both in RG 75.19.50, Reel 39.
196. Riordan to Foreman, Oct. 2, 1883, RG 75.19.63, Sent, Box 4.
197. Spencer to McLaughlin, Sept. 5, 1888, RG 75.19.113, Rec'd, Box 32.
198. Ashley to Adams, July 8, 1891, RG 75.19.50, Reel 40.
199. Gallagher to Upshaw, Dec. 4, 1886, RG 75.19.85, Sent, Box 53.
200. Matonajin to Leary, Nov. 7, 1889, RG 75.19.96, Rec'd, Box 5.
201. Wyman to Crazy Bear, Nov. 10, 1890, RG 75.19.21, Sent, Box 4.
202. Snider to McLaughlin, Oct. 8, 1883, RG 75.19.113, Rec'd, Box 29.
203. Phelps to McLaughlin, Feb. 2, 1883, RG 75.19.113, Rec'd, Box 29.
204. Spotted Horse to McLaughlin, May 15, 1889, *James McLaughlin Papers*, Reel 2.
205. Show-un-ah-cum-ig-ish-cung to McLaughlin, Sept. 11, 1886, RG 75.19.113, Rec'd, Box 30.
206. Yellow Hair to McLaughlin, May 26, 1880, RG 75.19.113, Rec'd, Box 26.
207. Gray Eagle to McLaughlin, June 9, 1888, RG 75.19.113, Rec'd, Box 31.
208. Feather-in-the-Ear to Sec. Int., July 25, 1890, RG 75.4, Rec'd, 22983, Box 645.
209. *ARCIA*, 1879, 184.
210. *Philadelphia Inquirer*, Aug. 9, 1879.

Chapter 4

1. See Young, "Intertribal Religious Movements"; Young and Gooding, "Celebrations and Giveaways." Scholars have made the distinction between social and religious dances in Native life before and during the early reservation years. Performances could be seen as entertainment. Rituals of religious dance could be stripped away for a more social setting, but social dancing was not absent of structure or ceremonial elements. Some scholars hypothesized that because of US government intervention, religious dancing diminished during the 1880s. See Wissler, "General Discussion of Shamanistic and Dancing Societies," 862; Hassrick, *The Sioux*, 160.
2. Swan to McLaughlin, Sept. 11, 1883, RG 75.19.113, Rec'd, Box 29.
3. For more on the Poncas' predicament, see Dando-Collins, *Standing Bear Is a Person*, 17–21.
4. Howell to Howell, Feb. 25, 1877, Howell Family Papers, Box 9, HM 67091, Huntington.
5. Howard, *The Ponca Tribe*, 33–36.
6. See Mathes and Lowitt, *The Standing Bear Controversy*.
7. Whiteman to Miles, May 13, 1879, RG 75.19.10, Reel 22.
8. CIA to Gallagher, Feb. 19, 1889, RG 75.19.85, Rec'd from OIA, Box 9; Gallagher to Upshaw, Jan. 9, 1889, RG 75.4, Rec'd, Letter 3787, Box 502.
9. CIA to Cook, Oct. 15, 1880, RG 75.19.96, Rec'd, Box 2. Bear Thunder told the police that he and his brother (who was from Rosebud but was traveling with Bear Thunder) were well armed.
10. Ibid.; the Rosebud agent later claimed that Spotted Tail was "innocent of the charge of interfering in the affairs at Cheyenne River"; see CIA to Cook, Jan. 15, 1881, RG 75.19.96, Rec'd, Box 3. Also in 1880, Bull Ghost (Tatankawangi or Bull's Ghost) and three other Yanktonai headmen at Standing Rock visited Crow Creek in order to circulate a petition that would have the Yanktonais at Standing Rock moved to Crow Creek with the Lower Yanktonais. Days later, the Crow Creek agent reported that another man from Standing Rock, No Hand, had visited only to "make disturbances and dissatisfaction." Without any more specifics on what No Hand was doing, the agent arrested him and sent him back to Standing Rock. See Dougherty to Standing Rock Agent, Aug. 12, 1880, RG 75.19.113, Rec'd, Box 26.
11. McLaughlin to CIA, Oct. 19, 1881, Standing Rock Letterpress Copybook, MSS S-3052, YCWA.
12. McGillycuddy to CIA, Nov. 1, 1881, RG 75.19.113, Rec'd, Box 27; CIA to McLaughlin, Nov. 8, 1881, RG 75.19.113, Rec'd, Box 27.
13. CIA to McLaughlin, Oct. 26, 1881, RG 75.19.113, Rec'd, Box 27.

14. CIA telegram to McGillycuddy, Nov. 17, 1881, RG 75.19.85, Rec'd, Box 26.
15. McGillycuddy to Wright, June 14, 1883, RG 75.19.85, Sent, Box 53; McGillycuddy to Wright, June 26, 1883, RG 75.19.96, Rec'd, Box 5.
16. *ARCIA*, 1876, 96.
17. Spencer to McLaughlin, Feb. 19, 1887, RG 75.19.113, Rec'd, Box 31.
18. Cowen to McLaughlin, June 30, 1887, RG 75.19.113, Rec'd, Box 31.
19. Day to Crook, Jan. 26, 1889, RG 75.4, Rec'd, 5119, Box 504.
20. CIA to Gallagher, Dec. 17, 1888, RG 75.19.85, Box 9.
21. Travel Pass, Sept. 8, 1885, RG 75.19.85, Sent, Box 53; Gallagher to Crow Agent, Dec. 3, 1888, RG 75.19.85, Sent, Box 54; Travel Pass, Sept. 4, 1883, RG 75.19.85, Sent, Box 53.
22. Day to Crook, Jan. 26, 1889, RG 75.4, Rec'd, 5119, Box 504.
23. Ostler, *The Plains Sioux*, 222.
24. *ARCIA*, 1887, 134; Williamson to CIA, Sept. 27, 1886, RG 75.19.21, Sent to CIA, Box 3; Williamson to Heth, Oct. 28, 1886, RG 75.19.21, Sent, Box 3.
25. *Billings (MT) Gazette*, March 26, 1887.
26. CIA Circular, Feb. 2, 1887, RG 75.19.50, Reel 40.
27. *Billings Gazette*, March 26, 1887.
28. Spencer to Gallagher, March 5, 1887, RG 75.19.96, Sent, Vol. 15.
29. Spencer to CIA, Oct. 20, 1887, RG 75.4, Rec'd, 27900, Box 28; Rzeczkowski, *Uniting the Tribes*, 97. For a thorough treatment on Sword Bearer and Crow Nation, see Hoxie, *Parading through History*, 154–68.
30. Spencer to CIA, Oct. 19, 1887, RG 75.19.96, Sent, Vol. 16; Upshaw to McLaughlin, Oct. 20, 1887, RG 75.19.113, Rec'd, Box 31.
31. Cole to Ruger, Oct. 26, 1887, THRP, MSS S-2699, Box 1.
32. See THRP, Folder "Correspondence Concerning the Crow, Cheyenne, and Sioux Tribes 1887–1890," MSS S-2699, Box 2.
33. Spencer to CIA, Oct. 19, 1887, RG 75.19.96, Sent, Vol. 16.
34. CIA Circular, Oct. 29, 1887, RG 75.19.50, Reel 40.
35. Acting CIA telegram to McLaughlin, Oct. 27, 1887, RG 75.19.113, Rec'd, Box 31.
36. *Billings Gazette*, Nov. 7, 1887; Armstrong to Ruger, Nov. 3, 1887, THRP, MSS S-2699, Box 2. The Crow party traveled west on the Northern Pacific from Billings, Montana Territory (just northwest of their reserve), to Spokane, Washington Territory, then south to the train station at Farmington, Idaho Territory, where they met Nez Perces waiting with horses. From there, they traveled sixty miles on horseback to Fort Lapwai on the Nez Perce Reservation.
37. *New York Times*, Aug. 26, 1888.
38. Wheaton to Asst. Adj. Gen., Sept. 7, 1888, THRP, MSS S-2699, Box 2.
39. McLaughlin to CIA, Feb. 23, 1888, RG 75.19.113, Sent to CIA, Box 2.

40. *ARCIA*, 1888, 55.
41. McChesney to McLaughlin, July 11, 1889, RG 75.19.113, Rec'd, Box 32. For more on the Crook Commission and the Sioux Bill, see Ostler, *The Plains Sioux*, 232–39.
42. Ft. Berthold Agent to CIA, June 17, 1889, RG 75.4, Rec'd, 16552, Box 529.
43. Ashley to Woods, Sept. 19, 1890, RG 75.19.10, Reel 32.
44. Gallagher to Wind River Agent, July 3, 1889, RG 75.19.85, Sent, Box 54.
45. Gallagher to Foster, Aug. 20, 1889, RG 75.19.85, Sent, Box 54.
46. Ibid. For more on Gallagher's strategy, see Ostler, *The Plains Sioux*, 236–37.
47. Selwyn to Foster, Nov. 25, 1890, RG 75.4, SC 188.
48. Copy of Burt to Asst. Adj. Gen. Dep. of the Platte, June 25, 1889, RG 75.4, Rec'd, 18670, Box 535. According to Black Coal, an Arapaho leader, the Oglalas had assisted them with their farming.
49. Gallagher to Wind River Agent, Oct. 28, 1889, RG 75.19.85, Sent, Box 54. Three of the men were put in the guardhouse and "given a good lecture" for leaving without permission on their return to Pine Ridge in the spring of 1890; see Gallagher to CIA, June 10, 1890, *LSCIAPR*, RBIA Microfilm Pub. M1282, Reel 10.
50. White to Pine Ridge Agent, Oct. 10, 1889, RG 75.19.85, Rec'd, Box 27.
51. Gallagher to CIA, June 10, 1890, *LSCIAPR*, RBIA Microfilm Pub. M1282, Reel 10.
52. *ARCIA*, 1876, 25.
53. Young, "Powwow Power."
54. Spier, "The Sun Dance of the Plains Indians"; Walker, "The Sun Dance"; Holler, *Black Elk's Religion*; DeMallie, "The Lakota Ghost Dance," 400; Dorsey, *The Arapaho Sun Dance*.
55. Shimkin, "Wind River Shoshone Sun Dance," 407.
56. Mooney, "Calendar History of the Kiowa Indians"; Kracht, "Kiowa Powwows," 325.
57. Spier, "The Sun Dance of the Plains Indians," 451–527.
58. Lewis, *Neither Wolf nor Dog*, 57; Opler, "The Integration of the Sun Dance in Ute Religion"; Smith, *Ethnography of the Northern Utes*, 208.
59. Opler, "The Integration of the Sun Dance in Ute Religion," 571.
60. Spier, "The Sun Dance of the Plains Indians," 516–17.
61. Lowie, "Sun Dance of the Shoshoni, Ute, and Hidatsa," 405.
62. Smith, *Ethnography of the Northern Utes*, 211.
63. *ARCIA*, 1886, 131. Some Kiowas visited and danced at the Pawnee Agency in the summer of 1886 as well; see Osborne to Hall, July 15, 1886, RG 75.19.50, Reel 40.
64. Ellis, "'We Don't Want Your Rations, We Want This Dance'"; Ellis, "'There Is No Doubt.'"

65. The courts were established at agencies beginning in 1883 to settle disputes between tribal members and punish minor crimes. They were composed of prominent men on the reservations who were typically chosen by the agents.
66. Ashley to Wood, June 24, 1890, RG 75.19.10, Reel 32.
67. Adams to Ashley, May 9, 1890, RG 75.19.50, Reel 18; Ashley to Adams, May 12, 1890, RG 75.19.10, Reel 39; Ashley to Adams, May 20, 1890, RG 75.19.10, Reel 32.
68. Ashley to Adams, April 14, 1890, RG 75.19.50, Reel 39. The previous year, agents at both reservations allowed Whirlwind and twenty-four others to visit the Kiowa, Comanche, and Wichita Reservation (four hundred had wanted to go); see Ashley telegram to Adams, July 13, 1889; Ashley to Adams, July 31, 1889; Ashley to Adams, Aug. 1, 1889, all in RG 75.19.50, Reel 40.
69. Gallagher to Wright, Oct. 2, 1889, 75.19.96, Rec'd, Box 5.
70. Wright to Gallagher, Sept. 30, 1889; Cartwright to Wright, Oct. 1, 1889, both in RG 75.4, Rec'd, 28215, Box 559.
71. Ruger telegram to Adj. Gen., June 17, 1890, RG 75.4, Rec'd, 19129, Box 634. The dancers decided to end their gathering (which also involved horse racing) three days early after they were told that the white settlers had panicked.
72. Saketopa to McLaughlin, Jan. 3, 1888, *James McLaughlin Papers*, Reel 2; McLaughlin to CIA, Oct. 1, 1890, RG 75.4, Rec'd, 30921, Box 668.
73. McLaughlin to CIA, Oct. 1, 1890, RG 75.4, Rec'd, 30921, Box 668.
74. *ARCIA*, 1886, 99.
75. *ARCIA*, 1885, 61.
76. *ARCIA*, 1888, 65.
77. *ARCIA*, 1886, 51; Kelly to McChesney, May 28, 1889, RG 75.19.11, Box 251; Fisherman to CIA, Jan. 21, 1890, RG 75.4, Rec'd, 2490, Box 589.
78. McLaughlin to McChesney, May 27, 1890, RG 75.19.11, Box 251.
79. Riggs and Stroh to CIA, Nov. 24, 1890, RG 75.4, Rec'd, 36576, Box 681.
80. Henry Rice to CIA, Oct. 30, 1890, RG 75.4, Rec'd, 33937, Box 675.
81. Kusick to CIA, Nov. 13, 1890, RG 75.4, Rec'd, 35513, Box 679. Parties of Sisseton Sioux visited the Mille Lac, Red Lake, and White Earth Chippewa bands of Wisconsin in 1889 and 1890 to dance; see Rice to CIA, Oct. 30, 1890, RG 75.4, Rec'd, 33937, Box 675; McKusick to CIA, Nov.13, 1890, RG 75.4, Rec'd, 35513, Box 679. Some Santees engaged in dances with some Winnebagos at both the Santee Reservation and the Winnebago Reservation in 1890; see Riggs to CIA, Nov. 24, 1890, RG 75.4, Rec'd, 36576, Box 681; Helms to CIA, Nov. 24, 1890, RG 75.4, SC 188, Box 199; Ashley to CIA, Jan. 22, 1891, RG 75.4, SC 188, Box 200. Dancing visits were common as far east as the Green Bay Agency in

Wisconsin, where some Menominees would receive Potawatomi, Winnebago, and Ojibwe visitors; see *ARCIA*, 1888, 239.
82. Bowman to Miles, May 27, 1882; Bowman to Miles, May 23, 1882, both in RG 75.19.10, Reel 22.
83. Wood to Davis, October 14, 1890, RG 75.19.77, Reel 17.
84. *ARCIA*, 1889, 75.
85. *ARCIA*, 1886, 66.
86. Wade to Cmd. Off. Ft. Reno, Sept. 28, 1889, RG 75.4, Rec'd, 30434, Box 564.
87. Ashley to CIA, May 20, 1890, RG 75.19.10, Sent, Reel 32.
88. Myers to CIA, May 16, 1889, RG 75.4, Rec'd, 13673, Box 522.
89. Myers to CIA, Aug. 1, 1889, RG 75.4, Rec'd, 21983, Box 543. Military assistance was requested to prevent the dance because the agent believed that the Kiowas would hold the dance without permission; see Acting Sec. of War to CIA, June 7, 1889, RG 75.4, Rec'd, 15339, Box 526.
90. Little Wound et al. to Cleveland, Dec. 10, 1888, RG 75.19.85, Misc. Sent, Box 54; Ostler, *The Plains Sioux*, 180; Fletcher, *Lakota Ceremonies*, 297–308.
91. *ARCIA*, 1883, xv.
92. Riggs, *Dakota Grammar, Texts, and Ethnography*, 229; Schusky, *The Forgotten Sioux*, 107; McGillycuddy to Newall, July 8, 1879, RG 75.19.85, Sent, Box 52.
93. "Proceedings of Council Held at Sun Dance," June 1, 1879, RG 75.19.85, Sent, Box 52.
94. Stephan to CIA, Aug. 1, 1882, Standing Rock Letterpress Copybook, MSS S-3052, YCWA.
95. Bad Moccasin to Dougherty, June 13, 1881, RG 75.19.20, Rec'd, Box 2; Ostler, *The Plains Sioux*, 173–79.
96. Fletcher, "The Elk Mystery or Festival," 280; Ostler, *The Plains Sioux*, 172–73; McGillycuddy telegram to Fletcher, Alice Fletcher Papers, MS 4558, Series 1, Box 1, NAA.
97. Wright to CIA, July 21, 1883, RG 75.19.96, Sent, Vol. 11.
98. McGillycuddy to McLaughlin, June 1, 1884, RG 75.19.113, Rec'd, Box 29.
99. Ostler, *The Plains Sioux*, 176–79.
100. Gallagher to Fast Horse, Aug. 8, 1888; Gallagher to Ruger, Aug. 18, 1888, both in RG 75.19.85, Sent, Box 54. Fast Horse was instructed not to "precipitate a conflict" with the "runaways."
101. Gallagher to Upshaw, Nov. 14, 1888, RG 75.19.85, Sent, Box 54.
102. Gallagher to Upshaw, Nov. 18, 1888, RG 75.19.85, Sent, Box 54.
103. Gallagher to Upshaw, May 8, 1889, RG 75.19.85, Sent, Box 54; *Registers of Letters Received, 1881–1907*, Microfilm Pub. P2186, Reel 40, 12932; *Indian Chieftain* (Vinita, OK), May 16, 1889.

104. Copy of Ruger to Asst. Adj. Gen. Div. Missouri, May 9, 1889, RG 75.4, Rec'd, 13043, Box 521; Copy of Ruger to Asst. Adj. Gen. Div. Missouri, May 10, 1889, RG 75.4, Rec'd, 13580, Box 522.
105. *Weekly Chieftain*, May 16, 1888.
106. Copy of Ruger to Asst. Adj. Gen. Div. Missouri, May 24, 1889, RG 75.4, Rec'd, 156XX (illegible), Box 527.
107. Upshaw to CIA, March 19, 1890, RG 75.4, Rec'd, 9281, Box 607.
108. *Weekly Chieftain*, May 16, 1889.
109. Upshaw to CIA, July 18, 1889, RG 75.4, Rec'd, 20238, Box 539; Gallagher to Upshaw, July 3, 1889, RG 75.19.85, Misc. Sent, Box 54.
110. CIA to Upshaw, Aug.10, 1889, RG 75.4, Sent, Land, 15596.
111. CIA to Upshaw, Aug. 12, 1889, RG 75.4, Sent, Land, 18366.
112. Cowell to Fields, May 26, 1888, RG 75.19.30, Rec'd, Box 2.
113. Fields to Cowell, June 2, 1888, RG 75.19.30, Sent, Box 1; Fields to Otis, June 7, 1888, RG 75.19.30, Sent, Box 1; Fields to Otis, June 15, 1888, RG 75.19.30, Sent, Box 1. For more on the experiences of the Cree refugees and the complications of the US-Canadian border in their history, see Rensink, *Native but Foreign*.
114. Dorsey, "The Arapaho Sun Dance," 23.
115. Office of H. W. Taylor to White, July 3, 1888, RG 75.19.50, Reel 47.
116. Kracht, *Kiowa Belief and Ritual*, 263–64; Clark to Hunt, July 26, 1881, RG 75.19.10, Reel 47; CIA to Lone Wolf and Caddo Jake, Feb. 16, 1887, RG 75.19.50, Reel 35.
117. Eggleston to Ft. Sill Comm. Off., July 14, 1881, RG 75.19.50, Reel 47.
118. Clark to Miles, Aug. 15, 1881, RG 75.19.10, Reel 45; Ft. Sill Comm. Off. to Miles, July 8, 1881, RG 75.19.10, Reel 45; Hunt to Miles, July 17, 1881, RG 75.19.10, Reel 32; Clark to Miles, July 22, 1881, RG 75.19.10, Reel 45; Mooney, "Calendar History of the Kiowa Indians."
119. Bowman to Hunt, May 23, 1882, RG 75.19.50, Reel 47; Kracht, *Kiowa Belief and Ritual*, 269.
120. Williams to White, July 2, 1888, RG 75.19.50, Reel 40.
121. CIA to Myers, June 4, 1889, RG 75.19.50, Reel 47; CIA to Myers, RG 75.19.50, Reel 47; Ellis, "'There Is No Doubt,'" 561–62.
122. Ashley to Adams, April 14, 1890, RG 75.19.50, Reel 39; CIA to Adams, July 10, 1890, RG 75.19.50, Reel 47; CIA to Adams, July 24, 1890, RG 75.19.50, Reel 47.
123. CIA to Adams, July 12, 1890, RG 75.19.50, Reel 35.
124. Kracht, *Kiowa Belief and Ritual*, 264–65.
125. Mooney, "Calendar History of the Kiowa Indians," 385.
126. Davis to *Indian Helper* (Carlisle, PA), Aug. 11, 1886, in *Morning Star* (Carlisle, PA), Sept. 1886. See "Richard Davis," RG 75.20.3, Series 1327, Box 7, folder 305, accessible at Carlisle Indian School Digital Resource Center, http://carlisleindian.dickinson.edu.

127. *Indian Helper*, Sept. 7, 1888.
128. He Dog and Little Eagle to Sword, June 20, 1882, RG 75.19.96, Rec'd, Box 4. Eight years later, Little Eagle was listed as one of twenty-one Ghost Dance "leaders" at Rosebud; see Reynolds telegram to CIA, Nov. 21, 1890, RG 75.4, SC 188, Box 199. For more on Sword, see Red Shirt, *George Sword's Warrior Narratives*.
129. Eagle Hawk telegram to Sword, June 23, 1882, RG 75.19.96, Rec'd, Box 4.
130. Big Head to Stewart, Feb. 12, 1883, RG 75.19.113, Rec'd, Box 29.
131. Tuttle to CIA, undated, rec'd May 5, 1890, RG 75.4, Rec'd, 13928, Box 619.
132. Wissler, "General Discussion of Shamanistic and Dancing Societies," 862; Young, "Powwow Power," 124–29.
133. Kracht, "Kiowa Powwows," 330.
134. Wright to CIA, Jan. 23, 1891, RG 75.19.96, Sent, Vol. 20. Most whites had little knowledge of the complexities of Native dancing. A white spectator might confuse an Omaha Dance with another, and many dances were generically referred to as War, Scalp, Squaw, and even Grass Dances.
135. Morledge, photographs, "Pine Ridge Agency, S. D.," 1890, X-31389; "Sioux Indians Dancing the Scalp Dance, P. R. Agc S. D.," 1890, X-31407; "Omaha Dancers P. R. Agency, S. D. with painted war horse," July 3, 1891, X-31298, all from Western History and Genealogy Digital Collections, Denver Public Library. Many white visitors to reservations enjoyed the novelty of dancing and hoped to witness the events. At the Southern Ute Agency in Colorado, an employee of the US Land Office was reprimanded for soliciting the Utes to perform a variety of dances in November 1890; see CIA to Comm. of the Gen. Land Office, Jan. 2, 1891, RG 75.4, Sent, Land, 36838.
136. Awakuni-Swetland, *Dance Lodges of the Omaha People*, 44. For a description of an Oglala Omaha Dance, see Webb, "The Omaha Dance of the Oglalas October 2, 1894."
137. Tully to CIA, Dec. 1, 1890, RG 75.4, Rec'd, 37882, Box 684.
138. Kracht, "Kiowa Powwows," 330; Mooney, *Ghost-Dance Religion*, 901, 920–21, 1038.
139. Interview with Left Hand and Row of Lodges, March 18, 1895, Alice Fletcher Papers, MS 4558, Series 1, Box 30, NAA.
140. Wissler, "General Discussion of Shamanistic and Dancing Societies," 868–71.
141. Little Wound et al. to Cleveland, Dec. 10, 1888, RG 75.19.85, Misc. Sent, Box 54.
142. *Executive Documents of the Senate of the United States for the First Session of the Fifty-Second Congress, 1891–'92*, 42–43. Young Man Afraid of His Horses died of pneumonia in 1893 on his way to the Crow Reservation for a visit.

Chapter 5

1. *New York Times*, Nov. 16, 1890; *New York Herald*, Nov. 23, 1890, reprinted in Grinnell, "Account of the Northern Cheyennes Concerning the Messiah Superstition," 61–69; Grinnell to Dunbar, Nov. 22, 1890; Grinnell to Fannin, Nov. 22, 1890; Grinnell to Jackson, Dec. 1, 1890, all in GBGP, MS 1388, Box 2, Reel 3.
2. Chapman to Gibbons, Dec. 6, 1890, in *Annual Report of the Secretary of War, 1891*, 191–94.
3. Hittman, *Wovoka*, 19, 27–34, 36–43, 63. Hittman's study on Wovoka is the most comprehensive. See also Dangberg, "Wovoka"; Stewart, "Contemporary Document on Wovoka"; Moses, "Jack Wilson and the Indian Service"; Moses, "'The Father Tells Me So'"; Warren, *God's Red Son*, 56–58, 66–68, 83, 98–139.
4. Chapman to Gibbons, Dec. 6, 1890. An Indian scout named Arthur Chapman, who provided the US government with accurate information on Wovoka, was the first man to interview Wovoka in an official capacity.
5. Mooney, *Ghost-Dance Religion*, 771–72.
6. Chapman to John Gibbons, Dec. 6, 1890.
7. Mooney, *Ghost-Dance Religion*, 771–72.
8. Ibid.
9. For a description of an 1888 Paiute Round Dance gathering, see *Reno Gazette*, May 9, 1888.
10. Wovoka sent a letter to the agent at Pyramid Lake in February 1890, intending it to be forwarded to Washington. The prophet was curious whether the US government saw him as an authentic prophet; see Hittman, *Wovoka*, 18.
11. For more on the initial spread, see Hittman, *Wovoka*, 63–103.
12. Blakely to Bowman, Sept. 30, 1890, copy in War Dept. to Sec. Int., Oct. 22, 1890, RG 75.4, SC 188, Box 199.
13. Mooney, *Ghost-Dance Religion*, 814–15.
14. Opler, "The Southern Ute of Colorado," 188–90. The Southern Ute agent was apparently oblivious to any dancing at his agency; he reported that his Indians were "free from any taint of the Ghost Dance" in early December 1890 and January 1891; see Ute Agent to CIA, Dec. 1, 1890; Ute Agent to CIA, Nov. 24, 1890; Ute Agent to CIA, Jan. 3, 1891, all in RG 75.19.18, Outgoing Corres., Box 2.
15. Mooney, *Ghost-Dance Religion*, 802, 805, 806.
16. Ibid., 804.
17. Du Bois, *The 1870 Ghost Dance*; Hittman, "The 1870 Ghost Dance at the Walker River Reservation," 247–78; Smoak, *Ghost Dances and Identity*,

113–51. Wodziwob, the 1870 Ghost Dance leader, prophesized that dead Indians would return to the world on a train coming from the East; see DuBois, 5.
18. *Lyon County (NV) Times*, Aug. 3, 1889.
19. Ruuska, "Ghost Dancing and the Iron Horse."
20. Mooney, *Ghost-Dance Religion*, 807.
21. Western Shoshones intermarried with Eastern Shoshones at Fort Hall and Wind River.
22. Quoted in Vander, *Shoshone Ghost Dance Religion*, 43.
23. Fisher to CIA, Nov. 26, 1890, RG 75.4, SC 188, Box 199.
24. Mooney, *Ghost-Dance Religion*, 807.
25. Dyer, "The Jack Wilson Story," Special Collections, University of Nevada Libraries, Reno, transcribed in Hittman, *Wovoka*, 247–55.
26. *Reno Evening Gazette*, Dec. 16, 1890; *Sacramento Daily*, Dec. 17, 1890.
27. *Mohave County (AZ) Miner*, Dec. 12, 1891. For more on Chemehuevis and the Ghost Dance, see Trafzer, *A Chemehuevi Song*, 121–22, 180–81.
28. *Daily Nevada State Journal*, Jan. 10, 1891.
29. *Los Angeles Herald*, Associated Press, Nov. 18, 1890.
30. Mooney, *Ghost-Dance Religion*, 807.
31. Shimkin, "Dynamics of Recent Wind River Shoshone History," 451–62. Dick Washakie, an informant for Shimkin, told Shimkin that the group arrived in 1890 on the railroad to Lander, Wyoming, but the track to Lander was not completed until 1906. The nearest rail station to Wind River in 1890 was at Rawlins, Wyoming, on the Union Pacific line, around 115 miles from Wind River; see *Report of the Secretary of War, First Session of the Fifty-Second Congress*, 549.
32. Mooney, *Ghost-Dance Religion*, 894.
33. Shimkin, "Dynamics of Recent Wind River Shoshone History," 457.
34. McCoy, *Tim McCoy Remembers the West*, 213–15. Tim McCoy was a former movie star cowboy who met Wovoka, Sage, Yellow Calf, Kicking Bear, and Short Bull in 1924. His book was not published until 1977, and he spoke with Sage and Yellowcalf thirty-five years after their encounter with Wovoka. It is not clear how well McCoy actually "remembered the West" or if he took notes during his interview with the men, but this is the only surviving testimony of Sage and Yellow Calf. Other historians (Kehoe, Hittman, and Fowler) have used McCoy in their studies.
35. Shimkin, "Dynamics of Recent Wind River Shoshone History," 457.
36. Fletcher interview with Left Hand and Row of Lodges, March 18, 1895, Alice Fletcher Papers, MS 4558, Series 1, Box 30, NAA.
37. Ashley to CIA, Jan. 30, 1890, RG 75.19.10, Sent, Reel 32. Chief Left Hand should not be confused with Chief Land Hand the elder (Niwot), who died from wounds he sustained at the Sand Creek Massacre in 1864.

The men were not related. Left Hand the elder was fluent in English. Left Hand the younger was not.
38. Mooney, *Ghost-Dance Religion*, 894.
39. The Wind River Reservation was one hundred miles north of the Union Pacific line. A stop at Wind River meant a two-hundred-mile round trip on foot or horseback.
40. *ARCIA*, 1890, 178. During the fall of 1889, Black Coyote was dealing with the serious illness of his son, Harry Mann, who was living across the country at the Carlisle Indian School. His son survived the illness; see Pratt to Black Coyote, Sept. 26, 1889, RHPP, Box 10–15; "Harry Mann," RG 75.20.3, Series 1328, Box 2, accessible at Carlisle Indian School Digital Collection, http://carlisleindian.dickinson.edu.
41. Ashley to CIA, Aug. 4, 1890, RG 75.4, Rec'd, 24229, Box 648.
42. Ashley to Wheeler, June 20, 1890; Ashley to Hays, Nov. 26, 1890, both in RG 75.19.10, Sent, Reel 32; Mooney, *Ghost-Dance Religion*, 895. Mooney states that Little Chief and Bark headed to Wind River, but the men's pass has Pine Ridge and Tongue River as their destinations.
43. Grinnell to Merrill, May 1, 1890, GBGP, MS 1388, Box 1, Reel 2.
44. Ashley to Fosher, April 24, 1890, RG 75.19.10, Sent, Reel 32.
45. Upshaw to CIA, April 20, 1890, RG 75.4, Rec'd, 13759, Box 617.
46. *New York Sun*, April 27, 1890; *Chicago Tribune*, April 27, 1890. Paul Boynton and Robert Burns were interpreters for Ashley in 1890; see *Indian Helper*, Dec. 19, 1890.
47. *New York Sun*, April 27, 1890; *Chicago Tribune*, April 27, 1890.
48. Upshaw to CIA, April 20, 1890, RG 75.4, Rec'd, 13159, Box 617; *ARCIA*, 1890, 135. Troops arrived at Tongue River on April 13, 1890, and peacefully dispersed the crowd.
49. Ashley to CIA, Aug. 4, 1890, RG 75.4, Rec'd, 24229, Box 648.
50. Mooney, *Ghost-Dance Religion*, 907.
51. *Fairfield (IA) Ledger*, July 9, 1890, clipping in Adams to CIA, July 16, 1890, RG 75.4, Rec'd, 22313, Box 643. William W. Junkin was a part owner of the *Fairfield Ledger* according to Charles Adams.
52. For a compilation of government reports on Jack Wilson, see Hittman, *Wovoka*, 269–91.
53. *Brown County (KS) World*, Jan. 16, 1891. The reporter noted that "those in the tribe who can read believe in the 'Messiah craze.'"
54. This map visualizes all the known trips between reservations from the beginning of 1888 through the end of 1891 that concerned the Ghost Dance. I know many more trips were made during this period, but these are the trips that I can document with certainty. Most of this documentation comes from the reservation records held in regional National Archives. See my note for map 2 in chapter 3 for information regarding the limitations of these records.

55. Interview with Left Hand and Row of Lodges, March 18, 1895, Alice Fletcher Papers, MS 4558, Series 1, Box 30, NAA.
56. Selwyn to Foster, Nov. 25, 1890, RG 75.4, SC 188, Box 199. Selwyn's letter was written at the request of his agent at Yankton in November 1890 during a period when the US government was investigating the origins and extent of the dance; see Foster to CIA, Nov. 25, 1890, RG 75.4, SC 188, Box 199.
57. Smith, *Ethnography of the Northern Utes*, 216–20; Lewis, *Neither Wolf nor Dog*, 32, 57; Jones, *The Sun Dance of the Northern Ute*, 239–41.
58. Levine, ed., *Witness*, 407.
59. Ibid., xxxii. Josephine Waggoner was employed at two schools at Standing Rock (the Episcopal Saint Elizabeth and the Congregationalist school near Fort Yates).
60. Selwyn to Foster, Nov. 25, 1890, RG 75.4, SC 188, Box 199; Mooney, *Ghost-Dance Religion*, 798, 819; Utley, *Last Days*, 67; Hyde, *A Sioux Chronicle*, 239; Ostler, *The Plains Sioux*, 243. Selwyn did not specify the language used in the letters, but they most likely would have been in English (unless they were written by a Dakota or a Lakota). Selwyn received his education under the patronage of a Philadelphia businessman. He was employed at various positions in the Sioux agencies. For more on Selwyn, see Warren, *God's Red Son*, 232–35.
61. Ruger Notes, Dec. 1890, THRP, MSS S-2699, Box 2.
62. *Malvern Ledger*, March 12, 1891. For more on Short Bull, see Andersson, *A Whirlwind Passed through Our Country*, 37, 40–41; Warren, *God's Red Son*, 147–50; 179–90.
63. George Sword, "Wanagi Wacipi toranpi owicakiyakapi kin lee," Dec. 7, 1891, MS 936, NAA. Revised and annotated translation in Andersson, *A Whirlwind Passed through Our Country*, 250–57. Rani-Henrik Andersson believes that, among Lakotas, "Spirit Dance" is a better translation of what Lakotas called the "Ghost Dance," *wanagi wachipi kin*; see Andersson, 8n12.
64. Crager, "As Narrated by Short Bull," Buffalo Bill Museum and Grave, Golden, Colo., annotated in Andersson, *A Whirlwind Passed through Our Country*, 40–56.
65. Miller, *Ghost Dance*, 30; Diary of Rev. Edward Ashley, Sep. 3, 1890, Edward Ashley Papers, 1883–1931, Episcopal Diocese of South Dakota Archives, Augustana University Center for Western Studies. Also published in *South Dakota Churchman*, Jan.–Feb., March, and April, 1932. For more on Kicking Bear and Short Bull, see Andersson, *A Whirlwind Passed through Our Country*, 37–38, 83–84.
66. Notes from John Holland, Head Farmer Cheyenne River, Nov.–Dec. 1890, THRP, MSS S-2699, Box 1.
67. Eastman, *Sister to the Sioux*, 97, 137.

68. Selwyn to Foster, Nov. 25, 1890, RG 75.4, SC 188, Box 199; Royer to CIA, Nov. 8, 1890, RG 75.4, SC 188, Box 199; McLaughlin, "The 'Indian Messiah Doctrine,'" November 1890, *James McLaughlin Papers*, Reel 20; Mooney, *Ghost-Dance Religion*, 820; Utley, *Last Days*, 60–65; Kehoe, *The Ghost Dance*, 48–49. Mooney and many later studies have suggested that two separate Sioux delegations traveled to Mason Valley to find Wovoka, but the conflicting timelines in the primary sources are most likely describing the same, single delegation. See Andersson, *The Lakota Ghost Dance of 1890*, 31–32.
69. Crager, "As Narrated by Short Bull."
70. Sword, "The Story of the Ghost Dance," 28. The Pine Ridge delegates left their reservation without their agent's knowledge, something that happened regularly as demonstrated in chapter 3; see Gallagher to Wind River Agent, Oct. 28, 1890, RG 75.19.85, Sent, Box 54.
71. There were three Lakota men who were part of the Lakota delegation, Broken Arm, Elk Horn, and Kicks Back, who decided to separate from the party at Wind River (before it headed southwest toward Nevada) and head northwest to investigate in Oregon. They went without permission and stayed at the Umatilla Agency for two weeks in March 1890. The men gathered an unknown amount of knowledge about the Messiah while conversing with the Umatillas through sign language. The Umatilla agent knew about Smohalla's 1855 and 1856 "messiah craze" that "agitated" the Indians in eastern Oregon and Washington and did not want a repeat of those beliefs in 1890. The agent bought the three Lakota men train tickets and sent them back to Pine Ridge; see *ARCIA*, 1891, 529. For more on Smohalla, see Mooney, *Ghost-Dance Religion*, 708–45; Ruby and Brown, *Dreamer-Prophets of the Columbia Plateau*.
72. "Proceedings of a Council Held with the Cheyennes on Tongue River, Montana, Nov. 18th, 1890," RG 75.4, SC 188, Box 199; "Statement of the Cheyenne 'Porcupine' of Meeting with the New 'Christ,'" copy in Ruger to Adj. Gen., June 25, 1890, RG 75.4, SC 188, Box 199.
73. *Billings (MT) Gazette*, April 7, 1935.
74. Chapman to Gibbons, Dec. 6, 1890, 194.
75. "Statement of the Cheyenne 'Porcupine' of Meeting with the New 'Christ.'"
76. Myrick, *Railroads of Nevada and Eastern California*, 166–81; Due, "The Carson and Colorado Railroad," 260.
77. Gregory to Sears, Feb. 18, 1890, RG 75.19.129, Box 314.
78. *Reno Evening Gazette*, Feb. 19, 1890.
79. *Reno Evening Gazette*, March 1, 1890.
80. Selwyn to Foster, Nov. 25, 1890, RG 75.4, SC 188, Box 199; Chapman to Gibbons, Dec. 6, 1890; Kicking Bear, "I Bring You Word from Your Fathers, the Ghosts," reproduced in McLaughlin, *My Friend the Indian*,

197–201; Mooney, *Ghost-Dance Religion*, 818–20; Hittman, *Wovoka*, 231–36, 271–72.
81. "Statement of the Cheyenne 'Porcupine' of Meeting with the New 'Christ.'"
82. Ibid.
83. Upshaw telegram to CIA, June 5, 1890, RG 75.4, Rec'd, 17190, Box 629; Sec. of Int. to Sec. of War, June 5, 1890, RG 75.4, Rec'd, 17767, Box 630; "Statement of the Cheyenne 'Porcupine' of Meeting with the New 'Christ.'" The army already had fairly accurate knowledge of Porcupine's experience in May 1890; see Carroll to Post Adj. Ft. Custer, May 7, 1890, RG 75.4, Rec'd, 19493, Box 635. For Kicking Bear's testimony, see McLaughlin, "The 'Indian Messiah Doctrine,'" November 1890, *James McLaughlin Papers*, Reel 20.
84. "Proceedings of a council held with the Cheyennes on Tongue River, Montana, Nov. 18th, 1890," RG 75.4, SC 188, Box 199. Porcupine's words were recorded by interpreters Fr. Van Der Velden and "an Indian girl at the school."
85. Crager, "As Narrated by Short Bull." Crager transcribed and translated Short Bull's testimony while the two were traveling with Buffalo Bill's Wild West Show. Crager's comments are in parentheses. See Maddra, *Hostiles?*, 12; Andersson, *A Whirlwind Passed through Our Country*, 47. Historian Louis Warren concluded that Wovoka, knowing that he was speaking to a group of Plains Indians (and later Short Bull personally), may have intentionally addressed "the needs of his Plains followers"; see Warren, *God's Red Son*, 186–87.
86. Crager, "As Narrated by Short Bull." Good Thunder saw his son who had died years before in war; see Sword, "The Story of the Ghost Dance," 30.
87. See DeMallie, "The Lakota Ghost Dance"; Warren, *God's Red Son*, 185–209; Maddra, *Hostiles?*, 45–62; Andersson, *The Lakota Ghost Dance of 1890*, 37–40; Overholt, "Short Bull, Black Elk, Sword, and the Meaning of the Ghost Dance," 171–95.
88. Fisher to CIA, Nov. 26, 1890, RG 75.4, SC 188, Box 199. In an interview, Short Bull stated that Kicking Bear and Yellow Breast did not go farther than Wind River with him and Turning Hip. *Malvern Ledger*, March 12, 1891.
89. DeMallie, "The Lakota Ghost Dance," 387. See also Andersson, *The Lakota Ghost Dance of 1890*, 298–300.
90. For studies on individual tribes and the Ghost Dance, see Kracht, "The Kiowa Ghost Dance," 452–77; Brown, "The Ghost Dance Religion among the Oklahoma Cheyenne"; Lesser, *The Pawnee Ghost Dance Hand Game*; Dobyns and Euler, *The Ghost Dance of 1889 among the Pai Indians*; Logan, "The Ghost Dance among the Paiute"; Stoffle

et al., "Ghost Dancing the Grand Canyon"; Dempsey, "Blackfoot Ghost Dance"; Vander, *Shoshone Ghost Dance Religion.*
91. DeMallie, "The Lakota Ghost Dance," 387.
92. See Andersson, *A Whirlwind Passed through Our Country*, 19, 37–141.
93. Plumb to CIA, Nov. 8, 1890, RG 75.4, SC 188, Box 199.
94. *Omaha Daily Bee*, April 27, 1890.
95. Scobey to CIA, Nov. 21, 1890, RG 75.4, SC 188, Box 199.
96. *Omaha Daily Bee*, April 12, 1890.
97. Ostler, *Plains Sioux*, 248–49. See also letters written by believers in part 3 of this book.
98. *Reno Gazette*, May 9, 1888.
99. Stewart, *Peyote Religion*, 66; Hittman, *Wovoka*, 35.
100. Warren, *God's Red Son*, 122.
101. Maddra, *Hostiles?*, 42.
102. For recent works that try to understand the meaning of the movement, see Overholt, "Short Bull, Black Elk, Sword, and the Meaning of the Ghost Dance"; Andersson, *A Whirlwind Passed through Our Country*; Warren, *God's Red Son*, 9–18. Andersson presents the direct opinions of Lakota dancers and nonbelievers. Warren sums up the Ghost Dance as "a modern religion that offered believers a means to reconcile the seeming contradictions between Indian identity and twentieth-century survival," 378.
103. Fletcher interview with Left Hand and Row of Lodges, March 18, 1895, Alice Fletcher Papers, MS 4558, Series 1, Box 30, NAA.
104. *Word Carrier*, Feb. 1890. It is not clear where or how the student heard this story, the student wrote that he or she "heard" it "from the West," but it is likely that the student received this news in a letter from home considering that he or she wrote the letter during the winter months, a time when boarding school students did not visit home.
105. *Chadron (NE) Democrat*, May 8, 1890.
106. Selwyn to Foster, Nov. 25, 1890, RG 75.4, SC 188, Box 199.
107. Waggoner's written memory of the letters is reproduced in Levine, ed., *Witness*, 175–76, and annotated in Andersson, *A Whirlwind Passed through Our Country*, 354–62. Original in Josephine Waggoner Papers, Museum of the Fur Trade, Chadron, Nebraska. Also see Waggoner interview in Walter S. Campbell Collection, Box 105, Folder 41, WHC. For more on Thunder Hawk, see Levine, ed., *Witness*, 417–21.
108. *Harper's Weekly*, Dec. 6, 1890.
109. "Statement of the Cheyenne 'Porcupine' of Meeting with the New 'Christ.'"
110. "Proceedings of a Council Held with the Cheyennes on Tongue River, Montana, Nov. 18th, 1890."

111. Carroll to Post Adj. Ft. Custer, May 7, 1890, RG 75.4, Rec'd, 19493, Box 635.
112. Clark to Spencer, Dec. 4, 1890, LFSP, MSS 596.
113. Gallagher to CIA, June 10, 1890, RG 75.4, SC 188, Box 199; Sword, "The Story of the Ghost Dance," 30.
114. Gallagher to CIA, June 10, 1890, RG 75.4, SC 188, Box 199.
115. Pine Ridge leaders complained. Young Man Afraid said his people were "penned up like so many cattle, not however for slaughter, for if that was the intention they would furnish us enough to eat to make us fat"; see Transcript of Council at Pine Ridge, July 22, 1890, RG 75.4, Rec'd, 23071, Box 41.
116. Mooney, *Ghost-Dance Religion*, 817.
117. Gallagher to CIA, June 14, 1890, RG 75.4, SC 188, Box 199; Wright to CIA, June 16, 1890, RG 75.4, SC 188, Box 199; Carroll to Post Adj. Ft. Custer, May 7, 1890, RG 75.4, Rec'd, 19493, Box 635.
118. Selwyn to Foster, Nov. 25, 1890, RG 75.4, SC 188, Box 199.
119. Gallagher to CIA, June 10, 1890, RG 75.4, SC 188, Box 199.
120. Selwyn to Foster, Nov. 25, 1890, RG 75.4, SC 188, Box 199.
121. Crooked Nose to Brother, undated, published in *Red Man* (Carlisle, PA), Oct./Nov. 1890.
122. Janis to Mixed Bloods, Oct. 1890, THRP, MSS S-2699, Box 2. Nettie Janis was the daughter of Nicholas Janis, a French American, and Martha Janis (He Bear), an Oglala. The 1890 Pine Ridge census lists the children of Nicholas and Martha, and Nettie seems to be listed as "Nellie." I believe Nettie was named after her aunt Eleonitte Janis. Nettie died in 1894.
123. Map 4 visualizes the known links of correspondence concerning the Ghost Dance from the beginning of 1889 through the end of 1894. The lines that connect the reservations represent one or more letters that passed between those reservations (or off-reservation boarding schools). I know that other reservations were likely linked through correspondence concerning the Ghost Dance, but I have only mapped specific letters that can be documented with certainty between specific reservations (I did not, for instance, include a link on the map between Walker River and the Lakota reservations even though there is general evidence that Walker River Paiutes and Lakotas exchanged letters concerning the Ghost Dance). There are also letters that I know about but do not know their origin or destination, which therefore cannot be mapped. For instance, an Oglala Lakota working for a traveling medicine show received letters from his relatives back at Pine Ridge about the new Messiah; see *Pioneer Press* (St. Paul, MN), Nov. 23, 1890.

124. Ruger to Adj. Gen., June 25, 1890, RG 75.4, SC 188, Box 199. Ruger added that the dance excited interest, "particularly the Arapahos and Cheyennes and those nearly related to them."
125. Blair to CIA, Jan. 2, 1891, RG 75.4, SC 188, Box 200.
126. Higheagle to Najinhkte, Dec. 7, 1890, reproduced in Vestal, *New Sources of Indian History*, 42.
127. *Southern Workman* 19, no. 12 (1890): 121. Martin High Eagle was an Indian policeman at Standing Rock and was involved in the attempted arrest and death of Sitting Bull in December 1890.
128. *Reno Evening Gazette*, Nov. 25, 1890.
129. *New York Times*, Dec. 22, 1890. Like many "Messiah Craze" reports, this story ran in papers across the country.
130. *Omaha Daily Bee*, Nov. 20, 1890; *Black Hills Daily Times*, Nov. 22, 1890.

Chapter 6

1. Kellogg to Asst. Adj. Gen. Dept. of the Platte, Oct. 27, 1890, RG 75.4, SC 188, Box 199.
2. Warner to CIA, Nov. 28, 1890; Sears to CIA, Nov. 17, 1890, both in RG 75.4, SC 188, Box 199. Agent S. S. Sears learned Wovoka's identity (Jack Wilson) from a Hualapai living far away in Arizona.
3. Utley, *Last Days*, 75–76.
4. Reynolds to CIA, Sept. 25, 1890, RG 75.4, SC 188, Box 199.
5. A reporter in Nevada testified to the secrecy among Paiutes, noting that Paiutes he had known for twenty-five years would not tell him about the Messiah; see *Salt Lake (UT) Tribune*, Nov. 30, 1890.
6. Hyde to Sec. Int., May 29, 1890, RG 75.4, SC 188, Box 199.
7. McChesney to CIA, June 16, 1890, RG 75.4, SC 188, Box 199; Mooney, *Ghost-Dance Religion*, 843; Robinson, *A History of the Dakota or Sioux Indians*, 469; Kehoe, *The Ghost Dance*, 14.
8. Hyde may have been the wealthiest man in South Dakota at the turn of the century and was convicted of fraudulent advertising of land in 1912 but was pardoned by President Taft. The intentions of his report may have been pure, but he was undoubtedly invested in the lands surrounding the Lakota reservations. For more on Hyde, see Robinson, *History of South Dakota*, 829–30; Kingsbury, *South Dakota*, 981.
9. McChesney to CIA, June 16, 1890, RG 75.4, SC 188, Box 199.
10. Acting CIA to Gallagher, June 7, 1890, RG 75.19.85, Rec'd from OIA, Box 9.
11. McChesney to CIA, June 16, 1890, RG 75.4, SC 188, Box 199.
12. Gallagher to CIA, June 14, 1890, RG 75.4, SC 188, Box 199.

13. Wright to CIA, June 16, 1890, RG 75.4, SC 188, Box 199.
14. Ibid.
15. For Wright and others in Indian Affairs, a "progressive" Indian valued Americanizing education and other aspects of white American society. For discussions on the terms used by agents and others, "progressives" and "nonprogressives" or "traditionalists" in relation to the Ghost Dance, see Andersson, *The Lakota Ghost Dance of 1890*, 46–48, 76, 80–81; Andersson, *A Whirlwind Passed through Our Country*; Warren, *God's Red Son*, 212–14.
16. McChesney to CIA, June 16, 1890, RG 75.4, SC 188, Box 199.
17. *Daily Huronite* (Huron, SD), June 18, 1890.
18. Bryan telegram to Carter, June 12, 1890, RG 75.4, GRBIA, Rec'd, 18013, Box 631; "Memo. Rel. to No. Cheyenne Outbreak," RBIA, RG 75.4, GRBIA, Rec'd, 18609, Box 633. Two "renegade Bannock Indians" were making some sort of trouble at Tongue River in April 1890, and Agent R. L. Upshaw recommended they be arrested by the army. Before that could happen, Upshaw sent them back to Fort Hall; see Ruger to Adj. Gen., May 20, 1890, RG 75.4, GRBIA, Rec'd, 19493, Box 635.
19. Upshaw to CIA, June 19, 1890, RG 75.4, Rec'd, 19377, Box 635; Clover, *On Special Assignment*, 47–54; *Chicago Tribune*, June 13, 1890.
20. Ruger Notes, Dec. 1890, THRP, MSS S-2699, Box 2.
21. Upshaw telegram to CIA, June 5, 1890, RG 75.4, GRBIA, Rec'd, 17190, Box 629; Sec. of Int. to Sec. of War, June 5, 1890, RG 75.4, GRBIA, Rec'd, 17767, Box 630.
22. Upshaw to CIA, June 19, 1890, RG 75.4, GRBIA, Rec'd, 19377, Box 635.
23. Ruger to Asst. Adj. Gen. Div. of the Missouri, June 20, 1890, copy in RBIA, RG 75.4, Rec'd, 20626, Box 638. A Sioux man and two women were at the Sac and Fox Agency in the summer of 1890 and reportedly told the people there about a "big fight"; see Sac and Fox Agent to CIA, Nov. 27, 1890, RG 75.4, SC 188, Box 199.
24. *Billings Gazette*, April 7, 1935.
25. Selwyn to Foster, November 25, 1890, RG 75.4, SC 188, Box 199.
26. Edward Roan Bear recalled that when Kicking Bear, Short Bull, and Low Dog brought the dance to Big Foot's camp, he emphasized that the dead would come back "through this secret belief." See Edward Roan Bear Papers, 1953–1954, MS 20121, State Historical Society of North Dakota, Bismarck. A group of Crow Creek Sioux went to dance at the Sisseton Reservation without permission in June 1890, although it is not known if it was a Ghost Dance; see Crawford et al. to CIA, June 21, 1890; Crawford et al. to CIA, June (undated) 1890, both in RG 75.4, SC 188, Box 199; McKusick to CIA, July 3, 1890, RG 75.4, GRBIA, Rec'd, 20600, Box 638.
27. Adams to CIA, Nov. 5, 1890, RG 75.4, SC 188, Box 199.

28. Ibid.
29. Davis to Asst. Adj. Gen., Dec. 23, 1890, RG 75.4, SC 188, Box 199.
30. Mooney, *Ghost-Dance Religion*, 909–11. See chapter 1 regarding Kiowas and their penchant for pictographic correspondence.
31. Palmer to CIA, April 8, 1891, RG 75.4, SC 188, Box 200.
32. Ibid.; Palmer to CIA, March 2, 1891, RG 75.4, SC 188, Box 200. Eventually, in April 1891, more than three months after the Wounded Knee Massacre, the agent determined that the mail coming in from Pine Ridge would not cause trouble.
33. Dorchester to CIA, April 30, 1891, RG 75.4, SC 188, Box 200.
34. Running Antelope et al. to Sec. Int., March 20, 1891, *James McLaughlin Papers*, Roll 2. Among several other charges, the men accused McLaughlin of favoring only Catholic Indians.
35. Ashley to Adams, May 12, 1890, RG 75.19.10, Sent, Reel 32.
36. Ashley to Adams, May 20, 1890, RG 75.19.10, Sent, Reel 32; Ashley to CIA, August 4, 1890, RG 75.4, GRBIA, Rec'd, 24229, Box 648; Adams to CIA, July 6, 1890, RG 75.19.50, Sent, Reel 18.
37. Ashley to Wheeler, June 20, 1890, RG 75.19.10, Sent, Reel 32.
38. Ashley to Wood, July 23, 1890; Ashley to Wood, July 29, 1890, both in RG 75.19.10, Sent, Reel 32.
39. Ashley to Adams, May 21, 1890; Ashley to Adams, May 22, 1890, both in RG 75.19.10, Sent, Reel 32.
40. Mooney, *Ghost-Dance Religion*, 908.
41. Ibid.
42. Ibid., 802. Caddos, who lived on the same reservation as the Kiowas, also danced around a pole, or *ee-chá*; see Newkumet and Meredith, *Hasinai*, 69.
43. CIA to Adams, July 10, 1890, RG 75.19.50, Reel 47.
44. Adams to CIA, July 16, 1890, RG 75.4, GRBIA, Rec'd, 22313, Box 643.
45. *Fairfield (IA) Ledger*, July 9, 1890.
46. Davis to Asst. Adj. Gen., Dec. 23, 1890, RG 75.4, SC 188, Box 199.
47. CIA to Adams, July 12, 1890, RG 75.19.50, Reel 35.
48. *Fairfield Ledger*, July 9, 1890. Comm. Morgan thought Junkin should "be called to the impropriety" for authorizing the dance; see CIA to Sec. Int., July 21, 1890, RG 75.4, Sent, Misc., Vol. 5. Junkin later defended himself against the commissioner's displeasure by stating that he did all he could to prevent the dances and that he doubted anyone else would have done differently; see Junkin to CIA, Aug. 9, 1890, RG 75.4, Rec'd, 24987, Box 650; Adams to CIA, July 16, 1890, RG 75.4, Rec'd, 22313, Box 643.
49. Given telegram to CIA, July 18, 1890, RG 75.4, Rec'd, 22043, Box 642.
50. CIA telegram to Given, July 18, 1890, RG 75.4, Sent, Misc., Vol. 5; CIA to Adams, July 24, 1890, RG 75.19.50, Reel 47.

51. Adams telegram to CIA, July 20, 1890, RG 75.4, Rec'd, 22264, Box 643.
52. Adams to CIA, July 16, 1890, RG 75.4, Rec'd, 22313, Box 643.
53. Williams to Adj. Gen., Aug. 1, 1890, RG 75.4, Rec'd, 25370, Box 651.
54. Ashley to Fosher, June 12, 1890, RG 75.19.10, Sent, Reel 32.
55. Ashley to Hays, Nov. 26, 1890, RG 75.19.10, Sent, Reel 32.
56. Scott to Post Adj. Ft. Sill, Feb. 10, 1891, RG 75.4, SC 188, Box 200.
57. Davis to Asst. Adj. Gen., Dec. 23, 1890, RG 75.4, SC 188, Box 199.
58. Mooney, *Ghost-Dance Religion*, 895.
59. Ashley telegram to Adams, Sept. 19, 1890, RG 75.19.50, Reel 40.
60. Wade to Asst. Adj. Gen., Dec. 26, 1890, RG 75.4, SC 188, Box 199.
61. *Daily Alta* (San Francisco, CA), Nov. 26, 1890; Mooney, *Ghost-Dance Religion*, 902; Grinnell to White Eagle, Dec. 4, 1890; Grinnell to Coons, Dec. 13, 1890, both in GBGP, MS 1388, Box 2, Reel 3.
62. Grinnell, "Account of the Northern Cheyennes," 63.
63. Davis to Asst. Adj. Gen., Dec. 23, 1890, RG 75.4, SC 188, Box 199; Newkumet and Meredith, *Hasinai*, 57, 69; Mooney, *Ghost-Dance Religion*, 1095.
64. Ashley to Woodson, Dec. 4, 1890, RG 75.19.10, Sent, Reel 32; *Cherokee Telephone* (Tahlequah, OK), December 4, 1890.
65. *Sacramento Daily*, December 25, 1890.
66. *Norman (OK) Transcript*, Dec. 27, 1890.
67. Blackfeet Agent to Ft. Belknap Agent, Nov. 29, 1890, RG 75.19.3, Sent, Box 6.
68. Ashley to Hays, Nov. 26, 1890, RG 75.19.10, Sent, Reel 32; Mooney, *Ghost-Dance Religion*, 895; *New York Times*, November 24, 1890.
69. Pass for White Elk, Oct. 29, 1890, RG 75.19.77, Reel 7.
70. Lesser, *The Pawnee Ghost Dance Hand Game*, 239.
71. Mayhugh to CIA, Nov. 24, 1890, RG 75.4, SC 188, Box 200.
72. The intertribal visits that were allowed in the fall of 1890 were closely watched. A group of Poncas, for instance, was assigned police escorts in November 1890 during their visit to the Kiowa, Comanche, and Wichita and Cheyenne-Arapaho Agencies; see Woods travel pass, Nov. 1, 1890, RG 75.19.77, Reel 17. That same month, Pine Ridge's agent D. F. Royer sent two policemen along with fourteen Oglalas on their journey to the Crow Reservation; see Royer to Wyman, Nov. 3, 1890, RG 75.19.85, Sent, Box 54.
73. Copy of Blakely to Bowman, Sept. 30, 1890, RG 75.19.132, Box 385A.
74. CIA to Sears, Nov. 7, 1890; CIA to Plumb, Nov. 7, 1890, both in RG 75.19.132, Box 385A.
75. *Mohave County (AZ) Miner*, Nov. 29, 1890; *Mohave County Miner*, Dec. 6, 1890.
76. Lake et al. to Murphy, Dec. 10, 1890, RG 75.4, Rec'd, 39770, Box 688.

77. *Daily Nevada State Journal*, Jan. 17, 1891; *Daily Nevada State Journal*, Jan. 14, 1891.
78. *Salt Lake Tribune*, Nov. 30, 1890.
79. Plumb to CIA, Nov. 11, 1890, RG 75.19.132, Box 372.
80. Plumb to CIA, Dec. 6, 1890, two letters; Plumb to CIA, Dec. 9, 1890, all in RG 75.19.132, Box 372. Dancing was planned to occur one week each month until the spring, "at which time the medicine men tell them that the messiah will come bringing with him all the Indians that have died." The commissioner instructed Agent Plumb to do what he could to stop the dancing, but said not to "inflame the minds of the Indians and incite them to such insubordination as would require force to repress"; see CIA to Plumb, Dec. 18, 1890, RG 75.19.132, Box 385A.
81. Kellogg to Asst. Adj. Gen., Oct. 27, 1890, RG 75.4, SC 188, Box 199; *New York Times*, Nov. 16, 1890.
82. Fowler, *Arapahoe Politics*, 102.
83. Royer to CIA, Nov. 8, 1890, RG 75.4, SC 188, Box 199. Kicking Bear seems to have been joined with Sells-the-Pistol as the leading proponents of the dance at Pine Ridge; see Jensen, ed., *The Indian Interviews of Eli S. Ricker*, 145.
84. Sword, "The Story of the Ghost Dance," 30–31. Kicking Bear witnessed dancers collapsing during the prolonged ceremony, seemingly dying and coming back to life. While unconscious, the dancers saw dead relatives and friends. For more on Sword, see Lee, "Warriors in Ranks," 268, 277, 303; Overholt, "Short Bull, Black Elk, Sword, and the Meaning of the Ghost Dance," 171–95. For more on the mistranslation of Sword's own account and how that resulted in a misunderstanding of the so-called ghost-shirts and, in turn, a misunderstanding among whites that the Ghost Dance was militant, see Andersson, *A Whirlwind Passed through Our Country*, 250–57.
85. Ostler, *The Plains Sioux*, 274. According to Rev. Edward Ashley, Kicking Bear sent people feathers symbolizing invitations to become dancers; see Diary of Rev. Edward Ashley, Dec. 5, 1890, Edward Ashley Papers.
86. McLaughlin, "The 'Indian Messiah Doctrine,'" Nov. 1890, *James McLaughlin Papers*, Roll 20. Sitting Bull had asked Agent McLaughlin on several occasions for permission to visit Cheyenne River, Pine Ridge, and Rosebud, but was denied the opportunity. Agent McLaughlin believed Sitting Bull wanted to involve himself in the dance.
87. Mooney, *Ghost-Dance Religion*, 847. Sitting Bull allowed the dancing at his camp to continue despite the disapproval of Agent McLaughlin. For a Native testimony on Sitting Bull's involvement in the dance, see Owen Lovejoy's article in the *Word Carrier*, Nov. 1890.

88. *Black Hills Weekly* (Deadwood, SD), Oct. 24, 31, 1890; Diary of Rev. Edward Ashley, Nov. 4, 1890, Edward Ashley Papers.
89. Hennisee to Cheyenne River Agent, Aug. 25, 1890, RG 75.19.11, Box 251. High Hawk became a Ghost Dancing "hostile" who helped lead a number of Rosebud Brulés into the Badlands in December 1890; see *ARCIA*, 1891, 180.
90. Given to CIA, Sept. 9, 1890, RG 75.4, Rec'd, 28577, Box 661.
91. Reynolds to CIA, Sept. 25, 1890, RG 75.4, SC 188, Box 199.
92. Wyman to Northern Pacific Railroad Agent, July 21, 1890; Wyman to Simmons, Aug. 11, 1890; Wyman to Murphy, Sept. 10, 1890; Wyman to Cooper, Sept.18, 1890; Wyman to Royer, Oct. 21, 1890, all in RG 75.19.21, Sent, Box 4. There is no evidence that suggests that these visits were made because of the Ghost Dance, but one can assume that the movement was a topic of discussion among the groups.
93. Wyman to Agent, July 2, 1890; Wyman to Agent, Aug. 30, 1890, both in RG 75.19.21, Sent, Box 4.
94. Wyman to Pine Ridge and Rosebud Agents, July 19, 1890, RG 75.19.21, Sent, Box 4. The party was told to "behave themselves properly" and not to accept presents from the Sioux.
95. Crow Agent to Penny, Jan. 3, 1895, RG 75.4, SC 188, Box 200.
96. Wyman to Crazy Bear, Nov. 10, 1890, RG 75.19.21, Sent, Box 4.
97. Wyman to Arnold, Dec. 9, 1890, RG 75.19.21, Sent, Box 5. In September 1890, Red Cloud and a party of other Oglalas visited Wind River so that Red Cloud could enjoy the health benefits of the hot springs there. Red Cloud was not a supporter of the dance, but he undoubtedly knew plenty about it. The agents at Pine Ridge and Wind River still allowed the visit, even though the US government was concerned about the dance's spread. See Kellogg to Asst. Adj. Gen., Oct. 27, 1890, RG 75.4, SC 188, Box 199.
98. *Ninth Annual Report of the Executive Committee of the Indian Rights Association*, 29; Ostler, *The Plains Sioux*, 274.
99. Ostler, *The Plains Sioux*, 274n32.
100. Ibid., 274.
101. Cook to Hare, September 8, 1890, copy in Hare to CIA, Sept. 11, 1890; Reynolds to CIA, Sept. 25, 1890, both in RG 75.4, SC 188, Box 199; *ARCIA*, 1890, 49; Ostler, *The Plains Sioux*, 275. Whites suspected that the popularity of the dance on the Lakota agencies was related to the people's unhappiness with the meager rations they were receiving that year; Cook to Hare, Sept. 8, 1890, copy in Hare to CIA, Sept. 11, 1890, RG 75.4, SC 188, Box 199. Hunger was rampant, and Lakota leaders had been pleading for months for the food they were owed; see American Horse et al. to Sec. Int., Mar. 6, 1890, RG 75.4, Rec'd, 7445. Fast Thunder

told officials in July 1890, "You have a family, you know how a man feels when he sees his wife and children starving"; see Transcript of Council at Pine Ridge, July 22, 1890, RG 75.4, Rec'd, 23071.
102. McLaughlin to CIA, Oct. 17, 1890, RG 75.4, SC 188, Box 199.
103. Murphy to CIA, Dec. 1, 1890, RG 75.19.31, Sent, Box 1.
104. Palmer to CIA, Oct. 31, 1890, RG 75.4, Rec'd, 34242, Box 675.
105. Palmer to CIA, Nov. 4, 1890, RG 75.4, SC 188, Box 199.
106. Ibid.; Palmer telegram to CIA, Nov. 5, 1890, RG 75.4, SC 188, Box 199.
107. Palmer to CIA, Dec. 1, 1890, RG 75.4, SC 188, Box 199.
108. Palmer, Nov. 10, 1890, RG 75.4, SC 188, Box 199.
109. Ruger to Assist. Adj. Gen., Nov. 16, 1890, THRP, MSS S-2699, Box 2.
110. Royer to Acting CIA, Oct. 30, 1890, RG 75.4, SC 188, Box 199.
111. At White Clay Creek, Royer counted 600 dancers under Torn Belly, His Fight, Bear Bone, and Jack Red Cloud. He estimated 300 dancers at Medicine Root Creek under Little Wound and 150 at Porcupine Creek under Knife Chief, Iron Bird, and Whetstone. There were around 230 at Wounded Knee Creek under Big Road, Shell Boy, and Good Thunder, who had accompanied Kicking Bear to see Wovoka.
112. Royer to CIA, Nov. 8, 1890, RG 75.4, SC 188, Box 199; CIA to Sec. Int., Nov. 12, 1890, RG 75.4, Sent, Land, Letter Books 207–8. Kicking Bear's brother, Flying Hawk, was allowed to transfer to Pine Ridge from Standing Rock with his family in September 1890; see Gallagher to McLaughlin, Sept. 29, 1890, RG 75.19.113, Rec'd, Box 33.
113. Royer telegram to CIA, Nov. 11, 1890; Royer telegram to CIA, Nov. 13, 1890, both in RG 75.4, SC 188, Box 199.
114. Royer telegram to CIA, Nov. 15, 1890, RG 75.4, SC 188, Box 199.
115. Ostler, *The Plains Sioux*, 291–94.
116. CIA to Sec. Int., Nov. 13, 1890, RG 75.4, Sent, Land, Letter Books 207–8.
117. For more on party politics and its role in the Wounded Knee Massacre, see Richardson, *Wounded Knee*. Richardson argues that President Benjamin Harrison's decision to send troops was also influenced by his Republican Party's inability to attract voters in the new western states they had just created, including North and South Dakota. In a move that proved popular to the white settlers there, the Harrison administration wanted a show of strength.
118. Royer to Barber, Nov. 24, 1890, RG 75.19.85, Sent, Box 54.
119. Cooper telegram to CIA, Nov. 21, 1890, RG 75.4, SC 188, Box 200; unknown telegram to Royer, Nov. 28, 1890, RG 75.19.85, Rec'd, Box 154; Wright to CIA, June 3, 1891, RG 75.19.96, Sent, Vol. 20. Lakotas were not the only ones nervous about the situation soon after the troop arrival. Brig. Gen. John Brooke confessed to an executive of the Union Pacific that he believed Indian warriors were gathering faster than the army

could reinforce his "little army"; see Kimball to Kimball, Nov. 23, 1890, Thomas Lord Kimball Papers, Box 1, Huntington.
120. Wright to CIA, May 18, 1891, RG 75.19.96, Sent, Vol. 20.
121. Ostler, *The Plains Sioux*, 311. The presence of troops also made the settlers in the region panic; see Ostler, *The Plains Sioux*, 306–9.
122. See CIA to Kiowa Agency, Nov. 22, 1890, RG 75.19.50, Reel 47.
123. Steel to Simmons, Nov. 29, 1890, RG 75.19.30, Rec'd 1877–1915, Box 2.
124. Steel to CIA, Dec. 1, 1890, RG 75.19.3, Sent, Box 1; Steel to Simmons, Nov. 29, 1890, RG 75.19.30, Rec'd 1877–1915, Box 2.
125. Steel to CIA, Dec. 16, 1890, RG 75.19.3, Sent, Box 1.
126. Steel to CIA, Jan. 1, 1891, RG 75.19.3, Sent, Box 1.
127. Grinnell to Jackson, Dec. 1, 1890, GBGP, MS 1388, Box 2, Reel 3. Weeks later, Agent Steel told Grinnell that the "Messiah craze" had not taken hold of the Piegan Blackfeet; see Grinnell to Steel, Jan. 12, 1891, GBGP, MS 1388, Box 2, Reel 3.
128. Simmons to Van Valzah, Nov. 21, 1890, RG 75.19.30, Rec'd 1877–1915, Box 2.
129. Simmons to CIA, Dec. 5, 1890, RG 75.4, Rec'd, 38204, Box 685.
130. Simmons to CIA, Nov. 29, 1890, RG 75.4, SC 188, Box 199.
131. Wright to CIA, Dec. 5, 1890, RG 75.4, SC 188, Box 199.
132. Wright to CIA, March 10, 1891, RG 75.4, SC 188, Box 200.
133. Palmer to Ruger, Nov. 15, 1890, THRP, MSS S-2699, Box 2.
134. Dixon telegram to Acting CIA, Nov. 21, 1890, RG 75.4, SC 188, Box 199.
135. Dixon telegram to CIA, Nov. 28, 1890, RG 75.4, SC 188, Box 199.
136. Dixon to Ruger, Dec. 15, 1890, RG 75.19.20, Sent, Box 2. The arrested were Slow Grower, Crazy Bear, Chasing Crane, Eagle Thunder, From Above, Gunny Sack Lodge, Bear Elk, Little Man, John Logan, Grinder, Running Rattler, Winter Chaser, Fool Elk, Butten, Pretty Voice Hawk, Blue Dog, and Shooting.
137. Foster to CIA, Nov. 25, 1890, RG 75.4, SC 188, Box 199.
138. *Omaha Daily Bee*, Nov. 20, 1890.
139. Foster to CIA, Nov. 25, 1890, RG 75.4, SC 188, Box 199; Selwyn to Foster, Nov. 22, 1890, RG 75.4, SC 188, Box 199. White Swan is now underwater. A series of dams on the Missouri River covered the area in the 1950s.
140. Tully to CIA, Dec. 1, 1890, RG 75.4, Rec'd, 37882, Box 684.
141. "Proceedings of a Council Held with the Cheyennes on Tongue River, Montana, Nov. 18th, 1890"; Palmer to CIA, Oct. 29, 1890, RG 75.4, SC 188, Box 199.
142. Notes of Perain Palmer, 1890, THRP, MSS S-2699, Box 2.
143. Palmer to CIA, Dec. 1, 1890, RG 75.4, SC 188, Box 199.
144. Ibid.; Notes of Perain Palmer, 1890, THRP, MSS S-2699, Box 2.

145. No Heart to Palmer, Nov. 5, 1890, RG 75.19.11, Box 570.
146. Palmer to CIA, Dec. 9, 1890, RG 75.4, SC 188, Box 199; Palmer to CIA, Jan. 5, 1891, RG 75.4, GRBIA, Rec'd, 1516, Box 695.
147. Ruger Notes, Dec. 1890, THRP, MSS S-2699, Box 2.
148. Narcelle to Palmer, Dec. 12, 1890, RG 75.19.11, Box 570.
149. Cooper to Murphy, Dec. 1, 1890, RG 75.19.31, Rec'd, Box 1.
150. Notes of Perain Palmer, 1890, THRP, MSS S-2699, Box 2. Around three hundred men, women, and children ignored ration day at Cheyenne River in mid-December and remained at Big Foot's camp, Hump's camp, or Cherry Creek to dance; see "Indians Absent and Not Drawing Rations," Dec. 22, 1890, RG 75.19.11, Box 364.
151. *Pioneer Press* (St. Paul, MN), Nov. 22, 1890.
152. White Buffalo Man to Sitting Bull, Nov. 11, 1890, reproduced in Vestal, *New Sources of Indian History*, 38–39.
153. Spotted Mountain Sheep to Kills Standing, Dec. 7, 1890, reproduced in Vestal, *New Sources of Indian History*, 41–42.

Chapter 7

1. *Sacramento (CA) Daily Union*, Nov. 30, 1890.
2. McLaughlin to CIA, Nov. 15, 1890, *James McLaughlin Papers*, Reel 21.
3. *Omaha (NE) Daily Bee*, Nov. 18, 1890. The *Omaha Bee* also reported, just below the Miles interview, that armed Indians in North Dakota were coming south to kill white settlers, outrageous speculation that never came to pass, like many other reports during those months.
4. Andersson, *The Lakota Ghost Dance of 1890*, 137.
5. Ibid., 138.
6. *Harper's Weekly*, Dec. 6, 1890.
7. Ibid.
8. *Chicago Tribune*, Nov. 30, 1890; *Omaha Daily Bee*, Nov. 30, 1890.
9. See Watson, "The Last Indian War"; Kerstetter, "Spin Doctors at Santee"; Andersson, *Lakota Ghost Dance of 1890*, 192–250; Bearor, "The *Illustrated American* and the Lakota Ghost Dance"; Coward, *The Newspaper Indian*.
10. Locke to Pratt, June 23, 1890, RG 75.4, Rec'd, 22502, Box 644; Andersson, *The Lakota Ghost Dance of 1890*, 192–250.
11. *Indian Helper* (Carlisle, PA), Dec. 26, 1890.
12. Ibid.; Pratt to Fire Thunder, Dec. 2, 1890, RHPP, MSS S-1174, Box 10.
13. *Indian Helper*, Dec. 26, 1890.
14. Andersson, *The Lakota Ghost Dance of 1890*, 211.

15. *Chicago Tribune*, Dec. 6, 1890. Daylight seems to be of Muscogee and/or Quapaw descent (Hadjo is a Muscogee surname), but other studies have called him (probably incorrectly) a Sioux or even an Oglala; see Johnson, *The Red Record of the Sioux*, 267; Rausch and Schepp, eds., *Native American Voices*, 140; Moquin, ed., *Great Documents*, 90.
16. *Sacramento Daily*, Dec. 27, 1890; *Salt Lake Tribune*, Dec. 7, 1890.
17. Cox, *Muting White Noise*, 36–37.
18. Davis to Asst. Adj. Gen., Dec. 23, 1890, RG 75.4, SC 188, Box 199.
19. Scott to Post Adj. Ft. Sill, Jan. 18, 1891, RG 75.4, SC 188, Box 200. For more on Lieutenant Scott, see Scott, *Some Memoirs of a Soldier*; Meadows, ed., *Through Indian Sign Language*.
20. Bales to Adams, Jan. 7, 1891, RG 75.19.50, Reel 93.
21. Robbins to Shoup, Nov. 26, 1890; Robbins to CIA, Dec. 3, 1890, both in RG 75.4, SC 188, Box 199.
22. Waugh to CIA, Dec. 2, 1890, RG 75.4, SC 188, Box 199.
23. Tally, Dec. 8, 1890, RG 75.4, Rec'd, 38945, Box 687.
24. Fosher to CIA, Dec. 3, 1890, RG 75.4, SC 188, Box 199; Simmons to CIA, Jan. 5, 1891, RG 75.4, Rec'd, 528, Box 693. The Yankton agent reported that most at his agency were "close and interested observers" of what was happening on the Lakota reservations; see Foster to CIA, Nov. 25, 1890, RG 75.4, SC 188, Box 199.
25. Sac and Fox Agent to CIA, Jan. 9, 1891, RG 75.4, SC 188, Box 200.
26. Elk et al. to Buckskin Charley et al., June 21, 1890, RG 75.19.18, Decimal Files, Box 2.
27. Ignacio et al. to Sevaro, Dec. 27, 1890, RG 75.19.18, Decimal Files, Box 2.
28. Wood to Acting CIA, Nov. 28, 1890, RG 75.4, Rec'd, 36857, Box 681.
29. Eastman to Wood, Nov. 11, 1890, RG 75.4, SC 188, Box 199.
30. *Southern Workman* 19, no. 12 (1890): 121.
31. Zanjani, "The Indian Massacre That Never Happened," 119–29.
32. *Belmont (MA) Courier*, Nov. 15, 1890; *White Pine News* (Ely, NV), Nov. 28, 1890. See Zanjani, "The Indian Massacre That Never Happened," 122–23; *Nevada State Journal*, Jan. 14, 1891.
33. Wolf Chief to Harrison, Dec. 8, 1890, RG 75.4, Rec'd, 39465, Box 688. Wolf Chief wrote a similar letter to Commissioner Morgan a month later, after Wounded Knee; see Wolf Chief to CIA, Jan. 4, 1891, RG 75.4, Rec'd, 1535, Box 695.
34. Parker to Editor, Dec. 7, 1890, RG 75.4, SC 188, Box 199.
35. Adams to CIA, Jan. 14, 1891, RG 75.4, SC 188, Box 200.
36. Scott to Comm. Off. Ft. Sill, Dec. 9, 1890, RG 75.4, SC 188, Box 199.
37. *Omaha Daily Bee*, April 12, 1890.
38. *Omaha Daily Bee*, Jan. 8, 1891.

39. See Bobtail Horse's comments about Abe Somers (sometimes "Summers") in "Proceedings of a Council held April 15, 1890," in RBIA, RG 75.4, Rec'd, 19493, Box 635. Bobtail Horse said, "The Agent don't tell us any of the news that comes from Washington. We don't know what the White Father does or says about us. We want this man (pointing to Abe Summers) to talk for us. I am afraid this man (Jules) don't talk straight for us."
40. Somers to Dear Friends, (undated), copy in Meserve to CIA, Jan. 27, 1892; Meserve to CIA, Jan. 25, 1892, both in RG 75.4, SC 188, Box 200; Gatschet, "Report of an Indian Visit to Jack Wilson," 108–11. It seems Somers made two trips to Tongue River and two trips to Haskell between late 1890 and January 1892. Gatschet wrote that Somers was at Haskell in February 1891, and Superintendent Meserve told the commissioner that Somers had "entered" Haskell in January 1892 after spending time in Montana with the Northern Cheyennes.
41. Somers to Dear Friends, (undated), copy in Meserve to CIA, Jan. 27, 1892, RG 75.4, SC 188, Box 200; Gatschet, "Report of an Indian Visit to Jack Wilson," 108–11. Somers enrolled at Carlisle in August 1882 at the age of sixteen and became a member of the First Presbyterian Church of Carlisle in early 1884. He left Carlisle in July 1888. See "Henry North," RBIA, RG 75.20.3, Carlisle, Entry 1327, Box 4, Card 151; Cowell, ed., *Arapaho Stories, Songs, and Prayers*, 8–9.
42. Pratt to Standing Elk, Jan. 25, 1889, RHPP, MSS S-1174, Box 10–14.
43. Murie to Wood, Dec. 6, 1891, RG 75.19.77, Reel 19.
44. Martha Blaine thought that Murie's "strong words about leading his people on the true path of Christianity may have been sincere, but they also appear to be aimed at obtaining the agent's approval"; see Blaine, *Some Things Are Not Forgotten*, 64.
45. Murie to Wood, Dec. 6, 1891, RG 75.19.77, Reel 19.
46. Dixon to CIA, April 10, 1891, RG 75.4, SC 188, Box 200.
47. Mooney, *Ghost-Dance Religion*, 817.
48. Panken to Sec. Int., Dec. 10, 1890, RG 75.4, Rec'd, 39955, Box 689; Fosher to CIA, Dec. 3, 1890, RG 75.4, SC 188, Box 199.
49. *Sacramento Daily*, Dec. 25, 1890.
50. Maddra, *Hostiles?*, 47.
51. Davis to Asst. Adj. Gen., Dec. 23, 1890, RG 75.4, SC 188, Box 199.
52. Swift Bear et al. to Harrison, Oct. 23, 1890, RG 75.4, Rec'd, 33608, Box 674.
53. Royer to Acting CIA, Nov. 27, 1890, RG 75.4, SC 188, Box 199.
54. Sword to CIA, Nov. (undated) 1890, RG 75.4, Rec'd, 36111, Box 680.
55. Ashley to McLaughlin, Nov. 19, 1890, *James McLaughlin Papers*, Reel 2.
56. Andersson, *The Lakota Ghost Dance of 1890*, 175.

57. Ibid., 46.
58. Ostler, *The Plains Sioux*, 311–12. At Pine Ridge, the looters intentionally left the churches and mission houses untouched; see Cook to Bishop, Dec. 1, 1890, THRP, MSS S-2699, Box 2.
59. Capt. to Wright, Dec. 13, 1890, RG 75.19.96, Rec'd, Box 5; Capt. to Foster, Dec. 13, 1890, RG 75.4, Rec'd, 39424, Box 688; CIA to Wright, Dec. 26, 1890, RG 75.4, Sent, Land, Letter Books 209–10; Wright to CIA, Jan. 2, 1891, RG 75.19.96, Sent, Vol. 20; Wright to Whom It May Concern, Jan. 7, 1891, RG 75.19.96, Sent, Vol. 20; Wright to Farnsworth, Jan. 9, 1891, RG 75.19.96, Sent, Vol. 20.
60. American Horse to Landy, Dec. 1, 1890, American Horse Papers, MSS S-903, YCWA.
61. Ibid.; American Horse to Landy, Dec. 22, 1890, American Horse Papers, MSS S-903, YCWA.
62. Ring Thunder to Spencer, Dec. 5, 1890; Parmelee to Spencer, Dec. 5, 1890, both in LFSP, MSS 596.
63. Good Voice to Spencer, Dec. 15, 1890, LFSP, MSS 596.
64. Little Soldier to McLaughlin, Dec. 31, 1890, copy in Campbell Collection, Box 104, Folder 6, WHC. This is probably Eugene Little Solider, a private in the Indian police at Standing Rock. He was twenty-seven years old in 1890. Gray Eagle was against the Ghost Dance; he volunteered to accompany the police who went to arrest Sitting Bull. Little Soldier was also a part of the arresting force.
65. Courtis to Spencer, Dec. 19, 1890, LFSP, MSS 596. Big Turkey was baptized at the Catholic mission just before he joined the hostiles, "probably to put himself in rapport with the Messiah," W. C. Courtis, the postmaster at Rosebud, surmised.
66. Courtis to Spencer, Dec. 19, 1890, LFSP, MSS 596.
67. Sweeney to Royer, Nov. 22, 1890, MS 3176, Ayer Collection, Newberry Library, Chicago.
68. *New York Times*, Nov. 23, 1890.
69. Bettelyoun to Cox, Dec. 6, 1890, RG 75.4, SC 188, Box 199.
70. Sitting Bull to McLaughlin, Nov. 22, 1890, THRP, MSS S-2699, Box 2; *Pioneer Press*, Nov. 11, 1890. Sometime in December, Sitting Bull received a letter from some Pine Ridge Ghost Dancers. They wanted him to travel to Pine Ridge because, as lieutenant of police Bull Head explained it, "God was to appear to them." Sitting Bull may have decided to visit Pine Ridge to "learn more about" the movement, but he was killed before he got the chance. See Brings Plenty to Sitting Bull, (undated), reproduced in Vestal, *New Sources of Indian History*, 39–40; Carnigan to McLaughlin, Dec. 14, 1890, RG 75.4, SC 188, Box 199; Aaron Beede Journal, Orin G. Libby Papers, MS 10085, Box 37, State Historical

Society of North Dakota, Bismarck. Sitting Bull told Rev. Aaron Beede that he did not want to keep children out of school during that winter: "I want them to go to school, but they must learn this religion *wocekiye*—as soon as they have learned this religion they shall go back to school."

71. Sitting Bull to McLaughlin, Dec. 11, 1890, copy in Campbell Collection, 114, WHC. March Diedrich offers a more readable version of the letter in *Sitting Bull: The Collected Speeches*, 181.
72. McLaughlin to Sitting Bull, Dec. 13, 1890, *James McLaughlin Papers*, Reel 20.
73. Ibid.
74. McLaughlin sent two copies of a letter meant for Sitting Bull with his Indian police on their infamous mission to arrest Sitting Bull on December 15, 1890, one written in English and one in Dakota, perhaps to ensure that Sitting Bull understood the situation; see McLaughlin to CIA, Dec. 24, 1890, *Reports and Correspondence Related to the Army Investigations of the Battle at Wounded Knee*, Reel 1. For more on the event, see McLaughlin to Welsh, Jan. 19, 1891, IRAP, Reel 17; Primeau to Afraid of Bear, Dec. 12, 1890, copy in Campbell Collection, 114, WHC; McLaughlin to Bull Head, Dec. 14, 1890, copy in Campbell Collection, 114, WHC; Ostler, *The Plains Sioux*, 320–26.
75. Ostler, *The Plains Sioux*, 326.
76. Grass and Gall to McLaughlin, Dec. 15, 1890, copy in Campbell Collection, 114, WHC.
77. Breast to Palmer, Dec. 16, 1890, RG 75.19.11, Box 251. Breast could not inform his agent in person because he was guarding his horses, so he sent the letter and asked for five or six policemen to come.
78. Quoted in Hultgren, "'To Be Examples to . . . Their People,'" 28.
79. Pawnee Tom to McLaughlin, Dec. 27, 1890, RG 75.19.113, Rec'd, Box 33.
80. Mooney, *Ghost-Dance Religion*, 861.
81. Egna to Hodgkiss, Dec. 18, 1890; Hodgkiss to Palmer, Dec. 19, 1890, both in RG 75.19.11, Box 581.
82. For a more detailed look at this negotiation process, see Ostler, *The Plains Sioux*, 327–37. American Horse was told by one returned "hostile" sometime before December 22 that half of those in the Badlands "would come way but the other half threaten them so they could not come"; see American Horse to Landy, Dec. 22, 1890, American Horse Papers, MSS S-903, YCWA.
83. *Washington (DC) Evening Star*, Jan. 28, 1891.
84. Jensen, ed., *The Indian Interviews of Eli S. Ricker*, 195. Joseph Horn Cloud, who was around nineteen years old in 1890, recalled this in 1906.
85. Ibid., 208–9
86. Sky Bull to Spencer, Dec. 26, 1890, LFSP, MSS 596.

87. Sky Bull referred to General William S. Harney, who created the peace proposal following the Sioux Expeditions of 1855–56. Others complained about soldiers sexually abusing Indian girls and women. One white father of two girls of mixed descent told his daughters to stay away from Pine Ridge because "nine out of every ten girls that come back here have gone to ruin. . . . The soldiers are here and it has a demoralizing effect on them"; see Nelson to Daughters, Dec. 26, 1890, copy in RBIA, RG 75.4, Rec'd, 1386, Box 695. Mary Cox told the commissioner that two girls were begging to be sent back to the Lincoln Institute because of the soldiers; see McHenry Cox to CIA, Jan. 9, 1891, RG 75.4, Rec'd, 1386, Box 695.
88. Pretty Eagle to Spencer, Dec. 28, 1890, LFSP, MSS 596. Spencer was interviewed in December 1890; see *Democrat & Chronicle* (Rochester, NY), Dec. 6, 1890.
89. Sky Bull et al. to Spencer, (undated) 1891, LFSP, MSS 596.
90. Stelzer to Spencer, LFSP, MSS 596. Stelzer thought that the "war" would "soon be over" since their "friends" Crow Dog and Two Strike had come into the agency. He also reported that three of the Indian police had left the force; two of them deserted and joined the hostile camp in the Badlands.
91. Courtis to Spencer, Dec. 25, 1890, LFSP, MSS 596. Courtis was an English-born trader at Rosebud married to Emma War Bonnet, an Oglala. He was a postmaster at Rosebud for twenty-nine years; see Jorgensen, *Before Homesteads*, 108; 1880 United States Federal Census, June 1, 1880, Rosebud Agency, Meyer, Dakota Territory, Household ID: 8,732,153.
92. The events that led to the Wounded Knee Massacre have fascinated historians, and study after study has analyzed the motivations and actions of agents, politicians, generals, and Ghost Dancers in an attempt to explain how seemingly peaceful dancing led to the deaths of hundreds. See Greene, *American Carnage*; Utley, *Last Days*; Richardson, *Wounded Knee*; Lauderdale, *After Wounded Knee*; Coleman, *Voices of Wounded*; Jensen et al., eds., *Eyewitness at Wounded Knee*; Maddra, *Hostiles?*, 45–62; Ostler, *The Plains Sioux*, 294–306; Andersson, *The Lakota Ghost Dance of 1890*; Warren, *God's Red Son*.
93. Eagle Horse to Spencer, Jan. 9, 1891, LFSP, MSS 596.
94. Half Iron to IRA, Feb. 1, 1891, *IRAP*, Reel 15.
95. Royer to CIA, Jan. 5, 1891, RG 75.4, Rec'd, 1214, Box 694; Davis to Royer, Jan. 1891, RG 75.4, Rec'd, 4922, Box 702.
96. Lauderdale to Lauderdale, Jan. 10, 1891, John Vance Lauderdale Papers, MSS S-1317, Box 11, YCWA.
97. Lauderdale to Lauderdale, Jan. 4, 1891, John Vance Lauderdale Papers, MSS S-1317, Box 11, YCWA.

98. Clow, "The Lakota Ghost Dance after 1890," 324–26.
99. Diary of Rev. Edward Ashley, Jan. 23, 1891, Edward Ashley Papers.
100. Palmer to CIA, April 25, 1891, RG 75.4, SC 188, Box 200.
101. *Omaha Daily Bee*, April 30, 1891; *McCook (NE) Tribune*, May 8, 1891. Some of the progressives, or "friendlies," at Pine Ridge and Rosebud thought that Two Strike would continue to be "obstinate and misleading"; see Primeau to Blackburn, March 3, 1891, RG 75.4, Rec'd, 10173, Box 714. Louis Primeau, the Standing Rock interpreter and a man of mixed descent, believed that there was a "danger" of violence between the two factions, the nonprogressives and the "friendlies," during the spring of 1891 at Rosebud and Pine Ridge. The growing rift between the two sides after Wounded Knee has largely been unexplored by historians. In addition to the differences between them, the progressive "friendlies" felt hurt for not being selected to travel to Washington, DC, after Wounded Knee. See Red Cloud to Pollock, Feb. 5, 1891, RG 75.4, Rec'd, 5164, Box 703; Red Cloud to Belk, Jan. 26, 1891, RG 75.4, SC 188, Box 200; Good Lance to CIA, Jan. 30, 1891, RG 75.4, SC 188, Box 200; Wright to CIA, Jan. 23, 1891, RG 75.19.96, Sent, Vol. 20.
102. *McCook Tribune*, May 8, 1891.
103. *Washington Evening Star*, Jan. 28, 1891. This interview with Young Man Afraid of His Horses, Big Road, Little Wound, Crow Dog, Two Strike, Long Bull, and Hump was reprinted in other papers.
104. Cousin to Baldwin, Jan. 19, 1891, Frank Baldwin Papers, Box 16, Huntington.
105. Gregory to Warner, Jan. 5, 1891; Gregory to Warner, Jan. 7, 1891, both in RG 75.19.129, Box 314; *Nevada State Journal*, Jan. 4, 1891.
106. Interview with Left Hand and Row of Lodges, March 18, 1895, Alice Fletcher Papers, MS 4558, Series 1, Box 30, NAA.

Chapter 8

1. Hittman, *Wovoka*, 273.
2. *Daily Nevada State Journal*, Jan. 10, 1891.
3. *Reno Gazette*, Jan. 13, 1891.
4. *Elko (NV) Independent*, Jan. 10, 1891.
5. "Number and names of Indians absent and not drawing Rations," Dec. 22, 1890, RG 75.19.11, Box 364.
6. *Malvern (IA) Ledger*, March 12, 1891.
7. *Omaha (NE) Daily Bee*, Jan. 8, 1891.
8. Wright to CIA, May 18, 1891, RG 75.19.96, Sent, Vol. 20.

9. CIA telegram to Penny, March 20, 1891, RG 75.19.85, Telegrams Rec'd, Box 721; Palmer to CIA, March 2, 1891, RG 75.4, SC 188, Box 200.
10. Bad Water in Rump to White Back, March 30, 1891, translated copy in Lee to Asst. Adj. Gen., April 20, 1891, RG 75.4, SC 188, Box 200.
11. Many Eagles to Sister, March 5, 1891, reproduced in Vestal, *New Sources of Indian History*, 60. Vestal records a slightly different translation in Campbell Collection, Box 114, Folder 6, WHC. Vestal said he acquired the letter in 1929 in Agent James McLaughlin's papers; see Campbell to Roberts, Aug. 4, 1939, Campbell Collection, Box 108, Folder 14, WHC.
12. Industrious to One Bull, March 4, 1891, reproduced in Vestal, *New Sources of Indian History*, 59. Industrious criticized the dancers in the letter, but he also admitted that it was good to see "the Indian camped as in early life. . . . It would make you feel good to see them." For more on One Bull and Sitting Bull, see Vestal, *Champion of the Sioux*, 313.
13. *Reno Gazette*, Feb. 26, 1891.
14. Blaine, *Some Things Are Not Forgotten*, 56–59.
15. Noble to Wood, Jan. 15, 1892, RG 75.4, SC 188, Box 200.
16. Wood to White, Dec. 19, 1891, RG 75.19.77, Reel 18.
17. Wood to CIA, Jan. 15, 1892, RG 75.4, SC 188, Box 200.
18. Wood to CIA, Jan. 26, 1892, RG 75.4, SC 188, Box 200.
19. Matlock to Pratt, Sept. 29, 1892, RHPP, MSS S-1174, Box 6.
20. Clow, "The Lakota Ghost Dance after 1890," 327–30. John Stands in Timber remembered that after Ghost Dancing was banned at Pine Ridge, some believers began fasting in secret; see Stands in Timber, *A Cheyenne Voice*, 154–57.
21. Cleveland to Welsh, Feb. 24, 1891, copy in Welsh to CIA, March 2, 1891, RG 75.4, Rec'd, 8149, Box 709. Cleveland was given "free access to all papers, letters, people, etc." at Pine Ridge by the acting agent.
22. Ibid.
23. Acting CIA to Tully, April 1, 1891, RG 75.19.117, Rec'd 1890–1924, Box 5.
24. Ibid.
25. Penny to Asst. Adj. Gen., March 17, 1891, *LSCIAPR*, Reel 11.
26. Sumner to Penny, March 1, 1891, RG 75.19.85, Rec'd, Box 31.
27. Sumner to Penny, March 13, 1891, RG 75.19.85, Rec'd, Box 31.
28. Lt. Col. W. F. Drum to Asst. Adj. Gen. Dept. of Dakota, April 29, 1891, copy in Asst. Adj. Gen. to Penny, May 15, 1891, RG 75.19.85, Rec'd, Box 28. Whitebull was tasked to gauge the attitude of those at Pine Ridge and Rosebud. During his thirty-day investigation, Whitebull spoke with informants and relatives about the Ghost Dance and the possibility of any further trouble. Some at Pine Ridge would not talk to Whitebull while others said that they were going to go to war with the whites. Whitebull's

relatives, who thought that another outbreak of violence might be near, were afraid that Whitebull might be murdered for poking around.
29. Wright to CIA, May 18, 1891, RG 75.19.96, Sent, Vol. 20.
30. Penny to Wright, May 28, 1891, RG 75.19.85, Sent, Box 54; Penny to Earnest, May 30, 1891, RG 75.19.85, Sent, Box 54.
31. Penny to CIA, Oct. 15, 1891, RG 75.4, SC 188, Box 200.
32. Spotted Horse to Penny, Oct. 20, 1891, RG 75.19.85, Rec'd, Box 28. Although he was not a supporter of the Ghost Dance, Spotted Horse did ask permission to hold Omaha dances on Mondays and Tuesdays following issue (of rations) days rather than on Mondays and Fridays, as allowed, and permission to dance with visitors if they came.
33. Acting Agent to CIA, March 3, 1892, RG 75.4, SC 188, Box 200.
34. Plumb to CIA, Dec. 6, 1890, RG 75.4, SC 188, Box 199; Plumb to CIA, Jan. 10, 1890, RG 75.4, SC 188, Box 200; Plumb to CIA, Jan. 6, 1891, RG 75.19.132, Box 372.
35. Mayhugh to Harrison, Jan. 9, 1891, RG 75.4, SC 188, Box 200. In fact, some messengers sent by headmen at Fort Hall (probably Shoshones) asked Mayhugh to visit them to discuss the Ghost Dance. The Fort Hall headmen knew Mayhugh had been to Walker Lake to investigate Wovoka, and they wanted to learn more. For other reports of Nevada dancing in January, see *Salt Lake (UT) Tribune*, Jan. 9, 1891. See also Mayhugh to CIA, Nov. 24, 1890, RG 75.4, SC 188, Box 200.
36. Wright to CIA, May 18, 1891, RG 75.19.96, Sent, Vol. 20.
37. Penny to Earnest, May 30, 1891, RG 75.19.85, Sent, Box 54.
38. McLaughlin to CIA, April 2, 1892, RG 75.4, SC 188, Box 200.
39. Pratt to Kendall, Jan. 6, 1891, RHPP, MSS S-1174, Box 10–18. James Mooney claimed that the Ghost Dance only reached Pueblos at Taos, "who performed the dance merely as a pastime"; see Mooney, *Ghost-Dance Religion*, 805.
40. Pattee et al. to Dixon, Oct. 28, 1891, RG 75.4, SC 188, Box 200.
41. Miller to Harrison, Nov. (undated) 1891, RG 75.4, SC 188, Box 200.
42. Swift Bird to Palmer, Nov. 20, 1891, RG 75.19.11, Box 570.
43. Washakie et al. to Harrison, Jan. 31, 1891, RG 75.4, Rec'd, 5896, Box 704; Fosher to CIA, Dec. 3, 1890, RG 75.4, SC 188, Box 199.
44. Panken to Sec. Int., Dec. 10, 1890, RG 75.4, Rec'd, 39955, Box 689; *Omaha Daily Bee*, Feb. 8, 1890.
45. *Omaha Daily Bee*, Feb. 10, 1890; Mooney, *Ghost-Dance Religion*, 808; Fowler, *Arapahoe Politics*, 122. Yellow Eagle, a Northern Arapaho and former Genoa student, led the investigation (joined by Goes in Lodge, Black Bear, Washington, and Michael Goodman).
46. Fosher to CIA, Dec. 3, 1890, RG 75.4, SC 188, Box 199.

47. North to Meserve, undated, copy in in Meserve to CIA, Jan. 27, 1892, RG 75.4, SC 188, Box 200.
48. Gallagher telegram to Adams, Sept. 11, 1890, RG 75.19.50, Reel 40; CIA to Adams, Sept. 8, 1890, RG 75.19.50, Rec'd, Reel 40; Adams to CIA, March 21, 1891, RG 75.19.50, Sent, Reel 19.
49. Mooney, *Ghost-Dance Religion*, 908–9. Once Apiatan made it to Pine Ridge in October, he informed Agent Adams that he wanted to investigate the Messiah farther west at Wind River. Adams agreed and mailed forty-seven dollars, raised by the Kiowas, to the Pine Ridge agent to give to Apiatan for his eventual train ride back home; see Adams to Gallagher, Oct. 10, 1890, RG 75.19.50, Sent, Reel 19.
50. Fosher to Adams, Nov. 19, 1890, RG 75.19.50, Rec'd, Reel 40; Scott, *Some Memoirs of a Soldier*, 149. Because Wind River sat one hundred miles north of the tracks, Apiatan did not reach the agency until November 19.
51. Apiatan to Big Tree et al., Nov. 17, 1890, RG 75.19.50, Rec'd, Reel 39.
52. Fosher to Adams, Nov. 19, 1890, RG 75.19.50, Rec'd, Reel 40.
53. Adams to Fosher, Nov. (date illegible) 1890, RG 75.19.50, Sent, Reel 19.
54. Fisher to Adams, Aug. 15, 1891, RG 75.19.50, Rec'd, Reel 50.
55. Warner to Adams, Dec. 26, 1890, RG 75.19.50, Rec'd, Reel 39.
56. *Daily Nevada State Journal*, Jan. 14, 1981.
57. *Daily Territorial Enterprise* (NV), Jan. 3, 1891; Scott to Post Adj. Ft. Sill, Feb. 22, 1891, RG 75.4, SC 188, Box 200.
58. For an example of the descriptions of Wovoka that reached Indian Territory, see Somers to Dear Friends, undated, copy in Meserve to CIA, Jan. 27, 1892, RG 75.4, SC 188, Box 200; Gatschet, "Report of an Indian Visit to Jack Wilson," 108–11.
59. Scott to Ft. Adj. Ft. Sill, Jan. 30, 1891, RG 75.4, SC 188, Box 200; Mooney, *Ghost-Dance Religion*, 913.
60. *Daily Nevada State Journal*, Jan. 14, 1891.
61. Fisher to Adams, Aug. 15, 1891, RG 75.19.50, Rec'd, Reel 50.
62. Apiatan to Adams, Jan. 26, 1891, RG 75.19.50, Rec'd, Reel 50. An interpreter at the Saint Stephen's Mission in Wind River wrote the letter for Apiatan.
63. Adams to Apiatan, Feb. 10, 1891, RG 75.19.50, Sent, Reel 19. Regrettably, Adams did not send the letter to Pine Ridge; he sent it to Saint Stephen's, even though Apiatan told him he was about to go to Pine Ridge.
64. Adams to CIA, Feb. 4, 1891, RG 75.4, SC 188, Box 200. Adams claimed he had "no sympathy whatever with a sentimental or theoretic view of the matter."
65. Adams wanted to use extra police and troops to stop the dancing at his reserve (and disarm the Indians) the previous November and

December 1890, but Indian Affairs and the military resisted that strategy; see Adams to CIA, Nov. 29, 1890, RG 75.4, Rec'd, 37264, Box 683; Scott, *Some Memoirs of a Soldier*, 149.
66. Mooney, *Ghost-Dance Religion*, 912–13.
67. Scott to Ft. Adj. Ft. Sill, Jan. 30, 1891, RG 75.4, SC 188, Box 200.
68. Fisher to Adams, Aug. 15, 1891, RG 75.19.50, Rec'd, Reel 50.
69. Ashley to Adams, Jan. 31, 1891, RG 75.19.10, Sent, Reel 32.
70. Scott to Post Adj. Ft. Sill, Feb. 22, 1891, RG 75.4, SC 188, Box 200; Mooney, *Ghost-Dance Religion*, 913–14.
71. Deere to Adams, Dec. 29, 1890, RG 75.19.50, Reel 47.
72. Kracht, "The Kiowa Ghost Dance," 452–77.
73. *Record Union* (Sacramento, CA), March 13, 1891; *Baltimore Sun*, March 25, 1891.
74. Mooney, *Ghost-Dance Religion*, 914; Mooney, "The Indian Ghost Dance," 173; Kracht, "The Kiowa Ghost Dance," 459.
75. Barber to Baldwin, Sept. 26, 1895, RG 75.19.50, Reel 47. The dancers disguised their beliefs by renaming their dance and behaving calmly when the agent inspected their gathering.
76. This according to Maryetta Reeside, a non-Native Baptist missionary; see Reeside to Baldwin, Nov. 19, 1895, RG 75.19.50, Reel 47. For more on Reeside and the success of Baptists among Kiowas, see Kracht, *Religious Revitalization among the Kiowas*, 55–58.
77. Agent Baldwin punished three hundred Ghost Dancers in 1897; *Valentine (NE) Democrat*, Sept. 2, 1897.
78. CIA to Day, March 26, 1892, RG 75.19.50, Rec'd, Reel 50.
79. CIA to Day, Jan. 2, 1892, RG 75.19.50, Reel 47.
80. Supt. in Charge to CIA, Sept. 30, 1930, RG 75.19.50, Rec'd, Reel 50.
81. The Fort Hall agent wrote to Agent Adams at the Kiowa Reserve curious to know if Apiatan did in fact denounce Wovoka as a fraud; see Fisher to Adams, Aug. 15, 1891, RG 75.19.50, Rec'd, Reel 50.
82. Casper Edson left Carlisle in Nov. 1890 after spending the better part of a decade there; see "Casper Edson," RBIA, RG 75.20.3, Carlisle, Entry 1327, Box 3, Card 138, accessible at Carlisle Indian School Digital Collection, http://carlisleindian.dickinson.edu. Carlisle's superintendent told Casper's mother in 1889 that he spoke about her son "in the highest terms"; see Pratt to Black Woman, Oct. 19, 1889, RHPP, MSS S-1174, Box 10–15.
83. Ashley to CIA, Aug. 22, 1891, RG 75.4, SC 188, Box 200.
84. *Indian Helper*, Nov. 14, 1890. See also *Indian Helper*, Dec. 19, 1890.
85. Mooney, *Ghost-Dance Religion*, 900. A number of Southern Arapaho headmen asked for the dismissal of Capt. Frank Tall Bull from the Indian police in December 1890; see Ashley to CIA, Dec. 17, 1890, RG 75.4, Rec'd, 39382.

86. An orphan and member of Left Hand's band, Woolworth was at Carlisle from 1881 to 1887. He worked as a scout at Fort Reno for twenty-five dollars a month in 1890 and lived in his sister's tepee; see *Red Man* (Carlisle, PA), June 1890; Fowler, *Wives and Husbands*, 134.
87. Mooney to Henshaw, Jan. 19, 1891; Mooney to Henshaw, Jan. 27, 1891, both in BAE, Series 1, Box 109, NAA.
88. Johnston. to Asst. Adj. Gen., Aug. 13, 1891, RG 75.4, SC 188, Box 200.
89. Ibid.
90. Warner to Fisher, Aug. 19, 1891, RG 75.4, SC 188, Box 200. Brig. Gen. John Brooke "strongly" approved of Warner's recommendation. In May, Warner's farmer-in-charge at Walker River reported that Paiutes were living peacefully and that "the Jack Wilson business is more of talk than anything of reality"; see Gregory to Warner, May 1, 1891; Gregory to Warner, May 25, 1891, both in RG 75.19.129, Box 314.
91. *Morning Appeal* (Carson City, NV), Aug. 13, 1891; *Reno Gazette-Journal*, Aug. 18, 1891.
92. Mooney, *Ghost-Dance Religion*, 900. Government documents never mention the additional members of Edson, Little Raven, and Red Wolf's delegation.
93. Mooney, *Ghost-Dance Religion*, 780–81.
94. Ibid., 781. Moony indicated that "the rest of the letter had been erased."
95. Ashley to CIA, Dec. 29, 1891, RG 75.4, SC 188, Box 200.
96. Fletcher interview with Left Hand and Row of Lodges, Alice Fletcher Papers, MS 4558, Series 1, Box 30, NAA. In the fall 1895, Richard Davis, the Carlisle-educated Southern Cheyenne, reported another four-day Ghost Dance, and among those dancing were three school girls from the Seger Colony; see Davis to Pratt, Nov. 25, 1895, RHPP, MSS S-1174, Box 2.
97. Mooney to Powell, June 21, 1893, BAE, Series 1, Box 109, NAA.
98. *New York Sun*, Jan. 13, 1892; *Fresno (CA) Weekly Republican*, Oct. 28, 1892; *Weekly Gazette and Stockman* (Reno, NV), Nov. 10, 1892; *Wichita (KS) Eagle*, Jan. 27, 1893; Gatschet, "Report of an Indian Visit to Jack Wilson," 111. The October group included four Arapahos: Sitting Bull, Washee, Black Bear, and Hanatcha-thiak, and one Cheyenne "half-blood" named Edward Geary (Le Guerrier). It was Sitting Bull and Washee's second trip. Wovoka was not pleased with the visits, according to a government farmer, and was no longer advocating Ghost Dancing there or anywhere. Wovoka's reluctance to interact with foreign visitors was also reported in 1894, this time by the *Nevada State Journal* and Johnson Sides (the well-known Paiute previously mentioned in this study), who did not like Wovoka. The newspaper claimed that Johnson Sides witnessed Wovoka ignoring a Pawnee who had just completed his

long trip from Indian Territory. The Pawnee man, who had permission from Indian Affairs to visit, became convinced that Wovoka "was a false prophet" and decided he "would so tell" the Pawnees back home; see *Nevada State Journal*, Aug. 21, 1894. In 1893, the Mason Valley newspaper printed an article supposedly debunking Wovoka's "trick" miracles; see *Mason Valley (NV) Tidings*, June 10, 1893.
99. *New York Times*, Nov. 20, 1890.
100. *Proceedings of the Ninth Annual Meeting of the Lake Mohonk Conference*, 8.
101. *Indian Helper*, Jan. 16, 1891; "Paul Boyton," RBIA, RG 75.20.3, Carlisle, Entry 1327, Box 3, Card 132. For more on Seger, see Perry, "The Indians' Friend, John H. Seger," 570–590; Mann, *Cheyenne and Arapaho Education*, 28–32, 97–100.
102. Stewart, *Peyote Religion*, 107. For more on Boyton, see Berthrong, *The Cheyenne and Arapaho Ordeal*, 313–14.
103. Mooney, *Ghost-Dance Religion*, 972–73.
104. See Pratt to CIA, Dec. 6, 1889, RHPP, MSS S-1174, Box 10.
105. It is important to note that former boarding school students were not the only literate Indians on reservations. Agency schools taught hundreds of students on the reservations, and many of them became fluent in English and learned how to read and write. For statistics at one agency, see Pine Ridge School Reports, 1882–1936, RG 75.19.85, Box 1112. There are stories of specific Ghost Dance participants who were educated on the reservations; see Stands in Timber, *A Cheyenne Voice*, 153–55; Stands in Timber, *Cheyenne Memories*, 258–59.
106. For more on Morgan and his mission, see Prucha, *American Indian Policy in Crisis*, 292–327. Congressional appropriations for Indian education in 1877 were only $20,000. In 1892, they were $2,291,650; see Welsh, "A Crisis in the Cause of Indian Education."
107. For a longer discussion, see Gage, "Intertribal Communication," 355–91.
108. Scott to Ft. Adj. Ft. Sill, Jan. 30, 1891, RG 75.4, SC 188, Box 200. Smith Curley was murdered in 1905; see *Wichita Daily Eagle*, June 7, 1905.
109. Scott to Ft. Adj. Ft. Sill, Jan. 30, 1891, RG 75.4, SC 188, Box 200.
110. Courtis to Spencer, Dec. 19, 1890, LFSP, MSS 596. For more on Stewart, see Gage, "Intertribal Communication," 370–73; "Raymond Stewart," RBIA, RG 75.20.3, Carlisle, Entry 1327, Box 37, Card 1812.
111. Pierre to CIA, Feb. 6, 1891, RG 75.4, Rec'd, 5287, Box 703. See "Brule Iron Eagle Feather," RBIA, RG 75.20.3, Carlisle, Entry 1327, Box 37, Card 1789; "Plenty Living Bear," RBIA, RG 75.20.3, Carlisle, Entry 1327, Box 37, Card 1797. Paul Eagle Star was killed while performing in the Buffalo Bill Wild West Show in August 1891; see *Sheffield & Rotherham (Great Britain) Independent*, Aug. 26, 1891.

112. *Pittsburg (PA) Daily Post*, Jan. 26, 1891; *Indiana Gazette*, Jan. 28, 1891.
113. *ARCIA*, 1889, 94.
114. *Red Man* (Carlisle, PA), Feb./March 1891; Gage, "Intertribal Communication," 374–91. For a look at how R. H. Pratt blamed the Catholic Indian schools he despised for the Ghost Dance and Wounded Knee, thus deflecting responsibility off his former students, see Tatonetti, "Catholics, Carlisle, and Casting Stones."
115. *Twenty-Two Years' Work*, 489–93.
116. Welsh, "A Crisis in the Cause of Indian Education."
117. *Eighth Annual Report of the Executive Committee of the Indian Rights Association*, 4–5; *Ninth Annual Report of the Executive Committee of the Indian Rights Association*, 3–4.
118. Fletcher, "The Indian Messiah," 59–60. Mooney wrote that "none of the Christian Indians took any part in the disturbance" on the Lakota reservations; see *Ghost-Dance Religion*, 852.
119. *Los Angeles Herald*, Feb. 5, 1893.
120. Mooney to Powell, June 21, 1893, BAE, Series 1, Box 109, NAA.
121. Watson to Penny, Jan. 3, 1895, RG 75.4, SC 188, Box 200.
122. Dyer, "The Jack Wilson Story," Special Collections, University of Nevada Libraries, Reno. On Grant Left Hand, see Mooney, *Ghost-Dance Religion*, 1038–39.
123. Ibid.; Dyer, Tape 17, Margaret M. Wheat Papers, 83–24, Special Collections, University of Nevada Libraries, Reno, transcribed in Hittman, *Wovoka*, 256. Wovoka continued to receive similar letters until at least 1911; see Dangberg, "Letters to Jack Wilson," 279–96.
124. Hittman, *Wovoka*, 25–26. It seems Wovoka "went underground" after army scout A. I. Chapman interrogated him in December 1890. By the time James Mooney visited him in 1892, Wovoka, according to Dyer, "was not exactly hiding nor had he run away"; he had "prudently . . . remove[d] his camp to the sound end of the valley . . . in a brush big enough to hide from the casual observer"; see Hittman, *Wovoka*, 21.
125. Warner to CIA, Dec. 7, 1892, RG 75.4, SC 188, Box 200. Warner told the farmer-in-charge at Walker River to conduct a more thorough investigation of Wovoka in November 1892. The farmer found that there had been several delegations "from eastern tribes" that came to "interview the Messiah." Some were "pleased" with Wovoka and some were not, but there was no cause for alarm; see Hammond to Warner, Nov. 22, 1892, RG 75.19.129, Box 314.
126. *Silver State* (Unionville, NV), Nov. 9, 1892. See Logan, "The Ghost Dance among the Paiute," 276.
127. Warner to CIA, Dec. 7, 1892, RG 75.4, SC 188, Box 200.

128. He reportedly successfully predicted a snowstorm at the beginning of the new year in 1892, and the number of foreign Indians visiting him via rail increased "remarkably"; see *Morning Appeal* (Carson City, NV), Jan. 13, 1892. In October 1891 it was reported that four Paiutes from outside Mason Valley were planning to kill Wovoka for reasons unknown, but it seems nothing came of it. Among those four were supposedly Natchez and Lee Winnemucca; see Hammond to Warner, Oct. 28, 1891, RG 75.19.129, Box 314.
129. Mooney, *Ghost-Dance Religion*, 808.
130. Ibid., 809; Mooney to Powell, June 21, 1893, BAE, Series 1, Box 109, NAA; Fowler, *Arapahoe Politics*, 124.
131. Mooney to Powell, June 21, 1893, BAE, Series 1, Box 109, NAA.
132. Ibid.
133. Smoot to Nichols, Aug. 23, 1894, RG 75.19.50, Reel 47.
134. Mooney, *Ghost-Dance Religion*, 914; Kracht, *Kiowa Belief and Ritual*, 272; Kracht, "The Kiowa Ghost Dance," 452–77.

Conclusion

1. Among Delawares, see *Brooklyn (NY) Daily Eagle*, March 16, 1900; among Kiowas, see *Evening Times* (Washington, DC), June 18, 1900; among Southern Arapahos, see *Reno (NV) Gazette*, Feb. 23, 1904. Wovoka remained prominent among Paiutes and received foreign visitors well into the 1900s, even heading to visit eastern tribes himself before his death in 1932; see *Nevada State Journal*, May 19, 1906, Sept. 1, 1914; *Yerington (NV) Times*, May 21, 1910, Aug. 24, 1912, July 5, 1913, Feb. 7, 1914, Nov. 28, 1914, March 11, 1916, Aug. 12, 1916, Oct. 18, 1922; *Reno Gazette*, March 10, 1920, Oct. 4, 1932. For more on Wovoka's twentieth-century life, see Hitman, *Wovoka*, 167–78; Warren, *God's Red Son*, 396–99.
2. Kehoe, "The Ghost Dance Religion in Saskatchewan, Canada"; Dangberg, "Letters to Jack Wilson."
3. *Yerington Times*, Jan. 29, 1910.
4. Dangberg, "Wovoka," 40–53. Among the correspondents were Bear Comes Out (Hunkpapa Lakota) at Standing Rock, Fast Horse (Yankton) at Fort Peck, Cloud Horse (Oglala Lakota) at Pine Ridge, and F. W. Antelope (Northern Arapaho) at Wind River. James Roberts, a Catholic Assiniboine at Fort Peck, near the Canadian border, wrote to Wovoka frequently, but none of his letters survive.
5. Kehoe, "The Ghost Dance Religion in Saskatchewan, Canada," 300.

6. Ibid., 301; Ahenakew and Wolfart, eds., *They Knew Both Sides of Medicine*, 115. My thanks to Maddie Reddon for telling me about Alice Ahenakew.
7. See Stewart, *Peyote Religion*; Slotkin, *The Peyote Religion*; Maroukis, *The Peyote Road*; La Barre, *The Peyote Cult*.
8. Browning to Baldwin, Aug. 4, 1896; Farmers Report of Delos Lonewolf, July 1, 1898; Aitson to Walker, Oct. 31, 1898, all in RG 75.19.50, Reel 47.
9. Stewart, *Peyote Religion*, 121.
10. Maroukis, *The Peyote Road*, 34–5; Link, "The Iron Horse in Indian Country," 193–201; Newkumet and Meredith, *Hasinai*, 69. Maroukis argues that although the Ghost Dance was "not related to" peyotism, the dance "indirectly facilitated the spread" of it because of the many "intertribal contacts that occurred with the" Ghost Dance. As this study demonstrates, many of those intertribal contacts were already established before the Ghost Dance, and as Maroukis and others demonstrate, peyotism was also being disseminated before the Ghost Dance.
11. Kracht, "The Kiowa Ghost Dance," 468.
12. Ibid.
13. Ibid., 468–70.
14. "Copy of a Letter in Lakota from John Anuwakte to Zitkalaciqala Teziska, August 10, 1896," MS 1397, NAA, translated into English by J. N. B. Hewitt.
15. Wissler, *Indian Cavalcade*, 344.
16. Thompson to CIA, March 30, 1892, RG 75.4, SC 188, Box 200; Brown to CIA, April 18, 1892, RG 75.4, Rec'd, 15084, Box 850. Tall Bull was described by officials as a dissatisfied Lakota from Cheyenne River who settled at Pine Ridge without permission.
17. Penny to CIA, Nov. 22, 1894, RG 75.4, SC 188, Box 200. The letter was given to the agent at Pine Ridge by Kicking Bear and several other headmen. It is not clear why the men gave the agent the letter; the agent only states that it was done for his "information."
18. Bollard and Wheeler to Sioux Chiefs, Sept. 17, 1894, copy in Penny to CIA, Nov. 22, 1894, RG 75.4, SC 188, Box 200. Joe Wheeler's agent called him the "wealthiest and one of the most influential" Shoshones at Fort Hall. "He dresses wholly in citizens' clothes, favors schools and civilization, and is a man of honesty and integrity"; see *ARCIA*, 1890, 77. In December 1894, some Lakotas at Rosebud, including Big Turkey and High Shield, reportedly organized a Ghost Dance; see *El Reno (OK) Eagle*, Dec. 28, 1894.
19. See Penny to CIA, May 15, 1891, RG 75.4, Rec'd, 18317, Box 734; Mooney to Gatschet, July 14, 1891, BAE, Series 1, Box 109, NAA; Penny

to CIA, Aug. 12, 1891, RG 75.4, Rec'd, 29367, Box 766; Brown to CIA, March 7, 1892, RG 75.4, Rec'd, 9440, Box 961; Brown to CIA, June 27, 1892, RG 75.4, Rec'd, 23877, Box 881; Brown to CIA, Aug. 1, 1892, RG 75.4, Rec'd, 28412–13, Box 893.
20. Wooten to Ellis, Nov. 21, 1895, RG 75.19.129, Box 249.
21. Hammond to Strother, July 21, 1891, RG 75.19.129, Box 314.
22. Pueblo Travel Pass, Dec. 5, 1894, RG 75.19.50, Reel 40.
23. *ARCIA*, 1897, 225.
24. Randlett to Kiowa Agent, Sept. 26, 1893, RG 75.19.50, Rec'd, Reel 39.

Bibliography

National Archives

RG 75.4. Records of the Bureau of Indian Affairs. General Records of the Bureau of Indian Affairs. National Archives and Records Administration, Washington, DC.

RG 75.4. Records of the Bureau of Indian Affairs. General Records of the Bureau of Indian Affairs, Special Cases, 1821–1907, SC 188. National Archives and Records Administration, Washington, DC.

RG 75.19.3. Records of the Bureau of Indian Affairs. Blackfeet Agency. National Archives and Records Administration, Broomfield, Colorado.

RG 75.19.10. Records of the Bureau of Indian Affairs. Cheyenne and Arapaho. National Archives and Records Administration, Oklahoma Historical Society, Oklahoma City.

RG 75.19.11. Records of the Bureau of Indian Affairs. Cheyenne River. National Archives and Records Administration, Oklahoma Historical Society, Oklahoma City.

RG 75.19.18. Records of the Bureau of Indian Affairs. Consolidated Ute. National Archives and Records Administration, Broomfield, Colorado.

RG 75.19.20. Records of the Bureau of Indian Affairs. Crow Creek. National Archives and Records Administration, Kansas City, Missouri.

RG 75.19.21. Records of the Bureau of Indian Affairs, Crow Agency. National Archives and Records Administration. Broomfield, Colorado.

RG 75.19.30. Records of the Bureau of Indian Affairs. Ft. Belknap. National Archives and Records Administration. Broomfield, Colorado.

RG 75.19.31. Records of the Bureau of Indian Affairs. Ft. Berthold. National Archives and Records Administration, Kansas City, Missouri.

RG 75.19.35. Records of the Bureau of Indian Affairs. Ft. Peck. National Archives and Records Administration, Broomfield, Colorado.

RG 75.19.50. Records of the Bureau of Indian Affairs. Kiowa Comanche and Wichita. National Archives and Records Administration, Oklahoma Historical Society, Oklahoma City.

RG 75.19.63. Records of the Bureau of Indian Affairs. Navajo. National Archives and Records Administration, Riverside, California.

RG 75.19.77. Records of the Bureau of Indian Affairs. Pawnee Ponca Otoe. National Archives and Records Administration, Oklahoma Historical Society, Oklahoma City.

RG 75.19.85. Records of the Bureau of Indian Affairs. Pine Ridge. National Archives and Records Administration, Kansas City, Missouri.

RG 75.19.96. Records of the Bureau of Indian Affairs. Rosebud. National Archives and Records Administration, Kansas City, Missouri.

RG 75.19.113. Records of the Bureau of Indian Affairs. Standing Rock. National Archives and Records Administration, Kansas City, Missouri.

RG 75.19.117. Records of the Bureau of Indian Affairs. Tongue River. National Archives and Records Administration, Broomfield, Colorado.

RG 75.19.132. Records of the Bureau of Indian Affairs. Western Shoshone. National Archives and Records Administration, San Bruno, California.

RG 75.20.3. Records of the Bureau of Indian Affairs. Records of the Carlisle Indian Industrial School. National Archives and Records Administration, Washington, DC.

Other Archival Sources

American Horse Papers. MSS S-903. Yale Collection of Western Americana, Beinecke Rare Book and Manuscript Library, Yale University.

Ashley, Edward, Papers, 1883–1931. Episcopal Diocese of South Dakota Archives, Augustana University Center for Western Studies.

Ayer, Edward E., Collection. Newberry Library, Chicago.

Baird, George William, Papers. MSS S-878 B163. Yale Collection of Western Americana, Beinecke Rare Book and Manuscript Library, Yale University.

Baldwin, Frank, Papers. The Huntington Library, San Marino, California.

Battey, Thomas, Papers. The Huntington Library, San Marino, California.

Beede, Aaron, Journal. Orin G. Libby Papers. MS 10085. Box 37. State Historical Society of North Dakota, Bismarck.

Burnham, Mary D., Papers. MSS S-2157. Yale Collection of Western Americana, Beinecke Rare Book and Manuscript Library, Yale University.

Campbell, Walter S., Collection. Western History Collections, University of Oklahoma Libraries.

Charging Crow, Alex. "History of the Lakotas as Told by Alex Charging Crow." Adee Dodge Papers. WA MSS S-2701 Series III. Box 40. Yale Collection of Western Americana, Beinecke Rare Book and Manuscript Library, Yale University.

Dorsey, John O., Papers. MS 4800. National Anthropological Archives, Smithsonian Institution, Washington, DC.
Dyer, Ed A. "The Jack Wilson Story." NC03. Special Collections, University Libraries, University of Nevada Libraries.
Fisher, Stanton G., Papers. MS106, Folder 15. Idaho State Historical Society, Boise.
"From Warrior to Saint: The Journey of David Pendleton Oakerhater." Oklahoma State University Library Digital Collection. https://dc.library.okstate.edu/digital/collection/oaker.
Grinnell, George Bird, Papers. MS 1388. Manuscripts and Archives, Yale University Library.
Howell Family Papers. HM 66800–67889. The Huntington Library, San Marino, California.
Kimball, Thomas Lord, Papers. The Huntington Library, San Marino, California.
Lauderdale, John Vance, Papers. MSS S-1317. Yale Collection of Western Americana, Beinecke Rare Book and Manuscript Library, Yale University.
Pratt, Richard Henry, Papers. MSS S-1174. Yale Collection of Western Americana, Beinecke Rare Book and Manuscript Library, Yale University.
Records of the Bureau of American Ethnology. National Anthropological Archives, Smithsonian Institution, Washington, DC.
Roan Bear, Edward, Papers, 1953–1954. MS 20121. State Historical Society of North Dakota, Bismarck.
Ruger, Thomas Howard, Papers. MSS S-2699. Yale Collection of Western Americana, Beinecke Rare Book and Manuscript Library, Yale University.
Schuyler, Walter Scribner, Papers. WS 71. The Huntington Library, San Marino, California.
Spencer, Lebbeus Foster, Papers. MSS 596. History Colorado, Stephen H. Hart Library and Research Center, Denver.
Standing Rock Letterpress Copybook. MSS S-3052, WA MSS S-2157. Yale Collection of Western Americana, Beinecke Rare Book and Manuscript Library, Yale University.
Walker, Dr. James R., Collection. MSS 653. History Colorado, Stephen H. Hart Library and Research Center, Denver.
Wheat, Margaret M., Papers, 83–24. Special Collections, University Libraries, University of Nevada Libraries.
White Earth Letter Book, 1876–1877. MSS S-3097. Yale Collection of Western Americana, Beinecke, Rare Book and Manuscript Library, Yale University.

Microfilm Publications

James McLaughlin Papers. Richardson, ND: Assumption College, 1968.
Indian Rights Association Papers, 1864–1973. Historical Society of Pennsylvania. Glen Rock, NJ: Microfilming Corp. of America, 1974.
Letters Received by the Office of Indian Affairs 1824–1881. Microcopy No. 234, Roll 768, Santee Sioux Agency, 1871–1876. Washington, DC: National Archives Microfilm Publications, 1958.
Letters Sent to the Office of Indian Affairs by the Pine Ridge Agency 1875–1914. National Archives Microfilm Publication M1282. Washington, DC: National Archives Microfilm Publications, 1985.
Registers of Letters Received, 1881–1907. Records of the Bureau of Indian Affairs, National Archives Microfilm Publication P2186. Washington, DC: National Archives Microfilm Publications.
Reports and Correspondence Related to the Army Investigations of the Battle at Wounded Knee and to the Sioux Campaign of 1890–1891. National Archives Microfilm Publications. Washington, DC: National Archives and Records Service, 1975.

Government Publications and Records

Annual Report of the Commissioner of Indian Affairs to the Secretary of the Interior. 1851, 1868, 1870, 1872–1892, 1897. Washington, DC: Government Printing Office, 1869–92.
Annual Report of the Postal Master General of the United States. 1870–1890. Washington, DC: Government Printing Office, 1871–91.
Annual Report of the Secretary of War, 1891. Vol. 1. Washington, DC: Government Printing Office, 1892.
1880 United States Federal Census.
Executive Documents of the Senate of the United States for the Second Session of the Fifty-First Congress. Washington, DC: Government Printing Office, 1891.
Executive Documents of the Senate of the United States for the First Session of the Fifty-Second Congress, 1891–92. Vol. 5. Washington, DC: Government Printing Office, 1892.
Executive Documents of the Senate of the United States for the Second Session of the Fifty-Third Congress, 1893–1894. Washington, DC: Government Printing Office, 1895.
Journal of the Senate of the United States of America, Being the Second Session of the Fifty-First Congress, Begun and Held at the City of Washington December 1, 1890. Washington, DC: Government Printing Office, 1891.

Report of the Secretary of War, First Session of the Fifty-Second Congress. Washington, DC: Government Printing Office, 1892.
Testimony Taken by the Committee on Indian Affairs of the Senate in Relation to Leases of Lands in the Indian Territory and other Reservations. Washington, DC: Government Printing Office, 1885.
United States Congress. *Congressional Record.* 48th Congress, 1st Session. Washington, DC: Government Printing Office, 1884.
United States Postal Guide. Vol. 11, no. 1, January 1889. Washington, DC: Brodix Publishing, 1889.

Published Primary Sources

Andreas, A. T. *Andreas' Historical Atlas of Dakota.* Chicago: R. R. Donnelley, Lakeside Press, 1884.
Battey, Thomas C. *The Life and Adventures of a Quaker among the Indians.* Boston: Lee and Shepard, 1876.
Brice, James. *Reminiscences of Ten Years Experience on the Western Plains.* Kansas City, MO: privately printed, 1905.
Clover, Samuel T. *On Special Assignment.* Boston: Lothrop Publishing, 1903.
Crager, George. "As Narrated by Short Bull." Golden, CO: Buffalo Bill Museum and Grave, 1891. Transcribed in Maddra, *Hostiles?*
Dorsey, James Owen. *The Cegiha Language.* Department of the Interior, Contributions to North American Ethnology. Washington, DC: Government Printing Office, 1890.
———. *Omaha and Ponka Letters.* Smithsonian Institution, Bureau of Ethnology. Washington, DC: Government Printing Office, 1891.
Hinman, Samuel D. *Journal of the Rev. S. D. Hinman, Missionary to the Santee Sioux Indians.* Philadelphia: McCalla & Stavely, 1869.
Indian Rights Association. *Are the Eastern Industrial Training Schools for Indian Children a Failure?* Philadelphia, 1886.
———. *Eighth Annual Report of the Executive Committee of the Indian Rights Association, for the Year Ending December 15th, 1890.* Philadelphia, 1891.
———. *Ninth Annual Report of the Executive Committee of the Indian Rights Association, for the Year Ending December 15th, 1891.* Philadelphia, 1892.
Journal of the Sixth Annual Session of the General Council of Indian Territory. Lawrence, KS: Republican Journal Steam Printing, 1875.
Proceedings of the Ninth Annual Meeting of the Lake Mohonk Conference of Friends of the Indian 1891. Lake Mohonk, NY: Lake Mohonk Conference, 1891.

Reinhardt, Richard, ed. *Out West on the Overland Trail: Across the Continent Excursion with Leslie's Magazine in 1877 and the Overland Trip in 1967.* Sanger, CA: American West, 1967.

Ross, Alexander. *The Red River Settlement: Its Rise, Progress, and Present State.* London: Smith, Elder, 1856.

Standing Bear, Luther. *My People, the Sioux.* Lincoln: University of Nebraska Press, 1975.

Sword, George. "The Story of the Ghost Dance." *The Folk-Lorist* 1 (1892): 28–31.

"Treaty between the United States Government and the Navajo Indians Signed at Fort Sumner, New Mexico Territory on June 1, 1868," National Archives Catalog, https://catalog.archives.gov/id/6173067.

Twenty-Two Years' Work of the Hampton Normal and Agricultural Institute at Hampton, Virginia. Hampton, VA: Hampton Normal Press, 1893.

Walker, Francis. *The Indian Question.* Boston: James R. Osgood, 1874.

Welsh, Herbert. "A Crisis in the Cause of Indian Education." Philadelphia: Indian Rights Association, 1892.

Winnemucca, Sarah. *A Century of Dishonor: A Sketch of the United States Government's Dealings with Some of the Indian Tribe.* New York: Harper, 1881.

Secondary Sources

Adams, David Wallace. *Education for Extinction: American Indians and the Boarding School Experience, 1875–1928.* Lawrence: University Press of Kansas, 1995.

Andersson, Rani-Henrik. *The Lakota Ghost Dance of 1890.* Lincoln: University of Nebraska Press, 2008.

———. *A Whirlwind Passed through Our Country: Lakota Voices of the Ghost Dance.* Norman: University of Oklahoma Press, 2018.

Awakuni-Swetland, Mark. *Dance Lodges of the Omaha People.* 2nd ed. Lincoln: University of Nebraska Press, 2008.

Barber, Bernard. "Acculturation and Messianic Movements." *American Sociological Review* 6, no. 5 (1941): 663–69.

Barney, Garold D. *Mormons, Indians, and the Ghost Dance.* Lanham, MD: University Press of America, 1986.

Bearor, Karen A. "The *Illustrated American* and the Lakota Ghost Dance." *American Periodicals* 21, no. 2 (2011): 143–63.

Bell, Genevieve. "Telling Stories out of School: Remembering the Carlisle Industrial School, 1879–1918." PhD diss., Stanford University, 1998.

Berthrong, Donald J. *The Cheyenne and Arapaho Ordeal: Reservation and Agency Life in the Indian Territory, 1875–1907.* Norman: University of Oklahoma Press, 1976.

———. *The Southern Cheyennes.* Norman: University of Oklahoma Press, 1963.

Blackhawk, Ned. *Violence over the Land: Indians and Empires in the Early American West.* Cambridge, MA: Harvard University Press, 2009.

Blaine, Garland James, and Martha Royce Blaine. "Pa-Re-Su A-Ri-Ra-Ke: The Hunters That Were Massacred." *Nebraska History* 58 (1977): 342–58.

Blakeslee, Donald J. "The Plains Interband Trade System: An Ethnohistoric and Archaeological Investigation." PhD diss., University of Wisconsin–Milwaukee, 1975.

Bleed, Peter. "Indians and Japanese Swords on the North Plains Frontier." *Nebraska History* 68 (1987): 112–15.

Blevins, Cameron. "The Postal West: Spatial Integration and the American West, 1865–1902." PhD diss., Stanford University, 2015.

Boughter, Judith A. *Betraying the Omaha Nation, 1790–1916.* Norman: University of Oklahoma Press, 1998.

Bray, Kingsley M. "Lakota Statesmen and the Horse Creek Treaty of 1851." *Nebraska History* 98, no. 3 (Fall 2017): 153–75.

———. "Lone Horn's Peace: A New View of Sioux-Crow Relations, 1851–1848." *Nebraska History* 66 (1985): 28–47.

Brown, Dee. *Hear That Lonesome Whistle Blow.* New York: Touchstone, 1977.

Brown, Donald N. "The Ghost Dance Religion among the Oklahoma Cheyenne." *Chronicles of Oklahoma* 30 (1952–53): 408–16.

Buechel, Eugene. *A Grammar of Lakota: The Language of the Teton Sioux Indians.* Saint Francis, SD: Saint Francis Mission, 1939.

Burns, Louis F. *A History of the Osage People.* Tuscaloosa: University of Alabama Press, 2004.

Cahill, Cathleen D. *Federal Fathers and Mothers: A Social History of the United States Indian Service, 1869–1933.* Chapel Hill: University of North Carolina Press, 2011.

Canfield, Gae Whitney. *Sarah Winnemucca of the Northern Paiutes.* Norman: University of Oklahoma Press, 1983.

Canku, Clifford, and Michael Simon. *The Dakota Prisoner of War Letters, Dakota Kaskapi Okicize Wowapi.* Saint Paul: Minnesota Historical Society Press, 2013.

"Captain Amberson G. Shaw." In *Compendium of History, Reminiscence and Biography of Western Nebraska*, 492–93. Chicago: Alden Publishing, 1909.

Carpenter, Cari M., and Carolyn Sorisio, eds. *The Newspaper Warrior: Sarah Winnemucca Hopkins's Campaign for American Indian Rights, 1864–1891.* Lincoln: University of Nebraska Press, 2015.

Cheyfitz, Eric, ed. *The Columbia Guide to American Indian Literatures of the United States since 1945.* New York: Columbia University Press, 2006.

Child, Brenda J. *Boarding School Seasons: American Indian Families, 1900–1940.* Lincoln: University of Nebraska Press, 1998.

Clow, Richmond L. "The Lakota Ghost Dance after 1890." *South Dakota History* 20 (1990): 323–33.

———. "Mad Bear: William S. Harney and the Sioux Expedition of 1855–56." *Nebraska History* 61 (1980): 132–51.

Coates, Lawrence G. "The Mormons and the Ghost Dance." *Dialogue: A Journal of Mormon Thought* 18 (1985): 89–111.

Coleman, Michael C. *American Indian Children at School, 1850–1930.* Oxford: University Press of Mississippi, 1993.

Coleman, William S. E. *Voices of Wounded Knee.* Lincoln: University of Nebraska Press, 2000.

Coward, John M. *The Newspaper Indian: Native American Identity in the Press, 1820–90.* Urbana: University of Illinois Press, 1999.

Cowell, Andrew, ed. *Arapaho Stories, Songs, and Prayers.* Norman: University of Oklahoma Press, 2014.

Cox, James H. *Muting White Noise: Native American and European American Novel Traditions.* Norman: University of Oklahoma Press, 2006.

Crum, Steven J. *The Road on Which We Came: A History of the Western Shoshone.* Salt Lake City: University of Utah Press, 1994.

Cutler, Lee. "Lawrie Tatum and the Kiowa Agency: 1869–1873." *Arizona and the West* 13, no. 3 (Autumn 1971): 237–38.

Dakota Presbytery Council. *The Dakota Mission, Past and Present.* Minneapolis, MN: Tribune Job, 1886.

Dangberg, Grace. "Letters to Jack Wilson, the Paiute Prophet." *Anthropological Papers* (Bureau of American Ethnology) 55, bulletin 164 (1957): 279–96.

———. "Wovoka." *Nevada Historical Society Quarterly* 11, no. 2 (1968): 5–53.

Davis, Jeffrey E. *Hand Talk: Sign Language among American Indian Nations.* New York: Cambridge University Press, 2010.

DeMallie, Raymond J. "The Lakota Ghost Dance: An Ethnohistorical Account." *Pacific Historical Review* 51, no. 4 (1982): 385–405.

———. "Santee." In *Handbook of North American Indians*, vol. 13, edited by William C. Sturtevant. Washington, DC: Smithsonian Institution, 2001.

———. "Sioux before 1850." In *Handbook of North American Indians*, vol. 13, edited by William C. Sturtevant. Washington, DC: Smithsonian Institution, 2001.

———, ed. *The Sixth Grandfather: Black Elk's Teachings Given to John G. Neihardt*. Lincoln: University of Nebraska Press, 1984.

———. "These Have No Ears: Narrative and the Ethnohistorical Method." *Ethnohistory* 40, no. 4 (1993): 515–38.

———. "Touching the Pen: Plains Indian Treaty Councils in Ethnohistorical Perspective." In *Major Problems in American Indian History*, edited by Albert Hurtado and Peter Iverson, 344–55. Lexington, MA: D. C. Heath, 1994.

———. "Yankton and Yanktonai." In *Handbook of North American Indians*, vol. 13, edited by William C. Sturtevant. Washington, DC: Smithsonian Institution, 2001.

DeMallie, Raymond J., and Douglas R. Parks. "Plains Indian Native Literatures." *boundary 2* 19, no. 3 (1992): 105–47.

Dempsey, Hugh A. "Blackfoot Ghost Dance." Glenbow-Atlanta Institute Occasional Papers 3. Calgary: Glenbow-Atlanta Institute, 1968.

———*The Vengeful Wife and Other Blackfoot Stories*. Norman, OK: University of Oklahoma Press, 2003.

Diedrich, March. *Sitting Bull: The Collected Speeches*. Rochester, MN: Coyote Books, 1998.

Dobyns, Henry F., and Robert C. Euler. *The Ghost Dance of 1889 among the Pai Indians of Northwestern Arizona*. Prescott, AZ: Prescott College Press, 1967.

Dorsey, George A. *The Arapaho Sun Dance: The Ceremony of the Offerings Lodge*. Anthropological Series 4. Chicago: Field Columbian Museum, 1903.

Dorsey, James Owen. "The Arapaho Sun Dance." *Field Museum Publication* (Chicago) 75, vol. 4 (1903).

Du Bois, Cora. *The 1870 Ghost Dance*. Anthropological Records 3, no. 1. Berkley: University of California Press, 1939.

Due, John F. "The Carson and Colorado Railroad." *Economic Geography* 27, no. 3 (1951): 251–67.

Eastman, Elaine Goodale. "The Ghost Dance War and Wounded Knee Massacre of 1890–91." *Nebraska History* 26, no. 1 (1945): 26–42.

———. "A Hasty Conclusion." *Midland Monthly* 2, no. 3 (1894): 192–99.

———. *Pratt, the Red Man's Moses*. Norman: University of Oklahoma Press, 1935.

———. *Sister to the Sioux, the Memoirs of Elaine Goodale Eastman, 1885–1891*. Lincoln: University of Nebraska Press, 1978.

Ellis, Clyde. "'There Is No Doubt . . . the Dances Should Be Curtailed': Indian Dances and Federal Policy on the Southern Plains, 1880–1930." *Pacific Historical Review* 70, no. 4 (2001): 543–69.

———. *To Change Them Forever: Indian Education at the Rainy Mountain Boarding School, 1893–1920.* Norman: University of Oklahoma Press, 1996.

———. "'We Don't Want Your Rations, We Want This Dance': The Changing Use of Song and Dance on the Southern Plains." *Western Historical Quarterly* 2, no. 2 (1999): 133–54.

Emery, Jacqueline. "Writing against Erasure: Native American Students at Hampton Institute and the Periodical Press." *American Periodicals* 22, no. 2 (2012): 178–98.

Enoch, Ross Alexander. *The Jesuit Mission to the Lakota Sioux: Pastoral Theology and Ministry, 1886–1945.* Kansas City, KS: Sheed and Ward, 1995.

Ewers, John C. "The Indian Trade of the Upper Missouri before Lewis and Clark: An Interpretation." *Bulletin of the Missouri Historical Society* 10 (1954): 429–46.

———. "Intertribal Warfare as the Precursor of Indian-White Warfare on the Northern Great Plains." *Western Historical Quarterly* 6 (Oct. 1975): 397–410.

Farr, William E. "Going Buffalo: Indian Hunting Migrations across the Rocky Mountains: Part 2, Civilian Permits, Army Escorts." *Montana: The Magazine of Western History* 54 (Spring 2004): 26–43.

Fear-Segal, Jacqueline. "Eyes in the Text: Marianna Burgess and the *Indian Helper*." In *Blue Pencils & Hidden Hands: Women Editing Periodicals, 1830–1910*, edited by Sharon Harris, 123–45. Boston: Northeastern University Press, 2004.

———. *White Man's Club: Schools and the Struggle of Indian Acculturation.* Lincoln: University of Nebraska Press, 2007.

Fear-Segal, Jacqueline, and Susan D. Rose, eds. *Carlisle Indian Industrial School: Indigenous Histories, Memories, and Reclamations.* Lincoln: University of Nebraska Press, 2016.

Fellman, Michael. *Citizen Sherman: A Life of William Tecumseh Sherman.* New York: Random House, 1995.

Fletcher, Alice C. "The Elk Mystery or Festival." *Reports of the Peabody Museum of American Archaeology and Ethnology* (Cambridge, MA) 3 (1887).

———. *Indian Education and Civilization.* Bureau of Education Special Report 1888. Washington, DC: Government Printing Office, 1888.

———. "The Indian Messiah." *Journal of American Folklore* 4, no. 12 (1891): 57–60.

———. *Lakota Ceremonies.* Sixteenth and Seventeenth Annual Report of the Trustees of the Peabody Museum of American Archeology and Ethnology. Cambridge, MA: 1884.

———. "A Phonetic Alphabet, Used by the Winnebago Tribe of Indians." *Journal of American Folklore* 3, no. 11 (1890): 299–301.

Fletcher, Alice C., and Frances La Flesche. *The Omaha Tribe*. Bureau of American Ethnology, 27th Annual Report, 1905–1906. Washington, DC: Government Printing Office, 1911.

Fowler, Loretta. *Arapahoe Politics, 1851–1978*. Lincoln: University of Nebraska Press, 1986.

Fuller, Wayne E. *The American Mail: Enlarger of the Common Life*. Chicago: University of Chicago Press, 1972.

Gage, Justin R. "Intertribal Communication, Literacy, and the Spread of the Ghost Dance." PhD diss., University of Arkansas, 2015.

Gatschet, Albert S. "Report of an Indian Visit to Jack Wilson, the Payute Messiah." *Journal of American Folklore* 6, no. 21 (1893): 108–11.

Gillmor, Frances, and Louisa Wade Wetherill. *Traders to the Navajos: The Story of The Wetherills of Kayenta*. Boston: Houghton Mifflin, 1934.

Glancy, Diane. *Fort Marion Prisoners and the Trauma of Native Education*. Lincoln: University of Nebraska Press, 2014.

Goodburn, Amy M. "Literacy Practices at the Genoa Industrial Indian School." *Great Plains Quarterly* 19 (Winter 1999): 35–52.

Gordon, Sarah. *Passage to Union: How the Railroads Transformed American Life, 1829–1929*. Chicago: Ivan R. Dee, 1996.

Graber, Jennifer. *The Gods of Indian Country: Religion and the Struggle for the American West*. New York: Oxford University Press, 2018.

Greene, Candace S., and Russell Thornton, eds. *The Year the Stars Fell: Lakota Winter Counts at the Smithsonian*. Lincoln: University of Nebraska Press, 2007.

Greene, Jerome. *American Carnage: Wounded Knee, 1890*. Norman: University of Oklahoma Press, 2014.

———. *Beyond Bear's Paw: The Nez Perce Indians in Canada*. Norman: University of Oklahoma Press, 2010.

Greenway, John. "The Ghost Dance, Some Reflections, with Evidence, on a Cult of Despair among the Indians of North America." *American West* 6, no. 4 (1969): 42–47.

Grinnell, George Bird. "Account of the Northern Cheyennes Concerning the Messiah Superstition." *Journal of American Folklore* 4, no. 12 (1891): 61–69.

Hagan, William T. "19th Century Indian Education Programs." In *Clash of Cultures: The American Indian Student in Higher Education*, edited by Roy H. Sandstrom, 96–101. Institute on the American Indian Student in Higher Education. Canton, NY: Saint Lawrence University, 1972.

Hall, Phillip S. *Reflections of the Badlands*. Freeman: University of South Dakota Press, 1993.

Hämäläinen, Pekka. *The Comanche Empire.* New Haven, CT: Yale University Press, 2008.
Harrington, John P. *Vocabulary of the Kiowa Language.* Smithsonian Institution Bulletin of the Bureau of American Ethnology 84. Washington, DC: Government Printing Office, 1928.
Hassrick, Royal. *The Sioux: Life and Customs of a Warrior Society.* Norman: University of Oklahoma Press, 1964.
Heaton, John W. *The Shoshone-Bannocks: Culture and Commerce at Fort Hall, 1870–1940.* Lawrence: University of Kansas Press, 2005.
Henkin, David M. *The Postal Age: The Emergence of Modern Communications in Nineteenth-Century America.* Chicago: University of Chicago Press, 2006.
Hertzberg, Hazel. *Search for an American Indian Identity: Modern Pan-Indian Movements.* Syracuse, NY: Syracuse University Press, 1971.
Hittman, Michael. "The 1870 Ghost Dance at the Walker River Reservation: A Reconstruction." *Ethnohistory* 20, no. 3 (1973): 247–78.
———. *Wovoka and the Ghost Dance.* Lincoln: University of Nebraska Press, 1997.
Holler, Clyde. *Black Elk's Religion: The Sun Dance and Lakota Catholicism.* Syracuse, NY: Syracuse University Press, 1995.
Hoxie, Frederick. "Crow Leadership amidst Reservation Oppression." In *State and Reservation: New Perspectives on Federal Indian Policy*, edited by George Castile and Robert Bee, 38–60. Tucson: University of Arizona Press, 1992.
———. "The End of the Savage: Indian Policy in the United States Senate, 1880–1900." *Chronicles of Oklahoma* 55 (1977): 157–79.
———. *The Final Promise: The Campaign to Assimilate the Indians, 1880–1920.* Lincoln: University of Nebraska Press, 1984.
———. *Parading through History: The Making of the Crow Nation in America 1805–1935.* New York: Cambridge University Press, 1995.
———. "Redefining Indian Education: Thomas J. Morgan's Program in Disarray." *Arizona and the West* 24, no. 1 (1982): 6–8.
Howard, James. *The Ponca Tribe.* Lincoln: University of Nebraska Press, 1995.
Hultgren, Mary Lou. "'To Be Examples to ... Their People': Standing Rock Sioux Students at Hampton Institute, 1878–1923 (Part Two)." *North Dakota History* (Fall 2001): 20–42.
Hungry Wolf, Beverly. *The Ways of My Grandmothers.* New York: Quill, 1982.
Hyde, George E. *A Sioux Chronicle.* Norman: University of Oklahoma Press, 1956.
———. *Spotted Tail's Folk: A History of the Brule Sioux.* Norman: University of Oklahoma Press, 1961.

Jensen, Richard E. "Big Foot's Followers at Wounded Knee." *Nebraska History* 71 (1990): 194–212.

———, ed. *The Indian Interviews of Eli S. Ricker, 1903–1919.* Lincoln: University of Nebraska Press, 2005.

Jensen, Richard E., R. Eli Paul, and John Carter, eds. *Eyewitness at Wounded Knee.* Lincoln: University of Nebraska Press, 1991.

Johns, Richard. *Spreading the News.* Cambridge, MA: Harvard University Press, 1995.

Johnson, Benjamin H. "Red Populism? T. A. Bland, Agrarian Radicalism, and the Debate over the Dawes Act." In *The Countryside in the Age of the Modern State*, edited by Catherine McNicol Stock and Robert D. Johnston, 15–37. Ithaca, NY: Cornell University Press, 2001.

Johnson, E. C. *Walker River Paiutes: A Tribal History.* Schurz, NV: Walker River Paiute Tribe, 1975.

Johnson, W. Fletcher. *The Red Record of the Sioux.* Philadelphia: Edgewood Publishing, 1891.

Jones, John A. *The Sun Dance of the Northern Ute.* Anthropological Papers 47, Bureau of American Ethnology Bulletin 157. Washington, DC: Government Printing Office, 1955.

Jorgensen, Gladys. *Before Homesteads in Tripp County and the Rosebud.* Freeman, SD: Pine Hill Press, 1974.

Josephy, Alvin M. *The Nez Perce Indians and the Opening of the Northwest.* New York: Houghton Mifflin, 1997.

Katanski, Amelia V. *Learning to Write 'Indian': The Boarding-School Experience and American Indian Literature.* Norman: University of Oklahoma Press, 2005.

Kehoe, Alice Beck. *The Ghost Dance: Ethnohistory and Revitalization.* 2nd ed. Long Grove, IL: Waveland Press, 2006.

———. "The Ghost Dance Religion in Saskatchewan, Canada." *Plains Anthropologist* 13 (1968): 296–304.

Kelly, Florence Finch. *Emerson's Wife: And Other Western Stories.* Chicago: A. C. McClurg, 1911.

Kerstetter, Todd. "Spin Doctors at Santee: Missionaries and the Dakota-Language Reporting of the Ghost Dance and Wounded Knee." *Western Historical Quarterly* 28, no. 1 (1997): 45–67.

Kingsbury, George Washington. *South Dakota: Its History and Its People.* Vol. 4. Chicago: S. J. Clarke Publishing, 1915.

Konkle, Maureen. "Indian Literacy, U.S. Colonialism, and Literary Criticism." *American Literature* 69, no. 3 (1997): 457–86.

Kracht, Benjamin R. *Kiowa Belief and Ritual.* Lincoln: University of Nebraska Press, 2017.

———. "The Kiowa Ghost Dance, 1894–1916: An Unheralded Revitalization Movement." *Ethnohistory* 39, no. 4 (1992): 452–77.

———. "Kiowa Powwows: Continuity in Ritual Practice." *American Indian Quarterly* 18 (Summer 1994): 321–48.

———. *Religious Revitalization among the Kiowas: The Ghost Dance, Peyote, and Christianity.* Lincoln: University of Nebraska Press, 2018.

Kreis, Karl Markus. *Lakota, Black Robes, and Holy Women: German Reports from the Indian Missions in South Dakota, 1886–1900.* Lincoln: University of Nebraska Press, 2000.

Kroeber, A. L. "The Bannock and Shoshone Languages." *American Anthropologist* 11, no. 2 (1909): 266–75.

Kueteman, K.B. "He Goes First: The Story of Episcopal Saint David Pendleton Oakerhater." Oklahoma State University Library Digital Collection. https://dc.library.okstate.edu/digital/collection/oaker/id/271/.

La Barre, Weston. *The Peyote Cult.* Norman: University of Oklahoma Press, 1976.

Lang, George. *Making Wawa: The Genesis of Chinook Jargon.* Vancouver: UBC Press, 2009.

Larson, Robert W. *Red Cloud: Warrior-Statesman of the Lakota Sioux.* Norman: University of Oklahoma Press, 1997.

Lauderdale, John Vance. *After Wounded Knee.* Lansing: Michigan State University Press, 1996.

Leap, William L. *American Indian English.* Salt Lake City: University of Utah Press, 1993.

Lee, Robert. "Warriors in Ranks: American Indian Units in the Regular Army, 1891–1897." *South Dakota History* 21, no. 3 (1991): 263–316.

Lesser, Alexander. "Cultural Significance of the Ghost Dance." *American Anthropologist* 45 (1933): 230–40.

———. *The Pawnee Ghost Dance Hand Game.* Lincoln: University of Nebraska Press, 1933.

Lewis, Bonnie Sue. "Leadership in the Native Tradition: Dakota and Nez Perce Presbyterian Pastors." *Journal of Presbyterian History* 77, no. 3 (Fall 1999): 153–66.

Lewis, David Rich. *Neither Wolf Nor Dog: American Indians, Environment, and Agrarian Change.* New York: Oxford University Press, 1994.

Link, Alessandra. "The Iron Horse in Indian Country: Native Americans and Railroads in the U.S. West, 1853–1924." PhD diss., University of Colorado, 2018.

Littlefield, Daniel F., Jr., and James W. Parins. *American Indian and Alaska Native Newspapers and Periodicals, 1826–1924.* Westport, CT: Greenwood Press, 1984.

Logan, Brad. "The Ghost Dance among the Paiute: An Ethnohistorical View of the Documentary Evidence." *Ethnohistory* 27, no. 3 (1980): 267–88.

Lomawaima, K. Tsianina. *They Called It Prairie Light: The Story of Chilocco Indian School.* Lincoln: University of Nebraska Press, 1995.
Lookingbill, Brad D. *War Dance at Fort Marion: Plain Indian War Prisoners.* Norman: University of Oklahoma Press, 2006.
Lowie, Robert H. *The Crow Indian.* New York: Farrar and Rinehart, 1935.
———. "Sun Dance of the Shoshoni, Ute, and Hidatsa." *Anthropological Papers of the American Museum of Natural History* 16, no. 7 (1921).
Lubetkin, M. John. *Jay Cooke's Gamble: The Northern Pacific Railroad, the Sioux, and the Panic.* Norman: University of Oklahoma Press, 2006.
Maddox, Lucy. *Citizen Indians: Native American Intellectuals, Race, and Reform.* Ithaca, NY: Cornell University Press, 2005.
Maddra, Sam A. *Hostiles? The Lakota Ghost Dance and Buffalo Bill's Wild West.* Norman: University of Oklahoma Press, 2006.
Mallery, Garrick. "Picture Writing of the American Indians." *Tenth Annual Report of the Bureau of Ethnology to the Secretary of the Smithsonian Institution, 1888–'89.* Washington, DC: Government Printing Office, 1893.
———. "Sign Language among North American Indians Compared with That among Other Peoples and Deaf-Mutes." *First Annual Report of the Bureau of Ethnology to the Secretary of the Smithsonian Institution, 1879–1880.* Washington, DC: Government Printing Office, 1881.
Mann, Henrietta. *Cheyenne and Arapaho Education, 1871–1982.* Boulder: University Press of Colorado, 1997.
Maroukis, Thomas C. *The Peyote Road: Religious Freedom and the Native American Church.* Norman: University of Oklahoma Press, 2010.
Maximillian, Alexander Philipp. *Travels in the Interior of North America.* London: Ackerman, 1843.
McCoy, Tim, and Ronald McCoy. *Tim McCoy Remembers the West: An Autobiography.* New York: Doubleday, 1977.
McGinnis, Anthony. *Counting Coup and Cutting Horses: Intertribal Warfare on the Northern Plains, 1738–1889.* Evergreen, CO: Cordillera Press, 1990.
McGrady, David. *Living with Strangers: The Nineteenth-Century Sioux and the Canadian-American Borderlands.* Lincoln: University of Nebraska Press, 2007.
McGregor, James H. *The Wounded Knee Massacre from Viewpoint of the Sioux.* Minneapolis, MN: Lund Press, 1940.
McLaughlin, James. *My Friend the Indian.* Boston: Houghton Mifflin, 1910.
Meadows, William C., ed. *Through Indian Sign Language: The Fort Sill Ledgers of Hugh Lenox Scott and Iseeo, 1889–1897.* Norman: University of Oklahoma Press, 2015.
Meyer, Roy. *History of the Santee.* Lincoln: University of Nebraska Press, 1967.
Miles, George. "To Hear an Old Voice: Rediscovering Native Americans in American History." In *Under an Open Sky: Rethinking America's Western*

Past, edited by William Cronon, George Miles, and Jay Gitlin. New York: W. W. Norton, 1992.

Miller, David Humphreys. *Ghost Dance*. New York: Duell, Sloan, and Pearce, 1959.

Mooney, James. "Calendar History of the Kiowa Indians." *Seventeenth Annual Report, Bureau of American Ethnology*, part 1. Washington, DC: Government Printing Office, 1898.

———. *The Ghost-Dance Religion and the Sioux Outbreak of 1890*. Extract from the *Fourteenth Annual Report of the Bureau of Ethnology*. Washington, DC: Government Printing Office, 1896.

———. "The Indian Ghost Dance." *Collections of the Nebraska State Historical Society* 16 (1911): 168–86.

Moquin, Wayne, ed. *Great Documents in American Indian History*. New York: Praeger, 1973.

Morgan, Mindy. *The Bearer of This Letter: Language Ideologies, Literacy Practices, and the Fort Belknap Indian Community*. Lincoln: University of Nebraska Press, 2009.

Morgan, Thisba Hutson. "Reminiscences of My Days in the Land of the Ogallala Sioux." *South Dakota Report and Historical Collections* 29 (1958): 21–62.

Moses, L. G. "'The Father Tells Me So!' Wovoka: The Ghost Dance Prophet." *American Indian Quarterly* 9, no. 3 (1985): 335–51.

———. "Jack Wilson and the Indian Service: The Response of the BIA to the Ghost Dance Prophet." *American Indian Quarterly* 5, no. 4 (1979): 295–316.

Myrick, David F. *Railroads of Nevada and Eastern California*. Vol. 1. Berkeley: Howell-North Books, 1962.

Nagel, Joane. *American Indian Ethnic Renewal: Red Power and the Resurgence of Identity and Culture*. Oxford: Oxford University Press, 1996.

Newkumet, Vynola Beaver, and Howard L. Meredith. *Hasinai: A Traditional History of the Caddo Confederacy*. College Station: Texas A&M University Press, 1988.

Olson, James C. *Red Cloud and the Sioux Problem*. Lincoln: University of Nebraska Press, 1965.

———. "Reservation Life: Breaking the Tribal Spirit, *Red Cloud vs. McGillycuddy*." In *The Western American Indian: Case Studies in Tribal History*, edited by Richard Ellis, 97–116. Lincoln: University of Nebraska Press, 1972.

Opler, Marvin K. "The Integration of the Sun Dance in Ute Religion." *American Anthropologist*, 43 (1941): 550–72;

———. "The Southern Ute of Colorado." In *Acculturation in Seven American Indian Tribes*, edited by Ralph Linton. New York: D. Appleton-Century, 1940.

Ostler, Jeffrey. *The Plains Sioux and U.S. Colonialism from Lewis and Clark to Wounded Knee.* Cambridge: Cambridge University Press, 2004.
Overholt, Thomas. "Short Bull, Black Elk, Sword, and the Meaning of the Ghost Dance." *Religion* 8, no. 2 (1978): 171–95.
Parks, Douglas R., and Robert Rankin. "Siouan Languages." In *Handbook of North American Indians*, vol. 13, edited by Raymond J. DeMallie. Washington, DC: Smithsonian Institution, 2001.
Paul, R. Eli. "Dakota Resources: The Investigation of Special Agent Cooper and Property Damage Claims in the Winter of 1890–1891." *South Dakota History* 24, no. 3 (1994): 212–35.
———. *The Nebraska Indian Wars Reader, 1865–1877.* Lincoln: University of Nebraska Press, 1998.
Perry, Dan. "The Indians' Friend, John H. Seger." *Chronicles of Oklahoma* 10, no. 4 (1932): 570–90.
Petter, Rodolphe. *English-Cheyenne Dictionary.* Kettle Falls, WA: Valdo Petter, 1915.
Pratt, R. H. *Battlefield and Classroom: Four Decades with the American Indian, 1867–1904.* New Haven, CT: Yale University Press, 1964.
Prucha, Francis Paul. *American Indian Policy in Crisis: Christian Reformers and the Indian, 1865–1900.* Norman: University of Oklahoma Press, 1976.
———. *The Churches and the Indian Schools, 1888–1912.* Lincoln: University of Nebraska Press, 1979.
———. *The Great Father: The United States Government and the American Indians.* Lincoln: University of Nebraska Press, 1995.
Rahn, Suzanne. "Young Eyewitnesses to History." In *St. Nicholas and Mary Mapes Dodge: The Legacy of a Children's Magazine Editor, 1873–1905*, edited by Susan R. Gannon, Suzanne Rahn, and Ruth Anne Thompson. New York: McFarland Books, 2004.
Rausch, David A., and Blair Schepp, eds. *Native American Voices.* Grand Rapids, MI: Baker Books, 1994.
Red Shirt, Delphine. *George Sword's Warrior Narratives: Compositional Processes in Lakota Oral Tradition.* Lincoln: University of Nebraska Press, 2016.
Rebhorn, Matthew. *Pioneer Performances: Staging the Frontier.* New York: Oxford University Press, 2012.
Reid, Joshua L. *The Sea Is My Country: The Maritime World of the Makahs.* New Haven, CT: Yale University Press, 2015.
Rensick, Brenden W. *Native but Foreign: Indigenous Immigrants and Refugees in the North American Borderlands.* College Station: Texas A&M University Press, 2018.
Renville, Mary Butler. *A Thrilling Narrative of Indian Captivity.* Lincoln: University of Nebraska Press, 2012.

Richardson, Heather Cox. *Wounded Knee: Party Politics and the Road to an American Massacre.* New York: Basic Books, 2010.

Riggs, Stephen R. *Dakota Grammar, Texts, and Ethnography.* Washington, DC: Government Printing Office, 1893.

Riley, Paul D. "The Battle of Massacre Canyon." *Nebraska History* 54 (1973): 220–49.

Robinson, Doanne. *A History of the Dakota or Sioux Indians.* South Dakota Historical Collections 2. Aberdeen, SD: News Printing, 1904.

———. *History of South Dakota, Personal Mention of Citizens of South Dakota.* Vol. 1. Logansport, IN: B. F. Bowen, 1904.

Rockwell, Stephen J. *Indian Affairs and the Administrative State in the Nineteenth Century.* New York: Cambridge University Press, 2010.

Ronda, James, and Carlos Schwantes. *The West the Railroads Made.* Seattle: University of Washington Press, 2008.

Royce Blaine, Martha. *Some Things Are Not Forgotten: A Pawnee Family Remembers.* Lincoln: University of Nebraska Press, 1997.

Ruby, Robert H., and John A. Brown. *Dreamer-Prophets of the Columbia Plateau: Smohalla and Skolaskin.* Norman: University of Oklahoma Press, 1989.

Ruuska, Alex. "Ghost Dancing and the Iron Horse: Surviving through Tradition and Technology." *Technology and Culture* 52 (July 2011): 574–97.

Rzeckzkowski, Frank. "The Crow Indians and the Bozeman Trail." *Montana: The Magazine of Western History* no. 4 (Winter 1999): 30–47.

———. *Uniting the Tribes: The Rise and Fall of Pan-Indian Community on the Crow Reservation.* Lawrence: University of Kansas Press, 2012.

Schusky, Ernest L. *The Forgotten Sioux: An Ethnohistory of the Lower Brule Reservation.* Chicago: Nelson-Hall, 1975.

Schwoch, James. *Wired into Nature: The Telegraph and the North American Frontier.* Urbana: University of Illinois Press, 2018.

Scott, Hugh Lenox. *Some Memoirs of a Soldier.* New York: Century, 1928.

Senier, Siobhan. *Voices of American Indian Assimilation and Resistance: Helen Hunt Jackson, Sarah Winnemucca, and Victoria Howard.* Norman: University of Oklahoma Press, 2001.

Shimkin, D. B. "Dynamics of Recent Wind River Shoshone History." *American Anthropologist* 44, no. 3 (1942): 451–62.

———. "Wind River Shoshone Sun Dance." *Anthropological Papers* 41, Smithsonian Institution, Bureau of American Ethnology Bulletin 151. Washington, DC: Government Printing Office, 1953.

Slotkin, James. *The Peyote Religion; A Study in Indian-White Relations.* Glencoe, IL: Free Press, 1956.

Smalling, Linda D. "From Satank to Joshua Given: The Assimilation of the Kiowas." MA Thesis, University of Central Oklahoma, 1994.

Smith, Anne M. *Ethnography of the Northern Utes.* Museum of New Mexico Papers in Anthropology 17. Santa Fe: Museum of New Mexico Press, 1974.

Smoak, Gregory E. *Ghost Dances and Identity.* Berkeley: University of California Press, 2006.

———. "The Mormons and the Ghost Dance of 1890." *South Dakota History* 16, no. 3 (1986): 269–94.

Spack, Ruth. *America's Second Tongue: American Indian Education and the Ownership of English, 1860–1900.* Lincoln: University of Nebraska Press, 2002.

Speroff, Leon. *Carlos Montezuma, M.D.: A Yavapai American Hero.* Portland, OR: Arnica Press, 2004.

Spier, Leslie. "The Sun Dance of the Plains Indians: Its Development and Diffusion." *Anthropological Papers of the American Museum of Natural History* 16 (1921): 451–527.

Sprague, Donovin A. *Images of America: The Rosebud Sioux.* Charleston, SC: Arcadia, 2005.

———. *Images of America: The Standing Rock Sioux.* Charleston, SC: Arcadia, 2005.

Stamm, Henry E. *People of Wind River: The Eastern Shoshones, 1825–1900.* Norman: University of Oklahoma Press, 1999.

Stands in Timber, John, and Margot Liberty. *Cheyenne Memories.* New Haven, CT: Yale University Press, 1998.

———. *A Cheyenne Voice: The Complete John Stands in Timber Interviews.* Norman: University of Oklahoma Press, 2013.

Stevenson, Winona. "Calling Badger and the Symbols of the Spirit Language: The Cree Origins of the Syllabic System." In *Native Historians Write Back: Decolonizing American Indian History*, edited by Susan A. Miller and James Riding In, 88–92. Lubbock: Texas Tech University Press, 2011.

Stewart Omer C. "Contemporary Document on Wovoka." *Ethnohistory* 4, no. 3 (1977): 219–22.

———. *Peyote Religion: A History.* Norman: University of Oklahoma Press, 1987.

Stoffle, Richard W., Lawrence Loendorf, Diane E. Austin, David B. Halmo, and Angelita Bulletts. "Ghost Dancing the Grand Canyon: Southern Paiute Rock Art, Ceremony, and Cultural Landscapes." *Current Anthropology* 41, no. 1 (2000): 11–38.

Stover, John F. *American Railroads.* Chicago: University of Chicago Press, 1961.

Swagerty, William. "Indian Trade in the Trans-Mississippi West to 1870." In *Handbook of North American Indians: History of Indian-White Relations*, edited by William C. Sturtevant. Washington, DC: Smithsonian Institution, 1988.

Szabo, Joyce M. *Art from Fort Marion: The Silberman Collection.* Norman: University of Oklahoma Press, 2007.

Tatonetti, Lisa. "Catholics, Carlisle, and Casting Stones: Richard Henry Pratt and the 1890 Ghost Dance." *Nineteenth-Century Contexts* 33, no. 3 (2011): 267–87.

Taylor, Alan. "Indian Lingua Francas." In *Language in the USA,* edited by Charles Ferguson and Shirley Brice Heath. New York: Cambridge University Press, 1981.

Thornton, Russell. *We Shall Live Again: The 1870 and 1890 Ghost Dance Movements as Demographic Revitalization.* Cambridge: Cambridge University Press, 1986.

Tong, Benson. *Susette LaFlesche Picotte, M.D.: Omaha Leader and Reformer.* Norman: University of Oklahoma Press, 1999.

Trafzer, Clifford E. *A Chemehuevi Song: The Resilience of a Southern Paiute Tribe.* Seattle: University of Washington Press, 2015.

Utley, Robert. *The Last Days of the Sioux Nation.* 2nd ed. New Haven, CT: Yale University Press, 2004.

———. "The Ordeal of Plenty Horses." *American Heritage* 26, no. 1 (1974): 15–19, 82–86.

van de Logt, Mark. *War Party in Blue: Pawnee Scouts in the U.S. Army.* Norman: University of Oklahoma Press, 2010.

Vander, Judith. *Shoshone Ghost Dance Religion: Poetry Songs and Great Basin Context.* Urbana: University of Illinois Press, 1997.

Vanderwerth, W. C., ed. *Indian Oratory: Famous Speeches by Noted Indian Chiefs.* Norman: University of Oklahoma Press, 1971.

Vestal, Stanley. *Champion of the Sioux.* Norman: University of Oklahoma Press, 1987.

———. *New Sources of Indian History, 1850–1891.* Norman: University of Oklahoma Press, 1934.

Victor, Frances Fuller. *Our Centennial Indian War and the Life of General Custer.* Norman: University of Oklahoma Press, 2011.

Vizenor, Gerald Robert. *The People Named the Chippewa: Narrative Histories.* Minneapolis: University of Minnesota Press, 1984.

Waite, Thornton. *The Railroad at Pocatello.* Charleston, SC: Arcadia, 2012.

Walker, James R. *Lakota Belief and Ritual.* Edited by Raymond J. DeMallie and Elaine A. Jahner. Lincoln: University of Nebraska Press, 1980.

———. "The Sun Dance and Other Ceremonies of the Oglala Division of the Teton Dakota." *Anthropological Papers of the American Museum of Natural History* 16, no. 2 (1917): 55–221.

Walker, Willard. "Native American Writing Systems." In *Language in the USA,* edited by Charles A. Ferguson and Shirley Brice Heath. New York: Cambridge University Press, 1981.

———. "The Winnebago Syllabary and the Generative Model." *Anthropological Linguistics* 16, no. 8 (1974): 393–414.
Wallace, Anthony. "Revitalization Movements." *American Anthropologist* 58 (1956): 264–81.
Warren, Louis. *God's Red Son: The Ghost Dance Religion and the Making of Modern America.* New York: Basic Books, 2017.
Watson, Elmo. "The Last Indian War, 1890–91: A Study of Newspaper Jingoism." *Journalism Quarterly* 20 (1943), 205–19.
Webb, H. G. "The Omaha Dance of the Oglalas October 2, 1894." Unpublished. Held in National Anthropological Archives. NAA MS 1394-B.
West, Elliott, *The Last Indian War: The Nez Perce Story.* New York: Oxford University Press, 2009.
———. "Listen Up: Hearing the Unheard in Western History." In *The Essential West: Collected Essays.* Norman: University of Oklahoma Press, 2012.
White, Eugene E. *Service on the Indian Reservations: Experiences of a Special Indian Agent While Inspecting Agencies and Serving as Agent for Various Tribes.* Little Rock: Diploma Press, Arkansas Democrat Company, 1893.
White, Richard. *It's Your Misfortune and None My Own: A New History of the American West.* Norman: University of Oklahoma Press, 1991.
———. *Railroaded: The Transcontinentals and the Making of Modern America.* New York: W. W. Norton, 2011.
———. "Using the Past: History and Native American Studies." In *Studying Native America*, edited by Russell Thornton. Madison: University of Wisconsin Press, 1999.
———. "The Winning of the West: The Expansion of the Western Sioux in the Eighteenth and Nineteenth Centuries." *Journal of American History* 65 (Sept. 1978) 319–43.
White Hat, Albert. *Reading and Writing the Lakota Language.* Edited by Jael Kampfe. Salt Lake City: University of Utah Press, 1999.
Wilson, Raymond. *Ohiyesa: Charles Eastman, Santee Sioux.* Urbana: University of Illinois Press, 1983.
Wissler, Clark. "General Discussion of Shamanistic and Dancing Societies." *American Museum of Natural History Anthropological Paper* 11, no. 12 (1916).
———. "General Discussion of Shamanistic and Dancing Societies." *Anthropological Papers of the American Museum of Natural History* 11, no. 12 (1916).
———. *Indian Cavalcade or Life on the Old-Time Indian Reservation.* New York: Sheridan House, 1938.
Wyss, Hilary. *Writing Indians: Literacy, Christianity, and Native Community in Early America.* Amherst: University of Massachusetts Press, 2000.

Young, Gloria A., and Erik D. Gooding. "Celebrations and Giveaways." In *Handbook of North American Indians*, vol. 13, edited by William C. Sturtevant. Washington, DC: Smithsonian Institution, 2001.

———. "Intertribal Religious Movements." In *Handbook of North American Indians*, vol. 13, edited by William C. Sturtevant, 996–1010. Washington, DC: Smithsonian Institution, 2001.

———. "Powwow Power: Perspectives on Historic and Contemporary Intertribalism," PhD diss., Indiana University, 1981.

Youngkin, S. Douglas. "'Hostile and Friendly': The 'Pygmalion Effect' at Cheyenne River Agency, 1873–1887." *South Dakota History* 7 (1977): 402–21.

Zanjani, Sally S. "The Indian Massacre That Never Happened." *Nevada Historical Quarterly* 31 (1988): 119–129.

———. *Sarah Winnemucca*. Lincoln: University of Nebraska Press, 2001.

Index

References to illustrations appear in italic type.

Absarokas. *See* Crows
Adams, Charles, 172–73, *174*, *175*, *176–77*, 223–24, *225*, 317n49
Adams, David Wallace, 9
Afraid of Bear (Lakota), 218
Afraid of Bears (Kiowa), 227, 241
"agency" ("Indian agency"; term), 253n31
Ahern, George, 37
Allotment Act of 1887. *See* Dawes Act (Severalty Act)
American Horse (Lakota), 35, 36, 37–38, 155, 202, 203, 218, 271n137; Ghost Dance, 155, 202; Wind River visit, 100
Anderson, W. W., 105, 127–28
Apaches: Hampton Institute, 30; prisoners, 265n33; schools, 25; travel and intertribal visits, 98, 100, 125; treaties, 24. *See also* Plains Apaches
Apiatan (Wooden Lance; Kiowa), *175*, 222–27, *232*, 241, 317n49
Apsáalookes. *See* Crows
Arapaho language, 19, 33
Arapahos, 3, 42; Crow relations, 20; Ghost Dance, 122, 149, 150; intertribal visits, 110, 150, 153, 319n98; Pawnee relations, 103; POWs, 29; Sun Dance, 123, 132, 133. *See also* Northern Arapahos; Southern Arapahos
Arikaras, 69; intertribal visits, 104; Lakota relations, 67, 69, 83, 184; Sioux relations, 83, 86
Armstrong, Samuel C., 53, 255n70
Army, US. *See* US Army
Ashley, Charles, 148, *174*, *175*, *177*, *178*, *226*, 227, 230

Ashley, Thomas, 202
assimilation, 17–18, 26–30, 63, 101
Assiniboines, 69, 86; Ghost Dance, 187, 239; intertribal visits, 87, 106; Sun Dance, 132
Atkins, J. D., 27

Bad Belly (Crow), 183, 236
Bad Water in Rump (Lakota), 214–15
Bannocks: free-living, 105; Ghost Dance, 143, 144–46, 155, 157; intertribal visits and meeting places, 93, 101, 109, 145–46, 157, 224, 228, 301n18; Nevada press on, 213; railroad use, 92; Wovoka visit and gifts, 224, 236–37. *See also* Fort Hall Reservation
Bannock War, 61
Battey, Thomas, 89, 91
Battle of Massacre Canyon, 87, 267n64
Beard, Dewey (Iron Hail), 208
Bear's Heart, James, *40*
Bear Thunder (Lakota), 116
Beaulieu, Theodore Hudon, 39
Bettelyoun, E. G., 205
Bible, 23, 26, 203
Big Beaver (Cheyenne), 156, 199–200
Big Bow (Kiowa), 100, 135, 245
Big Foot (Spotted Elk; Lakota), 181, 189, 207–8, 209, 218
Big Head (Lakota), 135
Big Road, Newton, 48
Big Road (Lakota), 155, 205, 207–8, 211
Big Tree (Kiowa), 176, 206, 241
Big Turkey (Lakota), 204, 268n82, 311n65, 323n18

bison: Lakotas and, 24, 69, 83, 87;
  Northern Cheyennes and, 68;
  population demise, 41, 42, 83, 87, 91,
  132, 133, 155, predicted return of, 122,
  146, 153, 154–55, 161, 172–73, 175;
  successful hunts, 98
Black Coal (Arapaho), 83, 201, 222, 223,
  287n48
Black Coyote (Arapaho), 133, 147, 148,
  149, 226, 228–29, 294n40
Blackfeet, 86–87, 275n25, 307n127;
  Ghost Dance, 157, 186–87;
  pictography, 19
Blackfeet Reservation, 86–87, 119;
  literacy, 31, 32; population, 10
Blackfoot Confederacy, 86
Black Hills, US taking of, 58, 188
Black Kettle (Cheyenne), 41–42
Black Sharp Nose, 229
Blue Tomahawk (Lakota), 55
boarding schools, 28–31, 51–56;
  Cheyenne River, 60, 210; Ghost
  Dance and, 232, 233; Nevada, 142;
  newspapers, 38, 54, 227; railroad travel
  and, 92; sexual abuse, 46. *See also*
  names of individual schools
Bobtail (Cheyenne), 53, 133
Bobtail Horse (Cheyenne), 310n39
Bollard, James, 243–44
Boynton, Paul, 231–33
Brave Bull (Lakota), 53, 73
Brice, James, 42
Briscoe, E. P., 105
Brooke, John, 185, 307n119, 319n90
Brulé Lakotas, 24, 28, 63, 70; Crow
  relations, 119–20; Ghost Dance, 153,
  154, 188, 190, 201; Sun Dance, 129,
  134–35; "troubles" of 1890, 208; visits
  and travel restrictions, 107, 109; after
  Wounded Knee Massacre, 218, 219.
  See also Rosebud Reservation
Buckskin Charley (Ute), 63, 83, 196
buffalo. *See* bison
Buffalo Bill's Wild West, 168, 267n62
Buffalo Hump (Cheyenne), 131
Bull Ghost (Tatankawangi), 285n10
Bull Head (Lakota), 206, 312n70

Caddo language, 19
Caddos, 25, 133, 174, 178, 216, 226, 241
Callahan, Sophia Alice, 195
calumets. *See* pipes, ceremonial
camas, 93
Campbell, Walter Stanley (Stanley
  Vestal), 37
Canada, 69; Blackfoot Confederacy, 87;
  Cree refugees from, 132; Ghost Dance
  transmittal, 184, 239; Lakotas, 61–62;
  Métis, 65, 69; Nez Perces, 61–62
C&C Railroad. *See* Carson & Colorado
  (C&C) Railroad
Captain Jim (Paiute), 79, 81
Captain Sam (Shoshone), 88
Carlisle Indian Industrial School, 30,
  36, 134, 232, 233; correspondence, 51,
  52–53, 54, 55; newspaper, 38; visits, 92
Carroll, Henry, 164, 172
Carson & Colorado (C&C) Railroad, 92,
  94, 145, 156, 228, 244, 277n71
Catholic Church, 34, 174; Dakota-
  language newspaper, 38; schools, 25
censorship and seizure of mail, 6, 48, 54,
  172–74, 190, 215, 218, 265n33
Central Pacific Railroad, 92, 93–94, 145,
  156, 228, 277–78n74
Charging Eagle (Lakota), 64
Chasing Crane (Lakota), 154
Chemehuevis, 25, 145
Cheyenne-Arapaho Reservation, 4, 7,
  20, 60; Boynton, 232; Ghost Dance,
  147, 148, 149, 165, 173, 174, 177, 178,
  221; intertribal dancing, 127, 134;
  intertribal visits, 99, 110, 115, 121,
  148, 227; languages, 19; literacy,
  25, 32; newspapers, 39; Poncas, 115;
  population, 10; railroads and, 96
Cheyenne language, 19, 33
Cheyenne River Reservation, 29, 35, 37,
  59–60, 64, 121, 170; Big Foot camp,
  207; dancing, 126; formation, 63; Ghost
  Dance, 154, 155, 171, 180–84 *passim*,
  188, 189, 207, 210; intertribal councils,
  114; intertribal visits, 84, 104, 110, 116,
  234; literacy, 32, 33; population, 10;
  raids, 86; travel restrictions, 99

Cheyennes, 3, 41–42; correspondence, 50, 53; Ghost Dance, 150; intertribal dancing, 130–31; intertribal visits, 99, 100, 107, 150; POWs, 29; railroad use, 96; Sun Dance, 133; Wyoming stockmen's fear of, 101. *See also* Northern Cheyennes; Southern Cheyennes

Cheyenne Transporter, 39

Christianity, 23, 113, 127, 195, 230, 231; in peyotism, 240. *See also* Bible; Catholic Church; Christian missionaries

Christian missionaries, 21–22, 23, 34, 253n28; Cheyenne-Arapaho Reservation, 232; Native-language instruction, 27; newspapers, 38, 39, 203; Quaker, 25; Santee Reservation, 38; Standing Rock, 37; Yankton Reservation, 26. *See also* mission schools

Cleveland, William, 217–18

Cloud Chief (Southern Cheyenne), 36, 48

Collins, Mary, 37

Comanche language, 19

Comanches, 4, 25, 42; Ghost Dance, 176, 178, 198; intertribal dancing, 125; intertribal visits, 86, 97, 110; Lakota language and, 18; POWs, 20, 29; Pueblo relations, 244; Sun Dance, 123; treaties, 24. *See also* Kiowa, Comanche, and Wichita Reservation

concentration camps, 61

Congress, US. *See* US Congress

Cooper, J. A., 188, 189

Courtis, William C., 209, 233–34

courts, 35, 39, 60, 73, 115, 288n65; tribal, 124, 288n65

Cowen, D. O., 117

Cozad, Below (Belo), 20–21

Crazy Bear (Lakota), 110, 183

Crees, 21, 69. *See also* Plains Crees

Crook Commission (1889), 121

Crow Creek Reservation, 25, 63; correspondence, 53, 64, 71; dancing, 127, 135; Ghost Dance, 188, 201; intertribal visits, 84, 105, 220, 285n10,

302n26; literacy, 32, 33; mission school, 51; population, 10; post office, 44

Crow Dance (Bird Dance), 136

Crow Dog (Lakota), 56, 187–88, 208

Crow Feather (Lakota), 59–60, 164

Crow Reservation: intertribal visits, 84, 87, 99, 104, 105, 110, 117–19, 181, 183; literacy, 32; population, 10; railroads and, 96

Crows, 20, 86, 118–20, 250n12; Dawes Act and, 118–19; Ghost Dance, 122, 182; intertribal dancing, 131; intertribal visits, 87, 93, 104, 105, 120, 153; Lakota relations, 20, 83, 104, 110, 118–20, 153, 181–83, 218, 236; railroad use, 93, 96; Sun Dance, 123; Wyoming stockmen's fear of, 101

Curley, Smith, 233

Dakota language, 23, 33–34, 42; in correspondence, 54, 57–58, *59*, 127, 163, 217, 242; newspapers, 38, 162, 203

Dakotas (people), 23, 65, 71; Ghost Dance, 201; intertribal visits, 103, 106; literacy, 33; pictography, 19; Sun Dance, 123. *See also* Crow Creek Reservation; Eastern Dakotas; Standing Rock Reservation; Western Dakotas

dances and dancing, 6, 136, 285n1; intertribal, 6, 81, 93, 102, 107, 113, 121–37, 288–89n81. *See also* Ghost Dance; Omaha Dance (Grass Dance); Paiute Round Dance; Sun Dance

Dátekâñ (Kiowa). *See* Pá-tépté (Kiowa)

Davis, Wirt, 173, 177

Dawes, Henry E. (school superintendent), 46

Dawes, Henry L. (politician), 35

Dawes Act (Severalty Act), 35, 39, 46, 70, 118–19, 120, 243

Dawes Sioux Bill (1884–88), 70, 118, 121, 171, 271n135

Day, George, 238

Daylight, John (Masse Hadjo), 195

Deaf Bull (Crow), 120

350 | Index

Deere, James, 226
Delaware language, 19
Delawares, 25, 216
DeMallie, Raymond J., 38, 160
Devil's Lake (Spirit Lake) Reservation, 31, 60; intertribal visits, 84, 98, 99, 108, 122; literacy, 32, 33; population, 10
Diné (Navajos). *See* Navajos
diseases, communicable, 68, 154, 280n119
Dixon, A. P., 188
Dorsey, J. Owen, 72, 132
Duck Valley Reservation. *See* Western Shoshone Reservation (Duck Valley)
Dumont, Gabriel, 69
Dyer, Ed, 145, 236, 237, 321n124

Eastern Dakotas, 33. *See also* Santee and Flandreau Agency; Santees; Sisseton Reservation; Sissetons; Wahpetons
Eastman, Charles, 197
Eastman, Elaine Goodale. *See* Goodale, Elaine
Edson, Casper, 227–30, *232*, 233
English language, 39–40, 193; forced use (English-only policy), 27, 54; learning, 23, 26–27, 29, 31, 53–54, 320n105; as lingua franca, 4, 50, 88; literacy statistics, 33–34; Wichitas, 25. *See also* literacy
espionage, 235–36, 237
Etokeah (Cheyenne and Lakota). *See* Hump (Cheyenne and Lakota)
Evans, James, 21–22
"exterminate the Indian within," 232, 233

farming, 68, 161, 164, 169, 180
Fast Horse (Lakota), 46, 130
Fast Thunder (Lakota), 202, 306n101
fear of Natives, 235; in agents, 185–86; among white settlers, 101, 119, 125, 171, 179, 194, 207, 235, 279n102
Feather-in-the-Ear (Dakota), 42–43, 49, 64, 68, 97, 111
Fire Thunder, Edgar, 194
Fire Thunder (Lakota), 155

Fisher, S. G., 228
Fletcher, Alice C., 22, 129, 152, 234–35
forged letters and passes, 110
Fort Assiniboine (Mont.), 132, 187
Fort Belknap Reservation, 69; Ghost Dance, 187; intertribal visits, 84, 87, 105, 132, 182, 186–87; literacy, 32; population, 10; railroads and, 96
Fort Bennett, 60, 186
Fort Berthold Reservation, 63–64, 69, 86; correspondence, 48, 67, 197–98; Ghost Dance, 184, 189; intertribal visits, 84, 86, 104, 105, 106, 108, 121, 182; literacy, 32; population, 10; railroads and, 96
Fort Bridger, 156
Fort Custer, 99, 183
Fort Hall Reservation, 83, 92, 104, 105, 243–44; Apiatan visits, 223, 224; Ghost Dance, 144–45, 155, 156, 160, 180, 237; intertribal visits, 84, 102, 109, 122, 180, 227, 228, 237; literacy, 32; population, 10; railroads and, 92, 93, 96, 144, 145
Fort Keogh, 43, 67, 68; intertribal visits, 84, 99, 100, 111
Fort Laramie Treaty (1851; Horse Creek Treaty), 24
Fort Laramie Treaty (1868), 118
Fort Marion, 20, 29, 30, 252n8, 255–56n70, 267n59
Fort Meade (S.Dak.), 186, 219
Fort Peck Reservation, 64; Ghost Dance, 161; intertribal visits, 84, 104, 106, 110, 117; literacy, 32, 33; population, 10; Sun Dance, 132
Fort Randall, 203
Fort Reno, 39, 148, 259n145, 319n86
Fort Robinson, 67, 185
Fort Sill, 90, 177, 260n145
Fort Simcoe, 61
Fort Totten, 60
Fort Washakie, 155, 169, 180
Fort Yates, 70, 206
Fosher, John, 148, 223–24
Foxes (Meskwakis), 22, 67, 103, 196, 252n17. *See also* Sac and Fox Reservations

French colonists, 18, 23, 165, 184
fur trade, 19–20, 23

Gall (Lakota), 69, 126, 207
Gallagher, H. D., 107, 109, 121, 122, 130–31, 185; Ghost Dance, 164–65, 170
gambling, 103
Gates, Merril, 231
General Allotment Act of 1887. *See* Dawes Act (Severalty Act)
Genoa Indian Industrial School, 38, 55, 173
Ghost Dance, 135–37; 1870 movement, 142, 144, 153; intertribal news dissemination, 141–68; Lakota "troubles" of 1890, 196, 197, 198, 201–12; Native correspondence, 141–42, 147–74, 183, 189–90, 195–215 *passim*, 219–25 *passim*, 229–30, 236–39 *passim*, 243–44; Native correspondence map, 167; Native critics, 221–27; peyotism and, 323n10; press coverage, 192–97, 198–99, 213; suppression attempts, 169–212; US Army and, 171–72, 176–77, 184–86, 187, 190, 221, 226–27; after Wounded Knee Massacre, 213–38, 315n20
Given, Joshua, 176, 181
Goodale, Elaine, 154–55, 203
Good Thunder (Lakota), 153, 155, 164, 181, 297n86, 306n111
Good Voice (Lakota), 204
government schools, 7, 17–18, 26, 27, 28, 141
Grant, Ulysses, 26, 27, 91
Grass, John, 110, 120, 207
Grasshopper (Cheyenne), 130–32
Gray Eagle (Lakota), 111, 204, 311n64
Great Lakes Algonquian Syllabary (Western Great Lakes Syllabary), 22
Great Plains Sign Language (Plains Indian Sign Language), 18, 20, 88–89
Great Sioux Reservation, 63, 73
Great Sioux War, 20, 58, 63, 69, 100, 118
Grinnell, George Bird, 6–7, 87, 141, 187

Gros Ventres, 69, 86, 197–98; Ghost Dance, 187; intertribal visits, 87, 96, 98, 104, 186
Grouard, Frank, 220

Half Iron, John, 48, 81, 209
Hampton Institute, 30, 34–35, *40*, 232; correspondence, 51, 53–54, 56, 166; Ghost Dance, 166, 234; newspapers, 38; prison-school pipeline, 255–56n70; visits, 92
Hanacha-Thiak (Arapaho). *See* Sitting Bull (Hanacha-Thiak; Arapaho)
Harney, William S., 208, 313n87
Harrison, Benjamin, 185, 306n117; letters to, 157, 197–98, 208, 220, 221
Haskell Institute, 52, 55, 166, 199, 222
Haworth, J. M., 99
Hayes, Rutherford B., 34, 40
He Dog (Lakota), 134, 202, 208, 217–18
Hidatsas, 67, 83, 86, 106, 184. *See also* Fort Berthold Reservation
High Chief (Cheyenne), 42
High Chief (Lakota), 96
Higheagle, Robert P., 166
High Hawk (Lakota), 181, 305n89
High Wolf (Lakota), 96, 175
Hinman, S. D., 23–24
Hittman, Michael, 161
Ho-Chunk language (Hoocąk), 22
Ho-Chunks (Winnebagos): Ghost Dance, 164; intertribal dancing, 126, 130; intertribal visits, 103; written language, 22. *See also* Winnebago Reservation
Hollow Horn Bear (Lakota), 109, 202
Hualapais, 143, 145, 179
Hultkranz, Åke, 144
Hump (Cheyenne and Lakota), 67, 181, 184, 189, 207
hunger, 46, 67, 133, 154, 202, 234, 306n101
Hunkpapa Lakotas, 56, 62, 63, 67, 86, 121, 204. *See also* Sitting Bull (Lakota); Standing Rock Reservation
Hurst, Joseph Henry, 210
Hyde, Charles L., 170, 300–301n8

Iapi Oaye, 38, 162, 203
Ignacio (Ute), 63, 83, 196
immigration, European, 27
Indian Helper, 38, 54, 227
Indian police. *See* police
Indian Rights Association, 81, 209, 217, 218, 234, 271n135
Indian schools. *See* schools
Industrious, Lawrence (Blihica), 215, 315n12
Iowas, 23, 178, 201
Iron Hail (Dewey Beard; Lakota), 208
Isadawah (Wichita), 66–67

jailing and imprisonment of Natives. *See* prisons and prisoners
Janis, Nettie, 165–66, 299n122
Jesuit missionaries, 23, 253n28
Jesus Christ: alleged appearances, visits, etc., 150, 163, 165, 177, 227
Johnston, W. H., 228
Junkin, William, 149, 175–76, 177

Kainais (Bloods), 87
Kichais (Keechis), 35, 216
Kickapoos, 56, 68, 150, 178
Kicking Bear (Lakota), 154, 155, 180–81, 207, 215, 233, 301n26, 304n84; brother, 306n112; influence in Canada, 239; letters, 163; Northern Arapaho relations, 180–81; Shoshone relations, 243; with Young Man Afraid, *182*
Kicking Bird (Kiowa), 25, 90
Kills Swimming, John (Nuwan Kte or Anuwakte), 242
"kill the Indian within," 232, 233
Kiowa, Comanche, and Wichita Reservation: Ghost Dance, 149, 166–67, 172–75, 177–79, 198, 216, 226, 238, 241; intertribal visits, 84, 100; languages, 4, 19; literacy, 32; name, 250n11; newspaper reading, 196–97; population, 10; travel policy, 99
Kiowa Agency, 25, 52, 177. *See also* Kiowa, Comanche, and Wichita Reservation
Kiowa language, 19, 33, 88

Kiowas, 41, 42; boarding school students, 51–52; correspondence, 52, 173; Crow Dance, 136; Ghost Dance, 149, 173, 175–77, 178, 181, 222–27, 238, 241; intertribal dancing, 125, 132–34, 136, 174, 241; intertribal visits, 86, 88–91, 100, 103, 110, 175, 245; Omaha Dance, 135; peyotism, 241; pictography, 19, 20–21; POWs, 20, 29; Pueblo relations, 244; sign language use, 88–89; Sun Dance, 123, 124, 128, 132–34, 238; treaties, 24; Ute relations, 245. *See also* Kiowa, Comanche, and Wichita Reservation
Klamath Reservation, 101
Kyle, S.Dak., 44

Lake Mohonk Conference (1891), 231
Lakota language, 18, 271n135
Lakotas, 3, 24, 25, 34–40; bands/distinctions, 63, 269n92; Canada, 61–62; Crow relations, 20, 83, 104, 110, 118–20, 153, 181–83, 218, 236; Dakota language literacy, 33; Ghost Dance, 147, 154, 155, 163–65, 170–75 *passim*, 180, 181, 183, 187–90, 201–2; Great Sioux War, 58, 63; intertribal councils, 114; intertribal dancing, 129–30, 131; intertribal visits, 87, 88, 102–10 *passim*, 116–19, 122, 125, 147, 155, 214, 220; mail use and correspondence, 42–44, 46, 48, 49, 53, 55, 57–61, 65–71; Mandan relations, 67, 83, 106, 184; Northern Cheyenne relations, 67–68; old enemies, 67, 86, 87, 106; Omaha Dance, 136–37; Pawnee relations, 58; pictography, 19; press coverage, 196; raiding and warfare, 83; schooling, 25, 53; Shoshone relations, 82, 83, 243–44; Sun Dance, 129–30; "troubles" of 1890, 196, 197, 198, 201–12; Washakie view, 222; Wovoka and, 150, 224; writing, 24. *See also* Brulé Lakotas; Hunkpapa Lakotas; Miniconjou Lakotas; *names of reservations*; Oglala Lakotas; Sans Arc Lakotas; Sihásapa Lakotas
Landy, Edwin, 37–38

Landy, James, 37–38, 203
languages, common. *See* lingua francas
languages, pidgin, 18
languages, written. *See* literacy
Lawyer, Archie, 62
Left Hand (the elder, ca. 1820s–64; Niwot), 294n37
Left Hand (ca. 1840–1911; Arapaho), 25, 35, 147, 152, 294n37
Left Hand, Grant, 229, 230, 233, 236
Lenapes. *See* Delawares
Like-the-Bear (Lakota), 35
lingua francas, 4, 18, 50, 88
literacy, 3, 4, 17–51, 54, 110, 141, 193, 250–51n21, 320n105
Little Chief (Arapaho), 17
Little Chief (Assiniboine), 105
Little Chief (Cheyenne), 133, 147
Little Eagle (Lakota), 134–35
Little Man (Cheyenne), 20, *21*
Little Raven (Arapaho), 25, 227–28
Little Soldier (Lakota), 204, 311n64
Little Thunder (Lakota), 217
Little Wolf (Arapaho), 42
Little Wound (Lakota), 36, 37, 81, 83, 121–22, 128; Ghost Dance, 155, 185, 197, 204–5; Lakota "troubles" of 1890, 204–5, 211–12; press relations, 194; on Sun Dance, 129, 204
Locke, Frank, 54, 194
Lone Dog, John, 117, 120
Lone Wolf (Kiowa), 133
Long Feather (Lakota), 117
Low Dog (Lakota), 181, 301n26
Lower Brule Reservation, 31, 218; dancing, 127; Ghost Dance, 188, 201; intertribal visits, 84, 105, 110; literacy, 32, 33; post office, 44
Ludlow, Helen, *40*

Maddra, Sam, 162
mail censorship. *See* censorship and seizure of mail
mail service. *See* US Postal Service
Mandans, 19–20, 48, 197–98; intertribal visits, 98, 104, 106; Lakota relations, 67, 83, 106, 184

Mantcu-nanba (Omaha), 42–43, 68
Many Eagles (Lakota), 215
maps, *12*, *80*, *151*, *167*
Marcisco (Ute), 83
Maroukis, Thomas C., 323n10
Massacre Canyon, Battle of, 87, 267n64
Masse Hadjo (John Daylight), 195
Mayhugh, John, 179, 220, 316n35
McChesney, Charles, 170, 171
McGillycuddy, Valentine, 235
McLaughlin, James, 125–26, 181, 183, 190, 221; awareness of Native literacy, 193; mail censorship and seizure, 173–74, 215; Sitting Bull relations, 205–6, 305n87, 312n74
medicine dolls, 124
Medicine Lodge Treaty, 24, 253n30
Meserve, Charles, 222, 310n40
Meskwakis. *See* Foxes (Meskwakis)
"Messiah." *See* Wovoka (Jack Wilson)
Métis, 65–66, 69
Miles, Nelson, 69, 193
Mille Lacs Band of Ojibwe, 127
Miniconjou Lakotas, 63, 154, 181, 187; Wounded Knee Massacre, 194, 207–10
mission schools, 23, 26, 27, 51
Missourias, 178
Mooney, James, 86, 136, 144–45, 222, 230; Kiowas, 149, 225, 226, 238; "Messiah Letter" and, 229; translation of Boynton song, 232–33; view of Apiatan, 223; Wind River, 237; on Wovoka, 142–43
Morgan, Thomas, 175, 176, 179, 185, 233; on education, 234; letters to, 170, 193, 197, 202, 216, 221
Mount Vernon Barracks (Ala.), 265n33
Murie, James, 200–201, 310n44

Najinhkte, Luke, 166, 190
Narcelle, Narcisse, 184, 189, 207
Natchez. *See* Winnemucca, Natchez
Native American Church, 240, 241
Native-language newspapers, 38, 162, 203
Navajos, 53; intertribal visits and travel, 86, 103, 106; population, 10; railroad use, 94–95, 106; reservation borders, 110

Nevada Reservation, 52, 224, 237; intertribal visits, 85, 224; literacy, 32; population, 10. See also Pyramid Lake Reservation; Walker River Reservation
newspapers. See press
Nez Perce Reservation: Ghost Dance news, 196; intertribal visits, 120, 182; literacy, 32, 33; population, 10; railroads and, 96
Nez Perces, 23, 61–62, 93, 196
Nez Perce War, 61
No Flesh (Lakota), 36, 73
nomad racial stereotype, 104, 106, 112
North, Henry Dawson (Henry Shave Head), 199, 222
Northern Arapahos, 7, 25, 50, 83, 201; Ghost Dance, 146, 147, 148, 180, 181; intertribal visits, 100, 146, 153–54, 180, 181. See also Wind River Reservation
Northern Cheyennes, 7, 25, 46, 50, 86, 130–33, 200; correspondence, 60, 148, 202; Crow relations, 119, 120; Ghost Dance, 147, 148, 149, 153, 158, 171, 172, 180, 199, 202; Great Sioux War, 58; Indian Territory, 60; intertribal dancing, 125, 180; intertribal visits, 99, 100, 107, 108, 115, 120, 180; Lakota relations, 67–68; Sun Dance, 130. See also Tongue River Reservation
Northern Pacific Railway, 92, 93, 96
Northern Paiutes, 61. See also Wovoka (Jack Wilson)
Northern Shoshones, 146
Northern Utes, 62–63, 83–84, 123–24, 196–97, 245, 268–69n85; Ghost Dance, 153; Lakota relations, 81–82; Wovoka investigation, 143. See also Uintah and Ouray Reservation; Uncompahgre Utes
No Water (Lakota), 71, 207–8, 217–18

off-reservation boarding schools. See boarding schools
Oglala Lakotas, 2, 24, 35, 118; Ghost Dance, 153, 154–55, 172; ghost lodge rites, 128; Sun Dance, 129; Ute relations, 81–83, 123; Wind River visit, 305n97. See also Pine Ridge Reservation
Ojibwe language, 18, 111, 127
Ojibwes (Chippewas), 39, 98, 111; intertribal dancing, 127, 288–89n81. See also White Earth Reservation
Omaha Dance (Grass Dance), 107, 125–26, 135–36, 209
Omaha language, 88
Omaha Reservation: literacy, 32, 33; population, 11
Omahas, 23, 40–41, 42, 45, 48; correspondence, 57, 62, 64–65, 68–69, 71–72, 88; Ghost Dance, 164; intertribal visits, 88, 103, 130; Omaha Dance, 135; smallpox, 68–69. See also Omaha Reservation
Opler, Marvin, 124
Osages, 23, 66–67, 103, 114, 123, 124
Ostler, Jeffrey, 28, 37, 181, 183
Otoes, 23, 103, 136. See also Ponca, Pawnee, and Otoe Reservation

Paiute language, 160
Paiute Round Dance, 143, 161
Paiutes, 7, 52, 79, 81, 160; farming, 161; Ghost Dance, 143–44, 145, 156, 157; intertribal meeting places, 93; intertribal visits, 86, 87–88, 102, 103, 109, 179, 224; Kiowa relations, 224; Nevada press on, 213; railroad use, 92–94, 95, 145; Ute relations, 153; Western Shoshone Reservation, 104, 105. See also Northern Paiutes
Palmer, Perain, 184–85, 189
pan-Indian views, 13, 79, 245; Young Man Afraid, 118, 137
Parker, Quanah, 198
Pá-tépté (Kiowa), 133, 135, 150
Pawnee language, 88
Pawnee Reservation, 59, 90, 91, 97, 114, 127, 200, 217. See also Ponca, Pawnee, and Otoe Reservation
Pawnees, 7, 42, 58–59, 207; advice to Poncas, 114; Ghost Dance, 178–79, 200–201, 216, 217; intertribal dancing,

127, 133; intertribal visits, 86–91, 103, 124; Lakota relations, 83; sign language use, 88–89. *See also* Pawnee Reservation; Ponca, Pawnee, and Otoe Reservation

Penny, Charles, 218–19, 220, 236

peyotism, 21, 232, 240–41, 323n10

Picket Pin, Charles (Red Cow or Spotted Horse; Oglala Lakota), 57–58, 267n62

pictography, 19–20, 173

Pine Ridge Reservation, 62; Apiatan visit, 223; Carlisle students, 30; Cheyennes, 67–68, 107, 108; correspondence, 46, 52, 54, 60, 64, 67–68, 70; council composition, 155; dancing, 129–30; drunken agency employees, 46; exodus of 1890, 189; "forlorn . . . concentration camp," 2; formation, 63; Ghost Dance, 83, 149, 153, 155, 163–75 *passim*, 180–85, 188, 202, 219–20, 235, 243, 315n20; intertribal dancing, 125, 129, 130–31, 175; intertribal visits, 99, 107–11, 115–21 *passim*, 155, 188, 219; intertribal visits (Arapahos), 100, 121, 122, 155, 180; intertribal visits (Cheyennes), 100, 108, 110, 115, 131; intertribal visits (Crows), 87, 99, 110, 182, 183, 303–4n72; intertribal visits (Kiowas), 223; intertribal visits (Ojibwes), 111; intertribal visits (Pawnees), 87; intertribal visits (Shoshones), 100, 121, 153, 243; intertribal visits (statistics), 84–85; intertribal visits (Utes), 102; literacy, 32, 33–34, 37; mail service, 43, 44; murder of white men (1893), 235; Omaha Dance, 135–36, 209; police, 68, 130, 134, 154, 164, 180–81, 202, 303n72; population, 11; schools, 28, 29; Tongue River relations, 108, 283n183; "troubles" of 1890, 204, 205, 207–10, 212, 218, 314n101; typical correspondence, 242; Ute visits, 83; after Wounded Knee Massacre, 215, 217, 218, 219, 221, 236; Young Man Afraid, 42, 43, 117, *182*, 218, 299n115. *See also* Wounded Knee Massacre

pipes, ceremonial, 42, 64

Plains Apaches, 176, 177, 178, 240, 244

Plains Crees, 86, 132, 239

Plains Indian Sign Language. *See* Great Plains Sign Language (Plains Indian Sign Language)

Plenty Eagles (Many Eagles; Lakota), 215

Plumb, William, 179–80

police, 183; Cheyenne-Arapaho, 110, 147, 227, 264–65n29, 319n85; Cheyenne River, 116, 184, 189, 221; Kiowa, Comanche, and Wichita, 226–27, 303n72; Pine Ridge, 68, 130, 134, 154, 164, 180–81, 202, 303n72; Ponca, Pawnee, and Otoe, 216; Rosebud, 107, 117, 121, 135; Standing Rock, 181

Ponca, Pawnee, and Otoe Reservation, 51, 61; dancing, 127; Ghost Dance, 200–201, 216; intertribal visits, 85, 175; literacy, 32; population, 11

Poncas, 42; correspondence, 48, 53, 57, 68–69, 71–72; Crow Dance, 136; forced removal, 114–15; Ghost Dance, 178; intertribal dancing, 125, 130; intertribal visits, 88, 89, 103, 121, 303n72; Lakota relations, 83; smallpox, 68–69

Poor Buffalo, 149, 245

Porcupine (Cheyenne), 155–56, 157–58, 163, 164, 171–72, 188–89, 199–200

Porter, Bradford, 68

post offices, 20, 259–60n145; censorship and, 174; Los Piños Agency (Colorado), *43*; Taos, *74*

Potawatomis, 56, 166, 289n81

Powell, John Wesley, 72

Pratt, Richard Henry, 29–30, 54, 55, 165, 200, 210; advice to prison chaplain, 265n33; Ghost Dance and, 234; letters to, 31, 36, 55, 221; Sun Dance and, 264–65n29

press, 38–40, 54, 192–97, 198–99, 213, 231, 235; coverage of Wovoka and Ghost Dance, 161, 162–63, 237, 320n98. *See also* Native-language newspapers

Pretty Eagle (Lakota), 202, 208

Pretty Owl (Lakota), *72*

Price, Hiram, 128
Primeau, Louis, 314n101
prisons and prisoners, 23, 61, 189, 217, 219, 220; Alabama, 265n33; Fort Marion, 20, 29, 30, 252n8, 255–56n70, 267n59
Pueblos, 100, 221, 244, 316n39
Pyramid Lake Reservation, 52; Ghost Dance, 156, 157; intertribal visits, 109, 156; railroads and, 92, 93, 94

Quapaw Reservation, 115, 195

railroads, 91–96, 145, 213; Ghost Dance and, 142, 144, 147, 156; peyotism and, 241
Raining Bird (Cree), 21–22
Red Buffalo (Kiowa), 241
Red Cloud, Jack, 82
Red Cloud (Lakota), 2, 34–35, 37, 65, 70–71, 128, 271n137; Ghost Dance, 155, 197; intertribal visits, 82, 83, 88, 93, 100, 305n97; letter from Sitting Bull, 217–18; on Sun Dance, 129; "troubles" of 1890, 207–8, 218
Red Cloud Agency, 63
Red Cow (Charles Picket Pin or Spotted Horse; Oglala Lakota), 57–58, 267n62
Red Deer, William, 219, 220
Red Eagle (Lakota), 116
Red Lake Reservation, 84, 98, 111, 127, 252n24
Red River Colony, 65
Red Wolf (Arapaho), 227–28
Red Wolf (Cheyenne), 36
Reed, Henry, 237
religious freedom, 128, 129, 174, 205–6, 243
Remington, Frederic, 193–94
Renville, Joseph, 23
Ridge Walker (Cheyenne), 156, 199–200
Riggs, Alfred, 27, 127
Ring Thunder (Lakota), 203–4
Roan Bear, Edward, 301–2n26
Roan Bear (Cheyenne), 131
Robinson, Fred, 239
Roman Catholic Church. *See* Catholic Church

Rosebud Reservation, 29, 30, 55, 56, 60, 64, 233; Carlisle students from, 55, 233; exodus of 1890, 186, 189, 305n89; formation, 63; Ghost Dance, 154, 155, 164, 170, 171, 181–87 *passim*, 217; intertribal dancing, 125, 129–30; intertribal visits and travel, 84, 99, 106, 110, 116, 117, 119, 122, 135, 187–88; literacy, 32, 33; Omaha Dance, 135; police, 107, 117, 121, 135; population, 11; Sitting Bull and, 70; Sun Dance, 129; "troubles" of 1890, 203, 205, 208, 211, 314n101; after Wounded Knee Massacre, 218, 219, 220
Round Dance, Paiute, 143, 161
Rowland, William, 172
Row of Lodges (Arapaho), 136, 152, 162, 212, 230
Royer, Daniel F., 180–81, 185, 186, 211, 303n72; Little Wound letter to, 204–5
Ruger, Thomas, 131, 171–72, 184–85
Running Antelope (Lakota), 173–74, 242, 268n82
Running Bull (Dakota), 46, 97
Rzeckzkowski, Frank, *Uniting the Tribes*, 250n12

Sac and Fox Reservations, 22, 196; intertribal visits, 103; literacy, 32; population, 11
Sacs (Sauks), 22, 67, 103
Sage (Nakash; Arapaho), 146, 147, 152, 161, 293n34
San Carlos Reservation, 11, 25, 30, 106
Sans Arc Lakotas, 59, 63, 110
Santana (Kiowa), 41
Santee and Flandreau Agency: literacy, 32, 33; population, 11
Santee Reservation, 38, 42; dancing, 126–27; intertribal visits, 85, 126
Santees, 18, 23, 63, 197; intertribal dancing, 126–27; letters, 48, 59–60, 81, 197, 209; literacy, 42; old enemies, 86
Sauks. *See* Sacs (Sauks)
schools, 25, 28, 30–31, 256n81; Ho-Chunk, 68; Pine Ridge, 28; Ponca, 51. *See also* boarding schools; government schools; mission schools

Schwan, Theodore, 60
Scobey, C. R. A., 161
Scott, Hugh Lennox, 195–96, 198, 225, 233
Seger, John, 232
Selwyn, William (Wicahaokdeum), 46, 153, 164–65, 172, 260n157
settlers, white. *See* white settlers
sexual abuse, 46, 313n87
Sharp Nose (Arapaho), 83, 222
Shawnees, 66
Sherman, William Tecumseh, 91
Shield, Luke, 62, 268n84
Shimkin, D. B., 123
Short Bull (Lakota), 153–60 *passim*, 164, 186, 203, 301n26; Little Thunder's son's vision of, 217; Raymond Stewart and, 233, 234; "troubles" of 1890, 205, 207, 208, 218
Shoshones, 3, 7, 144, 197; free-living, 105; Ghost Dance, 122, 143, 144, 145–46, 150, 179–80; intertribal meeting places, 93; intertribal visits, 87, 103, 145–46, 150, 153; Lakota relations, 82, 83, 243–44; Paiute relations, 87–88; railroad use, 92, 93–94, 95; schools, 25; Wyoming stockmen's fear of, 101. *See also* Fort Hall Reservation; Northern Shoshones; Western Shoshone Reservation (Duck Valley); Western Shoshones; Wind River Reservation
Shoshoni (language), 33
Sides, Johnson, 79, 81, 87–88, 157, 272–73n2, 277–78n74, 320n98
sign languages, 18, 20, 82, 88–89, 160, 177, 296n71
Sihásapa Lakotas, 67, 117
Simmons, A. O., 186, 187
Siouan languages, 23, 26. *See also* Dakota language; Lakota language; Omaha language
Sioux, 7; Christian missionizing, 253n28; Herbert Welsh on, 234; Hidatsa relations, 86. *See also* Dakota people; Great Sioux Reservation; Great Sioux War; Lakotas
Sioux Wahpeton Reserve (Saskatchewan), 239

Sisseton Reservation: Ghost Dance, 188; intertribal visits, 85, 302n26; literacy, 32, 33; population, 11
Sissetons, 23, 25, 65–66, 107, 188, 279n102; Canada, 239; intertribal dancing, 127. *See also* Devil's Lake (Spirit Lake) Reservation; Sisseton Reservation
Sitting Bull (Hanacha-Thiak; Arapaho), 155, 156, 164, 177, 178, 198, 217, 222; followers of, 225; Frank White and, 216; Smith Curley and, 233; after Wounded Knee Massacre, 226; Wovoka and, 225–26, 319n98
Sitting Bull (Lakota), 37, 39, 61–62, 69–70, 217–18; adopted son, 215; Dawes Act opposition, 118–19, 120; Ghost Dance, 181, 190, 305n87, 311–12n70; McLaughlin relations, 205–6, 305n87, 312n74; railroad and, 92; "troubles" of 1890 and death, 205–7, 311n64, 311–12n70, 312n74; Waggoner translation for, 153; Wolf Chief view, 198
Sky Bull (Lakota), 202, 208, 268n82
smallpox, 68, 280n119
Smith, Asa, 23
Smohalla (Wanapum), 296n71
Soldier Star (Lakota), 217–18
Somers, Abe, 199–200, 235
Southern Arapahos, 17, 50, 231–33; Crow Dance, 136; dancing, 128; Ghost Dance, 146, 147, 148, 178, 230; intertribal dancing, 238; intertribal visits, 86, 115, 244–45; POWs, 20; schooling, 25, 30; Sun Dance, 123, 132, 134; treaties, 24
Southern Cheyennes, 7, 199–200; correspondence, 48, 50, 55, 57, 202; Crow Dance, 136; intertribal dancing, 125, 135, 238, 241; Ghost Dance, 147, 148, 149, 165, 175, 178, 202, 230; intertribal visits, 86, 90, 100, 110, 115, 148, 244–45; Omaha Dance, 135; POWs, 20; schooling, 25, 30, 31; sign language use, 89; Sun Dance, 123, 132, 134; treaties, 24
Southern Ute Reservation, 85, 106; literacy, 32; population, 11

Southern Utes, 62–63, 93, 100, 102, 124, 196–97
Sowawick (Ute), 82–83, 93
Spack, Ruth, 30
Spencer, Lebbeus Foster, 204, 208
Spotted Horse (Hunkpapa Lakota), 110
Spotted Horse (Oglala Lakota), 202, 316n32
Spotted Horse (Red Cow or Charles Picket Pin; Oglala Lakota), 57–58, 267n62
Spotted Mountain Sheep (Lakota), 190
Spotted Tail (Lakota), 56, 65, 70, 111–12, 116
Spotted Tail Agency, 63
Spotted Tail Jr. *See* Young Spotted Tail
spying, 235–36, 237. *See also* censorship and seizure of mail
Standing Bear (Lakota), 173–74
Standing Bear (Ponca), 114, 115
Standing Bear, Luther, 44, 202
Standing Bear et al. v. Crook, 115
Standing Elk (Cheyenne), 200
Standing Elk (Hehaka Najin; Lakota), 34
Standing Rock Reservation, 39, 56, 57, 61, 62, 64, 67, 70, 71; Crow Creek relations, 285n10; dancing, 125–26, 129, 135; formation, 63; Ghost Dance, 163, 172, 181, 183, 189, 190, 202; intertribal visits, 84, 87, 99, 100, 104–11 *passim*, 116, 117, 120, 121; literacy, 32, 33; mail censorship and interception, 173–74, 190; police, 181; population, 11; schooling, 28, 34; "troubles" of 1890, 205–7; Waggoner, 153; after Wounded Knee Massacre, 217–18
Steel, George, 186–87
Stevenson, Winona. *See* Wheeler, Winona
Stewart, Omer, 161
Stewart, Raymond (Short Bull), 204, 233–34
Strikes the Ree (Yankton), 64
suicide, 62
Sun Chief (Pawnee), 58

Sun Dance, 6, 123–24, 146, 128–34, 237, 238, 264–65n29
surveillance and censorship of mail. *See* censorship and seizure of mail
Swan, Paul (White Swan; Swan; ca. 1838–1900; Lakota), 35, 97
Sweeney, John, 204–5
Swift Bear (Lakota), 73, 202, 203
Sword, George, 134–35, 154, 180–81, 202, 218
Sword Bearer (Wraps Up His Tail), 119–20, 150

Take Way From Crow, 57–58, *59*
Tall Bull, Frank, 227–28, 319n85
Tall Bull (Cheyenne; the younger), 67
Tall Bull (Lakota), 242–43, 323n16
Tall Sun (Cheyenne), 264–65n29
Taos, N.Mex., 316n39; post office, *74*
Tatanka Iyotake. *See* Sitting Bull (Lakota)
telegraph, 72–73, 131
Thunder Hawk (Brulé Lakota), 74, 268n82
Thunder Hawk (Hunkpapa Lakota), 163–64, 173–74
Thundering Herd, The (film), *240*
Tibbles, Thomas, 40–41
Tiokasin, John, 197
Tongue River Reservation, 68, 199, *199*; Ghost Dance, 147, 148, 149, 164, 171, 175, 178, 180, 188, 196; intertribal visits, 85, 100, 108, 109, 115–16, 120, 156, 182, 301n18; literacy, 32; Omaha Dance, 136; Pine Ridge relations, 108, 283n183; population, 11; Sun Dance, 130–31
trade and commerce, 82, 89, 93, 244; railroads and, 95, 96
treaties, 24, 118, 253n30
Trimmer, Mary, 59–60
Turtle-Following-His-Wife (Northern Cheyenne), 20, *21*
Two Crows (Omaha), 45
Two Strike (Lakota), 186, 187–88, 194, 204, 205, 208, 210–11, 218, 314n101; telegram use, 73

Uintah and Ouray Reservation, 196–97; correspondence, 50, 62–63, 196–97; Ghost Dance, 143; intertribal visits, 81–82, 85, 100, 245; literacy, 32; population, 11
Umatilla Reservation, 85, 93, 296n71
Uncompahgre Utes, *43*
Union Pacific Railroad, 91, 92, 93, 145, 156, 223, 307n119
Uniting the Tribes: The Rise and Fall of the Pan-Indian Community on the Crow Reservation (Rzeckzkowski), 250n12
Upshaw, Robert L., 109, 131, 149, 301n18
US Army, 58, 61, 102, 115, 125, 149, 197, 307n119; Ghost Dance and, 171–72, 176–77, 184–86, 187, 190, 221, 226–27; Lakota "troubles" of 1890, 195–96, 198, 201–12; military escorts, 98; officers as temporary agents, 82; Oglala enlistment, 215; Pine Ridge, 185, 190, 193; press relations, 193; railroad construction and, 91; Rosebud, 193; sexual abuse by soldiers, 313n87; Sun Dance and, 131, 134; Sword Bearer's death, 120; Wounded Knee Massacre and aftermath, 194, 207–10, 212, 213, 214, 218. *See also* Great Sioux War
US Congress, 26–27; Indian appropriations, 234
US Postal Service, 3, 41–44, 50, 141. *See also* censorship and seizure of mail; post offices
Utes, 50; Ghost Dance, 83, 122, 143, 153; intertribal visits, 81–83, 86, 100, 124, 153, 245; Lakota relations, 81–83, 123; Paiute relations, 153; Sun Dance, 123–24. *See also* Northern Utes; Southern Ute Reservation; Southern Utes

Vestal, Stanley, 37

Wade, J. F., 128, 178
Waggoner, Josephine, 153, 163–64, 235
Wahpetons, 25, 239
Walker, Francis, 1–2

Walker River Reservation, 52, 153, 157; intertribal visits, 142, 143, 144, 145, 187, 228; railroads and, 92, 94, 145
Wanamaker, John, 44
Wapaha, John, 23–24
Warner, C. C., 224, 228, 237
Warren, Louis, 161–62
Washakie, Dick, 145–46
Washakie (Shoshone), 145, 153, 155, 221–22
Washee (Arapaho), 147, 148, 319n98
Watson, J. J., 236, 238
Welsh, Herbert, 234
Western Dakotas. *See* Yanktonais; Yanktons
Western Great Lakes Syllabary, 22
Western Shoshone Reservation (Duck Valley), 45, 104–5, 282n148; Ghost Dance, 179–80, 220; intertribal visits, 88, 101, 109; literacy, 31, 32, 42; population, 11
Western Shoshones, 104, 109, 143, 145, 161
Wheeler, Joe, 243–44, 323n18
Wheeler, Winona, 22
Whip (Lakota), 59–60
Whirlwind (Southern Cheyenne), 31, 36, 99, 125
White, Eugene, 82, 107–8
White, Frank, 216–17
White Bird, Sam, 40, 203
White Buffalo (Cheyenne), 148, 178
White Buffalo Man (Lakota), 189–90
Whitebull, Charles, 219, 316n28
White Cloud (Kiowa), 178
White Eagle (Ponca), 48, 68
White Earth Progress, 39
White Earth Reservation, 39, 98, 127, 279n102
White Elk (Pawnee), 178–79
white settlers, 35, 58, 100, 170, 186; Arizona, 179; fear of Natives, 101, 119, 125, 171, 179, 194, 207, 235, 279n102; trade, 89
White Shield (Arikara), 86
White Shield (Cheyenne), 148, 178
White's Manual Labor Institute (Wabash, Ind.), 51, 196

White Swan (Swan; ca. 1838–1900; Lakota), 35, 97
Wichita Agency, 25, 56, 58, 99. *See also* Kiowa, Comanche, and Wichita Reservation
Wichita language, 19
Wichitas, 4, 19, 66–67, 226; Ghost Dance, 178, 216, 226; intertribal visits, 97, 124. *See also* Kiowa, Comanche, and Wichita Reservation
Wilkerson, Thomas, 23
Wilson, Jack. *See* Wovoka (Jack Wilson)
Wilson, John, 241
Wind River Reservation, 7, 177, 201, 222; Ghost Dance, 147, 148, 164, 180, 237; intertribal visits, 82, 83, 85, 93, 100, 121, 122, 146, 180; population, 11; schools, 25; Sun Dance, 123, 146, 237. *See also* Fort Washakie
Winnebago Reservation, 11, 22, 32, 33, 68, 85
Winnebagos. *See* Ho-Chunks (Winnebagos)
Winnemucca, Lee, 61, 322n128
Winnemucca, Natchez, 61, 87, 322n128
Winnemucca, Nevada, 92, 94, 102, 156
Winnemucca, Sarah, 61, 103
Wissler, Clark, 136
Wizi (Yanktonai), 35, 54
Wodziwob (Paiute), 142, 293n17
Wolf Chief (Mandan), 48, 197–98
Wolf Face (Southern Cheyenne), 36
Wood, J. M., 216–17
Wooden Lance (Kiowa). *See* Apiatan (Wooden Lance; Kiowa)
Woolworth, Arnold (Bagugi or Big Boy), 227, 319n86
Word Carrier, 38, 162
Wounded Knee Massacre, 194, 207–10, 212; aftermath, 212, 213, 214, 218, 224, 231, 234; Harrison, 306n117
Wovoka (Jack Wilson), 141–43, 156–66, 168, 179, 192, 212, *240*; "apostles" and emissaries, 143, 169, 171, 177, 188, 199–200; death, 322n1; errant beliefs about, 181; gifts received, 236–37; increasing secrecy, 237, 321n124; influence in Pine Ridge, 235; intertribal gathering of February–March 1890, 156–62; intertribal visits to, 143, 169, 212, 213, 222–30 *passim*, 237, 239, 277n71, 319–20n98, 321–22n125; Native critics, 221–27; red ochre, 228, 236, 239; transmission of teachings, 143–50, 152, 154, 156–64, 172–73, 233; Wounded Knee Massacre and, 224
Wright, J. George, 107, 129, 164, 170, 187–88, 220
Wyman, W. P., 105

Yakima Reservation, 61
Yanktonais, 25, 63, 65, 67, 285n10; boarding school students, 51; old enemies, 86; Wizi, 35, 54
Yankton Reservation, 25, 26, 49; dancing, 126; Ghost Dance, 188; intertribal visits, 85, 102, 110, 126; literacy, 32, 33; population, 11; sexual abuse, 46
Yanktons, 24, 42, 46, 65, 97; correspondence, 49, 62, 68, 97; dancing, 130; intertribal visits, 97, 102; old enemies, 86; smallpox, 68
Yellow Calf (Arapaho), 146, 147, 161, 293n34
Young Man Afraid of His Horses (Lakota), 42, 43, 117–18, 299n115; Cheyenne relations, 67; Crow visits, 117, 183, 251n28; death, 251n28; Ghost Dance, 155; with Kicking Bear, *182*; letter to Grover Cleveland, 2, 81, 128, 137; pan-Indian views, 13, 118, 137; "troubles" of 1890, 218
Young Spotted Tail, 62, 268n82

Zadoka, Percy, 35

www.ingramcontent.com/pod-product-compliance
Lightning Source LLC
Chambersburg PA
CBHW031426160426
43195CB00010BB/631